50% OFF
Online HSPT Prep Course!

Dear Customer,

Thank you for your purchase of this HSPT Study Guide. Included with your purchase is **discounted access to our online HSPT Course.** Many HSPT courses are needlessly expensive and don't deliver enough value. Our course provides the best HSPT prep material, and with discounted access, **you only pay half price**.

We have structured our online course to perfectly complement your printed study guide. The HSPT Online Course contains **in-depth lessons** that cover all the most important topics, **240+ video reviews** that explain difficult concepts, over **1,750 practice questions** to ensure you feel prepared, and more than **300 digital flashcards**, so you can study while you're on the go.

Online HSPT Prep Course

Topics Covered:
- Verbal Skills
    - Synonyms and Antonyms
    - Logic and Verbal Classification
- Reading Comprehension
    - Informational and Literary Texts
    - Figurative Language
- Language
    - Foundations of Grammar
    - Structure and Purpose of a Sentence
- Mathematics and Quantitative Skills
    - Fractions, Decimals, and Percentages
    - Polygons and Triangles

Course Features:
- HSPT Study Guide
    - Get content that complements our best-selling study guide.
- Full-Length Practice Tests
    - With over 1,750 practice questions, you can test yourself again and again.
- Mobile Friendly
    - If you need to study on the go, the course is easily accessible from your mobile device.
- HSPT Flashcards
    - Our course includes a flashcards mode with over 300 content cards for you to study.

To lock in your discounted access, visit mometrix.com/university/hspt or simply scan this QR code with your smartphone. At the checkout page, enter the discount code: **hspt50off**

If you have any questions or concerns, please contact us at support@mometrix.com.

Sincerely,

Access Your Online Resources

Don't miss out on the Online Resources included with your purchase!

Your purchase of this product unlocks access to our Online Resources page. Elevate your study experience with our **interactive practice test interface**, along with all of the additional resources that we couldn't include in this book.

Flip to the Online Resources section at the end of this book to find the link and a QR code to get started!

HSPT®

Prep Book 2025-2026

Secrets Study Guide for the Catholic High School Placement Test

2 Full-Length Practice Exams

225+ Online Video Tutorials

5th Edition

Copyright © 2025 by Mometrix Media LLC

All rights reserved. This product, or parts thereof, may not be reproduced, stored in a retrieval system, or transmitted in any form or by any means—electronic, mechanical, photocopy, recording, scanning, or other—except for brief quotations in critical reviews or articles, without the prior written permission of the publisher.

Written and edited by Matthew Bowling

Printed in the United States of America

This paper meets the requirements of ANSI/NISO Z39.48-1992 (Permanence of Paper).

Mometrix offers volume discount pricing to institutions. For more information or a price quote, please contact our sales department at sales@mometrix.com or 888-248-1219.

HSPT is a registered trademark of Scholastic Testing Service, Inc., which is not affiliated with Mometrix Test Preparation and does not endorse this product.

Paperback
ISBN 13: 978-1-5167-2835-0
ISBN 10: 1-5167-2835-1

Dear Future Exam Success Story

First of all, **THANK YOU** for purchasing Mometrix study materials!

Second, congratulations! You are one of the few determined test-takers who are committed to doing whatever it takes to excel on your exam. **You have come to the right place.** We developed these study materials with one goal in mind: to deliver you the information you need in a format that's concise and easy to use.

In addition to optimizing your guide for the content of the test, we've outlined our recommended steps for breaking down the preparation process into small, attainable goals so you can make sure you stay on track.

We've also analyzed the entire test-taking process, identifying the most common pitfalls and showing how you can overcome them and be ready for any curveball the test throws you.

Standardized testing is one of the biggest obstacles on your road to success, which only increases the importance of doing well in the high-pressure, high-stakes environment of test day. Your results on this test could have a significant impact on your future, and this guide provides the information and practical advice to help you achieve your full potential on test day.

Your success is our success

We would love to hear from you! If you would like to share the story of your exam success or if you have any questions or comments in regard to our products, please contact us at **800-673-8175** or **support@mometrix.com**.

Thanks again for your business and we wish you continued success!

Sincerely,
The Mometrix Test Preparation Team

Need more help? Check out our flashcards at:
http://MometrixFlashcards.com/HSPT

Table of Contents

- Introduction 1
- Secret Key #1 – Plan Big, Study Small 2
- Secret Key #2 – Make Your Studying Count 3
- Secret Key #3 – Practice the Right Way 4
- Secret Key #4 – Pace Yourself 6
- Secret Key #5 – Have a Plan for Guessing 7
- Test-Taking Strategies 10
- Five-Week HSPT Study Plan 15
  - Week 1: Reading 16
  - Week 2: Language; Verbal Skills 17
  - Week 3: Quantitative Skills; Mathematics 18
  - Week 4: Mathematics 19
  - Week 5: Practice Tests 20
- Reading 21
  - Ideas and Details 21
  - Craft and Structure 24
  - Integration of Ideas 32
  - Literary Elements 40
  - Literary Techniques 47
  - Vocabulary 52
  - Chapter Quiz 59
- Language 60
  - Parts of Speech 60
  - Agreement and Sentence Structure 68
  - Punctuation 85
  - Common Usage Mistakes 90
  - Spelling Conventions 95
  - The Writing Process 99
  - Outlining and Organizing Ideas 101
  - Coherence in Writing 105
  - Chapter Quiz 106
- Verbal Skills 107
  - Analogies 107
  - Logic and Verbal Classification 108
  - Synonyms and Antonyms 110
- Quantitative Skills 112
  - Sequences 112
  - Types of Reasoning 113
  - Practice 114

PRACTICE SOLUTIONS	116
MATHEMATICS	**118**
NUMBERS AND NUMERATION	118
MEASUREMENTS	137
GEOMETRY	139
ALGEBRA	158
STATISTICS AND PROBABILITY	189
CHAPTER QUIZ	199
OPTIONAL HSPT ASSESSMENTS	**200**
HSPT PRACTICE TEST #1	**201**
READING—COMPREHENSION	201
READING—VOCABULARY	211
LANGUAGE	214
VERBAL SKILLS	225
QUANTITATIVE SKILLS	233
MATHEMATICS	242
ANSWER KEY AND EXPLANATIONS FOR TEST #1	**257**
READING—COMPREHENSION	257
READING—VOCABULARY	259
LANGUAGE	260
VERBAL SKILLS	266
QUANTITATIVE SKILLS	269
MATHEMATICS	276
HSPT PRACTICE TEST #2	**287**
HOW TO OVERCOME TEST ANXIETY	**288**
ONLINE RESOURCES	**294**

Introduction

Thank you for purchasing this resource! You have made the choice to prepare yourself for a test that could have a huge impact on your future, and this guide is designed to help you be fully ready for test day. Obviously, it's important to have a solid understanding of the test material, but you also need to be prepared for the unique environment and stressors of the test, so that you can perform to the best of your abilities.

For this purpose, the first section that appears in this guide is the **Secret Keys**. We've devoted countless hours to meticulously researching what works and what doesn't, and we've boiled down our findings to the five most impactful steps you can take to improve your performance on the test. We start at the beginning with study planning and move through the preparation process, all the way to the testing strategies that will help you get the most out of what you know when you're finally sitting in front of the test.

We recommend that you start preparing for your test as far in advance as possible. However, if you've bought this guide as a last-minute study resource and only have a few days before your test, we recommend that you skip over the first two Secret Keys since they address a long-term study plan.

If you struggle with **test anxiety**, we strongly encourage you to check out our recommendations for how you can overcome it. Test anxiety is a formidable foe, but it can be beaten, and we want to make sure you have the tools you need to defeat it.

Secret Key #1 – Plan Big, Study Small

There's a lot riding on your performance. If you want to ace this test, you're going to need to keep your skills sharp and the material fresh in your mind. You need a plan that lets you review everything you need to know while still fitting in your schedule. We'll break this strategy down into three categories.

Information Organization

Start with the information you already have: the official test outline. From this, you can make a complete list of all the concepts you need to cover before the test. Organize these concepts into groups that can be studied together, and create a list of any related vocabulary you need to learn so you can brush up on any difficult terms. You'll want to keep this vocabulary list handy once you actually start studying since you may need to add to it along the way.

Time Management

Once you have your set of study concepts, decide how to spread them out over the time you have left before the test. Break your study plan into small, clear goals so you have a manageable task for each day and know exactly what you're doing. Then just focus on one small step at a time. When you manage your time this way, you don't need to spend hours at a time studying. Studying a small block of content for a short period each day helps you retain information better and avoid stressing over how much you have left to do. You can relax knowing that you have a plan to cover everything in time. In order for this strategy to be effective though, you have to start studying early and stick to your schedule. Avoid the exhaustion and futility that comes from last-minute cramming!

Study Environment

The environment you study in has a big impact on your learning. Studying in a coffee shop, while probably more enjoyable, is not likely to be as fruitful as studying in a quiet room. It's important to keep distractions to a minimum. You're only planning to study for a short block of time, so make the most of it. Don't pause to check your phone or get up to find a snack. It's also important to **avoid multitasking**. Research has consistently shown that multitasking will make your studying dramatically less effective. Your study area should also be comfortable and well-lit so you don't have the distraction of straining your eyes or sitting on an uncomfortable chair.

The time of day you study is also important. You want to be rested and alert. Don't wait until just before bedtime. Study when you'll be most likely to comprehend and remember. Even better, if you know what time of day your test will be, set that time aside for study. That way your brain will be used to working on that subject at that specific time and you'll have a better chance of recalling information.

Finally, it can be helpful to team up with others who are studying for the same test. Your actual studying should be done in as isolated an environment as possible, but the work of organizing the information and setting up the study plan can be divided up. In between study sessions, you can discuss with your teammates the concepts that you're all studying and quiz each other on the details. Just be sure that your teammates are as serious about the test as you are. If you find that your study time is being replaced with social time, you might need to find a new team.

Secret Key #2 – Make Your Studying Count

You're devoting a lot of time and effort to preparing for this test, so you want to be absolutely certain it will pay off. This means doing more than just reading the content and hoping you can remember it on test day. It's important to make every minute of study count. There are two main areas you can focus on to make your studying count.

Retention

It doesn't matter how much time you study if you can't remember the material. You need to make sure you are retaining the concepts. To check your retention of the information you're learning, try recalling it at later times with minimal prompting. Try carrying around flashcards and glance at one or two from time to time or ask a friend who's also studying for the test to quiz you.

To enhance your retention, look for ways to put the information into practice so that you can apply it rather than simply recalling it. If you're using the information in practical ways, it will be much easier to remember. Similarly, it helps to solidify a concept in your mind if you're not only reading it to yourself but also explaining it to someone else. Ask a friend to let you teach them about a concept you're a little shaky on (or speak aloud to an imaginary audience if necessary). As you try to summarize, define, give examples, and answer your friend's questions, you'll understand the concepts better and they will stay with you longer. Finally, step back for a big picture view and ask yourself how each piece of information fits with the whole subject. When you link the different concepts together and see them working together as a whole, it's easier to remember the individual components.

Finally, practice showing your work on any multi-step problems, even if you're just studying. Writing out each step you take to solve a problem will help solidify the process in your mind, and you'll be more likely to remember it during the test.

Modality

Modality simply refers to the means or method by which you study. Choosing a study modality that fits your own individual learning style is crucial. No two people learn best in exactly the same way, so it's important to know your strengths and use them to your advantage.

For example, if you learn best by visualization, focus on visualizing a concept in your mind and draw an image or a diagram. Try color-coding your notes, illustrating them, or creating symbols that will trigger your mind to recall a learned concept. If you learn best by hearing or discussing information, find a study partner who learns the same way or read aloud to yourself. Think about how to put the information in your own words. Imagine that you are giving a lecture on the topic and record yourself so you can listen to it later.

For any learning style, flashcards can be helpful. Organize the information so you can take advantage of spare moments to review. Underline key words or phrases. Use different colors for different categories. Mnemonic devices (such as creating a short list in which every item starts with the same letter) can also help with retention. Find what works best for you and use it to store the information in your mind most effectively and easily.

Secret Key #3 – Practice the Right Way

Your success on test day depends not only on how many hours you put into preparing, but also on whether you prepared the right way. It's good to check along the way to see if your studying is paying off. One of the most effective ways to do this is by taking practice tests to evaluate your progress. Practice tests are useful because they show exactly where you need to improve. Every time you take a practice test, pay special attention to these three groups of questions:

- The questions you got wrong
- The questions you had to guess on, even if you guessed right
- The questions you found difficult or slow to work through

This will show you exactly what your weak areas are, and where you need to devote more study time. Ask yourself why each of these questions gave you trouble. Was it because you didn't understand the material? Was it because you didn't remember the vocabulary? Do you need more repetitions on this type of question to build speed and confidence? Dig into those questions and figure out how you can strengthen your weak areas as you go back to review the material.

Additionally, many practice tests have a section explaining the answer choices. It can be tempting to read the explanation and think that you now have a good understanding of the concept. However, an explanation likely only covers part of the question's broader context. Even if the explanation makes perfect sense, **go back and investigate** every concept related to the question until you're positive you have a thorough understanding.

As you go along, keep in mind that the practice test is just that: practice. Memorizing these questions and answers will not be very helpful on the actual test because it is unlikely to have any of the same exact questions. If you only know the right answers to the sample questions, you won't be prepared for the real thing. **Study the concepts** until you understand them fully, and then you'll be able to answer any question that shows up on the test.

It's important to wait on the practice tests until you're ready. If you take a test on your first day of study, you may be overwhelmed by the amount of material covered and how much you need to learn. Work up to it gradually.

On test day, you'll need to be prepared for answering questions, managing your time, and using the test-taking strategies you've learned. It's a lot to balance, like a mental marathon that will have a big impact on your future. Like training for a marathon, you'll need to start slowly and work your way up. When test day arrives, you'll be ready.

Start with the strategies you've read in the first two Secret Keys—plan your course and study in the way that works best for you. If you have time, consider using multiple study resources to get different approaches to the same concepts. It can be helpful to see difficult concepts from more than one angle. Then find a good source for practice tests. Many times, the test website will suggest potential study resources or provide sample tests.

Practice Test Strategy

If you're able to find at least three practice tests, we recommend this strategy:

Untimed and Open-Book Practice

Take the first test with no time constraints and with your notes and study guide handy. Take your time and focus on applying the strategies you've learned.

Timed and Open-Book Practice

Take the second practice test open-book as well, but set a timer and practice pacing yourself to finish in time.

Timed and Closed-Book Practice

Take any other practice tests as if it were test day. Set a timer and put away your study materials. Sit at a table or desk in a quiet room, imagine yourself at the testing center, and answer questions as quickly and accurately as possible.

Keep repeating timed and closed-book tests on a regular basis until you run out of practice tests or it's time for the actual test. Your mind will be ready for the schedule and stress of test day, and you'll be able to focus on recalling the material you've learned.

Secret Key #4 – Pace Yourself

Once you're fully prepared for the material on the test, your biggest challenge on test day will be managing your time. Just knowing that the clock is ticking can make you panic even if you have plenty of time left. Work on pacing yourself so you can build confidence against the time constraints of the exam. Pacing is a difficult skill to master, especially in a high-pressure environment, so **practice is vital**.

Set time expectations for your pace based on how much time is available. For example, if a section has 60 questions and the time limit is 30 minutes, you know you have to average 30 seconds or less per question in order to answer them all. Although 30 seconds is the hard limit, set 25 seconds per question as your goal, so you reserve extra time to spend on harder questions. When you budget extra time for the harder questions, you no longer have any reason to stress when those questions take longer to answer.

Don't let this time expectation distract you from working through the test at a calm, steady pace, but keep it in mind so you don't spend too much time on any one question. Recognize that taking extra time on one question you don't understand may keep you from answering two that you do understand later in the test. If your time limit for a question is up and you're still not sure of the answer, mark it and move on, and come back to it later if the time and the test format allow. If the testing format doesn't allow you to return to earlier questions, just make an educated guess; then put it out of your mind and move on.

On the easier questions, be careful not to rush. It may seem wise to hurry through them so you have more time for the challenging ones, but it's not worth missing one if you know the concept and just didn't take the time to read the question fully. Work efficiently but make sure you understand the question and have looked at all of the answer choices, since more than one may seem right at first.

Even if you're paying attention to the time, you may find yourself a little behind at some point. You should speed up to get back on track, but do so wisely. Don't panic; just take a few seconds less on each question until you're caught up. Don't guess without thinking, but do look through the answer choices and eliminate any you know are wrong. If you can get down to two choices, it is often worthwhile to guess from those. Once you've chosen an answer, move on and don't dwell on any that you skipped or had to hurry through. If a question was taking too long, chances are it was one of the harder ones, so you weren't as likely to get it right anyway.

On the other hand, if you find yourself getting ahead of schedule, it may be beneficial to slow down a little. The more quickly you work, the more likely you are to make a careless mistake that will affect your score. You've budgeted time for each question, so don't be afraid to spend that time. Practice an efficient but careful pace to get the most out of the time you have.

Secret Key #5 – Have a Plan for Guessing

When you're taking the test, you may find yourself stuck on a question. Some of the answer choices seem better than others, but you don't see the one answer choice that is obviously correct. What do you do?

The scenario described above is very common, yet most test takers have not effectively prepared for it. Developing and practicing a plan for guessing may be one of the single most effective uses of your time as you get ready for the exam.

In developing your plan for guessing, there are three questions to address:

- When should you start the guessing process?
- How should you narrow down the choices?
- Which answer should you choose?

When to Start the Guessing Process

Unless your plan for guessing is to select C every time (which, despite its merits, is not what we recommend), you need to leave yourself enough time to apply your answer elimination strategies. Since you have a limited amount of time for each question, that means that if you're going to give yourself the best shot at guessing correctly, you have to decide quickly whether or not you will guess.

Of course, the best-case scenario is that you don't have to guess at all, so first, see if you can answer the question based on your knowledge of the subject and basic reasoning skills. Focus on the key words in the question and try to jog your memory of related topics. Give yourself a chance to bring the knowledge to mind, but once you realize that you don't have (or you can't access) the knowledge you need to answer the question, it's time to start the guessing process.

It's almost always better to start the guessing process too early than too late. It only takes a few seconds to remember something and answer the question from knowledge. Carefully eliminating wrong answer choices takes longer. Plus, going through the process of eliminating answer choices can actually help jog your memory.

Summary: Start the guessing process as soon as you decide that you can't answer the question based on your knowledge.

How to Narrow Down the Choices

The next chapter in this book (**Test-Taking Strategies**) includes a wide range of strategies for how to approach questions and how to look for answer choices to eliminate. You will definitely want to read those carefully, practice them, and figure out which ones work best for you. Here though, we're going to address a mindset rather than a particular strategy.

Your odds of guessing an answer correctly depend on how many options you are choosing from.

Number of options left	5	4	3	2	1
Odds of guessing correctly	20%	25%	33%	50%	100%

You can see from this chart just how valuable it is to be able to eliminate incorrect answers and make an educated guess, but there are two things that many test takers do that cause them to miss out on the benefits of guessing:

- Accidentally eliminating the correct answer
- Selecting an answer based on an impression

We'll look at the first one here, and the second one in the next section.

To avoid accidentally eliminating the correct answer, we recommend a thought exercise called **the $5 challenge**. In this challenge, you only eliminate an answer choice from contention if you are willing to bet $5 on it being wrong. Why $5? Five dollars is a small but not insignificant amount of money. It's an amount you could afford to lose but wouldn't want to throw away. And while losing $5 once might not hurt too much, doing it twenty times will set you back $100. In the same way, each small decision you make—eliminating a choice here, guessing on a question there—won't by itself impact your score very much, but when you put them all together, they can make a big difference. By holding each answer choice elimination decision to a higher standard, you can reduce the risk of accidentally eliminating the correct answer.

The $5 challenge can also be applied in a positive sense: If you are willing to bet $5 that an answer choice *is* correct, go ahead and mark it as correct.

Summary: Only eliminate an answer choice if you are willing to bet $5 that it is wrong.

Which Answer to Choose

You're taking the test. You've run into a hard question and decided you'll have to guess. You've eliminated all the answer choices you're willing to bet $5 on. Now you have to pick an answer. Why do we even need to talk about this? Why can't you just pick whichever one you feel like when the time comes?

The answer to these questions is that if you don't come into the test with a plan, you'll rely on your impression to select an answer choice, and if you do that, you risk falling into a trap. The test writers know that everyone who takes their test will be guessing on some of the questions, so they intentionally write wrong answer choices to seem plausible. You still have to pick an answer though, and if the wrong answer choices are designed to look right, how can you ever be sure that you're not falling for their trap? The best solution we've found to this dilemma is to take the decision out of your hands entirely. Here is the process we recommend:

Once you've eliminated any choices that you are confident (willing to bet $5) are wrong, select the first remaining choice as your answer.

Whether you choose to select the first remaining choice, the second, or the last, the important thing is that you use some preselected standard. Using this approach guarantees that you will not be enticed into selecting an answer choice that looks right, because you are not basing your decision on how the answer choices look.

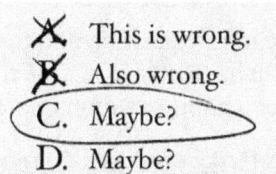

This is not meant to make you question your knowledge. Instead, it is to help you recognize the difference between your knowledge and your impressions. There's a huge difference between thinking an answer is right because of what you know, and thinking an answer is right because it looks or sounds like it should be right.

Summary: To ensure that your selection is appropriately random, make a predetermined selection from among all answer choices you have not eliminated.

Test-Taking Strategies

This section contains a list of test-taking strategies that you may find helpful as you work through the test. By taking what you know and applying logical thought, you can maximize your chances of answering any question correctly!

It is very important to realize that every question is different and every person is different: no single strategy will work on every question, and no single strategy will work for every person. That's why we've included all of them here, so you can try them out and determine which ones work best for different types of questions and which ones work best for you.

Question Strategies

☑ Read Carefully

Read the question and the answer choices carefully. Don't miss the question because you misread the terms. You have plenty of time to read each question thoroughly and make sure you understand what is being asked. Yet a happy medium must be attained, so don't waste too much time. You must read carefully and efficiently.

☑ Contextual Clues

Look for contextual clues. If the question includes a word you are not familiar with, look at the immediate context for some indication of what the word might mean. Contextual clues can often give you all the information you need to decipher the meaning of an unfamiliar word. Even if you can't determine the meaning, you may be able to narrow down the possibilities enough to make a solid guess at the answer to the question.

☑ Prefixes

If you're having trouble with a word in the question or answer choices, try dissecting it. Take advantage of every clue that the word might include. Prefixes can be a huge help. Usually, they allow you to determine a basic meaning. *Pre-* means before, *post-* means after, *pro-* is positive, *de-* is negative. From prefixes, you can get an idea of the general meaning of the word and try to put it into context.

☑ Hedge Words

Watch out for critical hedge words, such as *likely*, *may*, *can*, *often*, *almost*, *mostly*, *usually*, *generally*, *rarely*, and *sometimes*. Question writers insert these hedge phrases to cover every possibility. Often an answer choice will be wrong simply because it leaves no room for exception. Be on guard for answer choices that have definitive words such as *exactly* and *always*.

☑ Switchback Words

Stay alert for *switchbacks*. These are the words and phrases frequently used to alert you to shifts in thought. The most common switchback words are *but*, *although*, and *however*. Others include *nevertheless*, *on the other hand*, *even though*, *while*, *in spite of*, *despite*, and *regardless of*. Switchback words are important to catch because they can change the direction of the question or an answer choice.

☑ Face Value

When in doubt, use common sense. Accept the situation in the problem at face value. Don't read too much into it. These problems will not require you to make wild assumptions. If you have to go beyond creativity and warp time or space in order to have an answer choice fit the question, then you should move on and consider the other answer choices. These are normal problems rooted in reality. The applicable relationship or explanation may not be readily apparent, but it is there for you to figure out. Use your common sense to interpret anything that isn't clear.

Answer Choice Strategies

⊘ Answer Selection

The most thorough way to pick an answer choice is to identify and eliminate wrong answers until only one is left, then confirm it is the correct answer. Sometimes an answer choice may immediately seem right, but be careful. The test writers will usually put more than one reasonable answer choice on each question, so take a second to read all of them and make sure that the other choices are not equally obvious. As long as you have time left, it is better to read every answer choice than to pick the first one that looks right without checking the others.

⊘ Answer Choice Families

An answer choice family consists of two (in rare cases, three) answer choices that are very similar in construction and cannot all be true at the same time. If you see two answer choices that are direct opposites or parallels, one of them is usually the correct answer. For instance, if one answer choice says that quantity x increases and another either says that quantity x decreases (opposite) or says that quantity y increases (parallel), then those answer choices would fall into the same family. An answer choice that doesn't match the construction of the answer choice family is more likely to be incorrect. Most questions will not have answer choice families, but when they do appear, you should be prepared to recognize them.

⊘ Eliminate Answers

Eliminate answer choices as soon as you realize they are wrong, but make sure you consider all possibilities. If you are eliminating answer choices and realize that the last one you are left with is also wrong, don't panic. Start over and consider each choice again. There may be something you missed the first time that you will realize on the second pass.

⊘ Avoid Fact Traps

Don't be distracted by an answer choice that is factually true but doesn't answer the question. You are looking for the choice that answers the question. Stay focused on what the question is asking for so you don't accidentally pick an answer that is true but incorrect. Always go back to the question and make sure the answer choice you've selected actually answers the question and is not merely a true statement.

⊘ Extreme Statements

In general, you should avoid answers that put forth extreme actions as standard practice or proclaim controversial ideas as established fact. An answer choice that states the "process should be used in certain situations, if…" is much more likely to be correct than one that states the "process should be discontinued completely." The first is a calm rational statement and doesn't even make a definitive, uncompromising stance, using a hedge word *if* to provide wiggle room, whereas the second choice is far more extreme.

⊘ Benchmark

As you read through the answer choices and you come across one that seems to answer the question well, mentally select that answer choice. This is not your final answer, but it's the one that will help you evaluate the other answer choices. The one that you selected is your benchmark or standard for judging each of the other answer choices. Every other answer choice must be compared to your benchmark. That choice is correct until proven otherwise by another answer choice beating it. If you find a better answer, then that one becomes your new benchmark. Once you've decided that no other choice answers the question as well as your benchmark, you have your final answer.

ⓘ Predict the Answer

Before you even start looking at the answer choices, it is often best to try to predict the answer. When you come up with the answer on your own, it is easier to avoid distractions and traps because you will know exactly what to look for. The right answer choice is unlikely to be word-for-word what you came up with, but it should be a close match. Even if you are confident that you have the right answer, you should still take the time to read each option before moving on.

General Strategies

ⓘ Tough Questions

If you are stumped on a problem or it appears too hard or too difficult, don't waste time. Move on! Remember though, if you can quickly check for obviously incorrect answer choices, your chances of guessing correctly are greatly improved. Before you completely give up, at least try to knock out a couple of possible answers. Eliminate what you can and then guess at the remaining answer choices before moving on.

ⓘ Check Your Work

Since you will probably not know every term listed and the answer to every question, it is important that you get credit for the ones that you do know. Don't miss any questions through careless mistakes. If at all possible, try to take a second to look back over your answer selection and make sure you've selected the correct answer choice and haven't made a costly careless mistake (such as marking an answer choice that you didn't mean to mark). This quick double check should more than pay for itself in caught mistakes for the time it costs.

ⓘ Pace Yourself

It's easy to be overwhelmed when you're looking at a page full of questions; your mind is confused and full of random thoughts, and the clock is ticking down faster than you would like. Calm down and maintain the pace that you have set for yourself. Especially as you get down to the last few minutes of the test, don't let the small numbers on the clock make you panic. As long as you are on track by monitoring your pace, you are guaranteed to have time for each question.

ⓘ Don't Rush

It is very easy to make errors when you are in a hurry. Maintaining a fast pace in answering questions is pointless if it makes you miss questions that you would have gotten right otherwise. Test writers like to include distracting information and wrong answers that seem right. Taking a little extra time to avoid careless mistakes can make all the difference in your test score. Find a pace that allows you to be confident in the answers that you select.

ⓘ Keep Moving

Panicking will not help you pass the test, so do your best to stay calm and keep moving. Taking deep breaths and going through the answer elimination steps you practiced can help to break through a stress barrier and keep your pace.

Final Notes

The combination of a solid foundation of content knowledge and the confidence that comes from practicing your plan for applying that knowledge is the key to maximizing your performance on test day. As your foundation of content knowledge is built up and strengthened, you'll find that the strategies included in this chapter become more and more effective in helping you quickly sift through the distractions and traps of the test to isolate the correct answer.

Now that you're preparing to move forward into the test content chapters of this book, be sure to keep your goal in mind. As you read, think about how you will be able to apply this information on the test. If you've already seen sample questions for the test and you have an idea of the question format and style, try to come up with questions of your own that you can answer based on what you're reading. This will give you valuable practice applying your knowledge in the same ways you can expect to on test day.

Good luck and good studying!

Five-Week HSPT Study Plan

On the next few pages, we've provided an optional study plan to help you use this study guide to its fullest potential over the course of 5 weeks. If you have 10 weeks available and want to spread it out more, spend two weeks on each section of the plan.

Below is a quick summary of the subjects covered in each week of the plan.

- Week 1: Reading
- Week 2: Language; Verbal Skills
- Week 3: Quantitative Skills; Mathematics (Numbers and Numeration, Measurements, and Geometry)
- Week 4: Mathematics (Algebra, Statistics and Probability)
- Week 5: Practice Tests

Please note that not all subjects will take the same amount of time to work through.

Some chapters are followed by practice questions or a short chapter quiz. These quizzes are intended to help you check your knowledge of the material one chapter at a time, but they are not necessarily representative of the questions that you will encounter on the real test. We recommend taking each chapter quiz after reading through the chapter and reviewing any notes you made along the way.

Two full-length practice tests are included in this study guide. Take these practice tests without any reference materials a day or two before the real thing as practice runs to get yourself in the mode of answering questions at a good pace.

Week 1: Reading

INSTRUCTIONAL CONTENT

First, read carefully through the **Reading** chapter in this book, checking off your progress as you go:

- ❏ Ideas and Details
- ❏ Craft and Structure
- ❏ Integration of Ideas
- ❏ Literary Elements
- ❏ Literary Techniques
- ❏ Vocabulary

As you read, do the following:

- Highlight any sections, terms, or concepts you think are important
- Draw an asterisk (*) next to any areas you are struggling with
- Watch the review videos to gain more understanding of a particular topic
- Take notes in your notebook or in the margins of this book

After you've read through everything, go back and review any sections that you highlighted or that you drew an asterisk next to, referencing your notes along the way.

CHAPTER QUIZ

Once you've studied the content, take the chapter quiz. Check your answers against the provided answer key. For any questions that you got wrong, review that section of the guide once more.

Week 2: Language; Verbal Skills

INSTRUCTIONAL CONTENT

First, read carefully through the **Language** and **Verbal Skills** chapters in this book, checking off your progress as you go:

- ❏ Language
    - ❏ Parts of Speech
    - ❏ Agreement and Sentence Structure
    - ❏ Punctuation
    - ❏ Common Usage Mistakes
    - ❏ Spelling Conventions
    - ❏ The Writing Process
    - ❏ Outlining and Organizing Ideas
    - ❏ Coherence in Writing

- ❏ Verbal Skills
    - ❏ Analogies
    - ❏ Logic and Verbal Classification
    - ❏ Synonyms and Antonyms

As you read, do the following:

- Highlight any sections, terms, or concepts you think are important
- Draw an asterisk (*) next to any areas you are struggling with
- Watch the review videos to gain more understanding of a particular topic
- Take notes in your notebook or in the margins of this book

After you've read through everything, go back and review any sections that you highlighted or that you drew an asterisk next to, referencing your notes along the way.

CHAPTER QUIZ

Once you've studied the content, take the chapter quiz for the **Language** chapter. Check your answers against the provided answer key. For any questions that you got wrong, review that section of the guide once more.

Week 3: Quantitative Skills; Mathematics

INSTRUCTIONAL CONTENT

First, read carefully through the **Quantitative Skills** chapter and the first three sections of the **Mathematics** chapter in this book, checking off your progress as you go. The Mathematics chapter is quite long, so save the rest of it for next week.

- ❏ Quantitative Skills
    - ❏ Sequences
    - ❏ Types of Reasoning
    - ❏ Practice Questions

- ❏ Mathematics
    - ❏ Numbers and Numeration
    - ❏ Measurements
    - ❏ Geometry

As you read, do the following:

- Highlight any sections, terms, or concepts you think are important
- Draw an asterisk (*) next to any areas you are struggling with
- Watch the review videos to gain more understanding of a particular topic
- Take notes in your notebook or in the margins of this book

After you've read through everything, go back and review any sections that you highlighted or that you drew an asterisk next to, referencing your notes along the way.

PRACTICE QUESTIONS

Once you've studied the content, take the practice questions for the **Quantitative Skills** chapter. Check your answers against the provided answer key. For any questions that you got wrong, review that section of the guide once more.

Week 4: Mathematics

INSTRUCTIONAL CONTENT

First, read carefully through the rest of the **Mathematics** chapter in this book, checking off your progress as you go:

- ❏ Algebra
- ❏ Statistics and Probability

As you read, do the following:

- Highlight any sections, terms, or concepts you think are important
- Draw an asterisk (*) next to any areas you are struggling with
- Watch the review videos to gain more understanding of a particular topic
- Take notes in your notebook or in the margins of this book

After you've read through everything, go back and review any sections that you highlighted or that you drew an asterisk next to, referencing your notes along the way.

CHAPTER QUIZ

Once you've studied the content, take the chapter quiz. Check your answers against the provided answer key. For any questions that you got wrong, review that section of the guide once more.

Week 5: Practice Tests

Your success on test day depends not only on how many hours you put into preparing, but also on whether you prepared the right way. It's good to check to see if your studying is paying off. One of the most effective ways to do this is by taking practice tests to evaluate your progress. Practice tests are useful because they show exactly where you need to improve. Every time you take a practice test, pay special attention to these three groups of questions:

- The questions you got wrong
- The questions you had to guess on, even if you guessed right
- The questions you found difficult or slow to work through

This will show you exactly what your weak areas are, and where you need to devote more study time. Ask yourself why each of these questions gave you trouble. Was it because you didn't understand the material? Was it because you didn't remember the vocabulary? Do you need more repetitions on this type of question to build speed and confidence? Dig into those questions and figure out how you can strengthen your weak areas as you go back to review the material.

As you go along, keep in mind that the practice tests are just that: practice. Memorizing these questions and answers will not be very helpful on the actual test because it is unlikely to have any of the same exact questions. If you only know the right answers to the sample questions, you won't be prepared for the real thing. **Study the concepts** until you understand them fully, and then you'll be able to answer any question that shows up on the test.

PRACTICE TEST #1

Now that you've read over the instructional content, it's time to take a practice test. Complete Practice Test #1. Take this test with **no time constraints**, and feel free to reference the applicable sections of this guide as you go. Once you've finished, check your answers against the provided answer key. For any questions you answered incorrectly, review the answer rationale, and then **go back and review** the applicable sections of the book. The goal in this stage is to understand why you answered the question incorrectly, and make sure that the next time you see a similar question, you will get it right.

PRACTICE TEST #2

Next, complete Practice Test #2. This time, give yourself **2 hours and 30 minutes** to complete all of the questions. You should again feel free to reference the guide and your notes, but be mindful of the clock. If you run out of time before you finish all of the questions, mark where you were when time expired, but go ahead and finish taking the practice test. Once you've finished, check your answers against the provided answer key, and as before, review the answer rationale for any that you answered incorrectly and then go back and review the associated instructional content. Your goal is still to increase understanding of the content but also to get used to the time constraints you will face on the test.

Reading

Transform passive reading into active learning! After immersing yourself in this chapter, put your comprehension to the test by taking a quiz. The insights you gained will stay with you longer this way. Scan the QR code to go directly to the chapter quiz interface for this study guide. If you're using a computer, simply visit the online resources page at **mometrix.com/resources719/hspt-28350** and click the Chapter Quizzes link.

Ideas and Details

MAIN IDEAS AND SUPPORTING DETAILS
IDENTIFYING TOPICS AND MAIN IDEAS

One of the most important skills in reading comprehension is the identification of **topics** and **main ideas**. There is a subtle difference between these two features. The topic is the subject of a text (i.e., what the text is all about). The main idea, on the other hand, is the most important point being made by the author. The topic is usually expressed in a few words at the most while the main idea often needs a full sentence to be completely defined. As an example, a short passage might be written on the topic of penguins, and the main idea could be written as *Penguins are different from other birds in many ways*. In most nonfiction writing, the topic and the main idea will be **stated directly** and often appear in a sentence at the very beginning or end of the text. When being tested on an understanding of the author's topic, you may be able to skim the passage for the general idea by reading only the first sentence of each paragraph. A body paragraph's first sentence is often—but not always—the main **topic sentence** which gives you a summary of the content in the paragraph.

However, there are cases in which the reader must figure out an **unstated** topic or main idea. In these instances, you must read every sentence of the text and try to come up with an overarching idea that is supported by each of those sentences.

Note: The main idea should not be confused with the thesis statement. While the main idea gives a brief, general summary of a text, the thesis statement provides a **specific perspective** on an issue that the author supports with evidence.

> **Review Video: Topics and Main Ideas**
> Visit mometrix.com/academy and enter code: 407801

SUPPORTING DETAILS

Supporting details are smaller pieces of evidence that provide backing for the main point. In order to show that a main idea is correct or valid, an author must add details that prove their point. All texts contain details, but they are only classified as supporting details when they serve to reinforce some larger point. Supporting details are most commonly found in informative and persuasive texts. In some cases, they will be clearly indicated with terms like *for example* or *for instance*, or they will be enumerated with terms like *first*, *second*, and *last*. However, you need to be prepared for texts that do not contain those indicators. As a reader, you should consider whether the author's supporting details really back up his or her main point. Details can be factual and correct, yet they may not be **relevant** to the author's point. Conversely, details can be relevant, but be ineffective because they are based on opinion or assertions that cannot be proven.

> **Review Video: Supporting Details**
> Visit mometrix.com/academy and enter code: 396297

COMMON ORGANIZATIONS OF TEXTS

ORGANIZATION OF THE TEXT

The way a text is organized can help readers understand the author's intent and his or her conclusions. There are various ways to organize a text, and each one has a purpose and use. Usually, authors will organize information logically in a passage so the reader can follow and locate the information within the text. However, since not all passages are written with the same logical structure, you need to be familiar with several different types of passage structure.

> **Review Video: Sequence of Events in a Story**
> Visit mometrix.com/academy and enter code: 807512

CHRONOLOGICAL

When using **chronological** order, the author presents information in the order that it happened. For example, biographies are typically written in chronological order. The subject's birth and childhood are presented first, followed by their adult life, and lastly the events leading up to the person's death.

CAUSE AND EFFECT

One of the most common text structures is **cause and effect**. A **cause** is an act or event that makes something happen, and an **effect** is the thing that happens as a result of the cause. A cause-and-effect relationship is not always explicit, but there are some terms in English that signal causes, such as *since*, *because*, and *due to*. Furthermore, terms that signal effects include *consequently, therefore, this leads to*. As an example, consider the sentence *Because the sky was clear, Ron did not bring an umbrella*. The cause is the clear sky, and the effect is that Ron did not bring an umbrella. However, readers may find that sometimes the cause-and-effect relationship will not be clearly noted. For instance, the sentence *He was late and missed the meeting* does not contain any signaling words, but the sentence still contains a cause (he was late) and an effect (he missed the meeting).

> **Review Video: Cause and Effect**
> Visit mometrix.com/academy and enter code: 868099
>
> **Review Video: Rhetorical Strategy of Cause and Effect Analysis**
> Visit mometrix.com/academy and enter code: 725944

MULTIPLE EFFECTS

Be aware of the possibility for a single cause to have **multiple effects.** (e.g., *Single cause*: Because you left your homework on the table, your dog engulfed the assignment. *Multiple effects*: As a result, you receive a failing grade, your parents do not allow you to go out with your friends, you miss out on the new movie, and one of your classmates spoils it for you before you have another chance to watch it).

MULTIPLE CAUSES

Also, there is the possibility for a single effect to have **multiple causes.** (e.g., *Single effect*: Alan has a fever. *Multiple causes*: An unexpected cold front came through the area, and Alan forgot to take his multi-vitamin to avoid getting sick.) Additionally, an effect can in turn be the cause of another effect, in what is known as a cause-and-effect chain. (e.g., As a result of her disdain for procrastination, Lynn prepared for her exam. This led to her passing her test with high marks. Hence, her resume was accepted and her application was approved.)

CAUSE AND EFFECT IN PERSUASIVE ESSAYS

Persuasive essays, in which an author tries to make a convincing argument and change the minds of readers, usually include cause-and-effect relationships. However, these relationships should not always be taken at face value. Frequently, an author will assume a cause or take an effect for granted. To read a persuasive essay effectively, readers need to judge the cause-and-effect relationships that the author is presenting. For instance, imagine an author wrote the following: *The parking deck has been unprofitable because people would prefer to* *ride their bikes.* The relationship is clear: the cause is that people prefer to ride their bikes, and the effect is that the parking deck has been unprofitable. However, readers should consider whether this argument is conclusive. Perhaps there are other reasons for the failure of the parking deck: a down economy, excessive fees, etc. Too often, authors present causal relationships as if they are fact rather than opinion. Readers should be on the alert for these dubious claims.

PROBLEM-SOLUTION

Some nonfiction texts are organized to **present a problem** followed by a solution. For this type of text, the problem is often explained before the solution is offered. In some cases, as when the problem is well known, the solution may be introduced briefly at the beginning. Other passages may focus on the solution, and the problem will be referenced only occasionally. Some texts will outline multiple solutions to a problem, leaving readers to choose among them. If the author has an interest or an allegiance to one solution, he or she may fail to mention or describe accurately some of the other solutions. Readers should be careful of the author's agenda when reading a problem-solution text. Only by understanding the author's perspective and interests can one develop a proper judgment of the proposed solution.

COMPARE AND CONTRAST

Many texts follow the **compare-and-contrast** model in which the similarities and differences between two ideas or things are explored. Analysis of the similarities between ideas is called **comparison**. In an ideal comparison, the author places ideas or things in an equivalent structure, i.e., the author presents the ideas in the same way. If an author wants to show the similarities between cricket and baseball, then he or she may do so by summarizing the equipment and rules for each game. Be mindful of the similarities as they appear in the passage and take note of any differences that are mentioned. Often, these small differences will only reinforce the more general similarity.

> **Review Video: Compare and Contrast**
> Visit mometrix.com/academy and enter code: 798319

Thinking critically about ideas and conclusions can seem like a daunting task. One way to ease this task is to understand the basic elements of ideas and writing techniques. Looking at the ways different ideas relate to each other can be a good way for readers to begin their analysis. For instance, sometimes authors will write about two ideas that are in opposition to each other. Or, one author will provide his or her ideas on a topic, and another author may respond in opposition. The analysis of these opposing ideas is known as **contrast**. Contrast is often marred by the author's obvious partiality to one of the ideas. A discerning reader will be put off by an author who does not engage in a fair fight. In an analysis of opposing ideas, both ideas should be presented in clear and reasonable terms. If the author does prefer a side, you need to read carefully to determine the areas where the author shows or avoids this preference. In an analysis of opposing ideas, you should proceed through the passage by marking the major differences point by point with an eye that is looking for an explanation of each side's view. For instance, in an analysis of capitalism and communism, there is an importance in outlining each side's view on labor, markets, prices, personal responsibility, etc. Additionally, as you read through the passages, you should note whether the opposing views present each side in a similar manner.

SEQUENCE

Readers must be able to identify a text's **sequence**, or the order in which things happen. Often, when the sequence is very important to the author, the text is indicated with signal words like *first*, *then*, *next*, and *last*. However, a sequence can be merely implied and must be noted by the reader. Consider the sentence *He walked through the garden and gave water and fertilizer to the plants*. Clearly, the man did not walk through the garden before he collected water and fertilizer for the plants. So, the implied sequence is that he first collected water, then he collected fertilizer, next he walked through the garden, and last he gave water or fertilizer as necessary to the plants. Texts do not always proceed in an orderly sequence from first to last. Sometimes they begin at the end and start over at the beginning. As a reader, you can enhance your understanding of the passage by taking brief notes to clarify the sequence.

Review Video: Sequence
Visit mometrix.com/academy and enter code: 489027

Craft and Structure

AUTHOR'S PURPOSE

AUTHOR'S PURPOSE

Usually, identifying the author's **purpose** is easier than identifying his or her **position**. In most cases, the author has no interest in hiding his or her purpose. A text that is meant to entertain, for instance, should be written to please the reader. Most narratives, or stories, are written to entertain, though they may also inform or persuade. Informative texts are easy to identify, while the most difficult purpose of a text to identify is persuasion because the author has an interest in making this purpose hard to detect. When a reader discovers that the author is trying to persuade, he or she should be skeptical of the argument. For this reason, persuasive texts often try to establish an entertaining tone and hope to amuse the reader into agreement. On the other hand, an informative tone may be implemented to create an appearance of authority and objectivity.

An author's purpose is evident often in the **organization** of the text (e.g., section headings in bold font points to an informative text). However, you may not have such organization available to you in your exam. Instead, if the author makes his or her main idea clear from the beginning, then the likely purpose of the text is to **inform**. If the author begins by making a claim and provides various arguments to support that claim, then the purpose is probably to **persuade**. If the author tells a story or wants to gain the reader's attention more than to push a particular point or deliver information, then his or her purpose is most likely to **entertain**. As a reader, you must judge authors on how well they accomplish their purpose. In other words, you need to consider the type of passage (e.g., technical, persuasive, etc.) that the author has written and if the author has followed the requirements of the passage type.

Review Video: Understanding the Author's Intent
Visit mometrix.com/academy and enter code: 511819

INFORMATIONAL TEXTS

An **informational text** is written to educate and enlighten readers. Informational texts are almost always nonfiction and are rarely structured as a story. The intention of an informational text is to deliver information in the most comprehensible way. So, look for the structure of the text to be very clear. In an informational text, the thesis statement is one or two sentences that normally appears at the end of the first paragraph. The author may use some colorful language, but he or she is likely to put more emphasis on clarity and precision. Informational essays do not typically appeal to the emotions. They often contain facts and figures and rarely include the opinion of the author; however, readers should remain aware of the possibility for bias as those facts are presented. Sometimes a persuasive essay can resemble an informative essay, especially if the author maintains an even tone and presents his or her views as if they were established fact.

Review Video: Informational Text
Visit mometrix.com/academy and enter code: 924964

PERSUASIVE WRITING

In a persuasive essay, the author is attempting to change the reader's mind or **convince** him or her of something that he or she did not believe previously. There are several identifying characteristics of **persuasive writing**. One is **opinion presented as fact**. When authors attempt to persuade readers, they often present their opinions as if they were fact. Readers must be on guard for statements that sound factual but which cannot be subjected to research, observation, or experiment. Another characteristic of persuasive writing is **emotional language**. An author will often try to play on the emotions of readers by appealing to their sympathy or sense of morality. When an author uses colorful or evocative language with the intent of arousing the reader's passions, then the author may be attempting to persuade. Finally, in many cases, a persuasive text will give an **unfair explanation of opposing positions**, if these positions are mentioned at all.

ENTERTAINING TEXTS

The success or failure of an author's intent to **entertain** is determined by those who read the author's work. Entertaining texts may be either fiction or nonfiction, and they may describe real or imagined people, places, and events. Entertaining texts are often narratives or poems. A text that is written to entertain is likely to contain **colorful language** that engages the imagination and the emotions. Such writing often features a great deal of figurative language, which typically enlivens the subject matter with images and analogies.

Though an entertaining text is not usually written to persuade or inform, authors may accomplish both of these tasks in their work. An entertaining text may *appeal to the reader's emotions* and cause him or her to think differently about a particular subject. In any case, entertaining texts tend to showcase the personality of the author more than other types of writing.

DESCRIPTIVE TEXT

In a sense, almost all writing is descriptive, insofar as an author seeks to describe events, ideas, or people to the reader. Some texts, however, are primarily concerned with **description**. A descriptive text focuses on a particular subject and attempts to depict the subject in a way that will be clear to readers. Descriptive texts contain many adjectives and adverbs (i.e., words that give shades of meaning and create a more detailed mental picture for the reader). A descriptive text fails when it is unclear to the reader. A descriptive text will certainly be informative and may be persuasive and entertaining as well.

> **Review Video: Descriptive Texts**
> Visit mometrix.com/academy and enter code: 174903

EXPRESSION OF FEELINGS

When an author intends to **express feelings**, he or she may use **expressive and bold language**. An author may write with emotion for any number of reasons. Sometimes, authors will express feelings because they are describing a personal situation of great pain or happiness. In other situations, authors will attempt to persuade the reader and will use emotion to stir up the passions. This kind of expression is easy to identify when the writer uses phrases like *I felt* and *I sense*. However, readers may find that the author will simply describe feelings without introducing them. As a reader, you must know the importance of recognizing when an author is expressing emotion and not to become overwhelmed by sympathy or passion. Readers should maintain some **detachment** so that they can still evaluate the strength of the author's argument or the quality of the writing.

> **Review Video: Emotional Language in Literature**
> Visit mometrix.com/academy and enter code: 759390

EXPOSITORY PASSAGE

An **expository** passage aims to **inform** and enlighten readers. Expository passages are nonfiction and usually center around a simple, easily defined topic. Since the goal of exposition is to teach, such a passage should be as clear as possible. Often, an expository passage contains helpful organizing words, like *first*, *next*, *for example*, and *therefore*. These words keep the reader **oriented** in the text. Although expository passages do not need to feature colorful language and artful writing, they are often more effective with these features. For a reader, the challenge of expository passages is to maintain steady attention. Expository passages are not always about subjects that will naturally interest a reader, so the writer is often more concerned with **clarity** and

comprehensibility than with engaging the reader. By reading actively, you can ensure a good habit of focus when reading an expository passage.

> **Review Video: Expository Passages**
> Visit mometrix.com/academy and enter code: 256515

NARRATIVE PASSAGE

A **narrative** passage is a story that can be fiction or nonfiction. However, there are a few elements that a text must have in order to be classified as a narrative. First, the text must have a **plot** (i.e., a series of events). Narratives often proceed in a clear sequence, but this is not a requirement. If the narrative is good, then these events will be interesting to readers. Second, a narrative has **characters**. These characters could be people, animals, or even inanimate objects—so long as they participate in the plot. Third, a narrative passage often contains **figurative language** which is meant to stimulate the imagination of readers by making comparisons and observations. For instance, a *metaphor*, a common piece of figurative language, is a description of one thing in terms of another. *The moon was a frosty snowball* is an example of a metaphor. In the literal sense this is obviously untrue, but the comparison suggests a certain mood for the reader.

TECHNICAL PASSAGE

A **technical** passage is written to *describe* a complex object or process. Technical writing is common in medical and technological fields, in which complex ideas of mathematics, science, and engineering need to be explained *simply* and *clearly*. To ease comprehension, a technical passage usually proceeds in a very logical order. Technical passages often have clear headings and subheadings, which are used to keep the reader oriented in the text. Additionally, you will find that these passages divide sections up with numbers or letters. Many technical passages look more like an outline than a piece of prose. The amount of **jargon** or difficult vocabulary will vary in a technical passage depending on the intended audience. As much as possible, technical passages try to avoid language that the reader will have to research in order to understand the message, yet readers will find that jargon cannot always be avoided.

> **Review Video: Technical Passages**
> Visit mometrix.com/academy and enter code: 478923

READING INFORMATIONAL TEXTS
LANGUAGE USE
LITERAL AND FIGURATIVE LANGUAGE

As in fictional literature, informational text also uses both **literal language**, which means just what it says, and **figurative language**, which imparts more than literal meaning. For example, an informational text author might use a simile or direct comparison, such as writing that a racehorse "ran like the wind." Informational text authors also use metaphors or implied comparisons, such as "the cloud of the Great Depression." Imagery may also appear in informational texts to increase the reader's understanding of ideas and concepts discussed in the text.

> **Review Video: Figurative Language**
> Visit mometrix.com/academy and enter code: 584902

EXPLICIT AND IMPLICIT INFORMATION

When informational text states something explicitly, the reader is told by the author exactly what is meant, which can include the author's interpretation or perspective of events. For example, a professor writes, "I have seen students go into an absolute panic just because they weren't able to complete the exam in the time they were allotted." This explicitly tells the reader that the students were afraid, and by using the words "just because," the writer indicates their fear was exaggerated out of proportion relative to what happened. However, another professor writes, "I have had students come to me, their faces drained of all color, saying

'We weren't able to finish the exam.'" This is an example of implicit meaning: the second writer did not state explicitly that the students were panicked. Instead, he wrote a description of their faces being "drained of all color." From this description, the reader can infer that the students were so frightened that their faces paled.

> **Review Video: Explicit and Implicit Information**
> Visit mometrix.com/academy and enter code: 735771

MAKING INFERENCES ABOUT INFORMATIONAL TEXT

With informational text, reader comprehension depends not only on recalling important statements and details, but also on reader inferences based on examples and details. Readers add information from the text to what they already know to draw inferences about the text. These inferences help the readers to fill in the information that the text does not explicitly state, enabling them to understand the text better. When reading a nonfictional autobiography or biography, for example, the most appropriate inferences might concern the events in the book, the actions of the subject of the autobiography or biography, and the message the author means to convey. When reading a nonfictional expository (informational) text, the reader would best draw inferences about problems and their solutions, and causes and their effects. When reading a nonfictional persuasive text, the reader will want to infer ideas supporting the author's message and intent.

STRUCTURES OR ORGANIZATIONAL PATTERNS IN INFORMATIONAL TEXTS

Informational text can be **descriptive**, appealing to the five senses and answering the questions what, who, when, where, and why. Another method of structuring informational text is sequence and order. **Chronological** texts relate events in the sequence that they occurred, from start to finish, while how-to texts organize information into a series of instructions in the sequence in which the steps should be followed. **Comparison-contrast** structures of informational text describe various ideas to their readers by pointing out how things or ideas are similar and how they are different. **Cause and effect** structures of informational text describe events that occurred and identify the causes or reasons that those events occurred. **Problem and solution** structures of informational texts introduce and describe problems and offer one or more solutions for each problem described.

DETERMINING AN INFORMATIONAL AUTHOR'S PURPOSE

Informational authors' purposes are why they write texts. Readers must determine authors' motivations and goals. Readers gain greater insight into a text by considering the author's motivation. This develops critical reading skills. Readers perceive writing as a person's voice, not simply printed words. Uncovering author motivations and purposes empowers readers to know what to expect from the text, read for relevant details, evaluate authors and their work critically, and respond effectively to the motivations and persuasions of the text. The main idea of a text is what the reader is supposed to understand from reading it; the purpose of the text is why the author has written it and what the author wants readers to do with its information. Authors state some purposes clearly, while other purposes may be unstated but equally significant. When stated purposes contradict other parts of a text, the author may have a hidden agenda. Readers can better evaluate a text's effectiveness, whether they agree or disagree with it, and why they agree or disagree through identifying unstated author purposes.

IDENTIFYING AUTHOR'S POINT OF VIEW OR PURPOSE

In some informational texts, readers find it easy to identify the author's point of view and purpose, such as when the author explicitly states his or her position and reason for writing. But other texts are more difficult, either because of the content or because the authors give neutral or balanced viewpoints. This is particularly true in scientific texts, in which authors may state the purpose of their research in the report, but never state their point of view except by interpreting evidence or data.

To analyze text and identify point of view or purpose, readers should ask themselves the following four questions:

1. With what main point or idea does this author want to persuade readers to agree?
2. How does this author's word choice affect the way that readers consider this subject?
3. How do this author's choices of examples and facts affect the way that readers consider this subject?
4. What is it that this author wants to accomplish by writing this text?

> Review Video: **Understanding the Author's Intent**
> Visit mometrix.com/academy and enter code: 511819
>
> Review Video: **Author's Position**
> Visit mometrix.com/academy and enter code: 827954

EVALUATING ARGUMENTS MADE BY INFORMATIONAL TEXT WRITERS

When evaluating an informational text, the first step is to identify the argument's conclusion. Then identify the author's premises that support the conclusion. Try to paraphrase premises for clarification and make the conclusion and premises fit. List all premises first, sequentially numbered, then finish with the conclusion. Identify any premises or assumptions not stated by the author but required for the stated premises to support the conclusion. Read word assumptions sympathetically, as the author might. Evaluate whether premises reasonably support the conclusion. For inductive reasoning, the reader should ask if the premises are true, if they support the conclusion, and if so, how strongly. For deductive reasoning, the reader should ask if the argument is valid or invalid. If all premises are true, then the argument is valid unless the conclusion can be false. If it can, then the argument is invalid. An invalid argument can be made valid through alterations such as the addition of needed premises.

USE OF RHETORIC IN INFORMATIONAL TEXTS

There are many ways authors can support their claims, arguments, beliefs, ideas, and reasons for writing in informational texts. For example, authors can appeal to readers' sense of **logic** by communicating their reasoning through a carefully sequenced series of logical steps to help "prove" the points made. Authors can appeal to readers' **emotions** by using descriptions and words that evoke feelings of sympathy, sadness, anger, righteous indignation, hope, happiness, or any other emotion to reinforce what they express and share with their audience. Authors may appeal to the **moral** or **ethical values** of readers by using words and descriptions that can convince readers that something is right or wrong. By relating personal anecdotes, authors can supply readers with more accessible, realistic examples of points they make, as well as appealing to their emotions. They can provide supporting evidence by reporting case studies. They can also illustrate their points by making analogies to which readers can better relate.

TECHNICAL LANGUAGE

TECHNICAL LANGUAGE

Technical language is more impersonal than literary and vernacular language. Passive voice makes the tone impersonal. For example, instead of writing, "We found this a central component of protein metabolism," scientists write, "This was found a central component of protein metabolism." While science professors have traditionally instructed students to avoid active voice because it leads to first-person ("I" and "we") usage, science editors today find passive voice dull and weak. Many journal articles combine both. Tone in technical science writing should be detached, concise, and professional. While one may normally write, "This chemical has to be available for proteins to be digested," professionals write technically, "The presence of this chemical is required for the enzyme to break the covalent bonds of proteins." The use of technical language appeals to both technical and non-technical audiences by displaying the author or speaker's understanding of the subject and suggesting their credibility regarding the message they are communicating.

TECHNICAL MATERIAL FOR NON-TECHNICAL READERS

Writing about **technical subjects** for **non-technical readers** differs from writing for colleagues because authors place more importance on delivering a critical message than on imparting the maximum technical content possible. Technical authors also must assume that non-technical audiences do not have the expertise to comprehend extremely scientific or technical messages, concepts, and terminology. They must resist the temptation to impress audiences with their scientific knowledge and expertise and remember that their primary purpose is to communicate a message that non-technical readers will understand, feel, and respond to. Non-technical and technical styles include similarities. Both should formally cite any references or other authors' work utilized in the text. Both must follow intellectual property and copyright regulations. This includes the author's protecting his or her own rights, or a public domain statement, as he or she chooses.

> **Review Video: Technical Passages**
> Visit mometrix.com/academy and enter code: 478923

NON-TECHNICAL AUDIENCES

Writers of technical or scientific material may need to write for many non-technical audiences. Some readers have no technical or scientific background, and those who do may not be in the same field as the authors. Government and corporate policymakers and budget managers need technical information they can understand for decision-making. Citizens affected by technology or science are a different audience. Non-governmental organizations can encompass many of the preceding groups. Elementary and secondary school programs also need non-technical language for presenting technical subject matter. Additionally, technical authors will need to use non-technical language when collecting consumer responses to surveys, presenting scientific or para-scientific material to the public, writing about the history of science, and writing about science and technology in developing countries.

USE OF EVERYDAY LANGUAGE

Authors of technical information sometimes must write using non-technical language that readers outside their disciplinary fields can comprehend. They should use not only non-technical terms, but also normal, everyday language to accommodate readers whose native language is different than the language the text is written in. For example, instead of writing that "eustatic changes like thermal expansion are causing hazardous conditions in the littoral zone," an author would do better to write that "a rising sea level is threatening the coast." When technical terms cannot be avoided, authors should also define or explain them using non-technical language. Although authors must cite references and acknowledge their use of others' work, they should avoid the kinds of references or citations that they would use in scientific journals—unless they reinforce author messages. They should not use endnotes, footnotes, or any other complicated referential techniques because non-technical journal publishers usually do not accept them. Including high-resolution illustrations, photos, maps, or satellite images and incorporating multimedia into digital publications will enhance non-technical writing about technical subjects. Technical authors may publish using non-technical language in e-journals, trade journals, specialty newsletters, and daily newspapers.

Reading Argumentative Writing
Author's Argument in Argumentative Writing

In argumentative writing, the argument is a belief, position, or opinion that the author wants to convince readers to believe as well. For the first step, readers should identify the **issue**. Some issues are controversial, meaning people disagree about them. Gun control, foreign policy, and the death penalty are all controversial issues. The next step is to determine the **author's position** on the issue. That position or viewpoint constitutes the author's argument. Readers should then identify the **author's assumptions**: things he or she accepts, believes, or takes for granted without needing proof. Inaccurate or illogical assumptions produce flawed arguments and can mislead readers. Readers should identify what kinds of **supporting evidence** the author offers, such as research results, personal observations or experiences, case studies, facts, examples, expert testimony and opinions, and comparisons. Readers should decide how relevant this support is to the argument.

> **Review Video: Argumentative Writing**
> Visit mometrix.com/academy and enter code: 561544

Evaluating an Author's Argument

The first three reader steps to **evaluate an author's argument** are to identify the **author's assumptions**, identify the **supporting evidence**, and decide **whether the evidence is relevant**. For example, if an author is not an expert on a particular topic, then that author's personal experience or opinion might not be relevant. The fourth step is to assess the **author's objectivity**. For example, consider whether the author introduces clear, understandable supporting evidence and facts to support the argument. The fifth step is evaluating whether the author's **argument is complete**. When authors give sufficient support for their arguments and also anticipate and respond effectively to opposing arguments or objections to their points, their arguments are complete. However, some authors omit information that could detract from their arguments. If instead they stated this information and refuted it, it would strengthen their arguments. The sixth step in evaluating an author's argumentative writing is to assess whether the **argument is valid**. Providing clear, logical reasoning makes an author's argument valid. Readers should ask themselves whether the author's points follow a sequence that makes sense, and whether each point leads to the next. The seventh step is to determine whether the author's **argument is credible**, meaning that it is convincing and believable. Arguments that are not valid are not credible, so step seven depends on step six. Readers should be mindful of their own biases as they evaluate and should not expect authors to conclusively prove their arguments, but rather to provide effective support and reason.

Evaluating an Author's Method of Appeal

To evaluate the effectiveness of an appeal, it is important to consider the author's purpose for writing. Any appeals an author uses in their argument must be relevant to the argument's goal. For example, a writer that argues for the reclassification of Pluto, but primarily uses appeals to emotion, will not have an effective argument. This writer should focus on using appeals to logic and support their argument with provable facts. While most arguments should include appeals to logic, emotion, and credibility, some arguments only call for one or two of these types of appeal. Evidence can support an appeal, but the evidence must be relevant to truly strengthen the appeal's effectiveness. If the writer arguing for Pluto's reclassification uses the reasons for Jupiter's classification as evidence, their argument would be weak. This information may seem relevant because it is related to the classification of planets. However, this classification is highly dependent on the size of the celestial object, and Jupiter is significantly bigger than Pluto. This use of evidence is illogical and does not support the appeal. Even when appropriate evidence and appeals are used, appeals and arguments lose their effectiveness when they create logical fallacies.

Evidence

The term **text evidence** refers to information that supports a main point or minor points and can help lead the reader to a conclusion about the text's credibility. Information used as text evidence is precise, descriptive, and factual. A main point is often followed by supporting details that provide evidence to back up a claim. For example, a passage may include the claim that winter occurs during opposite months in the Northern and

Southern hemispheres. Text evidence for this claim may include examples of countries where winter occurs in opposite months. Stating that the tilt of the Earth as it rotates around the sun causes winter to occur at different times in separate hemispheres is another example of text evidence. Text evidence can come from common knowledge, but it is also valuable to include text evidence from credible, relevant outside sources.

> **Review Video: Textual Evidence**
> Visit mometrix.com/academy and enter code: 486236

Evidence that supports the thesis and additional arguments needs to be provided. Most arguments must be supported by facts or statistics. A fact is something that is known with certainty, has been verified by several independent individuals, and can be proven to be true. In addition to facts, examples and illustrations can support an argument by adding an emotional component. With this component, you persuade readers in ways that facts and statistics cannot. The emotional component is effective when used alongside objective information that can be confirmed.

CREDIBILITY

The text used to support an argument can be the argument's downfall if the text is not credible. A text is **credible**, or believable, when its author is knowledgeable and objective, or unbiased. The author's motivations for writing the text play a critical role in determining the credibility of the text and must be evaluated when assessing that credibility. Reports written about the ozone layer by an environmental scientist and a hairdresser will have a different level of credibility.

> **Review Video: Author Credibility**
> Visit mometrix.com/academy and enter code: 827257

APPEAL TO EMOTION

Sometimes, authors will appeal to the reader's emotion in an attempt to persuade or to distract the reader from the weakness of the argument. For instance, the author may try to inspire the pity of the reader by delivering a heart-rending story. An author also might use the bandwagon approach, in which he suggests that his opinion is correct because it is held by the majority. Some authors resort to name-calling, in which insults and harsh words are delivered to the opponent in an attempt to distract. In advertising, a common appeal is the celebrity testimonial, in which a famous person endorses a product. Of course, the fact that a famous person likes something should not really mean anything to the reader. These and other emotional appeals are usually evidence of poor reasoning and a weak argument.

> **Review Video: Emotional Language in Literature**
> Visit mometrix.com/academy and enter code: 759390

COUNTER ARGUMENTS

When authors give both sides to the argument, they build trust with their readers. As a reader, you should start with an undecided or neutral position. If an author presents only his or her side to the argument, then they are not exhibiting credibility and are weakening their argument.

Building common ground with readers can be effective for persuading neutral, skeptical, or opposed readers. Sharing values with undecided readers can allow people to switch positions without giving up what they feel is important. People who may oppose a position need to feel that they can change their minds without betraying who they are as a person. This appeal to having an open mind can be a powerful tool in arguing a position without antagonizing other views. Objections can be countered on a point-by-point basis or in a summary paragraph. Be mindful of how an author points out flaws in counter arguments. If they are unfair to the other side of the argument, then you should lose trust with the author.

Integration of Ideas

MAKING AND EVALUATING PREDICTIONS

MAKING PREDICTIONS

When we read literature, **making predictions** about what will happen in the writing reinforces our purpose for reading and prepares us mentally. A **prediction** is a guess about what will happen next. Readers constantly make predictions based on what they have read and what they already know. We can make predictions before we begin reading and during our reading. Consider the following sentence: *Staring at the computer screen in shock, Kim blindly reached over for the brimming glass of water on the shelf to her side.* The sentence suggests that Kim is distracted, and that she is not looking at the glass that she is going to pick up. So, a reader might predict that Kim is going to knock over the glass. Of course, not every prediction will be accurate: perhaps Kim will pick the glass up cleanly. Nevertheless, the author has certainly created the expectation that the water might be spilled.

As we read on, we can test the accuracy of our predictions, revise them in light of additional reading, and confirm or refute our predictions. Predictions are always subject to revision as the reader acquires more information. A reader can make predictions by observing the title and illustrations; noting the structure, characters, and subject; drawing on existing knowledge relative to the subject; and asking "why" and "who" questions. Connecting reading to what we already know enables us to learn new information and construct meaning. For example, before third-graders read a book about Johnny Appleseed, they may start a KWL chart—a list of what they *Know*, what they *Want* to know or learn, and what they have *Learned* after reading. Activating existing background knowledge and thinking about the text before reading improves comprehension.

> **Review Video: Predictive Reading**
> Visit mometrix.com/academy and enter code: 437248

Test-taking tip: To respond to questions requiring future predictions, your answers should be based on evidence of past or present behavior and events.

EVALUATING PREDICTIONS

When making predictions, readers should be able to explain how they developed their prediction. One way readers can defend their thought process is by citing textual evidence. Textual evidence to evaluate reader predictions about literature includes specific synopses of the work, paraphrases of the work or parts of it, and direct quotations from the work. These references to the text must support the prediction by indicating, clearly or unclearly, what will happen later in the story. A text may provide these indications through literary devices such as foreshadowing. Foreshadowing is anything in a text that gives the reader a hint about what is to come by emphasizing the likelihood of an event or development. Foreshadowing can occur through descriptions, exposition, and dialogue. Foreshadowing in dialogue usually occurs when a character gives a warning or expresses a strong feeling that a certain event will occur. Foreshadowing can also occur through irony. However, unlike other forms of foreshadowing, the events that seem the most likely are the opposite of what actually happens. Instances of foreshadowing and irony can be summarized, paraphrased, or quoted to defend a reader's prediction.

> **Review Video: Textual Evidence for Predictions**
> Visit mometrix.com/academy and enter code: 261070

MAKING INFERENCES AND DRAWING CONCLUSIONS

Inferences are logical conclusions that readers make based on their observations and previous knowledge. An inference is based on both what is found in a passage or a story and what is known from personal experience. For instance, a story may say that a character is frightened and can hear howling in the distance. Based on both what is in the text and personal knowledge, it is a logical conclusion that the character is frightened because he hears the sound of wolves. A good inference is supported by the information in a passage.

IMPLICIT AND EXPLICIT INFORMATION

By inferring, readers construct meanings from text that are personally relevant. By combining their own schemas or concepts and their background information pertinent to the text with what they read, readers interpret it according to both what the author has conveyed and their own unique perspectives. Inferences are different from **explicit information**, which is clearly stated in a passage. Authors do not always explicitly spell out every meaning in what they write; many meanings are implicit. Through inference, readers can comprehend implied meanings in the text, and also derive personal significance from it, making the text meaningful and memorable to them. Inference is a natural process in everyday life. When readers infer, they can draw conclusions about what the author is saying, predict what may reasonably follow, amend these predictions as they continue to read, interpret the import of themes, and analyze the characters' feelings and motivations through their actions.

EXAMPLE OF DRAWING CONCLUSIONS FROM INFERENCES

Read the excerpt and decide why Jana finally relaxed.

> Jana loved her job, but the work was very demanding. She had trouble relaxing. She called a friend, but she still thought about work. She ordered a pizza, but eating it did not help. Then, her kitten jumped on her lap and began to purr. Jana leaned back and began to hum a little tune. She felt better.

You can draw the conclusion that Jana relaxed because her kitten jumped on her lap. The kitten purred, and Jana leaned back and hummed a tune. Then she felt better. The excerpt does not explicitly say that this is the reason why she was able to relax. The text leaves the matter unclear, but the reader can infer or make a "best guess" that this is the reason she is relaxing. This is a logical conclusion based on the information in the passage. It is the best conclusion a reader can make based on the information he or she has read. Inferences are based on the information in a passage, but they are not directly stated in the passage.

Test-taking tip: While being tested on your ability to make correct inferences, you must look for **contextual clues**. An answer can be true, but not the best or most correct answer. The contextual clues will help you find the answer that is the **best answer** out of the given choices. Be careful in your reading to understand the context in which a phrase is stated. When asked for the implied meaning of a statement made in the passage, you should immediately locate the statement and read the **context** in which the statement was made. Also, look for an answer choice that has a similar phrase to the statement in question.

> **Review Video: Inference**
> Visit mometrix.com/academy and enter code: 379203
>
> **Review Video: How to Support a Conclusion**
> Visit mometrix.com/academy and enter code: 281653

CRITICAL READING SKILLS
OPINIONS, FACTS, AND FALLACIES

Critical thinking skills are mastered through understanding various types of writing and the different purposes authors can have for writing different passages. Every author writes for a purpose. When you understand their purpose and how they accomplish their goal, you will be able to analyze their writing and determine whether or not you agree with their conclusions.

Readers must always be aware of the difference between fact and opinion. A **fact** can be subjected to analysis and proven to be true. An **opinion**, on the other hand, is the author's personal thoughts or feelings and may not be altered by research or evidence. If the author writes that the distance from New York City to Boston is about two hundred miles, then he or she is stating a fact. If the author writes that New York City is too crowded, then he or she is giving an opinion because there is no objective standard for overpopulation. Opinions are often supported by facts. For instance, an author might use a comparison between the population density of New York City and that of other major American cities as evidence of an overcrowded population. An opinion supported by facts tends to be more convincing. On the other hand, when authors support their opinions with other opinions, readers should employ critical thinking and approach the argument with skepticism.

> **Review Video: Distinguishing Fact and Opinion**
> Visit mometrix.com/academy and enter code: 870899

RELIABLE SOURCES

When you read an argumentative passage, you need to be sure that facts are presented to the reader from **reliable sources**. An opinion is what the author thinks about a given topic. An opinion is not common knowledge or proven by expert sources, instead the information is the personal beliefs and thoughts of the author. To distinguish between fact and opinion, a reader needs to consider the type of source that is presenting information, the information that backs-up a claim, and the author's motivation to have a certain point-of-view on a given topic. For example, if a panel of scientists has conducted multiple studies on the effectiveness of taking a certain vitamin, then the results are more likely to be factual than those of a company that is selling a vitamin and simply claims that taking the vitamin can produce positive effects. The company is motivated to sell their product, and the scientists are using the scientific method to prove a theory. Remember, if you find sentences that contain phrases such as "I think...", then the statement is an opinion.

BIASES

In their attempts to persuade, writers often make mistakes in their thought processes and writing choices. These processes and choices are important to understand so you can make an informed decision about the author's credibility. Every author has a point of view, but authors demonstrate a **bias** when they ignore reasonable counterarguments or distort opposing viewpoints. A bias is evident whenever the author's claims are presented in a way that is unfair or inaccurate. Bias can be intentional or unintentional, but readers should be skeptical of the author's argument in either case. Remember that a biased author may still be correct. However, the author will be correct in spite of, not because of, his or her bias.

A **stereotype** is a bias applied specifically to a group of people or a place. Stereotyping is considered to be particularly abhorrent because it promotes negative, misleading generalizations about people. Readers should be very cautious of authors who use stereotypes in their writing. These faulty assumptions typically reveal the author's ignorance and lack of curiosity.

> **Review Video: Bias and Stereotype**
> Visit mometrix.com/academy and enter code: 644829

PERSUASION AND RHETORIC
PERSUASIVE TECHNIQUES

To **appeal using reason**, writers present logical arguments, such as using "If... then... because" statements. To **appeal to emotions**, authors may ask readers how they would feel about something or to put themselves in another's place, present their argument as one that will make the audience feel good, or tell readers how they should feel. To **appeal to character**, **morality**, or **ethics**, authors present their points to readers as the right or most moral choices. Authors cite expert opinions to show readers that someone very knowledgeable about the subject or viewpoint agrees with the author's claims. **Testimonials**, usually via anecdotes or quotations regarding the author's subject, help build the audience's trust in an author's message through positive support from ordinary people. **Bandwagon appeals** claim that everybody else agrees with the author's argument and persuade readers to conform and agree, also. Authors **appeal to greed** by presenting their choice as cheaper, free, or more valuable for less cost. They **appeal to laziness** by presenting their views as more convenient, easy, or relaxing. Authors also anticipate potential objections and argue against them before audiences think of them, thereby depicting those objections as weak.

Authors can use **comparisons** like analogies, similes, and metaphors to persuade audiences. For example, a writer might represent excessive expenses as "hemorrhaging" money, which the author's recommended solution will stop. Authors can use negative word connotations to make some choices unappealing to readers, and positive word connotations to make others more appealing. Using **humor** can relax readers and garner their agreement. However, writers must take care: ridiculing opponents can be a successful strategy for appealing to readers who already agree with the author, but can backfire by angering other readers. **Rhetorical questions** need no answer, but create effect that can force agreement, such as asking the question, "Wouldn't you rather be paid more than less?" **Generalizations** persuade readers by being impossible to disagree with. Writers can easily make generalizations that appear to support their viewpoints, like saying, "We all want peace, not war" regarding more specific political arguments. **Transfer** and **association** persuade by example: if advertisements show attractive actors enjoying their products, audiences imagine they will experience the same. **Repetition** can also sometimes effectively persuade audiences.

> **Review Video: Using Rhetorical Strategies for Persuasion**
> Visit mometrix.com/academy and enter code: 302658

CLASSICAL AUTHOR APPEALS

In his *On Rhetoric,* ancient Greek philosopher Aristotle defined three basic types of appeal used in writing, which he called *pathos*, *ethos*, and *logos*. **Pathos** means suffering or experience and refers to appeals to the emotions (the English word *pathetic* comes from this root). Writing that is meant to entertain audiences, by making them either happy, as with comedy, or sad, as with tragedy, uses *pathos*. Aristotle's *Poetics* states that evoking the emotions of terror and pity is one of the criteria for writing tragedy. **Ethos** means character and connotes ideology (the English word *ethics* comes from this root). Writing that appeals to credibility, based on academic, professional, or personal merit, uses *ethos*. **Logos** means "I say" and refers to a plea, opinion, expectation, word or speech, account, opinion, or reason (the English word *logic* comes from this root.) Aristotle used it to mean persuasion that appeals to the audience through reasoning and logic to influence their opinions.

RHETORICAL DEVICES

- An **anecdote** is a brief story authors may relate to their argument, which can illustrate their points in a more real and relatable way.
- **Aphorisms** concisely state common beliefs and may rhyme. For example, Benjamin Franklin's "Early to bed and early to rise / Makes a man healthy, wealthy, and wise" is an aphorism.
- **Allusions** refer to literary or historical figures to impart symbolism to a thing or person and to create reader resonance. In John Steinbeck's *Of Mice and Men,* protagonist George's last name is Milton. This alludes to John Milton, who wrote *Paradise Lost*, and symbolizes George's eventual loss of his dream.

- **Satire** exaggerates, ridicules, or pokes fun at human flaws or ideas, as in the works of Jonathan Swift and Mark Twain.
- A **parody** is a form of satire that imitates another work to ridicule its topic or style.
- A **paradox** is a statement that is true despite appearing contradictory.
- **Hyperbole** is overstatement using exaggerated language.
- An **oxymoron** combines seeming contradictions, such as "deafening silence."
- **Analogies** compare two things that share common elements.
- **Similes** (stated comparisons using the words *like* or *as*) and **metaphors** (stated comparisons that do not use *like* or *as*) are considered forms of analogy.
- When using logic to reason with audiences, **syllogism** refers either to deductive reasoning or a deceptive, very sophisticated, or subtle argument.
- **Deductive reasoning** moves from general to specific, **inductive reasoning** from specific to general.
- **Diction** is author word choice that establishes tone and effect.
- **Understatement** achieves effects like contrast or irony by downplaying or describing something more subtly than warranted.
- **Chiasmus** uses parallel clauses, the second reversing the order of the first. Examples include T. S. Eliot's "Has the Church failed mankind, or has mankind failed the Church?" and John F. Kennedy's "Ask not what your country can do for you; ask what you can do for your country."
- **Anaphora** regularly repeats a word or phrase at the beginnings of consecutive clauses or phrases to add emphasis to an idea. A classic example of anaphora was Winston Churchill's emphasis of determination: "[W]e shall fight on the beaches, we shall fight on the landing grounds, we shall fight in the fields and in the streets, we shall fight in the hills; we shall never surrender..."

READING COMPREHENSION AND CONNECTING WITH TEXTS
COMPARING TWO STORIES

When presented with two different stories, there will be **similarities** and **differences** between the two. A reader needs to make a list, or other graphic organizer, of the points presented in each story. Once the reader has written down the main point and supporting points for each story, the two sets of ideas can be compared. The reader can then present each idea and show how it is the same or different in the other story. This is called **comparing and contrasting ideas**.

The reader can compare ideas by stating, for example: "In Story 1, the author believes that humankind will one day land on Mars, whereas in Story 2, the author believes that Mars is too far away for humans to ever step foot on." Note that the two viewpoints are different in each story that the reader is comparing. A reader may state that: "Both stories discussed the likelihood of humankind landing on Mars." This statement shows how the viewpoint presented in both stories is based on the same topic, rather than how each viewpoint is different. The reader will complete a comparison of two stories with a conclusion.

> **Review Video: How to Compare and Contrast**
> Visit mometrix.com/academy and enter code: 833765

OUTLINING A PASSAGE

As an aid to drawing conclusions, **outlining** the information contained in the passage should be a familiar skill to readers. An effective outline will reveal the structure of the passage and will lead to solid conclusions. An effective outline will have a title that refers to the basic subject of the text, though the title does not need to restate the main idea. In most outlines, the main idea will be the first major section. Each major idea in the passage will be established as the head of a category. For instance, the most common outline format calls for the main ideas of the passage to be indicated with Roman numerals. In an effective outline of this kind, each of the main ideas will be represented by a Roman numeral and none of the Roman numerals will designate minor details or secondary ideas. Moreover, all supporting ideas and details should be placed in the appropriate place on the outline. An outline does not need to include every detail listed in the text, but it should feature all of those that are central to the argument or message. Each of these details should be listed under the corresponding main idea.

> **Review Video: Outlining as an Aid to Drawing Conclusions**
> Visit mometrix.com/academy and enter code: 584445

USING GRAPHIC ORGANIZERS

Ideas from a text can also be organized using **graphic organizers**. A graphic organizer is a way to simplify information and take key points from the text. A graphic organizer such as a timeline may have an event listed for a corresponding date on the timeline, while an outline may have an event listed under a key point that occurs in the text. Each reader needs to create the type of graphic organizer that works the best for him or her in terms of being able to recall information from a story. Examples include a spider-map, which takes a main idea from the story and places it in a bubble with supporting points branching off the main idea. An outline is useful for diagramming the main and supporting points of the entire story, and a Venn diagram compares and contrasts characteristics of two or more ideas.

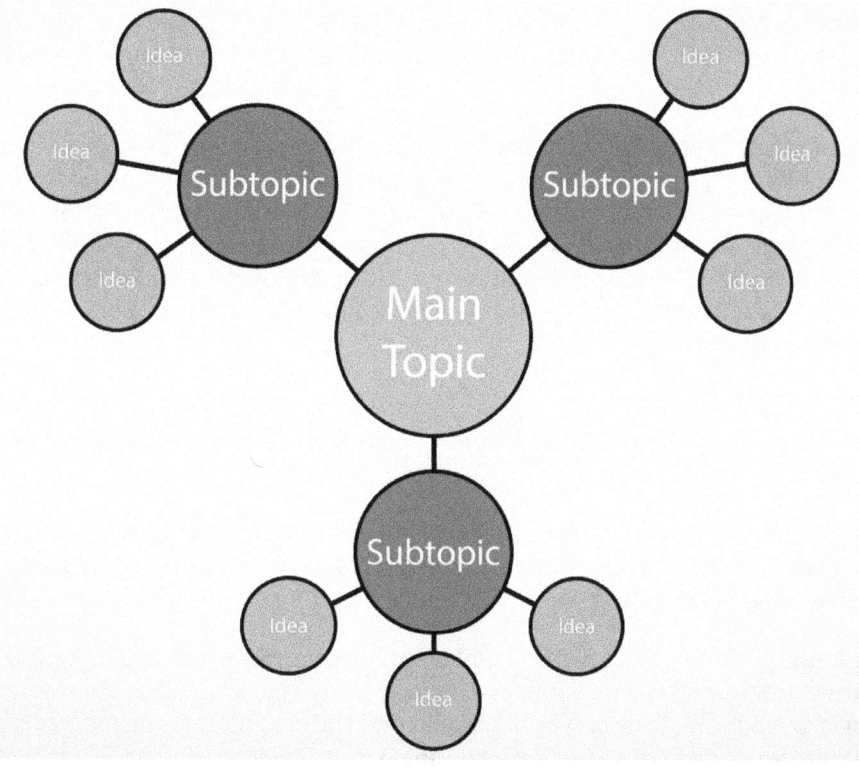

> **Review Video: Graphic Organizers**
> Visit mometrix.com/academy and enter code: 665513

MAKING LOGICAL CONCLUSIONS ABOUT A PASSAGE

A reader should always be drawing conclusions from the text. Sometimes conclusions are **implied** from written information, and other times the information is **stated directly** within the passage. One should always aim to draw conclusions from information stated within a passage, rather than to draw them from mere implications. At times an author may provide some information and then describe a counterargument. Readers should be alert for direct statements that are subsequently rejected or weakened by the author. Furthermore, you should always read through the entire passage before drawing conclusions. Many readers are trained to expect the author's conclusions at either the beginning or the end of the passage, but many texts do not adhere to this format.

Drawing conclusions from information implied within a passage requires confidence on the part of the reader. **Implications** are things that the author does not state directly, but readers can assume based on what the author does say. Consider the following passage: *I stepped outside and opened my umbrella. By the time I got to work, the cuffs of my pants were soaked.* The author never states that it is raining, but this fact is clearly implied. Conclusions based on implication must be well supported by the text. In order to draw a solid conclusion, readers should have **multiple pieces of evidence**. If readers have only one piece, they must be assured that there is no other possible explanation than their conclusion. A good reader will be able to draw many conclusions from information implied by the text, which will be a great help on the exam.

DRAWING CONCLUSIONS

A common type of inference that a reader has to make is **drawing a conclusion**. The reader makes this conclusion based on the information provided within a text. Certain facts are included to help a reader come to a specific conclusion. For example, a story may open with a man trudging through the snow on a cold winter day, dragging a sled behind him. The reader can logically **infer** from the setting of the story that the man is wearing heavy winter clothes in order to stay warm. Information is implied based on the setting of a story, which is why **setting** is an important element of the text. If the same man in the example was trudging down a beach on a hot summer day, dragging a surf board behind him, the reader would assume that the man is not wearing heavy clothes. The reader makes inferences based on their own experiences and the information presented to them in the story.

Test-taking tip: When asked to identify a conclusion that may be drawn, look for critical "hedge" phrases, such as *likely*, *may*, *can*, and *will often*, among many others. When you are being tested on this knowledge, remember the question that writers insert into these hedge phrases to cover every possibility. Often an answer will be wrong simply because there is no room for exception. Extreme positive or negative answers (such as always or never) are usually not correct. When answering these questions, the reader **should not** use any outside knowledge that is not gathered directly or reasonably inferred from the passage. Correct answers can be derived straight from the passage.

EXAMPLE

Read the following sentence from *Little Women* by Louisa May Alcott and draw a conclusion based upon the information presented:

> You know the reason Mother proposed not having any presents this Christmas was because it is going to be a hard winter for everyone; and she thinks we ought not to spend money for pleasure, when our men are suffering so in the army.

Based on the information in the sentence, the reader can conclude, or **infer**, that the men are away at war while the women are still at home. The pronoun *our* gives a clue to the reader that the character is speaking about men she knows. In addition, the reader can assume that the character is speaking to a brother or sister, since the term "Mother" is used by the character while speaking to another person. The reader can also come to the conclusion that the characters celebrate Christmas, since it is mentioned in the **context** of the sentence. In the sentence, the mother is presented as an unselfish character who is opinionated and thinks about the wellbeing of other people.

SUMMARIZING

A helpful tool is the ability to **summarize** the information that you have read in a paragraph or passage format. This process is similar to creating an effective outline. First, a summary should accurately define the main idea of the passage, though the summary does not need to explain this main idea in exhaustive detail. The summary should continue by laying out the most important supporting details or arguments from the passage. All of the significant supporting details should be included, and none of the details included should be irrelevant or insignificant. Also, the summary should accurately report all of these details. Too often, the desire for brevity in a summary leads to the sacrifice of clarity or accuracy. Summaries are often difficult to read because they omit all of the graceful language, digressions, and asides that distinguish great writing. However, an effective summary should communicate the same overall message as the original text.

> **Review Video: Summarizing Text**
> Visit mometrix.com/academy and enter code: 172903

PARAPHRASING

Paraphrasing is another method that the reader can use to aid in comprehension. When paraphrasing, one puts what they have read into their own words by rephrasing what the author has written, or one "translates" all of what the author shared into their own words by including as many details as they can.

EVALUATING A PASSAGE

It is important to understand the logical conclusion of the ideas presented in an informational text. **Identifying a logical conclusion** can help you determine whether you agree with the writer or not. Coming to this conclusion is much like making an inference: the approach requires you to combine the information given by the text with what you already know and make a logical conclusion. If the author intended for the reader to draw a certain conclusion, then you can expect the author's argumentation and detail to be leading in that direction.

One way to approach the task of drawing conclusions is to make brief **notes** of all the points made by the author. When the notes are arranged on paper, they may clarify the logical conclusion. Another way to approach conclusions is to consider whether the reasoning of the author raises any pertinent questions. Sometimes you will be able to draw several conclusions from a passage. On occasion these will be conclusions that were never imagined by the author. Therefore, be aware that these conclusions must be **supported directly by the text**.

EVALUATION OF SUMMARIES

A summary of a literary passage is a condensation in the reader's own words of the passage's main points. Several guidelines can be used in evaluating a summary. The summary should be complete yet concise. It should be accurate, balanced, fair, neutral, and objective, excluding the reader's own opinions or reactions. It should reflect in similar proportion how much each point summarized was covered in the original passage. Summary writers should include tags of attribution, like "Macaulay argues that" to reference the original author whose ideas are represented in the summary. Summary writers should not overuse quotations; they should only quote central concepts or phrases they cannot precisely convey in words other than those of the original author. Another aspect of evaluating a summary is considering whether it can stand alone as a coherent, unified composition. In addition, evaluation of a summary should include whether its writer has cited the original source of the passage they have summarized so that readers can find it.

MAKING CONNECTIONS TO ENHANCE COMPREHENSION

Reading involves thinking. For good comprehension, readers make **text-to-self**, **text-to-text**, and **text-to-world connections**. Making connections helps readers understand text better and predict what might occur next based on what they already know, such as how characters in the story feel or what happened in another text. Text-to-self connections with the reader's life and experiences make literature more personally relevant and meaningful to readers. Readers can make connections before, during, and after reading—including whenever the text reminds them of something similar they have encountered in life or other texts. The genre, setting, characters, plot elements, literary structure and devices, and themes an author uses allow a reader to make connections to other works of literature or to people and events in their own lives. Venn diagrams and other graphic organizers help visualize connections. Readers can also make double-entry notes: key content, ideas, events, words, and quotations on one side, and the connections with these on the other.

Literary Elements

PLOT AND STORY STRUCTURE

PLOT AND STORY STRUCTURE

The **plot** includes the events that happen in a story and the order in which they are told to the reader. There are several types of plot structures, as stories can be told in many ways. The most common plot structure is the chronological plot, which presents the events to the reader in the same order they occur for the characters in the story. Chronological plots usually have five main parts, the **exposition, rising action**, the **climax, falling action**, and the **resolution**. This type of plot structure guides the reader through the story's events as the characters experience them and is the easiest structure to understand and identify. While this is the most common plot structure, many stories are nonlinear, which means the plot does not sequence events in the same order the characters experience them. Such stories might include elements like flashbacks that cause the story to be nonlinear.

> **Review Video: How to Make a Story Map**
> Visit mometrix.com/academy and enter code: 261719

EXPOSITION

The **exposition** is at the beginning of the story and generally takes place before the rising action begins. The purpose of the exposition is to give the reader context for the story, which the author may do by introducing one or more characters, describing the setting or world, or explaining the events leading up to the point where the story begins. The exposition may still include events that contribute to the plot, but the **rising action** and main conflict of the story are not part of the exposition. Some narratives skip the exposition and begin the story with the beginning of the rising action, which causes the reader to learn the context as the story intensifies.

> **Review Video: Plot Line**
> Visit mometrix.com/academy and enter code: 944011

CONFLICT

A **conflict** is a problem to be solved. Literary plots typically include one conflict or more. Characters' attempts to resolve conflicts drive the narrative's forward movement. **Conflict resolution** is often the protagonist's primary occupation. Physical conflicts like exploring, wars, and escapes tend to make plots most suspenseful and exciting. Emotional, mental, or moral conflicts tend to make stories more personally gratifying or rewarding for many audiences. Conflicts can be external or internal. A major type of internal conflict is some inner personal battle, or **man versus self**. Major types of external conflicts include **man versus nature**, **man versus man**, and **man versus society**. Readers can identify conflicts in literary plots by identifying the protagonist and antagonist and asking why they conflict, what events develop the conflict, where the climax occurs, and how they identify with the characters.

Read the following paragraph and discuss the type of conflict present:

> Timothy was shocked out of sleep by the appearance of a bear just outside his tent. After panicking for a moment, he remembered some advice he had read in preparation for this trip: he should make noise so the bear would not be startled. As Timothy started to hum and sing, the bear wandered away.

There are three main types of conflict in literature: **man versus man**, **man versus nature**, and **man versus self**. This paragraph is an example of man versus nature. Timothy is in conflict with the bear. Even though no physical conflict like an attack exists, Timothy is pitted against the bear. Timothy uses his knowledge to "defeat" the bear and keep himself safe. The solution to the conflict is that Timothy makes noise, the bear wanders away, and Timothy is safe.

> **Review Video: Conflict**
> Visit mometrix.com/academy and enter code: 559550
>
> **Review Video: Determining Relationships in a Story**
> Visit mometrix.com/academy and enter code: 929925

RISING ACTION

The **rising action** is the part of the story where conflict **intensifies**. The rising action begins with an event that prompts the main conflict of the story. This may also be called the **inciting incident**. The main conflict generally occurs between the protagonist and an antagonist, but this is not the only type of conflict that may occur in a narrative. After this event, the protagonist works to resolve the main conflict by preparing for an altercation, pursuing a goal, fleeing an antagonist, or doing some other action that will end the conflict. The rising action is composed of several additional events that increase the story's tension. Most often, other developments will occur alongside the growth of the main conflict, such as character development or the development of minor conflicts. The rising action ends with the **climax**, which is the point of highest tension in the story.

CLIMAX

The **climax** is the event in the narrative that marks the height of the story's conflict or tension. The event that takes place at the story's climax will end the rising action and bring about the results of the main conflict. If the conflict was between a good protagonist and an evil antagonist, the climax may be a final battle between the two characters. If the conflict is an adventurer looking for heavily guarded treasure, the climax may be the adventurer's encounter with the final obstacle that protects the treasure. The climax may be made of multiple scenes, but can usually be summarized as one event. Once the conflict and climax are complete, the **falling action** begins.

FALLING ACTION

The **falling action** shows what happens in the story between the climax and the resolution. The falling action often composes a much smaller portion of the story than the rising action does. While the climax includes the end of the main conflict, the falling action may show the results of any minor conflicts in the story. For example, if the protagonist encountered a troll on the way to find some treasure, and the troll demanded the protagonist share the treasure after retrieving it, the falling action would include the protagonist returning to share the treasure with the troll. Similarly, any unexplained major events are usually made clear during the falling action. Once all significant elements of the story are resolved or addressed, the story's resolution will occur. The **resolution** is the end of the story, which shows the final result of the plot's events and shows what life is like for the main characters once they are no longer experiencing the story's conflicts.

RESOLUTION

The way the conflict is **resolved** depends on the type of conflict. The plot of any book starts with the lead up to the conflict, then the conflict itself, and finally the solution, or **resolution**, to the conflict. In **man versus man** conflicts, the conflict is often resolved by two parties coming to some sort of agreement or by one party triumphing over the other party. In **man versus nature** conflicts, the conflict is often resolved by man coming to some realization about some aspect of nature. In **man versus self** conflicts, the conflict is often resolved by the character growing or coming to an understanding about part of himself.

THEME

A **theme** is a central idea demonstrated by a passage. Often, a theme is a lesson or moral contained in the text, but it does not have to be. It also is a unifying idea that is used throughout the text; it can take the form of a common setting, idea, symbol, design, or recurring event. A passage can have two or more themes that convey its overall idea. The theme or themes of a passage are often based on **universal themes**. They can frequently be expressed using well-known sayings about life, society, or human nature, such as "Hard work pays off" or "Good triumphs over evil." Themes are not usually stated **explicitly**. The reader must figure them out by carefully reading the passage. Themes are created through descriptive language or events in the plot. The events of a story help shape the themes of a passage.

EXAMPLE

Explain why "if you care about something, you need to take care of it" accurately describes the theme of the following excerpt.

> Luca collected baseball cards, but he wasn't very careful with them. He left them around the house. His dog liked to chew. One day, Luca and his friend Bart were looking at his collection. Then they went outside. When Luca got home, he saw his dog chewing on his cards. They were ruined.

This excerpt tells the story of a boy who is careless with his baseball cards and leaves them lying around. His dog ends up chewing them and ruining them. The lesson is that if you care about something, you need to take care of it. This is the theme, or point, of the story. Some stories have more than one theme, but this is not really true of this excerpt. The reader needs to figure out the theme based on what happens in the story. Sometimes, as in the case of fables, the theme is stated directly in the text. However, this is not usually the case.

> **Review Video: Themes in Literature**
> Visit mometrix.com/academy and enter code: 732074

NARRATOR'S POINT OF VIEW

POINT OF VIEW

Another element that impacts a text is the author's point of view. The **point of view** of a text is the perspective from which a passage is told. An author will always have a point of view about a story before he or she draws up a plot line. The author will know what events they want to take place, how they want the characters to interact, and how they want the story to resolve. An author will also have an opinion on the topic or series of events which is presented in the story that is based on their prior experience and beliefs.

The two main points of view that authors use, especially in a work of fiction, are first person and third person. If the narrator of the story is also the main character, or *protagonist*, the text is written in first-person point of view. In first person, the author writes from the perspective of *I*. Third-person point of view is probably the most common that authors use in their passages. Using third person, authors refer to each character by using *he* or *she*. In third-person omniscient, the narrator is not a character in the story and tells the story of all of the characters at the same time.

> **Review Video: Point of View**
> Visit mometrix.com/academy and enter code: 383336

FIRST-PERSON NARRATION

First-person narratives let narrators express inner feelings and thoughts, especially when the narrator is the protagonist as Lemuel Gulliver is in Jonathan Swift's *Gulliver's Travels*. The narrator may be a close friend of the protagonist, like Dr. Watson in Sir Arthur Conan Doyle's *Sherlock Holmes*. Or, the narrator can be less involved with the main characters and plot, like Nick Carraway in F. Scott Fitzgerald's *The Great Gatsby*. When a narrator reports others' narratives, she or he is a "**frame narrator**," like the nameless narrator of Joseph Conrad's *Heart of Darkness* or Mr. Lockwood in Emily Brontë's *Wuthering Heights*. **First-person plural** is unusual but can be effective. Isaac Asimov's *I, Robot*, William Faulkner's *A Rose for Emily*, Maxim Gorky's *Twenty-Six Men and a Girl*, and Jeffrey Eugenides' *The Virgin Suicides* all use first-person plural narration. Author Kurt Vonnegut is the first-person narrator in his semi-autobiographical novel *Timequake*. Also unusual, but effective, is a **first-person omniscient** (rather than the more common third-person omniscient) narrator, like Death in Markus Zusak's *The Book Thief* and the ghost in Alice Sebold's *The Lovely Bones*.

SECOND-PERSON NARRATION

While **second-person** address is very commonplace in popular song lyrics, it is the least used form of narrative voice in literary works. Popular serial books of the 1980s like *Fighting Fantasy* or *Choose Your Own Adventure* employed second-person narratives. In some cases, a narrative combines both second-person and first-person voices, using the pronouns *you* and *I*. This can draw readers into the story, and it can also enable the authors to compare directly "your" and "my" feelings, thoughts, and actions. When the narrator is also a character in the story, as in Edgar Allan Poe's short story "The Tell-Tale Heart" or Jay McInerney's novel *Bright Lights, Big City*, the narrative is better defined as first-person despite it also addressing "you."

THIRD-PERSON NARRATION

Narration in the third person is the most prevalent type, as it allows authors the most flexibility. It is so common that readers simply assume without needing to be informed that the narrator is not a character in the story, or involved in its events. **Third-person singular** is used more frequently than **third-person plural**, though some authors have also effectively used plural. However, both singular and plural are most often included in stories according to which characters are being described. The third-person narrator may be either objective or subjective, and either omniscient or limited. **Objective third-person** narration does not include what the characters described are thinking or feeling, while **subjective third-person** narration does. The **third-person omniscient** narrator knows everything about all characters, including their thoughts and emotions, and all related places, times, and events. However, the **third-person limited** narrator may know everything about a particular character, but is limited to that character. In other words, the narrator cannot speak about anything that character does not know.

ALTERNATING-PERSON NARRATION

Although authors more commonly write stories from one point of view, there are also instances wherein they alternate the narrative voice within the same book. For example, they may sometimes use an omniscient third-person narrator and a more intimate first-person narrator at other times. In J. K. Rowling's series of *Harry Potter* novels, she often writes in a third-person limited narrative, but sometimes changes to narration by characters other than the protagonist. George R. R. Martin's series *A Song of Ice and Fire* changes the point of view to coincide with divisions between chapters. The same technique is used by Erin Hunter (a pseudonym for several authors of the *Warriors, Seekers,* and *Survivors* book series). Authors using first-person narrative sometimes switch to third-person to describe significant action scenes, especially those where the narrator was absent or uninvolved, as Barbara Kingsolver does in her novel *The Poisonwood Bible*.

> **Review Video: The Narrator of a Story**
> Visit mometrix.com/academy and enter code: 742528

SETTING, MOOD, AND TONE
SETTING AND TIME FRAME
A literary text has both a setting and time frame. A **setting** is the place in which the story as a whole is set. The **time frame** is the period in which the story is set. This may refer to the historical period the story takes place in or if the story takes place over a single day. Both setting and time frame are relevant to a text's meaning because they help the reader place the story in time and space. An author uses setting and time frame to anchor a text, create a mood, and enhance its meaning. This helps a reader understand why a character acts the way he does, or why certain events in the story are important. The setting impacts the **plot** and character **motivations**, while the time frame helps place the story in **chronological context**.

EXAMPLE
Read the following excerpt from The Adventures of Huckleberry Finn by Mark Twain and analyze the relevance of setting to the text's meaning:

> We said there warn't no home like a raft, after all. Other places do seem so cramped up and smothery, but a raft don't. You feel mighty free and easy and comfortable on a raft.

This excerpt from *The Adventures of Huckleberry Finn* by Mark Twain reveals information about the **setting** of the book. By understanding that the main character, Huckleberry Finn, lives on a raft, the reader can place the story on a river, in this case, the Mississippi River in the South before the Civil War. The information about the setting also gives the reader clues about the **character** of Huck Finn: he clearly values independence and freedom, and he likes the outdoors. The information about the setting in the quote helps the reader to better understand the rest of the text.

SYNTAX AND WORD CHOICE
Authors use words and **syntax**, or sentence structure, to make their texts unique, convey their own writing style, and sometimes to make a point or emphasis. They know that word choice and syntax contribute to the reader's understanding of the text as well as to the tone and mood of a text.

> **Review Video: Syntax**
> Visit mometrix.com/academy and enter code: 242280

MOOD AND TONE
Mood is a story's atmosphere, or the feelings the reader gets from reading it. The way authors set the mood in writing is comparable to the way filmmakers use music to set the mood in movies. Instead of music, though, writers judiciously select descriptive words to evoke certain **moods**. The mood of a work may convey joy, anger, bitterness, hope, gloom, fear, apprehension, or any other emotion the author wants the reader to feel. In addition to vocabulary choices, authors also use figurative expressions, particular sentence structures, and choices of diction that project and reinforce the moods they want to create. Whereas mood is the reader's emotions evoked by reading what is written, **tone** is the emotions and attitudes of the writer that she or he expresses in the writing. Authors use the same literary techniques to establish tone as they do to establish

mood. An author may use a humorous tone, an angry or sad tone, a sentimental or unsentimental tone, or something else entirely.

MOOD AND TONE IN THE GREAT GATSBY

To understand the difference between mood and tone, look at this excerpt from F. Scott Fitzgerald's *The Great Gatsby*. In this passage, Nick Caraway, the novel's narrator, is describing his affordable house, which sits in a neighborhood full of expensive mansions.

> "I lived at West Egg, the—well the less fashionable of the two, though this is a most superficial tag to express the bizarre and not a little sinister contrast between them. My house was at the very tip of the egg, only fifty yard from the Sound, and squeezed between two huge places that rented for twelve or fifteen thousand a season ... My own house was an eyesore, but it was a small eyesore, and it had been overlooked, so I had a view of the water, a partial view of my neighbor's lawn, and the consoling proximity of millionaires—all for eighty dollars a month."

In this description, the mood created for the reader does not match the tone created through the narrator. The mood in this passage is one of dissatisfaction and inferiority. Nick compares his home to his neighbors', saying he lives in the "less fashionable" neighborhood and that his house is "overlooked," an "eyesore," and "squeezed between two huge" mansions. He also adds that his placement allows him the "consoling proximity of millionaires." A literal reading of these details leads the reader to have negative feelings toward Nick's house and his economic inferiority to his neighbors, creating the mood.

However, Fitzgerald also conveys an opposing attitude, or tone, through Nick's description. Nick calls the distinction between the neighborhoods "superficial," showing a suspicion of the value suggested by the neighborhoods' titles, properties, and residents. Nick also undermines his critique of his own home by calling it "a small eyesore" and claiming it has "been overlooked." However, he follows these statements with a description of his surroundings, claiming that he has "a view of the water" and can see some of his wealthy neighbor's property from his home, and a comparison between the properties' rent. While the mental image created for the reader depicts a small house shoved between looming mansions, the tone suggests that Nick enjoys these qualities about his home, or at least finds it charming. He acknowledges its shortcomings, but includes the benefits of his home's unassuming appearance.

> **Review Video: Style, Tone, and Mood**
> Visit mometrix.com/academy and enter code: 416961

HISTORICAL AND SOCIAL CONTEXT

Fiction that is heavily influenced by a historical or social context cannot be comprehended as the author intended if the reader does not keep this context in mind. Many important elements of the text will be influenced by any context, including symbols, allusions, settings, and plot events. These contexts, as well as the identity of the work's author, can help to inform the reader about the author's concerns and intended meanings. For example, George Orwell published his novel *1984* in the year 1949, soon after the end of World War II. At that time, following the defeat of the Nazis, the Cold War began between the Western Allied nations and the Eastern Soviet Communists. People were therefore concerned about the conflict between the freedoms afforded by Western democracies versus the oppression represented by Communism. Orwell had also previously fought in the Spanish Civil War against a Spanish regime that he and his fellows viewed as oppressive. From this information, readers can infer that Orwell was concerned about oppression by totalitarian governments. This informs *1984*'s story of Winston Smith's rebellion against the oppressive "Big Brother" government, of the fictional dictatorial state of Oceania, and his capture, torture, and ultimate conversion by that government. Some literary theories also seek to use historical and social contexts to reveal deeper meanings and implications in a text.

CHARACTER DEVELOPMENT AND DIALOGUE

CHARACTER DEVELOPMENT

When depicting characters or figures in a written text, authors generally use actions, dialogue, and descriptions as characterization techniques. Characterization can occur in both fiction and nonfiction and is used to show a character or figure's personality, demeanor, and thoughts. This helps create a more engaging experience for the reader by providing a more concrete picture of a character or figure's tendencies and features. Characterizations also gives authors the opportunity to integrate elements such as dialects, activities, attire, and attitudes into their writing.

To understand the meaning of a story, it is vital to understand the characters as the author describes them. We can look for contradictions in what a character thinks, says, and does. We can notice whether the author's observations about a character differ from what other characters in the story say about that character. A character may be dynamic, meaning they change significantly during the story, or static, meaning they remain the same from beginning to end. Characters may be two-dimensional, not fully developed, or may be well developed with characteristics that stand out vividly. Characters may also symbolize universal properties. Additionally, readers can compare and contrast characters to analyze how each one developed.

A well-known example of character development can be found in Charles Dickens's *Great Expectations*. The novel's main character, Pip, is introduced as a young boy, and he is depicted as innocent, kind, and humble. However, as Pip grows up and is confronted with the social hierarchy of Victorian England, he becomes arrogant and rejects his loved ones in pursuit of his own social advancement. Once he achieves his social goals, he realizes the merits of his former lifestyle, and lives with the wisdom he gained in both environments and life stages. Dickens shows Pip's ever-changing character through his interactions with others and his inner thoughts, which evolve as his personal values and personality shift.

DIALOGUE

Effectively written dialogue serves at least one, but usually several, purposes. It advances the story and moves the plot, develops the characters, sheds light on the work's theme or meaning, and can, often subtly, account for the passage of time not otherwise indicated. It can alter the direction that the plot is taking, typically by introducing some new conflict or changing existing ones. **Dialogue** can establish a work's narrative voice and the characters' voices and set the tone of the story or of particular characters. When fictional characters display enlightenment or realization, dialogue can give readers an understanding of what those characters have discovered and how. Dialogue can illuminate the motivations and wishes of the story's characters. By using consistent thoughts and syntax, dialogue can support character development. Skillfully created, it can also represent real-life speech rhythms in written form. Via conflicts and ensuing action, dialogue also provides drama.

DIALOGUE IN FICTION

In fictional works, effectively written dialogue does more than just break up or interrupt sections of narrative. While **dialogue** may supply exposition for readers, it must nonetheless be believable. Dialogue should be dynamic, not static, and it should not resemble regular prose. Authors should not use dialogue to write clever similes or metaphors, or to inject their own opinions. Nor should they use dialogue at all when narrative would be better. Most importantly, dialogue should not slow the plot movement. Dialogue must seem natural, which means careful construction of phrases rather than actually duplicating natural speech, which does not necessarily translate well to the written word. Finally, all dialogue must be pertinent to the story, rather than just added conversation.

Literary Techniques

FIGURATIVE LANGUAGE
LITERAL AND FIGURATIVE MEANING

When language is used **literally**, the words mean exactly what they say and nothing more. When language is used **figuratively**, the words mean something beyond their literal meaning. For example, "The weeping willow tree has long, trailing branches and leaves" is a literal description. But "The weeping willow tree looks as if it is bending over and crying" is a figurative description—specifically, a **simile** or stated comparison. Another figurative language form is **metaphor**, or an implied comparison. A good example is the metaphor of a city, state, or city-state as a ship, and its governance as sailing that ship. Ancient Greek lyrical poet Alcaeus is credited with first using this metaphor, and ancient Greek tragedian Aeschylus then used it in *Seven Against Thebes,* and then Plato used it in the *Republic.*

FIGURES OF SPEECH

A **figure of speech** is a verbal expression whose meaning is figurative rather than literal. For example, the phrase "butterflies in the stomach" does not refer to actual butterflies in a person's stomach. It is a metaphor representing the fluttery feelings experienced when a person is nervous or excited—or when one "falls in love," which does not mean physically falling. "Hitting a sales target" does not mean physically hitting a target with arrows as in archery; it is a metaphor for meeting a sales quota. "Climbing the ladder of success" metaphorically likens advancing in one's career to ascending ladder rungs. Similes, such as "light as a feather" (meaning very light, not a feather's actual weight), and hyperbole, like "I'm starving/freezing/roasting," are also figures of speech. Figures of speech are often used and crafted for emphasis, freshness of expression, or clarity.

> **Review Video: Figures of Speech**
> Visit mometrix.com/academy and enter code: 111295

FIGURATIVE LANGUAGE

Figurative language extends past the literal meanings of words. It offers readers new insight into the people, things, events, and subjects covered in a work of literature. Figurative language also enables readers to feel they are sharing the authors' experiences. It can stimulate the reader's senses, make comparisons that readers find intriguing or even startling, and enable readers to view the world in different ways. When looking for figurative language, it is important to consider the context of the sentence or situation. Phrases that appear out of place or make little sense when read literally are likely instances of figurative language. Once figurative language has been recognized, context is also important to determining the type of figurative language being used and its function. For example, when a comparison is being made, a metaphor or simile is likely being used. This means the comparison may emphasize or create irony through the things being compared. Seven specific types of figurative language include: alliteration, onomatopoeia, personification, imagery, similes, metaphors, and hyperbole.

> **Review Video: Figurative Language**
> Visit mometrix.com/academy and enter code: 584902

ALLITERATION AND ONOMATOPOEIA

Alliteration describes a series of words beginning with the same sounds. **Onomatopoeia** uses words imitating the sounds of things they name or describe. For example, in his poem "Come Down, O Maid," Alfred Tennyson writes of "The moan of doves in immemorial elms, / And murmuring of innumerable bees." The word "moan" sounds like some sounds doves make, "murmuring" represents the sounds of bees buzzing.

Onomatopoeia also includes words that are simply meant to represent sounds, such as "meow," "kaboom," and "whoosh."

> **Review Video: Alliteration in Everyday Expressions**
> Visit mometrix.com/academy and enter code: 462837

PERSONIFICATION

Another type of figurative language is **personification**. This is describing a non-human thing, like an animal or an object, as if it were human. The general intent of personification is to describe things in a manner that will be comprehensible to readers. When an author states that a tree *groans* in the wind, he or she does not mean that the tree is emitting a low, pained sound from a mouth. Instead, the author means that the tree is making a noise similar to a human groan. Of course, this personification establishes a tone of sadness or suffering. A different tone would be established if the author said that the tree was *swaying* or *dancing*. Alfred Tennyson's poem "The Eagle" uses all of these types of figurative language: "He clasps the crag with crooked hands." Tennyson used alliteration, repeating /k/ and /kr/ sounds. These hard-sounding consonants reinforce the imagery, giving visual and tactile impressions of the eagle.

> **Review Video: Personification**
> Visit mometrix.com/academy and enter code: 260066

SIMILES AND METAPHORS

Similes are stated comparisons using "like" or "as." Similes can be used to stimulate readers' imaginations and appeal to their senses. Because a simile includes *like* or *as,* the device creates more space between the description and the thing being described than a metaphor does. If an author says that *a house was like a shoebox*, then the tone is different than the author saying that the house *was* a shoebox. Authors will choose between a metaphor and a simile depending on their intended tone.

Similes also help compare fictional characters to well-known objects or experiences, so the reader can better relate to them. William Wordsworth's poem about "Daffodils" begins, "I wandered lonely as a cloud." This simile compares his loneliness to that of a cloud. It is also personification, giving a cloud the human quality loneliness. In his novel *Lord Jim* (1900), Joseph Conrad writes in Chapter 33, "I would have given anything for the power to soothe her frail soul, tormenting itself in its invincible ignorance like a small bird beating about the cruel wires of a cage." Conrad uses the word "like" to compare the girl's soul to a small bird. His description of the bird beating at the cage shows the similar helplessness of the girl's soul to gain freedom.

> **Review Video: Similes**
> Visit mometrix.com/academy and enter code: 642949

A **metaphor** is a type of figurative language in which the writer equates something with another thing that is not particularly similar, instead of using *like* or *as*. For instance, *the bird was an arrow arcing through the sky*. In this sentence, the arrow is serving as a metaphor for the bird. The point of a metaphor is to encourage the reader to consider the item being described in a *different way*. Let's continue with this metaphor for a flying bird. You are asked to envision the bird's flight as being similar to the arc of an arrow. So, you imagine the flight to be swift and bending. Metaphors are a way for the author to describe an item *without being direct and obvious*. This literary device is a lyrical and suggestive way of providing information. Note that the reference for a metaphor will not always be mentioned explicitly by the author. Consider the following description of a forest in winter: *Swaying skeletons reached for the sky and groaned as the wind blew through them.* In this example, the author is using *skeletons* as a metaphor for leafless trees. This metaphor creates a spooky tone while inspiring the reader's imagination.

LITERARY EXAMPLES OF METAPHOR

A **metaphor** is an implied comparison, i.e., it compares something to something else without using "like", "as", or other comparative words. For example, in "The Tyger" (1794), William Blake writes, "Tyger Tyger, burning bright, / In the forests of the night." Blake compares the tiger to a flame not by saying it is like a fire, but by simply describing it as "burning." Henry Wadsworth Longfellow's poem "O Ship of State" (1850) uses an extended metaphor by referring consistently throughout the entire poem to the state, union, or republic as a seagoing vessel, referring to its keel, mast, sail, rope, anchors, and to its braving waves, rocks, gale, tempest, and "false lights on the shore." Within the extended metaphor, Wordsworth uses a specific metaphor: "the anchors of thy hope!"

TED HUGHES' ANIMAL METAPHORS

Ted Hughes frequently used animal metaphors in his poetry. In "The Thought Fox," a model of concise, structured beauty, Hughes characterizes the poet's creative process with succinct, striking imagery of an idea entering his head like a wild fox. Repeating "loneliness" in the first two stanzas emphasizes the poet's lonely work: "Something else is alive / Beside the clock's loneliness." He treats an idea's arrival as separate from himself. Three stanzas detail in vivid images a fox's approach from the outside winter forest at starless midnight—its nose, "Cold, delicately" touching twigs and leaves; "neat" paw prints in snow; "bold" body; brilliant green eyes; and self-contained, focused progress—"Till, with a sudden sharp hot stink of fox," he metaphorically depicts poetic inspiration as the fox's physical entry into "the dark hole of the head." Hughes ends by summarizing his vision of a poet as an interior, passive idea recipient, with the outside world unchanged: "The window is starless still; the clock ticks, / The page is printed."

> **Review Video: Metaphors in Writing**
> Visit mometrix.com/academy and enter code: 133295

METONYMY

Metonymy is naming one thing with words or phrases of a closely related thing. This is similar to metaphor. However, the comparison has a close connection, unlike metaphor. An example of metonymy is to call the news media *the press*. Of course, *the press* is the machine that prints newspapers. Metonymy is a way of naming something without using the same name constantly.

SYNECDOCHE

Synecdoche points to the whole by naming one of the parts. An example of synecdoche would be calling a construction worker a *hard hat*. Like metonymy, synecdoche is an easy way of naming something without having to overuse a name. The device allows writers to highlight pieces of the thing being described. For example, referring to businessmen as *suits* suggests professionalism and unity.

> **Review Video: Metonymy and Synecdoche**
> Visit mometrix.com/academy and enter code: 900306

HYPERBOLE

Hyperbole is excessive exaggeration used for humor or emphasis rather than for literal meaning. For example, in *To Kill a Mockingbird*, Harper Lee wrote, "People moved slowly then. There was no hurry, for there was nowhere to go, nothing to buy and no money to buy it with, nothing to see outside the boundaries of Maycomb County." This was not literally true; Lee exaggerates the scarcity of these things for emphasis. In "Old Times on the Mississippi," Mark Twain wrote, "I... could have hung my hat on my eyes, they stuck out so far." This is not literal, but makes his description vivid and funny. In his poem "As I Walked Out One Evening", W. H. Auden wrote, "I'll love you, dear, I'll love you / Till China and Africa meet, / And the river jumps over the mountain / And the salmon sing in the street." He used things not literally possible to emphasize the duration of his love.

UNDERSTATEMENT

Understatement is the opposite of hyperbole. This device discounts or downplays something. Think about someone who climbs Mount Everest. Then, they say that the journey was *a little stroll*. As with other types of figurative language, understatement has a range of uses. The device may show self-defeat or modesty as in the Mount Everest example. However, some may think of understatement as false modesty (i.e., an attempt to bring attention to you or a situation). For example, a woman is praised on her diamond engagement ring. The woman says, *Oh, this little thing?* Her understatement might be heard as stuck-up or unfeeling.

> **Review Video: Hyperbole and Understatement**
> Visit mometrix.com/academy and enter code: 308470

LITERARY DEVICES

LITERARY IRONY

In literature, irony demonstrates the opposite of what is said or done. The three types of irony are **verbal irony**, **situational irony**, and **dramatic irony**. Verbal irony uses words opposite to the meaning. Sarcasm may use verbal irony. One common example is describing something that is confusing as "clear as mud." For example, in his 1986 movie *Hannah and Her Sisters,* author, director, and actor Woody Allen says to his character's date, "I had a great evening; it was like the Nuremburg Trials." Notice these employ similes. In situational irony, what happens contrasts with what was expected. O. Henry's short story *The Gift of the Magi* uses situational irony: a husband and wife each sacrifice their most prized possession to buy each other a Christmas present. The irony is that she sells her long hair to buy him a watch fob, while he sells his heirloom pocket-watch to buy her the jeweled combs for her hair she had long wanted; in the end, neither of them can use their gifts. In dramatic irony, narrative informs audiences of more than its characters know. For example, in *Romeo and Juliet,* the audience is made aware that Juliet is only asleep, while Romeo believes her to be dead, which then leads to Romeo's death.

> **Review Video: Irony**
> Visit mometrix.com/academy and enter code: 374204

IDIOMS

Idioms create comparisons, and often take the form of similes or metaphors. Idioms are always phrases and are understood to have a meaning that is different from its individual words' literal meaning. For example, "break a leg" is a common idiom that is used to wish someone luck or tell them to perform well. Literally, the phrase "break a leg" means to injure a person's leg, but the phrase takes on a different meaning when used as an idiom. Another example is "call it a day," which means to temporarily stop working on a task, or find a stopping point, rather than literally referring to something as "a day." Many idioms are associated with a region or group. For example, an idiom commonly used in the American South is "'til the cows come home." This phrase is often used to indicate that something will take or may last for a very long time, but not that it will literally last until the cows return to where they reside.

ALLUSION

An allusion is an uncited but recognizable reference to something else. Authors use language to make allusions to places, events, artwork, and other books in order to make their own text richer. For example, an author may allude to a very important text in order to make his own text seem more important. Martin Luther King, Jr. started his "I Have a Dream" speech by saying "Five score years ago…" This is a clear allusion to President Abraham Lincoln's "Gettysburg Address" and served to remind people of the significance of the event. An author may allude to a place to ground his text or make a cultural reference to make readers feel included. There are many reasons that authors make allusions.

> **Review Video: Allusions**
> Visit mometrix.com/academy and enter code: 294065

Comic Relief

Comic relief is the use of comedy by an author to break up a dramatic or tragic scene and infuse it with a bit of **lightheartedness**. In William Shakespeare's *Hamlet*, two gravediggers digging the grave for Ophelia share a joke while they work. The death and burial of Ophelia are tragic moments that directly follow each other. Shakespeare uses an instance of comedy to break up the tragedy and give his audience a bit of a break from the tragic drama. Authors sometimes use comic relief so that their work will be less depressing; other times they use it to create irony or contrast between the darkness of the situation and the lightness of the joke. Often, authors will use comedy to parallel what is happening in the tragic scenes.

> **Review Video: Comic Relief**
> Visit mometrix.com/academy and enter code: 779604

Foreshadowing

Foreshadowing is a device authors use to give readers **hints** about events that will take place later in a story. Foreshadowing most often takes place through a character's dialogue or actions. Sometimes the character will know what is going to happen and will purposefully allude to future events. For example, consider a protagonist who is about to embark on a journey through the woods. Just before the protagonist begins the trip, another character says, "Be careful, you never know what could be out in those woods!" This alerts the reader that the woods may be dangerous and prompts the reader to expect something to attack the protagonist in the woods. This is an example of foreshadowing through warning. Alternatively, a character may unknowingly foreshadow later events. For example, consider a story where a brother and sister run through their house and knock over a vase and break it. The brother says, "Don't worry, we'll clean it up! Mom will never know!" However, the reader knows that their mother will most likely find out what they have done, so the reader expects the siblings to later get in trouble for running, breaking the vase, and hiding it from their mother.

Symbolism

Symbolism describes an author's use of a **symbol**, an element of the story that **represents** something else. Symbols can impact stories in many ways, including deepening the meaning of a story or its elements, comparing a story to another work, or foreshadowing later events in a story. Symbols can be objects, characters, colors, numbers, or anything else the author establishes as a symbol. Symbols can be clearly established through direct comparison or repetition, but they can also be established subtly or gradually over a large portion of the story. Another form of symbolism is **allusion**, which is when something in a story is used to prompt the reader to think about another work. Many well-known works use **Biblical allusions**, which are allusions to events or details in the Bible that inform a work or an element within it.

Vocabulary

WORD ROOTS AND PREFIXES AND SUFFIXES

AFFIXES

Affixes in the English language are morphemes that are added to words to create related but different words. Derivational affixes form new words based on and related to the original words. For example, the affix *–ness* added to the end of the adjective *happy* forms the noun *happiness.* Inflectional affixes form different grammatical versions of words. For example, the plural affix *–s* changes the singular noun *book* to the plural noun *books*, and the past tense affix *–ed* changes the present tense verb *look* to the past tense *looked.* Prefixes are affixes placed in front of words. For example, *heat* means to make hot; *preheat* means to heat in advance. Suffixes are affixes placed at the ends of words. The *happiness* example above contains the suffix *–ness*. Circumfixes add parts both before and after words, such as how *light* becomes *enlighten* with the prefix *en-* and the suffix *–en.* Interfixes create compound words via central affixes: *speed* and *meter* become *speedometer* via the interfix *–o–*.

> **Review Video: Affixes**
> Visit mometrix.com/academy and enter code: 782422

WORD ROOTS, PREFIXES, AND SUFFIXES TO HELP DETERMINE MEANINGS OF WORDS

Many English words were formed from combining multiple sources. For example, the Latin *habēre* means "to have," and the prefixes *in-* and *im-* mean a lack or prevention of something, as in *insufficient* and *imperfect*. Latin combined *in-* with *habēre* to form *inhibēre*, whose past participle was *inhibitus*. This is the origin of the English word *inhibit*, meaning to prevent from having. Hence by knowing the meanings of both the prefix and the root, one can decipher the word meaning. In Greek, the root *enkephalo-* refers to the brain. Many medical terms are based on this root, such as encephalitis and hydrocephalus. Understanding the prefix and suffix meanings (*-itis* means inflammation; *hydro-* means water) allows a person to deduce that encephalitis refers to brain inflammation and hydrocephalus refers to water (or other fluid) in the brain.

> **Review Video: Root Words in English**
> Visit mometrix.com/academy and enter code: 896380
>
> **Review Video: Determining Word Meanings**
> Visit mometrix.com/academy and enter code: 894894

PREFIXES

Knowing common prefixes is helpful for all readers as they try to determining meanings or definitions of unfamiliar words. For example, a common word used when cooking is *preheat*. Knowing that *pre-* means in advance can also inform them that *presume* means to assume in advance, that *prejudice* means advance judgment, and that this understanding can be applied to many other words beginning with *pre-*. Knowing that the prefix *dis-* indicates opposition informs the meanings of words like *disbar, disagree, disestablish,* and many more. Knowing *dys-* means bad, impaired, abnormal, or difficult informs *dyslogistic, dysfunctional, dysphagia,* and *dysplasia.*

SUFFIXES

In English, certain suffixes generally indicate both that a word is a noun, and that the noun represents a state of being or quality. For example, *-ness* is commonly used to change an adjective into its noun form, as with *happy* and *happiness, nice* and *niceness,* and so on. The suffix *–tion* is commonly used to transform a verb into its noun form, as with *converse* and *conversation or move* and *motion*. Thus, if readers are unfamiliar with the second form of a word, knowing the meaning of the transforming suffix can help them determine meaning.

Prefixes for Numbers

Prefix	Definition	Examples
bi-	two	bisect, biennial
mono-	one, single	monogamy, monologue
poly-	many	polymorphous, polygamous
semi-	half, partly	semicircle, semicolon
uni-	one	uniform, unity

Prefixes for Time, Direction, and Space

Prefix	Definition	Examples
a-	in, on, of, up, to	abed, afoot
ab-	from, away, off	abdicate, abjure
ad-	to, toward	advance, adventure
ante-	before, previous	antecedent, antedate
anti-	against, opposing	antipathy, antidote
cata-	down, away, thoroughly	catastrophe, cataclysm
circum-	around	circumspect, circumference
com-	with, together, very	commotion, complicate
contra-	against, opposing	contradict, contravene
de-	from	depart
dia-	through, across, apart	diameter, diagnose
dis-	away, off, down, not	dissent, disappear
epi-	upon	epilogue
ex-	out	extract, excerpt
hypo-	under, beneath	hypodermic, hypothesis
inter-	among, between	intercede, interrupt
intra-	within	intramural, intrastate
ob-	against, opposing	objection
per-	through	perceive, permit
peri-	around	periscope, perimeter
post-	after, following	postpone, postscript
pre-	before, previous	prevent, preclude
pro-	forward, in place of	propel, pronoun
retro-	back, backward	retrospect, retrograde
sub-	under, beneath	subjugate, substitute
super-	above, extra	supersede, supernumerary
trans-	across, beyond, over	transact, transport
ultra-	beyond, excessively	ultramodern, ultrasonic

Negative Prefixes

Prefix	Definition	Examples
a-	without, lacking	atheist, agnostic
in-	not, opposing	incapable, ineligible
non-	not	nonentity, nonsense
un-	not, reverse of	unhappy, unlock

Extra Prefixes

Prefix	Definition	Examples
for-	away, off, from	forget, forswear

Prefix	Definition	Examples
fore-	previous	foretell, forefathers
homo-	same, equal	homogenized, homonym
hyper-	excessive, over	hypercritical, hypertension
in-	in, into	intrude, invade
mal-	bad, poorly, not	malfunction, malpractice
mis-	bad, poorly, not	misspell, misfire
neo-	new	Neolithic, neoconservative
omni-	all, everywhere	omniscient, omnivore
ortho-	right, straight	orthogonal, orthodox
over-	above	overbearing, oversight
pan-	all, entire	panorama, pandemonium
para-	beside, beyond	parallel, paradox
re-	backward, again	revoke, recur
sym-	with, together	sympathy, symphony

Below is a list of common suffixes and their meanings:

ADJECTIVE SUFFIXES

Suffix	Definition	Examples
-able (-ible)	capable of being	tolerable, edible
-esque	in the style of, like	picturesque, grotesque
-ful	filled with, marked by	thankful, zestful
-ific	make, cause	terrific, beatific
-ish	suggesting, like	churlish, childish
-less	lacking, without	hopeless, countless
-ous	marked by, given to	religious, riotous

NOUN SUFFIXES

Suffix	Definition	Examples
-acy	state, condition	accuracy, privacy
-ance	act, condition, fact	acceptance, vigilance
-ard	one that does excessively	drunkard, sluggard
-ation	action, state, result	occupation, starvation
-dom	state, rank, condition	serfdom, wisdom
-er (-or)	office, action	teacher, elevator, honor
-ess	feminine	waitress, duchess
-hood	state, condition	manhood, statehood
-ion	action, result, state	union, fusion
-ism	act, manner, doctrine	barbarism, socialism
-ist	worker, follower	monopolist, socialist
-ity (-ty)	state, quality, condition	acidity, civility, twenty
-ment	result, action	Refreshment
-ness	quality, state	greatness, tallness
-ship	position	internship, statesmanship
-sion (-tion)	state, result	revision, expedition
-th	act, state, quality	warmth, width
-tude	quality, state, result	magnitude, fortitude

VERB SUFFIXES

Suffix	Definition	Examples
-ate	having, showing	separate, desolate
-en	cause to be, become	deepen, strengthen
-fy	make, cause to have	glorify, fortify
-ize	cause to be, treat with	sterilize, mechanize

NUANCE AND WORD MEANINGS

SYNONYMS AND ANTONYMS

When you understand how words relate to each other, you will discover more in a passage. This is explained by understanding **synonyms** (e.g., words that mean the same thing) and **antonyms** (e.g., words that mean the opposite of one another). As an example, *dry* and *arid* are synonyms, and *dry* and *wet* are antonyms.

There are many pairs of words in English that can be considered synonyms, despite having slightly different definitions. For instance, the words *friendly* and *collegial* can both be used to describe a warm interpersonal relationship, and one would be correct to call them synonyms. However, *collegial* (kin to *colleague*) is often used in reference to professional or academic relationships, and *friendly* has no such connotation.

If the difference between the two words is too great, then they should not be called synonyms. *Hot* and *warm* are not synonyms because their meanings are too distinct. A good way to determine whether two words are synonyms is to substitute one word for the other word and verify that the meaning of the sentence has not changed. Substituting *warm* for *hot* in a sentence would convey a different meaning. Although warm and hot may seem close in meaning, warm generally means that the temperature is moderate, and hot generally means that the temperature is excessively high.

Antonyms are words with opposite meanings. *Light* and *dark*, *up* and *down*, *right* and *left*, *good* and *bad*: these are all sets of antonyms. Be careful to distinguish between antonyms and pairs of words that are simply different. *Black* and *gray*, for instance, are not antonyms because gray is not the opposite of black. *Black* and *white*, on the other hand, are antonyms.

Not every word has an antonym. For instance, many nouns do not. What would be the antonym of *chair*? During your exam, the questions related to antonyms are more likely to concern adjectives. You will recall that adjectives are words that describe a noun. Some common adjectives include *purple*, *fast*, *skinny*, and *sweet*. From those four adjectives, *purple* is the item that lacks a group of obvious antonyms.

> **Review Video: Synonyms and Antonyms**
> Visit mometrix.com/academy and enter code: 105612

DENOTATIVE VS. CONNOTATIVE MEANING

The **denotative** meaning of a word is the literal meaning. The **connotative** meaning goes beyond the denotative meaning to include the emotional reaction that a word may invoke. The connotative meaning often takes the denotative meaning a step further due to associations the reader makes with the denotative meaning. Readers can differentiate between the denotative and connotative meanings by first recognizing how authors use each meaning. Most non-fiction, for example, is fact-based and authors do not use flowery, figurative language. The reader can assume that the writer is using the denotative meaning of words. In fiction, the author may use the connotative meaning. Readers can determine whether the author is using the denotative or connotative meaning of a word by implementing context clues.

> **Review Video: Connotation and Denotation**
> Visit mometrix.com/academy and enter code: 310092

Nuances of Word Meaning

A word's denotation is simply its objective dictionary definition. However, its connotation refers to the subjective associations, often emotional, that specific words evoke in listeners and readers. Two or more words can have the same dictionary meaning, but very different connotations. Writers use diction (word choice) to convey various nuances of thought and emotion by selecting synonyms for other words that best communicate the associations they want to trigger for readers. For example, a car engine is naturally greasy; in this sense, "greasy" is a neutral term. But when a person's smile, appearance, or clothing is described as "greasy," it has a negative connotation. Some words have even gained additional or different meanings over time. For example, *awful* used to be used to describe things that evoked a sense of awe. When *awful* is separated into its root word, awe, and suffix, -ful, it can be understood to mean "full of awe." However, the word is now commonly used to describe things that evoke repulsion, terror, or another intense, negative reaction.

> **Review Video: Word Usage in Sentences**
> Visit mometrix.com/academy and enter code: 197863

Using Context to Determine Meaning

Context Clues

Readers of all levels will encounter words that they have either never seen or have encountered only on a limited basis. The best way to define a word in **context** is to look for nearby words that can assist in revealing the meaning of the word. For instance, unfamiliar nouns are often accompanied by examples that provide a definition. Consider the following sentence: *Dave arrived at the party in hilarious garb: a leopard-print shirt, buckskin trousers, and bright green sneakers.* If a reader was unfamiliar with the meaning of garb, he or she could read the examples (i.e., a leopard-print shirt, buckskin trousers, and bright green sneakers) and quickly determine that the word means *clothing*. Examples will not always be this obvious. Consider this sentence: *Parsley, lemon, and flowers were just a few of the items he used as garnishes.* Here, the word *garnishes* is exemplified by parsley, lemon, and flowers. Readers who have eaten in a variety of restaurants will probably be able to identify a garnish as something used to decorate a plate.

> **Review Video: Reading Comprehension: Using Context Clues**
> Visit mometrix.com/academy and enter code: 613660

Using Contrast in Context Clues

In addition to looking at the context of a passage, readers can use contrast to define an unfamiliar word in context. In many sentences, the author will not describe the unfamiliar word directly; instead, he or she will describe the opposite of the unfamiliar word. Thus, you are provided with some information that will bring you closer to defining the word. Consider the following example: *Despite his intelligence, Hector's low brow and bad posture made him look obtuse.* The author writes that Hector's appearance does not convey intelligence. Therefore, *obtuse* must mean unintelligent. Here is another example: *Despite the horrible weather, we were beatific about our trip to Alaska.* The word *despite* indicates that the speaker's feelings were at odds with the weather. Since the weather is described as *horrible*, then *beatific* must mean something positive.

Substitution to Find Meaning

In some cases, there will be very few contextual clues to help a reader define the meaning of an unfamiliar word. When this happens, one strategy that readers may employ is **substitution**. A good reader will brainstorm some possible synonyms for the given word, and he or she will substitute these words into the sentence. If the sentence and the surrounding passage continue to make sense, then the substitution has revealed at least some information about the unfamiliar word. Consider the sentence: *Frank's admonition rang in her ears as she climbed the mountain.* A reader unfamiliar with *admonition* might come up with some substitutions like *vow, promise, advice, complaint,* or *compliment.* All of these words make general sense of the sentence, though their meanings are diverse. However, this process has suggested that an admonition is some

sort of message. The substitution strategy is rarely able to pinpoint a precise definition, but this process can be effective as a last resort.

Occasionally, you will be able to define an unfamiliar word by looking at the descriptive words in the context. Consider the following sentence: *Fred dragged the recalcitrant boy kicking and screaming up the stairs.* The words *dragged*, *kicking*, and *screaming* all suggest that the boy does not want to go up the stairs. The reader may assume that *recalcitrant* means something like unwilling or protesting. In this example, an unfamiliar adjective was identified.

Additionally, using description to define an unfamiliar noun is a common practice compared to unfamiliar adjectives, as in this sentence: *Don's wrinkled frown and constantly shaking fist identified him as a curmudgeon of the first order.* Don is described as having a *wrinkled frown and constantly shaking fist*, suggesting that a *curmudgeon* must be a grumpy person. Contrasts do not always provide detailed information about the unfamiliar word, but they at least give the reader some clues.

WORDS WITH MULTIPLE MEANINGS

When a word has more than one meaning, readers can have difficulty determining how the word is being used in a given sentence. For instance, the verb *cleave*, can mean either *join* or *separate*. When readers come upon this word, they will have to select the definition that makes the most sense. Consider the following sentence: *Hermione's knife cleaved the bread cleanly*. Since a knife cannot join bread together, the word must indicate separation. A slightly more difficult example would be the sentence: *The birds cleaved to one another as they flew from the oak tree.* Immediately, the presence of the words *to one another* should suggest that in this sentence *cleave* is being used to mean *join*. Discovering the intent of a word with multiple meanings requires the same tricks as defining an unknown word: look for contextual clues and evaluate the substituted words.

CONTEXT CLUES TO HELP DETERMINE MEANINGS OF WORDS

If readers simply bypass unknown words, they can reach unclear conclusions about what they read. However, looking for the definition of every unfamiliar word in the dictionary can slow their reading progress. Moreover, the dictionary may list multiple definitions for a word, so readers must search the word's context for meaning. Hence context is important to new vocabulary regardless of reader methods. Four types of context clues are examples, definitions, descriptive words, and opposites. Authors may use a certain word, and then follow it with several different examples of what it describes. Sometimes authors actually supply a definition of a word they use, which is especially true in informational and technical texts. Authors may use descriptive words that elaborate upon a vocabulary word they just used. Authors may also use opposites with negation that help define meaning.

EXAMPLES AND DEFINITIONS

An author may use a word and then give examples that illustrate its meaning. Consider this text: "Teachers who do not know how to use sign language can help students who are deaf or hard of hearing understand certain instructions by using gestures instead, like pointing their fingers to indicate which direction to look or go; holding up a hand, palm outward, to indicate stopping; holding the hands flat, palms up, curling a finger toward oneself in a beckoning motion to indicate 'come here'; or curling all fingers toward oneself repeatedly to indicate 'come on', 'more', or 'continue.'" The author of this text has used the word "gestures" and then followed it with examples, so a reader unfamiliar with the word could deduce from the examples that "gestures" means "hand motions." Readers can find examples by looking for signal words "for example," "for instance," "like," "such as," and "e.g."

While readers sometimes have to look for definitions of unfamiliar words in a dictionary or do some work to determine a word's meaning from its surrounding context, at other times an author may make it easier for readers by defining certain words. For example, an author may write, "The company did not have sufficient capital, that is, available money, to continue operations." The author defined "capital" as "available money," and heralded the definition with the phrase "that is." Another way that authors supply word definitions is with appositives. Rather than being introduced by a signal phrase like "that is," "namely," or "meaning," an appositive comes after the vocabulary word it defines and is enclosed within two commas. For example, an author may write, "The Indians introduced the Pilgrims to pemmican, cakes they made of lean meat dried and mixed with fat, which proved greatly beneficial to keep settlers from starving while trapping." In this example, the appositive phrase following "pemmican" and preceding "which" defines the word "pemmican."

DESCRIPTIONS

When readers encounter a word they do not recognize in a text, the author may expand on that word to illustrate it better. While the author may do this to make the prose more picturesque and vivid, the reader can also take advantage of this description to provide context clues to the meaning of the unfamiliar word. For example, an author may write, "The man sitting next to me on the airplane was obese. His shirt stretched across his vast expanse of flesh, strained almost to bursting." The descriptive second sentence elaborates on and helps to define the previous sentence's word "obese" to mean extremely fat. A reader unfamiliar with the word "repugnant" can decipher its meaning through an author's accompanying description: "The way the child grimaced and shuddered as he swallowed the medicine showed that its taste was particularly repugnant."

OPPOSITES

Text authors sometimes introduce a contrasting or opposing idea before or after a concept they present. They may do this to emphasize or heighten the idea they present by contrasting it with something that is the reverse. However, readers can also use these context clues to understand familiar words. For example, an author may write, "Our conversation was not cheery. We sat and talked very solemnly about his experience and a number of similar events." The reader who is not familiar with the word "solemnly" can deduce by the author's preceding use of "not cheery" that "solemn" means the opposite of cheery or happy, so it must mean serious or sad. Or if someone writes, "Don't condemn his entire project because you couldn't find anything good to say about it," readers unfamiliar with "condemn" can understand from the sentence structure that it means the opposite of saying anything good, so it must mean reject, dismiss, or disapprove. "Entire" adds another context clue, meaning total or complete rejection.

SYNTAX TO DETERMINE PART OF SPEECH AND MEANINGS OF WORDS

Syntax refers to sentence structure and word order. Suppose that a reader encounters an unfamiliar word when reading a text. To illustrate, consider an invented word like "splunch." If this word is used in a sentence like "Please splunch that ball to me," the reader can assume from syntactic context that "splunch" is a verb. We would not use a noun, adjective, adverb, or preposition with the object "that ball," and the prepositional phrase "to me" further indicates "splunch" represents an action. However, in the sentence, "Please hand that splunch to me," the reader can assume that "splunch" is a noun. Demonstrative adjectives like "that" modify nouns. Also, we hand someone some*thing*—a thing being a noun; we do not hand someone a verb, adjective, or adverb. Some sentences contain further clues. For example, from the sentence, "The princess wore the glittering splunch on her head," the reader can deduce that it is a crown, tiara, or something similar from the syntactic context, without knowing the word.

SYNTAX TO INDICATE DIFFERENT MEANINGS OF SIMILAR SENTENCES

The syntax, or structure, of a sentence affords grammatical cues that aid readers in comprehending the meanings of words, phrases, and sentences in the texts that they read. Seemingly minor differences in how the words or phrases in a sentence are ordered can make major differences in meaning. For example, two sentences can use exactly the same words but have different meanings based on the word order:

- "The man with a broken arm sat in a chair."
- "The man sat in a chair with a broken arm."

While both sentences indicate that a man sat in a chair, differing syntax indicates whether the man's or chair's arm was broken.

> **Review Video: Syntax**
> Visit mometrix.com/academy and enter code: 242280

DETERMINING MEANING OF PHRASES AND PARAGRAPHS

Like unknown words, the meanings of phrases, paragraphs, and entire works can also be difficult to discern. Each of these can be better understood with added context. However, for larger groups of words, more context is needed. Unclear phrases are similar to unclear words, and the same methods can be used to understand their meaning. However, it is also important to consider how the individual words in the phrase work together. Paragraphs are a bit more complicated. Just as words must be compared to other words in a sentence, paragraphs must be compared to other paragraphs in a composition or a section.

DETERMINING MEANING IN VARIOUS TYPES OF COMPOSITIONS

To understand the meaning of an entire composition, the type of composition must be considered. **Expository writing** is generally organized so that each paragraph focuses on explaining one idea, or part of an idea, and its relevance. **Persuasive writing** uses paragraphs for different purposes to organize the parts of the argument. **Unclear paragraphs** must be read in the context of the paragraphs around them for their meaning to be fully understood. The meaning of full texts can also be unclear at times. The purpose of composition is also important for understanding the meaning of a text. To quickly understand the broad meaning of a text, look to the introductory and concluding paragraphs. Fictional texts are different. Some fictional works have implicit meanings, but some do not. The target audience must be considered for understanding texts that do have an implicit meaning, as most children's fiction will clearly state any lessons or morals. For other fiction, the application of literary theories and criticism may be helpful for understanding the text.

Chapter Quiz

Ready to see how well you retained what you just read? Scan the QR code to go directly to the chapter quiz interface for this study guide. If you're using a computer, simply visit the online resources page at **mometrix.com/resources719/hspt-28350** and click the Chapter Quizzes link.

Language

Transform passive reading into active learning! After immersing yourself in this chapter, put your comprehension to the test by taking a quiz. The insights you gained will stay with you longer this way. Scan the QR code to go directly to the chapter quiz interface for this study guide. If you're using a computer, simply visit the online resources page at **mometrix.com/resources719/hspt-28350** and click the Chapter Quizzes link.

Parts of Speech

NOUNS

A noun is a person, place, thing, or idea. The two main types of nouns are **common** and **proper** nouns. Nouns can also be categorized as abstract (i.e., general) or concrete (i.e., specific).

COMMON NOUNS

Common nouns are generic names for people, places, and things. Common nouns are not usually capitalized.

Examples of common nouns:

People: boy, girl, worker, manager

Places: school, bank, library, home

Things: dog, cat, truck, car

> **Review Video: Nouns**
> Visit mometrix.com/academy and enter code: 344028

PROPER NOUNS

Proper nouns name specific people, places, or things. All proper nouns are capitalized.

Examples of proper nouns:

People: Abraham Lincoln, George Washington, Martin Luther King, Jr.

Places: Los Angeles, California; New York; Asia

Things: Statue of Liberty, Earth, Lincoln Memorial

Note: Some nouns can be either common or proper depending on their use. For example, when referring to the planet that we live on, *Earth* is a proper noun and is capitalized. When referring to the dirt, rocks, or land on our planet, *earth* is a common noun and is not capitalized.

GENERAL AND SPECIFIC NOUNS

General nouns are the names of conditions or ideas. **Specific nouns** name people, places, and things that are understood by using your senses.

General nouns:

Condition: beauty, strength

Idea: truth, peace

Specific nouns:

People: baby, friend, father

Places: town, park, city hall

Things: rainbow, cough, apple, silk, gasoline

COLLECTIVE NOUNS

Collective nouns are the names for a group of people, places, or things that may act as a whole. The following are examples of collective nouns: *class, company, dozen, group, herd, team,* and *public*. Collective nouns usually require an article, which denotes the noun as being a single unit. For instance, a choir is a group of singers. Even though there are many singers in a choir, the word choir is grammatically treated as a single unit. If we refer to the members of the group, and not the group itself, it is no longer a collective noun.

Incorrect: The *choir are* going to compete nationally this year.

Correct: The *choir is* going to compete nationally this year.

Incorrect: The *members* of the choir *is* competing nationally this year.

Correct: The *members* of the choir *are* competing nationally this year.

PRONOUNS

Pronouns are words that are used to stand in for nouns. A pronoun may be classified as personal, intensive, relative, interrogative, demonstrative, indefinite, and reciprocal.

Personal: *Nominative* is the case for nouns and pronouns that are the subject of a sentence. *Objective* is the case for nouns and pronouns that are an object in a sentence. *Possessive* is the case for nouns and pronouns that show possession or ownership.

Singular

	Nominative	Objective	Possessive
First Person	I	me	my, mine
Second Person	you	you	your, yours
Third Person	he, she, it	him, her, it	his, her, hers, its

Plural

	Nominative	Objective	Possessive
First Person	we	us	our, ours
Second Person	you	you	your, yours
Third Person	they	them	their, theirs

Intensive: I myself, you yourself, he himself, she herself, the (thing) itself, we ourselves, you yourselves, they themselves

Relative: which, who, whom, whose

Interrogative: what, which, who, whom, whose

Demonstrative: this, that, these, those

Indefinite: all, any, each, everyone, either/neither, one, some, several

Reciprocal: each other, one another

> **Review Video: Nouns and Pronouns**
> Visit mometrix.com/academy and enter code: 312073

VERBS

A verb is a word or group of words that indicates action or being. In other words, the verb shows something's action or state of being or the action that has been done to something. If you want to write a sentence, then you need a verb. Without a verb, you have no sentence.

TRANSITIVE AND INTRANSITIVE VERBS

A **transitive verb** is a verb whose action indicates a receiver. **Intransitive verbs** do not indicate a receiver of an action. In other words, the action of the verb does not point to an object.

   Transitive: He drives a car. | She feeds the dog.

   Intransitive: He runs every day. | She voted in the last election.

A dictionary will tell you whether a verb is transitive or intransitive. Some verbs can be transitive or intransitive.

ACTION VERBS AND LINKING VERBS

Action verbs show what the subject is doing. In other words, an action verb shows action. Unlike most types of words, a single action verb, in the right context, can be an entire sentence. **Linking verbs** link the subject of a sentence to a noun or pronoun, or they link a subject with an adjective. You always need a verb if you want a complete sentence. However, linking verbs on their own cannot be a complete sentence.

Common linking verbs include *appear, be, become, feel, grow, look, seem, smell, sound,* and *taste*. However, any verb that shows a condition and connects to a noun, pronoun, or adjective that describes the subject of a sentence is a linking verb.

Action: He sings. | Run! | Go! | I talk with him every day. | She reads.

Linking:

   Incorrect: I am.

   Correct: I am John. | The roses smell lovely. | I feel tired.

Note: Some verbs are followed by words that look like prepositions, but they are a part of the verb and a part of the verb's meaning. These are known as phrasal verbs, and examples include *call off*, *look up*, and *drop off*.

> **Review Video: Action Verbs and Linking Verbs**
> Visit mometrix.com/academy and enter code: 743142

VOICE

Transitive verbs may be in active voice or passive voice. The difference between active voice and passive voice is whether the subject is acting or being acted upon. When the subject of the sentence is doing the action, the verb is in **active voice**. When the subject is being acted upon, the verb is in **passive voice**.

Active: Jon drew the picture. (The subject *Jon* is doing the action of *drawing a picture*.)

Passive: The picture is drawn by Jon. (The subject *picture* is receiving the action from Jon.)

VERB TENSES

Verb **tense** is a property of a verb that indicates when the action being described takes place (past, present, or future) and whether or not the action is completed (simple or perfect). Describing an action taking place in the present (*I talk*) requires a different verb tense than describing an action that took place in the past (*I talked*). Some verb tenses require an auxiliary (helping) verb. These helping verbs include *am, are, is | have, has, had | was, were, will* (or *shall*).

Present: I talk	Present perfect: I have talked
Past: I talked	Past perfect: I had talked
Future: I will talk	Future perfect: I will have talked

Present: The action is happening at the current time.

Example: He *walks* to the store every morning.

To show that something is happening right now, use the progressive present tense: I *am walking*.

Past: The action happened in the past.

Example: She *walked* to the store an hour ago.

Future: The action will happen later.

Example: I *will walk* to the store tomorrow.

Present perfect: The action started in the past and continues into the present or took place previously at an unspecified time.

Example: I *have walked* to the store three times today.

Past perfect: The action was completed at some point in the past. This tense is usually used to describe an action that was completed before some other reference time or event.

Example: I *had eaten* already before they arrived.

Future perfect: The action will be completed before some point in the future. This tense may be used to describe an action that has already begun or has yet to begin.

Example: The project *will have been completed* by the deadline.

> **Review Video: Present Perfect, Past Perfect, and Future Perfect Verb Tenses**
> Visit mometrix.com/academy and enter code: 269472

CONJUGATING VERBS

When you need to change the form of a verb, you are **conjugating** a verb. The key forms of a verb are present tense (sing/sings), past tense (sang), present participle (singing), and past participle (sung). By combining these forms with helping verbs, you can make almost any verb tense. The following table demonstrate some of the different ways to conjugate a verb:

Tense	First Person	Second Person	Third Person Singular	Third Person Plural
Simple Present	I sing	You sing	He, she, it sings	They sing
Simple Past	I sang	You sang	He, she, it sang	They sang
Simple Future	I will sing	You will sing	He, she, it will sing	They will sing
Present Progressive	I am singing	You are singing	He, she, it is singing	They are singing
Past Progressive	I was singing	You were singing	He, she, it was singing	They were singing
Present Perfect	I have sung	You have sung	He, she, it has sung	They have sung
Past Perfect	I had sung	You had sung	He, she, it had sung	They had sung

MOOD

There are three **moods** in English: the indicative, the imperative, and the subjunctive.

The **indicative mood** is used for facts, opinions, and questions.

    Fact: You can do this.

    Opinion: I think that you can do this.

    Question: Do you know that you can do this?

The **imperative** is used for orders or requests.

    Order: You are going to do this!

    Request: Will you do this for me?

The **subjunctive mood** is for wishes and statements that go against fact.

    Wish: I wish that I were famous.

    Statement against fact: If I were you, I would do this. (This goes against fact because I am not you. You have the chance to do this, and I do not have the chance.)

ADJECTIVES

An **adjective** is a word that is used to modify a noun or pronoun. An adjective answers a question: *Which one? What kind?* or *How many?* Usually, adjectives come before the words that they modify, but they may also come after a linking verb.

Which one? The *third* suit is my favorite.

What kind? This suit is *navy blue*.

How many? I am going to buy *four* pairs of socks to match the suit.

> **Review Video: Descriptive Text**
> Visit mometrix.com/academy and enter code: 174903

ARTICLES

Articles are adjectives that are used to distinguish nouns as definite or indefinite. *A*, *an*, and *the* are the only articles. **Definite** nouns are preceded by *the* and indicate a specific person, place, thing, or idea. **Indefinite** nouns are preceded by *a* or *an* and do not indicate a specific person, place, thing, or idea.

Note: *An* comes before words that start with a vowel sound. For example, "Are you going to get an **u**mbrella?"

Definite: I lost *the* bottle that belongs to me.

Indefinite: Does anyone have *a* bottle to share?

> **Review Video: Function of Articles in a Sentence**
> Visit mometrix.com/academy and enter code: 449383

COMPARISON WITH ADJECTIVES

Some adjectives are relative and other adjectives are absolute. Adjectives that are **relative** can show the comparison between things. **Absolute** adjectives can also show comparison, but they do so in a different way. Let's say that you are reading two books. You think that one book is perfect, and the other book is not exactly perfect. It is not possible for one book to be more perfect than the other. Either you think that the book is perfect, or you think that the book is imperfect. In this case, perfect and imperfect are absolute adjectives.

Relative adjectives will show the different **degrees** of something or someone to something else or someone else. The three degrees of adjectives include positive, comparative, and superlative.

The **positive** degree is the normal form of an adjective.

Example: This work is *difficult*. | She is *smart*.

The **comparative** degree compares one person or thing to another person or thing.

Example: This work is *more difficult* than your work. | She is *smarter* than me.

The **superlative** degree compares more than two people or things.

Example: This is the *most difficult* work of my life. | She is the *smartest* lady in school.

> **Review Video: Adjectives**
> Visit mometrix.com/academy and enter code: 470154

ADVERBS

An **adverb** is a word that is used to **modify** a verb, an adjective, or another adverb. Usually, adverbs answer one of these questions: *When? Where? How?* and *Why?* The negatives *not* and *never* are considered adverbs. Adverbs that modify adjectives or other adverbs **strengthen** or **weaken** the words that they modify.

Examples:

He walks *quickly* through the crowd.

The water flows *smoothly* on the rocks.

Note: Adverbs are usually indicated by the morpheme *-ly*, which has been added to the root word. For instance, *quick* can be made into an adverb by adding *-ly* to construct *quickly*. Some words that end in *-ly* do not follow this rule and can behave as other parts of speech. Examples of adjectives ending in *-ly* include: *early, friendly, holy, lonely, silly,* and *ugly*. To know if a word that ends in *-ly* is an adjective or adverb, check your dictionary. Also, while many adverbs end in *-ly*, you need to remember that not all adverbs end in *-ly*.

Examples:

He is *never* angry.

You are *too* irresponsible to travel alone.

> **Review Video: Adverbs**
> Visit mometrix.com/academy and enter code: 713951
>
> **Review Video: Adverbs that Modify Adjectives**
> Visit mometrix.com/academy and enter code: 122570

COMPARISON WITH ADVERBS

The rules for comparing adverbs are the same as the rules for adjectives.

The **positive** degree is the standard form of an adverb.

Example: He arrives *soon*. | She speaks *softly* to her friends.

The **comparative** degree compares one person or thing to another person or thing.

Example: He arrives *sooner* than Sarah. | She speaks *more softly* than him.

The **superlative** degree compares more than two people or things.

Example: He arrives *soonest* of the group. | She speaks the *most softly* of any of her friends.

PREPOSITIONS

A **preposition** is a word placed before a noun or pronoun that shows the relationship between that noun or pronoun and another word in the sentence.

Common prepositions:

about	before	during	on	under
after	beneath	for	over	until
against	between	from	past	up
among	beyond	in	through	with
around	by	of	to	within
at	down	off	toward	without

Examples:

> The napkin is *in* the drawer.
>
> The Earth rotates *around* the Sun.
>
> The needle is *beneath* the haystack.
>
> Can you find "me" *among* the words?

> **Review Video: Prepositions**
> Visit mometrix.com/academy and enter code: 946763

CONJUNCTIONS

Conjunctions join words, phrases, or clauses and they show the connection between the joined pieces. **Coordinating conjunctions** connect equal parts of sentences. **Correlative conjunctions** show the connection between pairs. **Subordinating conjunctions** join subordinate (i.e., dependent) clauses with independent clauses.

COORDINATING CONJUNCTIONS

The **coordinating conjunctions** include: *and, but, yet, or, nor, for,* and *so*

Examples:

> The rock was small, *but* it was heavy.
>
> She drove in the night, *and* he drove in the day.

CORRELATIVE CONJUNCTIONS

The **correlative conjunctions** are: *either...or | neither...nor | not only...but also*

Examples:

Either you are coming *or* you are staying.

He *not only* ran three miles *but also* swam 200 yards.

> **Review Video: Coordinating and Correlative Conjunctions**
> Visit mometrix.com/academy and enter code: 390329
>
> **Review Video: Adverb Equal Comparisons**
> Visit mometrix.com/academy and enter code: 231291

SUBORDINATING CONJUNCTIONS

Common **subordinating conjunctions** include:

after	since	whenever
although	so that	where
because	unless	wherever
before	until	whether
in order that	when	while

Examples:

I am hungry *because* I did not eat breakfast.

He went home *when* everyone left.

> **Review Video: Subordinating Conjunctions**
> Visit mometrix.com/academy and enter code: 958913

INTERJECTIONS

Interjections are words of exclamation (i.e., audible expression of great feeling) that are used alone or as a part of a sentence. Often, they are used at the beginning of a sentence for an introduction. Sometimes, they can be used in the middle of a sentence to show a change in thought or attitude.

Common Interjections: Hey! | Oh, | Ouch! | Please! | Wow!

Agreement and Sentence Structure

SUBJECTS AND PREDICATES

SUBJECTS

The **subject** of a sentence names who or what the sentence is about. The subject may be directly stated in a sentence, or the subject may be the implied *you*. The **complete subject** includes the simple subject and all of its modifiers. To find the complete subject, ask *Who* or *What* and insert the verb to complete the question. The answer, including any modifiers (adjectives, prepositional phrases, etc.), is the complete subject. To find the **simple subject**, remove all of the modifiers in the complete subject. Being able to locate the subject of a sentence helps with many problems, such as those involving sentence fragments and subject-verb agreement.

Examples:

The small, red <u>car</u> is the one that he wants for Christmas.
(simple subject: car; complete subject: The small, red car)

The young <u>artist</u> is coming over for dinner.
(simple subject: artist; complete subject: The young artist)

> **Review Video: Subjects in English**
> Visit mometrix.com/academy and enter code: 444771

In **imperative** sentences, the verb's subject is understood (e.g., [You] Run to the store), but is not actually present in the sentence. Normally, the subject comes before the verb. However, the subject comes after the verb in sentences that begin with *There are* or *There was*.

Direct:

John knows the way to the park.	Who knows the way to the park?	John
The cookies need ten more minutes.	What needs ten minutes?	The cookies
By five o'clock, Bill will need to leave.	Who needs to leave?	Bill
There are five letters on the table for him.	What is on the table?	Five letters
There were coffee and doughnuts in the house.	What was in the house?	Coffee and doughnuts

Implied:

Go to the post office for me.	Who is going to the post office?	You
Come and sit with me, please?	Who needs to come and sit?	You

PREDICATES

In a sentence, you always have a predicate and a subject. The subject tells who or what the sentence is about, and the **predicate** explains or describes the subject. The predicate includes the verb or verb phrase and any direct or indirect objects of the verb, as well as any words or phrases modifying these.

Think about the sentence *He sings*. In this sentence, we have a subject (He) and a predicate (sings). This is all that is needed for a sentence to be complete. Most sentences contain more information, but if this is all the information that you are given, then you have a complete sentence.

Now, let's look at another sentence: *John and Jane sing on Tuesday nights at the dance hall.*

      subject   predicate
    John and Jane sing on Tuesday nights at the dance hall.

> **Review Video: Complete Predicate**
> Visit mometrix.com/academy and enter code: 293942

SUBJECT-VERB AGREEMENT

Verbs must **agree** with their subjects in number and in person. To agree in number, singular subjects need singular verbs and plural subjects need plural verbs. A **singular** noun refers to **one** person, place, or thing. A **plural** noun refers to **more than one** person, place, or thing. To agree in person, the correct verb form must be chosen to match the first, second, or third person subject. The present tense ending -s or -es is used on a verb if its subject is third person singular; otherwise, the verb's ending is not modified.

> **Review Video: Subject-Verb Agreement**
> Visit mometrix.com/academy and enter code: 479190

NUMBER AGREEMENT EXAMPLES:

                                  singular singular
                                  subject   verb
Single Subject and Verb: Dan calls home.

Dan is one person. So, the singular verb *calls* is needed.

                                plural   plural
                             subject   verb
Plural Subject and Verb: Dan and Bob call home.

More than one person needs the plural verb *call*.

PERSON AGREEMENT EXAMPLES:

First Person: I *am* walking.

Second Person: You *are* walking.

Third Person: He *is* walking.

COMPLICATIONS WITH SUBJECT-VERB AGREEMENT
WORDS BETWEEN SUBJECT AND VERB

Words that come between the simple subject and the verb have no bearing on subject-verb agreement.

Examples:

      singular   singular
      subject   verb
The joy of my life returns home tonight.

The phrase *of my life* does not influence the verb *returns*.

The question *(singular subject)* that still remains unanswered is *(singular verb)* "Who are you?"

Don't let the phrase "*that still remains…*" trouble you. The subject *question* goes with *is*.

COMPOUND SUBJECTS

A compound subject is formed when two or more nouns joined by *and*, *or*, or *nor* jointly act as the subject of the sentence.

JOINED BY AND

When a compound subject is joined by *and*, it is treated as a plural subject and requires a plural verb.

Examples:

You and Jon *(plural subject)* are *(plural verb)* invited to come to my house.

The pencil and paper *(plural subject)* belong *(plural verb)* to me.

JOINED BY OR/NOR

For a compound subject joined by *or* or *nor*, the verb must agree in number with the part of the subject that is closest to the verb (italicized in the examples below).

Examples:

Today or *tomorrow* *(subject)* is *(verb)* the day.

Stan or *Phil* *(subject)* wants *(verb)* to read the book.

Neither the pen nor *the book* *(subject)* is *(verb)* on the desk.

Either the blanket or *pillows* *(subject)* arrive *(verb)* this afternoon.

INDEFINITE PRONOUNS AS SUBJECT

An indefinite pronoun is a pronoun that does not refer to a specific noun. Some indefinite pronouns function as only singular, some function as only plural, and some can function as either singular or plural depending on how they are used.

ALWAYS SINGULAR

Pronouns such as *each*, *either*, *everybody*, *anybody*, *somebody*, and *nobody* are always singular.

Examples:

Each (singular subject) of the runners has (singular verb) a different bib number.

Is (singular verb) either (singular subject) of you ready for the game?

Note: The words *each* and *either* can also be used as adjectives (e.g., *each* person is unique). When one of these adjectives modifies the subject of a sentence, it is always a singular subject.

Everybody (singular subject) grows (singular verb) a day older every day.

Anybody (singular subject) is (singular verb) welcome to bring a tent.

ALWAYS PLURAL

Pronouns such as *both*, *several*, and *many* are always plural.

Examples:

Both (plural subject) of the siblings were (plural verb) too tired to argue.

Many (plural subject) have tried (plural verb), but none have succeeded.

DEPEND ON CONTEXT

Pronouns such as *some*, *any*, *all*, *none*, *more*, and *most* can be either singular or plural depending on what they are representing in the context of the sentence.

Examples:

All (singular subject) of my dog's food was (singular verb) still there in his bowl.

By the end of the night, all (plural subject) of my guests were (plural verb) already excited about coming to my next party.

OTHER CASES INVOLVING PLURAL OR IRREGULAR FORM

Some nouns are **singular in meaning but plural in form**: news, mathematics, physics, and economics.

The *news is* coming on now.

Mathematics is my favorite class.

Some nouns are plural in form and meaning, and have **no singular equivalent**: scissors and pants.

> Do these *pants come* with a shirt?
>
> The *scissors are* for my project.

Mathematical operations are **irregular** in their construction, but are normally considered to be **singular in meaning**.

> *One plus one is* two.
>
> *Three times three is* nine.

Note: Look to your **dictionary** for help when you aren't sure whether a noun with a plural form has a singular or plural meaning.

COMPLEMENTS

A complement is a noun, pronoun, or adjective that is used to give more information about the subject or object in the sentence.

DIRECT OBJECTS

A direct object is a noun or pronoun that tells who or what **receives** the action of the verb. A sentence will only include a direct object if the verb is a transitive verb. If the verb is an intransitive verb or a linking verb, there will be no direct object. When you are looking for a direct object, find the verb and ask *who* or *what*.

Examples:

> I took *the blanket*.
>
> Jane read *books*.

INDIRECT OBJECTS

An indirect object is a noun or pronoun that indicates what or whom the action had an **influence** on. If there is an indirect object in a sentence, then there will also be a direct object. When you are looking for the indirect object, find the verb and ask *to/for whom or what*.

Examples:

> We taught <u>the old dog</u> (indirect object) <u>a new trick</u> (direct object).
>
> I gave <u>them</u> (indirect object) <u>a math lesson</u> (direct object).

> **Review Video: Direct and Indirect Objects**
> Visit mometrix.com/academy and enter code: 817385

PREDICATE NOMINATIVES AND PREDICATE ADJECTIVES

As we looked at previously, verbs may be classified as either action verbs or linking verbs. A linking verb is so named because it links the subject to words in the predicate that describe or define the subject. These words are called predicate nominatives (if nouns or pronouns) or predicate adjectives (if adjectives).

Examples:

    My **father** is a **lawyer**.
    (subject) (predicate nominative)

    Your **mother** is **patient**.
    (subject) (predicate adjective)

PRONOUN USAGE

The **antecedent** is the noun that has been replaced by a pronoun. A pronoun and its antecedent **agree** when they have the same number (singular or plural) and gender (male, female, or neutral).

Examples:

    Singular agreement: *John* (antecedent) came into town, and *he* (pronoun) played for us.

    Plural agreement: *John and Rick* (antecedent) came into town, and *they* (pronoun) played for us.

To determine which is the correct pronoun to use in a compound subject or object, try each pronoun **alone** in place of the compound in the sentence. Your knowledge of pronouns will tell you which one is correct.

Example:

    Bob and (I, me) will be going.

    Test: (1) *I will be going* or (2) *Me will be going*. The second choice cannot be correct because *me* cannot be used as the subject of a sentence. Instead, *me* is used as an object.

    Answer: Bob and I will be going.

When a pronoun is used with a noun immediately following (as in "we boys"), try the sentence **without the added noun**.

Example:

    (We/Us) boys played football last year.

    Test: (1) *We played football last year* or (2) *Us played football last year*. Again, the second choice cannot be correct because *us* cannot be used as a subject of a sentence. Instead, *us* is used as an object.

    Answer: We boys played football last year.

> **Review Video: Pronoun Usage**
> Visit mometrix.com/academy and enter code: 666500
>
> **Review Video: Pronoun-Antecedent Agreement**
> Visit mometrix.com/academy and enter code: 919704

A pronoun should point clearly to the **antecedent**. Here is how a pronoun reference can be unhelpful if it is puzzling or not directly stated.

Unhelpful: Ron and Jim (antecedent) went to the store, and he (pronoun) bought soda.

Who bought soda? Ron or Jim?

Helpful: Jim (antecedent) went to the store, and he (pronoun) bought soda.

The sentence is clear. Jim bought the soda.

Some pronouns change their form by their placement in a sentence. A pronoun that is a **subject** in a sentence comes in the **subjective case**. Pronouns that serve as **objects** appear in the **objective case**. Finally, the pronouns that are used as **possessives** appear in the **possessive case**.

Examples:

Subjective case: *He* is coming to the show.

The pronoun *He* is the subject of the sentence.

Objective case: Josh drove *him* to the airport.

The pronoun *him* is the object of the sentence.

Possessive case: The flowers are *mine*.

The pronoun *mine* shows ownership of the flowers.

The word *who* is a subjective-case pronoun that can be used as a **subject**. The word *whom* is an objective-case pronoun that can be used as an **object**. The words *who* and *whom* are common in subordinate clauses or in questions.

Examples:

He knows who (subject) wants (verb) to come.

He knows the man whom (object) we want (verb) at the party.

CLAUSES

A clause is a group of words that contains both a subject and a predicate (verb). There are two types of clauses: independent and dependent. An **independent clause** contains a complete thought, while a **dependent (or subordinate) clause** does not. A dependent clause includes a subject and a verb, and may also contain objects or complements, but it cannot stand as a complete thought without being joined to an independent clause. Dependent clauses function within sentences as adjectives, adverbs, or nouns.

Example:

I am running (independent clause) because I want to stay in shape (dependent clause).

The clause *I am running* is an independent clause: it has a subject and a verb, and it gives a complete thought. The clause *because I want to stay in shape* is a dependent clause: it has a subject and a verb, but it does not express a complete thought. It adds detail to the independent clause to which it is attached.

> **Review Video: Clauses**
> Visit mometrix.com/academy and enter code: 940170
>
> **Review Video: Independent and Dependent Clauses**
> Visit mometrix.com/academy and enter code: 556903

TYPES OF DEPENDENT CLAUSES
ADJECTIVE CLAUSES

An **adjective clause** is a dependent clause that modifies a noun or a pronoun. Adjective clauses begin with a relative pronoun (*who, whose, whom, which,* and *that*) or a relative adverb (*where, when,* and *why*).

Also, adjective clauses usually come immediately after the noun that the clause needs to explain or rename. This is done to ensure that it is clear which noun or pronoun the clause is modifying.

Examples:

I learned the reason [independent clause] why I won the award. [adjective clause]

This is the place [independent clause] where I started my first job. [adjective clause]

An adjective clause can be an essential or nonessential clause. An essential clause is very important to the sentence. **Essential clauses** explain or define a person or thing. **Nonessential clauses** give more information about a person or thing but are not necessary to define them. Nonessential clauses are set off with commas while essential clauses are not.

Examples:

A person who works hard at first [essential clause] can often rest later in life.

Neil Armstrong, who walked on the moon, [nonessential clause] is my hero.

> **Review Video: Adjective Clauses and Phrases**
> Visit mometrix.com/academy and enter code: 520888

ADVERB CLAUSES

An **adverb clause** is a dependent clause that modifies a verb, adjective, or adverb. In sentences with multiple dependent clauses, adverb clauses are usually placed immediately before or after the independent clause. An adverb clause is introduced with words such as *after, although, as, before, because, if, since, so, unless, when, where,* and *while*.

Examples:

    When you walked outside, I called the manager.
    [*When you walked outside* = adverb clause]

    I will go with you unless you want to stay.
    [*unless you want to stay* = adverb clause]

Noun Clauses

A **noun clause** is a dependent clause that can be used as a subject, object, or complement. Noun clauses begin with words such as *how, that, what, whether, which, who,* and *why*. These words can also come with an adjective clause. Unless the noun clause is being used as the subject of the sentence, it should come after the verb of the independent clause.

Examples:

    The real mystery is how you avoided serious injury.
    [*how you avoided serious injury* = noun clause]

    What you learn from each other depends on your honesty with others.
    [*What you learn from each other* = noun clause]

Subordination

When two related ideas are not of equal importance, the ideal way to combine them is to make the more important idea an independent clause and the less important idea a dependent or subordinate clause. This is called **subordination**.

Example:

    Separate ideas: The team had a perfect regular season. The team lost the championship.

    Subordinated: Despite having a perfect regular season, *the team lost the championship*.

Phrases

A phrase is a group of words that functions as a single part of speech, usually a noun, adjective, or adverb. A **phrase** is not a complete thought and does not contain a subject and predicate, but it adds detail or explanation to a sentence, or renames something within the sentence.

Prepositional Phrases

One of the most common types of phrases is the prepositional phrase. A **prepositional phrase** begins with a preposition and ends with a noun or pronoun that is the object of the preposition. Normally, the prepositional phrase functions as an **adjective** or an **adverb** within the sentence.

Examples:

    The picnic is on the blanket.
    [*on the blanket* = prepositional phrase]

    I am sick with a fever today.
    [*with a fever* = prepositional phrase]

Among the many flowers, John found a four-leaf clover.
(prepositional phrase: Among the many flowers)

VERBAL PHRASES

A **verbal** is a word or phrase that is formed from a verb but does not function as a verb. Depending on its particular form, it may be used as a noun, adjective, or adverb. A verbal does **not** replace a verb in a sentence.

Examples:

Correct: **Walk** a mile daily. *(verb: Walk)*

This is a complete sentence with the implied subject *you*.

Incorrect: **To walk** a mile. *(verbal: To walk)*

This is not a sentence since there is no functional verb.

There are three types of verbal: **participles**, **gerunds**, and **infinitives**. Each type of verbal has a corresponding **phrase** that consists of the verbal itself along with any complements or modifiers.

PARTICIPLES

A **participle** is a type of verbal that always functions as an adjective. The present participle always ends with *-ing*. Past participles end with *-d*, *-ed*, *-n*, or *-t*. Participles are combined with helping verbs to form certain verb tenses, but a participle by itself cannot function as a verb.

Examples: dance | dancing | danced
(verb: dance; present participle: dancing; past participle: danced)

Participial phrases most often come right before or right after the noun or pronoun that they modify.

Examples:

(participial phrase:) Shipwrecked on an island, the boys started to fish for food.

(participial phrase:) Having been seated for five hours, we got out of the car to stretch our legs.

(participial phrase:) Praised for their work, the group accepted the first-place trophy.

GERUNDS

A **gerund** is a type of verbal that always functions as a **noun**. Like present participles, gerunds always end with *-ing*, but they can be easily distinguished from participles by the part of speech they represent (participles always function as adjectives). Since a gerund or gerund phrase always functions as a noun, it can be used as the subject of a sentence, the predicate nominative, or the object of a verb or preposition.

Examples:

We want to be known for [teaching the poor]().
- teaching = gerund
- teaching the poor = object of preposition

[Coaching this team]() is the best job of my life.
- Coaching = gerund
- Coaching this team = subject

We like [practicing our songs]() in the basement.
- practicing = gerund
- practicing our songs = object of verb

INFINITIVES

An **infinitive** is a type of verbal that can function as a noun, an adjective, or an adverb. An infinitive is made of the word *to* and the basic form of the verb. As with all other types of verbal phrases, an infinitive phrase includes the verbal itself and all of its complements or modifiers.

Examples:

[To join the team]() is my goal in life.
- To join = infinitive
- To join the team = noun

The animals have enough food [to eat]() for the night.
- to eat = infinitive
- to eat = adjective

People lift weights [to exercise their muscles]().
- to exercise = infinitive
- to exercise their muscles = adverb

> **Review Video: Verbals**
> Visit mometrix.com/academy and enter code: 915480

APPOSITIVE PHRASES

An **appositive** is a word or phrase that is used to explain or rename nouns or pronouns. Noun phrases, gerund phrases, and infinitive phrases can all be used as appositives.

Examples:

Terriers, [hunters at heart](), have been dressed up to look like lap dogs.

The noun phrase *hunters at heart* renames the noun *terriers*.

His plan, [to save and invest his money](), was proven as a safe approach.

The infinitive phrase explains what the plan is.

Appositive phrases can be **essential** or **nonessential**. An appositive phrase is essential if the person, place, or thing being described or renamed is too general for its meaning to be understood without the appositive.

Examples:

$$\overbrace{\text{essential}}$$
Two of America's Founding Fathers, George Washington and Thomas Jefferson, served as presidents.

$$\overbrace{\text{nonessential}}$$
George Washington and Thomas Jefferson, two Founding Fathers, served as presidents.

ABSOLUTE PHRASES

An absolute phrase is a phrase that consists of **a noun followed by a participle**. An absolute phrase provides **context** to what is being described in the sentence, but it does not modify or explain any particular word; it is essentially independent.

Examples:

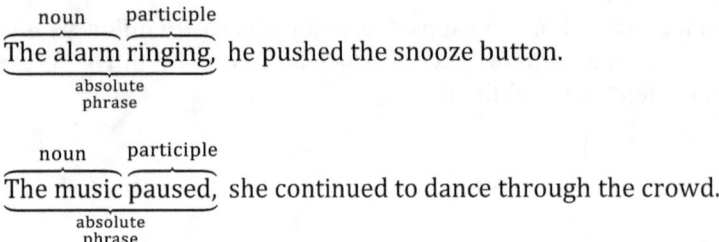

The alarm ringing, he pushed the snooze button.

The music paused, she continued to dance through the crowd.

PARALLELISM

When multiple items or ideas are presented in a sentence in series, such as in a list, the items or ideas must be stated in grammatically equivalent ways. For example, if two ideas are listed in parallel and the first is stated in gerund form, the second cannot be stated in infinitive form. (e.g., *I enjoy reading and to study.* [incorrect]) An infinitive and a gerund are not grammatically equivalent. Instead, you should write *I enjoy reading and studying* OR *I like to read and to study*. In lists of more than two, all items must be parallel.

Example:

Incorrect: He stopped at the office, grocery store, and the pharmacy before heading home.

The first and third items in the list of places include the article *the*, so the second item needs it as well.

Correct: He stopped at the office, *the* grocery store, and the pharmacy before heading home.

Example:

Incorrect: While vacationing in Europe, she went biking, skiing, and climbed mountains.

The first and second items in the list are gerunds, so the third item must be as well.

Correct: While vacationing in Europe, she went biking, skiing, and *mountain climbing*.

> **Review Video: Parallel Sentence Construction**
> Visit mometrix.com/academy and enter code: 831988

SENTENCE PURPOSE

There are four types of sentences: declarative, imperative, interrogative, and exclamatory.

A **declarative** sentence states a fact and ends with a period.

The football game starts at seven o'clock.

An **imperative** sentence tells someone to do something and generally ends with a period. An urgent command might end with an exclamation point instead.

Don't forget to buy your ticket.

An **interrogative** sentence asks a question and ends with a question mark.

Are you going to the game on Friday?

An **exclamatory** sentence shows strong emotion and ends with an exclamation point.

I can't believe we won the game!

SENTENCE STRUCTURE

Sentences are classified by structure based on the type and number of clauses present. The four classifications of sentence structure are the following:

Simple: A simple sentence has one independent clause with no dependent clauses. A simple sentence may have **compound elements** (i.e., compound subject or verb).

Examples:

Judy (single subject) watered (single verb) the lawn.

Judy and Alan (compound subject) watered (single verb) the lawn.

Judy (single subject) watered (compound verb) the lawn and pulled (compound verb) weeds.

Judy and Alan (compound subject) watered (compound verb) the lawn and pulled (compound verb) weeds.

Compound: A compound sentence has two or more independent clauses with no dependent clauses. Usually, the independent clauses are joined with a comma and a coordinating conjunction or with a semicolon.

Examples:

The time has come, (independent clause) and we are ready. (independent clause)

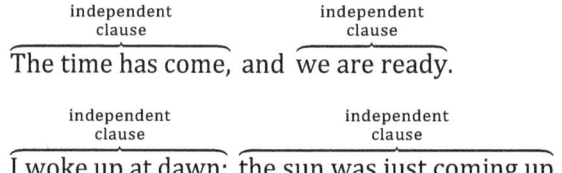

I woke up at dawn; (independent clause) the sun was just coming up. (independent clause)

Complex: A complex sentence has one independent clause and at least one dependent clause.

Examples:

Although he had the flu, [dependent clause] Harry went to work. [independent clause]

Marcia got married, [independent clause] after she finished college. [dependent clause]

Compound-Complex: A compound-complex sentence has at least two independent clauses and at least one dependent clause.

Examples:

John is my friend [independent clause] who went to India, [dependent clause] and he brought back souvenirs. [independent clause]

You may not realize this, [independent clause] but we heard the music [independent clause] that you played last night. [dependent clause]

> **Review Video: Sentence Structure**
> Visit mometrix.com/academy and enter code: 700478

Sentence variety is important to consider when writing an essay or speech. A variety of sentence lengths and types creates rhythm, makes a passage more engaging, and gives writers an opportunity to demonstrate their writing style. Writing that uses the same length or type of sentence without variation can be boring or difficult to read. To evaluate a passage for effective sentence variety, it is helpful to note whether the passage contains diverse sentence structures and lengths. It is also important to pay attention to the way each sentence starts and avoid beginning with the same words or phrases.

SENTENCE FRAGMENTS

Recall that a group of words must contain at least one **independent clause** in order to be considered a sentence. If it doesn't contain even one independent clause, it is called a **sentence fragment**.

The appropriate process for **repairing** a sentence fragment depends on what type of fragment it is. If the fragment is a dependent clause, it can sometimes be as simple as removing a subordinating word (e.g., when, because, if) from the beginning of the fragment. Alternatively, a dependent clause can be incorporated into a closely related neighboring sentence. If the fragment is missing some required part, like a subject or a verb, the fix might be as simple as adding the missing part.

Examples:

  Fragment: Because he wanted to sail the Mediterranean.

  Removed subordinating word: He wanted to sail the Mediterranean.

  Combined with another sentence: Because he wanted to sail the Mediterranean, he booked a Greek island cruise.

RUN-ON SENTENCES

Run-on sentences consist of multiple independent clauses that have not been joined together properly. Run-on sentences can be corrected in several different ways:

Join clauses properly: This can be done with a comma and coordinating conjunction, with a semicolon, or with a colon or dash if the second clause is explaining something in the first.

Example:

> **Incorrect**: I went on the trip, we visited lots of castles.
>
> **Corrected**: I went on the trip, and we visited lots of castles.

Split into separate sentences: This correction is most effective when the independent clauses are very long or when they are not closely related.

Example:

> **Incorrect**: The drive to New York takes ten hours, my uncle lives in Boston.
>
> **Corrected**: The drive to New York takes ten hours. My uncle lives in Boston.

Make one clause dependent: This is the easiest way to make the sentence correct and more interesting at the same time. It's often as simple as adding a subordinating word between the two clauses or before the first clause.

Example:

> **Incorrect**: I finally made it to the store and I bought some eggs.
>
> **Corrected**: When I finally made it to the store, I bought some eggs.

Reduce to one clause with a compound verb: If both clauses have the same subject, remove the subject from the second clause, and you now have just one clause with a compound verb.

Example:

> **Incorrect**: The drive to New York takes ten hours, it makes me very tired.
>
> **Corrected**: The drive to New York takes ten hours and makes me very tired.

Note: While these are the simplest ways to correct a run-on sentence, often the best way is to completely reorganize the thoughts in the sentence and rewrite it.

> **Review Video: Fragments and Run-on Sentences**
> Visit mometrix.com/academy and enter code: 541989

DANGLING AND MISPLACED MODIFIERS

DANGLING MODIFIERS

A dangling modifier is a dependent clause or verbal phrase that does not have a clear logical connection to a word in the sentence.

Example:

Incorrect: <u>Reading each magazine article</u>, the stories caught my attention. *(dangling modifier)*

The word *stories* cannot be modified by *Reading each magazine article*. People can read, but stories cannot read. Therefore, the subject of the sentence must be a person.

Corrected: <u>Reading each magazine article</u>, I was entertained by the stories. *(gerund phrase)*

Example:

Incorrect: <u>Ever since childhood</u>, my grandparents have visited me for Christmas. *(dangling modifier)*

The speaker in this sentence can't have been visited by her grandparents when *they* were children, since she wouldn't have been born yet. Either the modifier should be clarified or the sentence should be rearranged to specify whose childhood is being referenced.

Clarified: <u>Ever since I was a child</u>, my grandparents have visited for Christmas. *(dependent clause)*

Rearranged: <u>Ever since childhood</u>, I have enjoyed my grandparents visiting for Christmas. *(adverb phrase)*

MISPLACED MODIFIERS

Because modifiers are grammatically versatile, they can be put in many different places within the structure of a sentence. The danger of this versatility is that a modifier can accidentally be placed where it is modifying the wrong word or where it is not clear which word it is modifying.

Example:

Incorrect: She read the book to a crowd <u>that was filled with beautiful pictures</u>. *(modifier)*

The book was filled with beautiful pictures, not the crowd.

Corrected: She read the book <u>that was filled with beautiful pictures</u> to a crowd. *(modifier)*

Example:

Ambiguous: Derek saw a bus nearly hit a man <u>on his way to work</u>. *(modifier)*

Was Derek on his way to work or was the other man?

Derek: <u>On his way to work</u>, Derek saw a bus nearly hit a man. *(modifier)*

The other man: Derek saw a bus nearly hit a man <u>who was on his way to work</u>. *(modifier)*

SPLIT INFINITIVES

A split infinitive occurs when a modifying word comes between the word *to* and the verb that pairs with *to*.

Example: To *clearly* explain vs. To explain clearly | To *softly* sing vs. To sing softly

Though considered improper by some, split infinitives may provide better clarity and simplicity in some cases than the alternatives. As such, avoiding them should not be considered a universal rule.

DOUBLE NEGATIVES

Standard English allows **two negatives** only when a **positive** meaning is intended. (e.g., The team was *not displeased* with their performance.) Double negatives to emphasize negation are not used in standard English.

Negative modifiers (e.g., never, no, and not) should not be paired with other negative modifiers or negative words (e.g., none, nobody, nothing, or neither). The modifiers *hardly, barely*, and *scarcely* are also considered negatives in standard English, so they should not be used with other negatives.

Punctuation

END PUNCTUATION

PERIODS

Use a period to end all sentences except direct questions and exclamations. Periods are also used for abbreviations.

Examples: 3 p.m. | 2 a.m. | Mr. Jones | Mrs. Stevens | Dr. Smith | Bill, Jr. | Pennsylvania Ave.

Note: An abbreviation is a shortened form of a word or phrase.

QUESTION MARKS

Question marks should be used following a **direct question**. A polite request can be followed by a period instead of a question mark.

Direct Question: What is for lunch today? | How are you? | Why is that the answer?

Polite Requests: Can you please send me the item tomorrow. | Will you please walk with me on the track.

> **Review Video: Question Marks**
> Visit mometrix.com/academy and enter code: 118471

EXCLAMATION MARKS

Exclamation marks are used after a word group or sentence that shows much feeling or has special importance. Exclamation marks should not be overused. They are saved for proper **exclamatory interjections**.

Example: We're going to the finals! | You have a beautiful car! | "That's crazy!" she yelled.

> **Review Video: Exclamation Points**
> Visit mometrix.com/academy and enter code: 199367

COMMAS

The comma is a punctuation mark that can help you understand connections in a sentence. Not every sentence needs a comma. However, if a sentence needs a comma, you need to put it in the right place. A comma in the wrong place (or an absent comma) will make a sentence's meaning unclear.

These are some of the rules for commas:

Use Case	Example
Before a **coordinating conjunction** joining independent clauses	Bob caught three fish, and I caught two fish.
After an **introductory phrase**	After the final out, we went to a restaurant to celebrate.
After an **adverbial clause**	Studying the stars, I was awed by the beauty of the sky.
Between **items in a series**	I will bring the turkey, the pie, and the coffee.
For **interjections**	Wow, you know how to play this game.
After *yes* and *no* responses	No, I cannot come tomorrow.
Separate **nonessential modifiers**	John Frank, who coaches the team, was promoted today.
Separate **nonessential appositives**	Thomas Edison, an American inventor, was born in Ohio.
Separate **nouns of direct address**	You, John, are my only hope in this moment.
Separate **interrogative tags**	This is the last time, correct?
Separate **contrasts**	You are my friend, not my enemy.
Writing **dates**	July 4, 1776, is an important date to remember.
Writing **addresses**	He is meeting me at 456 Delaware Avenue, Washington, D.C., tomorrow morning.
Writing **geographical names**	Paris, France, is my favorite city.
Writing **titles**	John Smith, PhD, will be visiting your class today.
Separate **expressions like** *he said*	"You can start," she said, "with an apology."

A comma is also used **between coordinate adjectives** not joined with *and*. However, not all adjectives are coordinate (i.e., equal or parallel). To determine if your adjectives are coordinate, try connecting them with *and* or reversing their order. If it still sounds right, they are coordinate.

Incorrect: The kind, brown dog followed me home.

Correct: The kind, loyal dog followed me home.

> **Review Video: When to Use a Comma**
> Visit mometrix.com/academy and enter code: 786797

SEMICOLONS

The semicolon is used to join closely related independent clauses without the need for a coordinating conjunction. Semicolons are also used in place of commas to separate list elements that have internal commas. Some rules for semicolons include:

Use Case	Example
Between closely connected independent clauses **not connected with a coordinating conjunction**	You are right; we should go with your plan.
Between independent clauses **linked with a transitional word**	I think that we can agree on this; however, I am not sure about my friends.
Between items in a **series that has internal punctuation**	I have visited New York, New York; Augusta, Maine; and Baltimore, Maryland.

> **Review Video: How to Use Semicolons**
> Visit mometrix.com/academy and enter code: 370605

COLONS

The colon is used to call attention to the words that follow it. When used in a sentence, a colon should only come at the **end** of a **complete sentence**. The rules for colons are as follows:

Use Case	Example
After an independent clause to **make a list**	I want to learn many languages: Spanish, German, and Italian.
For **explanations**	There is one thing that stands out on your resume: responsibility.
To give a **quote**	He started with an idea: "We are able to do more than we imagine."
After the **greeting in a formal letter**	To Whom It May Concern:
Show **hours and minutes**	It is 3:14 p.m.
Separate a **title and subtitle**	The essay is titled "America: A Short Introduction to a Modern Country."

> **Review Video: Using Colons**
> Visit mometrix.com/academy and enter code: 868673

PARENTHESES

Parentheses are used for additional information. Also, they can be used to put labels for letters or numbers in a series. Parentheses should be not be used very often. If they are overused, parentheses can be a distraction instead of a help.

Examples:

> **Extra Information**: The rattlesnake (see Image 2) is a dangerous snake of North and South America.
>
> **Series**: Include in the email (1) your name, (2) your address, and (3) your question for the author.

> **Review Video: Parentheses**
> Visit mometrix.com/academy and enter code: 947743

QUOTATION MARKS

Use quotation marks to close off **direct quotations** of a person's spoken or written words. Do not use quotation marks around indirect quotations. An indirect quotation gives someone's message without using the person's exact words. Use **single quotation marks** to close off a quotation inside a quotation.

Direct Quote: Nancy said, "I am waiting for Henry to arrive."

Indirect Quote: Henry said that he is going to be late to the meeting.

Quote inside a Quote: The teacher asked, "Has everyone read 'The Gift of the Magi'?"

Quotation marks should be used around the titles of **short works**: newspaper and magazine articles, poems, short stories, songs, television episodes, radio programs, and subdivisions of books or websites.

Examples:

"Rip Van Winkle" (short story by Washington Irving)

"O Captain! My Captain!" (poem by Walt Whitman)

Although it is not standard usage, quotation marks are sometimes used to highlight **irony** or the use of words to mean something other than their dictionary definition. This type of usage should be employed sparingly, if at all.

Examples:

| The boss warned Frank that he was walking on "thin ice." | Frank is not walking on real ice. Instead, he is being warned to avoid mistakes. |
| The teacher thanked the young man for his "honesty." | The quotation marks around *honesty* show that the teacher does not believe the young man's explanation. |

> **Review Video: Quotation Marks**
> Visit mometrix.com/academy and enter code: 884918

Periods and commas are put **inside** quotation marks. Colons and semicolons are put **outside** the quotation marks. Question marks and exclamation points are placed inside quotation marks when they are part of a quote. When the question or exclamation mark goes with the whole sentence, the mark is left outside of the quotation marks.

Examples:

Period and comma	We read "The Gift of the Magi," "The Skylight Room," and "The Cactus."
Semicolon	They watched "The Nutcracker"; then, they went home.
Exclamation mark that is a part of a quote	The crowd cheered, "Victory!"
Question mark that goes with the whole sentence	Is your favorite short story "The Tell-Tale Heart"?

APOSTROPHES

An apostrophe is used to show **possession** or the **deletion of letters in contractions**. An apostrophe is not needed with the possessive pronouns *his, hers, its, ours, theirs, whose*, and *yours*.

Singular Nouns: David's car | a book's theme | my brother's board game

Plural Nouns that end with -s: the scissors' handle | boys' basketball

Plural Nouns that end without -s: Men's department | the people's adventure

> Review Video: **When to Use an Apostrophe**
> Visit mometrix.com/academy and enter code: 213068
>
> Review Video: **Punctuation Errors in Possessive Pronouns**
> Visit mometrix.com/academy and enter code: 221438

HYPHENS

Hyphens are used to **separate compound words**. Use hyphens in the following cases:

Use Case	Example
Compound numbers from 21 to 99 when written out in words	This team needs twenty-five points to win the game.
Written-out fractions that are used as adjectives	The recipe says that we need a three-fourths cup of butter.
Compound adjectives that come before a noun	The well-fed dog took a nap.
Unusual compound words that would be hard to read or easily confused with other words	This is the best anti-itch cream on the market.

Note: This is not a complete set of the rules for hyphens. A dictionary is the best tool for knowing if a compound word needs a hyphen.

> Review Video: **Hyphens**
> Visit mometrix.com/academy and enter code: 981632

DASHES

Dashes are used to show a **break** or a **change in thought** in a sentence or to act as parentheses in a sentence. When typing, use two hyphens to make a dash. Do not put a space before or after the dash. The following are the functions of dashes:

Use Case	Example
Set off parenthetical statements or an **appositive with internal punctuation**	The three trees—oak, pine, and magnolia—are coming on a truck tomorrow.
Show a **break or change in tone or thought**	The first question—how silly of me—does not have a correct answer.

ELLIPSIS MARKS

The ellipsis mark has **three** periods (...) to show when **words have been removed** from a quotation. If a **full sentence or more** is removed from a quoted passage, you need to use **four** periods to show the removed text and the end punctuation mark. The ellipsis mark should not be used at the beginning of a quotation. The ellipsis mark should also not be used at the end of a quotation unless some words have been deleted from the end of the final quoted sentence.

Example:

"Then he picked up the groceries...paid for them...later he went home."

BRACKETS

There are two main reasons to use brackets:

Use Case	Example
Placing **parentheses inside of parentheses**	The hero of this story, Paul Revere (a silversmith and industrialist [see Ch. 4]), rode through towns of Massachusetts to warn of advancing British troops.
Adding **clarification or detail to a quotation** that is not part of the quotation	The father explained, "My children are planning to attend my alma mater [State University]."

> **Review Video: Brackets**
> Visit mometrix.com/academy and enter code: 727546

Common Usage Mistakes

COMMONLY CONFUSED WORDS

WHICH, THAT, AND WHO

The words *which*, *that*, and *who* can act as **relative pronouns** to help clarify or describe a noun.

Which is used for things only.

   Example: Andrew's car, *which is old and rusty*, broke down last week.

That is used for people or things. *That* is usually informal when used to describe people.

   Example: Is this the only book *that Louis L'Amour wrote*?

   Example: Is Louis L'Amour the author *that wrote Western novels*?

Who is used for people or for animals that have an identity or personality.

   Example: Mozart was the composer *who wrote those operas*.

   Example: John's dog, *who is called Max*, is large and fierce.

THEN AND THAN

Then is an adverb that indicates sequence or order:

   Example: I'm going to run to the library and then come home.

Than is special-purpose word used only for comparisons:

   Example: Susie likes chips more than candy.

SAW AND SEEN

Saw is the past-tense form of *see*.

> Example: I saw a turtle on my walk this morning.

Seen is the past participle of *see*.

> Example: I have seen this movie before.

AFFECT AND EFFECT

There are two main reasons that *affect* and *effect* are so often confused: 1) both words can be used as either a noun or a verb, and 2) unlike most homophones, their usage and meanings are closely related to each other. Here is a quick rundown of the four usage options:

Affect (n): feeling, emotion, or mood that is displayed

> Example: The patient had a flat *affect*. (i.e., his face showed little or no emotion)

Affect (v): to alter, to change, to influence

> Example: The sunshine *affects* the plant's growth.

Effect (n): a result, a consequence

> Example: What *effect* will this weather have on our schedule?

Effect (v): to bring about, to cause to be

> Example: These new rules will *effect* order in the office.

The noun form of *affect* is rarely used outside of technical medical descriptions, so if a noun form is needed on the test, you can safely select *effect*. The verb form of *effect* is not as rare as the noun form of *affect*, but it's still not all that likely to show up on your test. If you need a verb and you can't decide which to use based on the definitions, choosing *affect* is your best bet.

HOMOPHONES

Homophones are words that sound alike (or similar) but have different **spellings** and **definitions**. A homophone is a type of **homonym**, which is a pair or group of words that are pronounced or spelled the same, but do not mean the same thing.

TO, TOO, AND TWO

To can be an adverb or a preposition for showing direction, purpose, and relationship. See your dictionary for the many other ways to use *to* in a sentence.

> Examples: I went to the store. | I want to go with you.

Too is an adverb that means *also, as well, very,* or *in excess*.

> Examples: I can walk a mile too. | You have eaten too much.

Two is a number.

> Example: You have two minutes left.

THERE, THEIR, AND THEY'RE

There can be an adjective, adverb, or pronoun. Often, *there* is used to show a place or to start a sentence.

>Examples: I went there yesterday. | There is something in his pocket.

Their is a pronoun that is used to show ownership.

>Examples: He is their father. | This is their fourth apology this week.

They're is a contraction of *they are*.

>Example: Did you know that they're in town?

KNEW AND NEW

Knew is the past tense of *know*.

>Example: I knew the answer.

New is an adjective that means something is current, has not been used, or is modern.

>Example: This is my new phone.

ITS AND IT'S

Its is a pronoun that shows ownership.

>Example: The guitar is in its case.

It's is a contraction of *it is*.

>Example: It's an honor and a privilege to meet you.

Note: The *h* in honor is silent, so *honor* starts with the vowel sound *o*, which must have the article *an*.

YOUR AND YOU'RE

Your is a pronoun that shows ownership.

>Example: This is your moment to shine.

You're is a contraction of *you are*.

>Example: Yes, you're correct.

HOMOGRAPHS

Homographs are words that share the same spelling, but have different meanings and sometimes different pronunciations. To figure out which meaning is being used, you should be looking for context clues. The context clues give hints to the meaning of the word. For example, the word *spot* has many meanings. It can mean "a place" or "a stain or blot." In the sentence "After my lunch, I saw a spot on my shirt," the word *spot* means "a stain or blot." The context clues of "After my lunch" and "on my shirt" guide you to this decision. A homograph is another type of homonym.

BANK

>(noun): an establishment where money is held for savings or lending

>(verb): to collect or pile up

Content
- (noun): the topics that will be addressed within a book
- (adjective): pleased or satisfied
- (verb): to make someone pleased or satisfied

Fine
- (noun): an amount of money that acts a penalty for an offense
- (adjective): very small or thin
- (adverb): in an acceptable way
- (verb): to make someone pay money as a punishment

Incense
- (noun): a material that is burned in religious settings and makes a pleasant aroma
- (verb): to frustrate or anger

Lead
- (noun): the first or highest position
- (noun): a heavy metallic element
- (verb): to direct a person or group of followers
- (adjective): containing lead

Object
- (noun): a lifeless item that can be held and observed
- (verb): to disagree

Produce
- (noun): fruits and vegetables
- (verb): to make or create something

Refuse
- (noun): garbage or debris that has been thrown away
- (verb): to not allow

Subject
- (noun): an area of study
- (verb): to force or subdue

Tear
- (noun): a fluid secreted by the eyes
- (verb): to separate or pull apart

Commonly Misused Words and Phrases

A Lot

The phrase *a lot* should always be written as two words; never as *alot*.

>**Correct**: That's a lot of chocolate!

>**Incorrect**: He does that alot.

Can

The word *can* is used to describe things that are possible occurrences; the word *may* is used to described things that are allowed to happen.

>**Correct**: May I have another piece of pie?

>**Correct**: I can lift three of these bags of mulch at a time.

>**Incorrect**: Mom said we can stay up thirty minutes later tonight.

Could Have

The phrase *could of* is often incorrectly substituted for the phrase *could have*. Similarly, *could of, may of,* and *might of* are sometimes used in place of the correct phrases *could have, may have,* and *might have*.

>**Correct**: If I had known, I would have helped out.

>**Incorrect**: Well, that could of gone much worse than it did.

Myself

The word *myself* is a reflexive pronoun, often incorrectly used in place of *I* or *me*.

>**Correct**: He let me do it myself.

>**Incorrect**: The job was given to Dave and myself.

Off

The phrase *off of* is a redundant expression that should be avoided. In most cases, it can be corrected simply by removing *of*.

>**Correct**: My dog chased the squirrel off its perch on the fence.

>**Incorrect**: He finally moved his plate off of the table.

Supposed To

The phrase *suppose to* is sometimes used incorrectly in place of the phrase *supposed to*.

>**Correct**: I was supposed to go to the store this afternoon.

>**Incorrect**: When are we suppose to get our grades?

Try To

The phrase *try and* is often used in informal writing and conversation to replace the correct phrase *try to*.

>**Correct**: It's a good policy to try to satisfy every customer who walks in the door.

>**Incorrect**: Don't try and do too much.

Spelling Conventions

GENERAL SPELLING RULES

WORDS ENDING WITH A CONSONANT

Usually, the final consonant is **doubled** on a word before adding a suffix. This is the rule for single syllable words, words ending with one consonant, and multi-syllable words with the last syllable accented. The following are examples:

- *beg* becomes *begging* (single syllable)
- *shop* becomes *shopped* (single syllable)
- *add* becomes *adding* (already ends in double consonant, do not add another *d*)
- *deter* becomes *deterring* (multi-syllable, accent on last syllable)
- *regret* becomes *regrettable* (multi-syllable, accent on last syllable)
- *compost* becomes *composting* (do not add another *t* because the accent is on the first syllable)

WORDS ENDING WITH Y OR C

The general rule for words ending in *y* is to keep the *y* when adding a suffix if the **y is preceded by a vowel**. If the word **ends in a consonant and y** the *y* is changed to an *i* before the suffix is added (unless the suffix itself begins with *i*). The following are examples:

- *pay* becomes *paying* (keep the *y*)
- *bully* becomes *bullied* (change to *i*)
- *bully* becomes *bullying* (keep the *y* because the suffix is –*ing*)

If a word ends with *c* and the suffix begins with an *e, i,* or *y*, the letter *k* is usually added to the end of the word. The following are examples:

- panic becomes panicky
- mimic becomes mimicking

WORDS CONTAINING IE OR EI, AND/OR ENDING WITH E

Most words are spelled with an *i* before *e*, except when they follow the letter *c,* **or** sound like *a*. For example, the following words are spelled correctly according to these rules:

- piece, friend, believe (*i* before *e*)
- receive, ceiling, conceited (except after *c*)
- weight, neighborhood, veil (sounds like *a*)

To add a suffix to words ending with the letter *e*, first determine if the *e* is silent. If it is, the *e* will be kept if the added suffix begins with a consonant. If the suffix begins with a vowel, the *e* is dropped. The following are examples:

- *age* becomes *ageless* (keep the *e*)
- *age* becomes *aging* (drop the *e*)

An exception to this rule occurs when the word ends in *ce* or *ge* and the suffix *able* or *ous* is added; these words will retain the letter *e*. The following are examples:

- courage becomes courageous
- notice becomes noticeable

Words Ending with ISE or IZE

A small number of words end with *ise*. Most of the words in the English language with the same sound end in *ize*. The following are examples:

- advertise, advise, arise, chastise, circumcise, and comprise
- compromise, demise, despise, devise, disguise, enterprise, excise, and exercise
- franchise, improvise, incise, merchandise, premise, reprise, and revise
- supervise, surmise, surprise, and televise

Words that end with *ize* include the following:

- accessorize, agonize, authorize, and brutalize
- capitalize, caramelize, categorize, civilize, and demonize
- downsize, empathize, euthanize, idolize, and immunize
- legalize, metabolize, mobilize, organize, and ostracize
- plagiarize, privatize, utilize, and visualize

(Note that some words may technically be spelled with *ise*, especially in British English, but it is more common to use *ize*. Examples include *symbolize/symbolise* and *baptize/baptise*.)

Words Ending with CEED, SEDE, OR CEDE

There are only three words in the English language that end with *ceed*: *exceed, proceed,* and *succeed*. There is only one word in the English language that ends with *sede*: *supersede*. Most other words that sound like *sede* or *ceed* end with *cede*. The following are examples:

- concede, recede, and precede

Words Ending in ABLE OR IBLE

For words ending in *able* or *ible*, there are no hard and fast rules. The following are examples:

- adjustable, unbeatable, collectable, deliverable, and likeable
- edible, compatible, feasible, sensible, and credible

There are more words ending in *able* than *ible*; this is useful to know if guessing is necessary.

Words Ending in ANCE OR ENCE

The suffixes *ence, ency,* and *ent* are used in the following cases:

- the suffix is preceded by the letter *c* but sounds like *s* – *innocence*
- the suffix is preceded by the letter *g* but sounds like *j* – *intelligence, negligence*

The suffixes *ance, ancy,* and *ant* are used in the following cases:

- the suffix is preceded by the letter *c* but sounds like *k* – *significant, vacant*
- the suffix is preceded by the letter *g* with a hard sound – *elegant, extravagance*

If the suffix is preceded by other letters, there are no clear rules. For example: *finance, abundance,* and *assistance* use the letter *a*, while *decadence, competence,* and *excellence* use the letter *e*.

Words Ending in tion, sion, or cian

Words ending in *tion, sion,* or *cian* all sound like *shun* or *zhun*. There are no rules for which ending is used for words. The following are examples:

- action, agitation, caution, fiction, nation, and motion
- admission, expression, mansion, permission, and television
- electrician, magician, musician, optician, and physician (note that these words tend to describe occupations)

Words with the ai or ia Combination

When deciding if *ai* or *ia* is correct, the combination of *ai* usually sounds like one vowel sound, as in *Britain*, while the vowels in *ia* are pronounced separately, as in *guardian*. The following are examples:

- captain, certain, faint, hair, malaise, and praise (*ai* makes one sound)
- bacteria, beneficiary, diamond, humiliation, and nuptial (*ia* makes two sounds)

Rules for Plurals
Nouns Ending in ch, sh, s, x, or z

When a noun ends in the letters *ch, sh, s, x,* or *z*, an *es* instead of a singular *s* is added to the end of the word to make it plural. The following are examples:

- church becomes churches
- bush becomes bushes
- bass becomes basses
- mix becomes mixes
- buzz becomes buzzes

This is the rule with proper names as well; the Ross family would become the Rosses.

Nouns Ending in y or ay/ey/iy/oy/uy

If a noun ends with a **consonant and y**, the plural is formed by replacing the *y* with *ies*. For example, *fly* becomes *flies* and *puppy* becomes *puppies*. If a noun ends with a **vowel and y**, the plural is formed by adding an *s*. For example, *alley* becomes *alleys* and *boy* becomes *boys*.

Nouns Ending in f or fe

Most nouns ending in *f* or *fe* are pluralized by replacing the *f* with *v* and adding *es*. The following are examples:

- knife becomes knives; self becomes selves; wolf becomes wolves.

An exception to this rule is the word *roof; roof* becomes *roofs*.

Nouns Ending in o

Most nouns ending with a **consonant and o** are pluralized by adding *es*. The following are examples:

- hero becomes heroes; tornado becomes tornadoes; potato becomes potatoes

Most nouns ending with a **vowel and o** are pluralized by adding *s*. The following are examples:

- portfolio becomes portfolios; radio becomes radios; cameo becomes cameos.

An exception to these rules is seen with musical terms ending in *o*. These words are pluralized by adding *s* even if they end in a consonant and *o*. The following are examples: *soprano* becomes *sopranos*; *banjo* becomes *banjos*; *piano* becomes *pianos*.

LETTERS, NUMBERS, AND SYMBOLS

Letters and numbers become plural by adding an apostrophe and *s*. The following are examples:

- The *L's* are the people whose names begin with the letter *L*.
- They broke the teams down into groups of *3's*.
- The sorority girls were all *KD's*.

COMPOUND NOUNS

A **compound noun** is a noun that is made up of two or more words; they can be written with hyphens. For example, *mother-in-law* or *court-martial* are compound nouns. To make them plural, an *s* or *es* is added to the noun portion of the word. The following are examples: *mother-in-law* becomes *mothers-in-law*; *court-martial* becomes *courts-martial*.

EXCEPTIONS

Some words do not fall into any specific category for making the singular form plural. They are **irregular**. Certain words become plural by changing the vowels within the word. The following are examples:

- woman becomes women; goose becomes geese; foot becomes feet

Some words change in unusual ways in the plural form. The following are examples:

- mouse becomes mice; ox becomes oxen; person becomes people

Some words are the same in both the singular and plural forms. The following are examples:

- *Salmon*, *deer*, and *moose* are the same whether singular or plural.

COMMONLY MISSPELLED WORDS

accidentally	accommodate	accompanied	accompany
achieved	acknowledgment	across	address
aggravate	aisle	ancient	anxiety
apparently	appearance	arctic	argument
arrangement	attendance	auxiliary	awkward
bachelor	barbarian	beggar	beneficiary
biscuit	brilliant	business	cafeteria
calendar	campaign	candidate	ceiling
cemetery	changeable	changing	characteristic
chauffeur	colonel	column	commit
committee	comparative	compel	competent
competition	conceive	congratulations	conqueror
conscious	coolly	correspondent	courtesy
curiosity	cylinder	deceive	deference
deferred	definite	describe	desirable
desperate	develop	diphtheria	disappear
disappoint	disastrous	discipline	discussion
disease	dissatisfied	dissipate	drudgery
ecstasy	efficient	eighth	eligible
embarrass	emphasize	especially	exaggerate
exceed	exhaust	exhilaration	existence

explanation	extraordinary	familiar	fascinate
February	fiery	finally	forehead
foreign	foreigner	foremost	forfeit
ghost	glamorous	government	grammar
grateful	grief	grievous	handkerchief
harass	height	hoping	hurriedly
hygiene	hypocrisy	imminent	incidentally
incredible	independent	indigestible	inevitable
innocence	intelligible	intentionally	intercede
interest	irresistible	judgment	legitimate
liable	library	likelihood	literature
maintenance	maneuver	manual	mathematics
mattress	miniature	mischievous	misspell
momentous	mortgage	neither	nickel
niece	ninety	noticeable	notoriety
obedience	obstacle	occasion	occurrence
omitted	operate	optimistic	organization
outrageous	pageant	pamphlet	parallel
parliament	permissible	perseverance	persuade
physically	physician	possess	possibly
practically	prairie	preceding	prejudice
prevalent	professor	pronunciation	pronouncement
propeller	protein	psychiatrist	psychology
quantity	questionnaire	rally	recede
receive	recognize	recommend	referral
referred	relieve	religious	resistance
restaurant	rhetoric	rhythm	ridiculous
sacrilegious	salary	scarcely	schedule
secretary	sentinel	separate	severely
sheriff	shriek	similar	soliloquy
sophomore	species	strenuous	studying
suffrage	supersede	suppress	surprise
symmetry	temperament	temperature	tendency
tournament	tragedy	transferred	truly
twelfth	tyranny	unanimous	unpleasant
usage	vacuum	valuable	vein
vengeance	vigilance	villain	Wednesday
weird	wholly		

The Writing Process

BRAINSTORMING

Brainstorming is a technique that is used to find a creative approach to a subject. This can be accomplished by simple **free-association** with a topic. For example, with paper and pen, write every thought that you have about the topic in a word or phrase. This is done without critical thinking. You should put everything that comes to your mind about the topic on your scratch paper. Then, you need to read the list over a few times. Next, look for patterns, repetitions, and clusters of ideas. This allows a variety of fresh ideas to come as you think about the topic.

FREE WRITING

Free writing is a more structured form of brainstorming. The method involves taking a limited amount of time (e.g., 2 to 3 minutes) to write everything that comes to mind about the topic in complete sentences. When time expires, review everything that has been written down. Many of your sentences may make little or no sense, but the insights and observations that can come from free writing make this method a valuable approach. Usually, free writing results in a fuller expression of ideas than brainstorming because thoughts and associations are written in complete sentences. However, both techniques can be used to complement each other.

PLANNING

Planning is the process of organizing a piece of writing before composing a draft. Planning can include creating an outline or a graphic organizer, such as a Venn diagram, a spider-map, or a flowchart. These methods should help the writer identify their topic, main ideas, and the general organization of the composition. Preliminary research can also take place during this stage. Planning helps writers organize all of their ideas and decide if they have enough material to begin their first draft. However, writers should remember that the decisions they make during this step will likely change later in the process, so their plan does not have to be perfect.

DRAFTING

Writers may then use their plan, outline, or graphic organizer to compose their first draft. They may write subsequent drafts to improve their writing. Writing multiple drafts can help writers consider different ways to communicate their ideas and address errors that may be difficult to correct without rewriting a section or the whole composition. Most writers will vary in how many drafts they choose to write, as there is no "right" number of drafts. Writing drafts also takes away the pressure to write perfectly on the first try, as writers can improve with each draft they write.

REVISING, EDITING, AND PROOFREADING

Once a writer completes a draft, they can move on to the revising, editing, and proofreading steps to improve their draft. These steps begin with making broad changes that may apply to large sections of a composition and then making small, specific corrections. **Revising** is the first and broadest of these steps. Revising involves ensuring that the composition addresses an appropriate audience, includes all necessary material, maintains focus throughout, and is organized logically. Revising may occur after the first draft to ensure that the following drafts improve upon errors from the first draft. Some revision should occur between each draft to avoid repeating these errors. The **editing** phase of writing is narrower than the revising phase. Editing a composition should include steps such as improving transitions between paragraphs, ensuring each paragraph is on topic, and improving the flow of the text. The editing phase may also include correcting grammatical errors that cannot be fixed without significantly altering the text. **Proofreading** involves fixing misspelled words, typos, other grammatical errors, and any remaining surface-level flaws in the composition.

RECURSIVE WRITING PROCESS

However you approach writing, you may find comfort in knowing that the revision process can occur in any order. The **recursive writing process** is not as difficult as the phrase may make it seem. Simply put, the recursive writing process means that you may need to revisit steps after completing other steps. It also implies that the steps are not required to take place in any certain order. Indeed, you may find that planning, drafting, and revising can all take place at about the same time. The writing process involves moving back and forth between planning, drafting, and revising, followed by more planning, more drafting, and more revising until the writing is satisfactory.

> **Review Video: Recursive Writing Process**
> Visit mometrix.com/academy and enter code: 951611

Outlining and Organizing Ideas

Essays

Essays usually focus on one topic, subject, or goal. There are several types of essays, including informative, persuasive, and narrative. An essay's structure and level of formality depend on the type of essay and its goal. While narrative essays typically do not include outside sources, other types of essays often require some research and the integration of primary and secondary sources.

The basic format of an essay typically has three major parts: the introduction, the body, and the conclusion. The body is further divided into the writer's main points. Short and simple essays may have three main points, while essays covering broader ranges and going into more depth can have almost any number of main points, depending on length.

An essay's introduction should answer three questions:

1. What is the **subject** of the essay?

    If a student writes an essay about a book, the answer would include the title and author of the book and any additional information needed—such as the subject or argument of the book.

2. How does the essay **address** the subject?

    To answer this, the writer identifies the essay's organization by briefly summarizing main points and the evidence supporting them.

3. What will the essay **prove**?

    This is the thesis statement, usually the opening paragraph's last sentence, clearly stating the writer's message.

The body elaborates on all the main points related to the thesis, introducing one main point at a time, and includes supporting evidence with each main point. Each body paragraph should state the point in a topic sentence, which is usually the first sentence in the paragraph. The paragraph should then explain the point's meaning, support it with quotations or other evidence, and then explain how this point and the evidence are related to the thesis. The writer should then repeat this procedure in a new paragraph for each additional main point.

The conclusion reiterates the content of the introduction, including the thesis, to remind the reader of the essay's main argument or subject. The essay writer may also summarize the highlights of the argument or description contained in the body of the essay, following the same sequence originally used in the body. For example, a conclusion might look like: Point 1 + Point 2 + Point 3 = Thesis, or Point 1 → Point 2 → Point 3 → Thesis Proof. Good organization makes essays easier for writers to compose and provides a guide for readers to follow. Well-organized essays hold attention better and are more likely to get readers to accept their theses as valid.

Main Ideas, Supporting Details, and Outlining a Topic

A writer often begins the first paragraph of a paper by stating the **main idea** or point, also known as the **topic sentence**. The rest of the paragraph supplies particular details that develop and support the main point. One way to visualize the relationship between the main point and supporting information is by considering a table: the tabletop is the main point, and each of the table's legs is a supporting detail or group of details. Both professional authors and students can benefit from planning their writing by first making an outline of the topic. Outlines facilitate quick identification of the main point and supporting details without having to wade through the additional language that will exist in the fully developed essay, article, or paper. Outlining can also help readers to analyze a piece of existing writing for the same reason. The outline first summarizes the main idea in one sentence. Then, below that, it summarizes the supporting details in a numbered list. Writing the paper then consists of filling in the outline with detail, writing a paragraph for each supporting point, and adding an introduction and conclusion.

INTRODUCTION

The purpose of the introduction is to capture the reader's attention and announce the essay's main idea. Normally, the introduction contains 50-80 words, or 3-5 sentences. An introduction can begin with an interesting quote, a question, or a strong opinion—something that will **engage** the reader's interest and prompt them to keep reading. If you are writing your essay to a specific prompt, your introduction should include a **restatement or summarization** of the prompt so that the reader will have some context for your essay. Finally, your introduction should briefly state your **thesis or main idea**: the primary thing you hope to communicate to the reader through your essay. Don't try to include all of the details and nuances of your thesis, or all of your reasons for it, in the introduction. That's what the rest of the essay is for!

> **Review Video: Introduction**
> Visit mometrix.com/academy and enter code: 961328

THESIS STATEMENT

The thesis is the main idea of the essay. A temporary thesis, or working thesis, should be established early in the writing process because it will serve to keep the writer focused as ideas develop. This temporary thesis is subject to change as you continue to write.

The temporary thesis has two parts: a **topic** (i.e., the focus of your essay based on the prompt) and a **comment**. The comment makes an important point about the topic. A temporary thesis should be interesting and specific. Also, you need to limit the topic to a manageable scope. These three questions are useful tools to measure the effectiveness of any temporary thesis:

- Does the focus of my essay have enough interest to hold an audience?
- Is the focus of my essay specific enough to generate interest?
- Is the focus of my essay manageable for the time limit? Too broad? Too narrow?

The thesis should be a generalization rather than a fact because the thesis prepares readers for facts and details that support the thesis. The process of bringing the thesis into sharp focus may help in outlining major sections of the work. Once the thesis and introduction are complete, you can address the body of the work.

> **Review Video: Thesis Statements**
> Visit mometrix.com/academy and enter code: 691033

SUPPORTING THE THESIS

Throughout your essay, the thesis should be **explained clearly and supported** adequately by additional arguments. The thesis sentence needs to contain a clear statement of the purpose of your essay and a comment about the thesis. With the thesis statement, you have an opportunity to state what is noteworthy of this particular treatment of the prompt. Each sentence and paragraph should build on and support the thesis.

When you respond to the prompt, use parts of the passage to support your argument or defend your position. Using supporting evidence from the passage strengths your argument because readers can see your attention to the entire passage and your response to the details and facts within the passage. You can use facts, details, statistics, and direct quotations from the passage to uphold your position. Be sure to point out which information comes from the original passage and base your argument around that evidence.

BODY

In an essay's introduction, the writer establishes the thesis and may indicate how the rest of the piece will be structured. In the body of the piece, the writer **elaborates** upon, **illustrates**, and **explains** the thesis

statement. How writers arrange supporting details and their choices of paragraph types are development techniques. Writers may give examples of the concept introduced in the thesis statement. If the subject includes a cause-and-effect relationship, the author may explain its causality. A writer will explain or analyze the main idea of the piece throughout the body, often by presenting arguments for the veracity or credibility of the thesis statement. Writers may use development to define or clarify ambiguous terms. Paragraphs within the body may be organized using natural sequences, like space and time. Writers may employ **inductive reasoning**, using multiple details to establish a generalization or causal relationship, or **deductive reasoning**, proving a generalized hypothesis or proposition through a specific example or case.

> **Review Video: Drafting Body Paragraphs**
> Visit mometrix.com/academy and enter code: 724590

PARAGRAPHS

After the introduction of a passage, a series of body paragraphs will carry a message through to the conclusion. Each paragraph should be **unified around a main point**. Normally, a good topic sentence summarizes the paragraph's main point. A topic sentence is a general sentence that gives an introduction to the paragraph.

The sentences that follow support the topic sentence. However, though it is usually the first sentence, the topic sentence can come as the final sentence to the paragraph if the earlier sentences give a clear explanation of the paragraph's topic. This allows the topic sentence to function as a concluding sentence. Overall, the paragraphs need to stay true to the main point. This means that any unnecessary sentences that do not advance the main point should be removed.

The main point of a paragraph requires adequate development (i.e., a substantial paragraph that covers the main point). A paragraph of two or three sentences does not cover a main point. This is especially true when the main point of the paragraph gives strong support to the argument of the thesis. An occasional short paragraph is fine as a transitional device. However, a well-developed argument will have paragraphs with more than a few sentences.

METHODS OF DEVELOPING PARAGRAPHS

Common methods of adding substance to paragraphs include examples, illustrations, analogies, and cause and effect.

- **Examples** are supporting details to the main idea of a paragraph or a passage. When authors write about something that their audience may not understand, they can provide an example to show their point. When authors write about something that is not easily accepted, they can give examples to prove their point.
- **Illustrations** are extended examples that require several sentences. Well-selected illustrations can be a great way for authors to develop a point that may not be familiar to their audience.
- **Analogies** make comparisons between items that appear to have nothing in common. Analogies are employed by writers to provoke fresh thoughts about a subject. These comparisons may be used to explain the unfamiliar, to clarify an abstract point, or to argue a point. Although analogies are effective literary devices, they should be used carefully in arguments. Two things may be alike in some respects but completely different in others.
- **Cause and effect** is an excellent device to explain the connection between an action or situation and a particular result. One way that authors can use cause and effect is to state the effect in the topic sentence of a paragraph and add the causes in the body of the paragraph. This method can give an author's paragraphs structure, which always strengthens writing.

Types of Paragraphs

- A **paragraph of narration** tells a story or a part of a story. Normally, the sentences are arranged in chronological order (i.e., the order that the events happened). However, flashbacks (i.e., an anecdote from an earlier time) can be included.
- A **descriptive paragraph** makes a verbal portrait of a person, place, or thing. When specific details are used that appeal to one or more of the senses (i.e., sight, sound, smell, taste, and touch), authors give readers a sense of being present in the moment.
- A **process paragraph** is related to time order (i.e., First, you open the bottle. Second, you pour the liquid, etc.). Usually, this describes a process or teaches readers how to perform a process.
- **Comparing two things** draws attention to their similarities and indicates a number of differences. When authors contrast, they focus only on differences. Both comparing and contrasting may be done point-by-point, noting both the similarities and differences of each point, or in sequential paragraphs, where you discuss all the similarities and then all the differences, or vice versa.

Breaking Text into Paragraphs

For most forms of writing, you will need to use multiple paragraphs. As such, determining when to start a new paragraph is very important. Reasons for starting a new paragraph include:

- To mark off the introduction and concluding paragraphs
- To signal a shift to a new idea or topic
- To indicate an important shift in time or place
- To explain a point in additional detail
- To highlight a comparison, contrast, or cause and effect relationship

Paragraph Length

Most readers find that their comfort level for a paragraph is between 100 and 200 words. Shorter paragraphs cause too much starting and stopping and give a choppy effect. Paragraphs that are too long often test the attention span of readers. Two notable exceptions to this rule exist. In scientific or scholarly papers, longer paragraphs suggest seriousness and depth. In journalistic writing, constraints are placed on paragraph size by the narrow columns in a newspaper format.

The first and last paragraphs of a text will usually be the introduction and conclusion. These special-purpose paragraphs are likely to be shorter than paragraphs in the body of the work. Paragraphs in the body of the essay follow the subject's outline (e.g., one paragraph per point in short essays and a group of paragraphs per point in longer works). Some ideas require more development than others, so it is good for a writer to remain flexible. A paragraph of excessive length may be divided, and shorter ones may be combined.

Conclusion

Two important principles to consider when writing a conclusion are strength and closure. A strong conclusion gives the reader a sense that the author's main points are meaningful and important, and that the supporting facts and arguments are convincing, solid, and well developed. When a conclusion achieves closure, it gives the impression that the writer has stated all necessary information and points and completed the work, rather than simply stopping after a specified length. Some things to avoid when writing concluding paragraphs include:

- Introducing a completely new idea
- Beginning with obvious or unoriginal phrases like "In conclusion" or "To summarize"
- Apologizing for one's opinions or writing
- Repeating the thesis word for word rather than rephrasing it
- Believing that the conclusion must always summarize the piece

Coherence in Writing

COHERENT PARAGRAPHS

A smooth flow of sentences and paragraphs without gaps, shifts, or bumps will lead to paragraph **coherence**. Ties between old and new information can be smoothed using several methods:

- **Linking ideas clearly**, from the topic sentence to the body of the paragraph, is essential for a smooth transition. The topic sentence states the main point, and this should be followed by specific details, examples, and illustrations that support the topic sentence. The support may be direct or indirect. In **indirect support**, the illustrations and examples may support a sentence that in turn supports the topic directly.
- The **repetition of key words** adds coherence to a paragraph. To avoid dull language, variations of the key words may be used.
- **Parallel structures** are often used within sentences to emphasize the similarity of ideas and connect sentences giving similar information.
- Maintaining a **consistent verb tense** throughout the paragraph helps. Shifting tenses affects the smooth flow of words and can disrupt the coherence of the paragraph.

> **Review Video: How to Write a Good Paragraph**
> Visit mometrix.com/academy and enter code: 682127

SEQUENCE WORDS AND PHRASES

When a paragraph opens with the topic sentence, the second sentence may begin with a phrase like *first of all*, introducing the first supporting detail or example. The writer may introduce the second supporting item with words or phrases like *also*, *in addition*, and *besides*. The writer might introduce succeeding pieces of support with wording like, *another thing*, *moreover*, *furthermore*, or *not only that, but*. The writer may introduce the last piece of support with *lastly*, *finally*, or *last but not least*. Writers get off the point by presenting off-target items not supporting the main point. For example, a main point *my dog is not smart* is supported by the statement, *he's six years old and still doesn't answer to his name*. But *he cries when I leave for school* is not supportive, as it does not indicate lack of intelligence. Writers stay on point by presenting only supportive statements that are directly relevant to and illustrative of their main point.

> **Review Video: Sequence**
> Visit mometrix.com/academy and enter code: 489027

TRANSITIONS

Transitions between sentences and paragraphs guide readers from idea to idea and indicate relationships between sentences and paragraphs. Writers should be judicious in their use of transitions, inserting them sparingly. They should also be selected to fit the author's purpose—transitions can indicate time, comparison, and conclusion, among other purposes. Tone is also important to consider when using transitional phrases, varying the tone for different audiences. For example, in a scholarly essay, *in summary* would be preferable to the more informal *in short*.

When working with transitional words and phrases, writers usually find a natural flow that indicates when a transition is needed. In reading a draft of the text, it should become apparent where the flow is disrupted. At this point, the writer can add transitional elements during the revision process. Revising can also afford an opportunity to delete transitional devices that seem heavy handed or unnecessary.

> **Review Video: Transitions in Writing**
> Visit mometrix.com/academy and enter code: 233246

Types of Transitional Words

Time	afterward, immediately, earlier, meanwhile, recently, lately, now, since, soon, when, then, until, before, etc.
Sequence	too, first, second, further, moreover, also, again, and, next, still, besides, finally
Comparison	similarly, in the same way, likewise, also, again, once more
Contrasting	but, although, despite, however, instead, nevertheless, on the one hand... on the other hand, regardless, yet, in contrast
Cause and Effect	because, consequently, thus, therefore, then, to this end, since, so, as a result, if... then, accordingly
Examples	for example, for instance, such as, to illustrate, indeed, in fact, specifically
Place	near, far, here, there, to the left/right, next to, above, below, beyond, opposite, beside
Concession	granted that, naturally, of course, it may appear, although it is true that
Repetition, Summary, or Conclusion	as mentioned earlier, as noted, in other words, in short, on the whole, to summarize, therefore, as a result, to conclude, in conclusion
Addition	and, also, furthermore, moreover
Generalization	in broad terms, broadly speaking, in general

Review Video: Transition Words
Visit mometrix.com/academy and enter code: 707563

Review Video: How to Effectively Connect Sentences
Visit mometrix.com/academy and enter code: 948325

Chapter Quiz

Ready to see how well you retained what you just read? Scan the QR code to go directly to the chapter quiz interface for this study guide. If you're using a computer, simply visit the online resources page at **mometrix.com/resources719/hspt-28350** and click the Chapter Quizzes link.

Verbal Skills

Analogies

DETERMINE THE RELATIONSHIP

As you try to decide on how the words in question are connected, don't jump to understand the meaning of the words. Instead, see if you can find the **relationship** between the two words. To understand the relationship, you can start by creating a sentence that links the two words and puts them into perspective. At first, try to use a simple sentence to find a connection. Then, go through each answer choice and replace the words in the answer choices with the parts of your simple sentence. Depending on the question, you may need to make changes to your sentence to make it more specific.

EXAMPLE:

Wood is to fire as

Simple Sentence: *Wood* feeds a *fire* as

Wood is to fire as

    A. Farmer is to cow
    B. Gasoline is to engine

Using the simple sentence, you would state "Farmer feeds a cow" which is correct. Yet, the next answer choice "Gasoline feeds an engine" is also true. So, which is the correct answer? With this simple sentence, we need to be more **specific**.

Specific Sentences: "Wood feeds a fire and is consumed" / "Wood is burned in a fire"

These specific sentences show that answer choice (A) is incorrect and answer choice (B) is clearly correct. With the specific sentences, you have "Gasoline feeds an engine and is consumed" is correct. Also, "Farmer feeds a cow and is consumed" is clearly incorrect. If your simple sentence seems correct with more than one answer choice, then keep making changes until only one answer choice makes sense.

ELIMINATING SIMILARITIES

This method works well in the Analogies section and the Synonyms/Antonyms section. You can start by looking over the answer choices and see what clues they provide. If there are any common relationships between the pairs of terms, then those answer choices have to be **wrong**.

EXAMPLE:

Tough is to rugged as

    A. Soft is to hard
    B. Clear is to foggy
    C. Inhale is to exhale
    D. Rigid is to taut

In this example, tough and rugged are synonyms. Also, the first three answer choices are antonyms. You may not realize that taut and rigid are synonyms. However, it has to be correct. The reason is that you know the other answer choices all had the **same relationship** of being antonyms.

Word Types
Example:
Gardener is to hedge as

    A. Wind is to rock
    B. Woodcarver is to stick

In this example, you could start with a simple sentence of "Gardener cuts away at hedges." Now, both answer choices seem correct with this sentence. For choice (A), you can say that "Wind cuts away at rocks" due to erosion. For choice (B), you can say that a "Woodcarver cuts away at sticks." The difference is that a gardener is a person, and a woodcarver is a person. However, the wind is a thing, which makes answer choice (B) correct.

Face Value
When you are not sure about an answer, you should try to accept the problem at **face value**. Don't read too much into it. These problems will not ask you to make **impossible comparisons**. The test writers are not trying to throw you off with cheap tricks. If you have to make a stretch of the question to make a connection between the two terms, then you should start over and find another relationship. Don't make the problem more difficult. These are normal questions with differences in difficulty. Sometimes the terms that go together and their relationships may not be very clear. So, you will want to read over the question and answer choices carefully.

Example:
Odor is to smell as flavor is to

    A. believe
    B. know
    C. feel
    D. taste

Would a flavor be "known", "felt", "tasted", or "believed"? The analogy is about a synonym. So, answer choice D, which is "taste," is a synonym of flavor and is the best answer.

Read Carefully
To understand the analogies, you need to read the terms and answer choices **carefully**. You can miss the question because you misread the terms. Each question here has only a few words, so you can spend time reading them carefully. Yet, you cannot forget your time limit of the section. So, don't spend too much time on one question. Just focus on reading carefully and be sure to read all of the choices. You may find an answer choice that seems correct. Yet, when you finish reading over the choices, you may find a better choice.

Logic and Verbal Classification

Logic
These questions will provide you with three statements and then ask you that if the first two are true, what must the third statement be, whether true, false, or uncertain.

Look for the Obvious
Usually the nature of the first two statements will give a **clue** about what a truthful third statement will look like. Example: John runs faster than Mary. Bob runs faster than John.

Ask yourself what is probably going to be the true statement that you should expect to see as the third statement. It will likely be "Bob runs faster than Mary." Both of the given statements seem to be leading up to that statement.

If you expect that to be the third statement, then you can quickly look at the third statement and see if you are correct. If so, you know the third statement is true. If not, you will have to determine whether or not it is false or uncertain.

WATCH FOR INVERSIONS

Not only does the statement "Bob runs faster than Mary" seem to be a likely possibility, but also the **inverse**, which is "Mary runs slower than Bob".

Don't get caught off guard and think that your predicted answer isn't the third statement. It's inverse, which is equally true, may be provided.

Example 1:

John throws faster pitches than Kyle. Greg throws faster pitches than John. Kyle throws faster pitches than Greg. If the first two statements are true, then the third is:

A. True
B. False
C. Uncertain
D. An opinion

Example 2:

Allen sent in his taxes one day after Phil. Phil sent in his taxes before Blake. Blake sent in his taxes after Allen. If the first two statements are true, then the third is:

A. True
B. False
C. Uncertain
D. A contradiction

ANSWERS

Example 1: B: We can diagram the first two sentences as follows: John > Kyle and Greg > John. In other words, Greg throws faster pitches than John and Kyle. If those statements are true, then the third statement is certainly false.

Example 2: C: We can diagram this sentence as follows: Phil > Allen; Phil > Blake. In other words, Phil sent in his taxes before Allen and before Blake. We do not have enough information to determine whether Allen > Blake is true.

VERBAL CLASSIFICATION

These questions will give you a list of four words and ask you to determine which does not belong with the others.

FIND THE COMMON GROUND

The common ground is the characteristics that all of the words have in common. All but one that is. Once you've identified the **common characteristic** shared by three of the words, you know which is your correct answer, because it does not share that same characteristic.

Example:

A. bass
B. salmon
C. moose
D. tuna

In the example above, answer choices a, b, and d all share one thing in common. They are fish. The lone exception is answer choice c, which is moose and is not a species of fish.

WATCH OUT FOR GENERIC TYPES

Usually the answer choices will provide **specific** examples of a certain thing. If the more **generic** name of the common characteristic is given, it is usually wrong.

Example:

A. bass
B. salmon
C. fish
D. tuna

At first glance these all seem the same. They are all fish, right? Wrong. Three of them are species of fish. Answer choice c, "fish" is not a species of fish, but is rather the name of the category the other answer choices fall into.

Example:

A. football
B. basketball
C. tennis
D. sports

Notice the similarity in examples. Here again all four answer choices seem similar. The first three are types of sporting activities. The last is the name of the category the others fall into. Choice d does *not* belong.

Synonyms and Antonyms

When you understand how words relate to each other, you will discover more in a passage. This is explained by understanding **synonyms** (e.g., words that mean the same thing) and **antonyms** (e.g., words that mean the opposite of one another). As an example, *dry* and *arid* are synonyms, and *dry* and *wet* are antonyms. There are many pairs of words in English that can be considered synonyms, despite having slightly different definitions. For instance, the words *friendly* and *collegial* can both be used to describe a warm interpersonal relationship, and one would be correct to call them **synonyms**. However, *collegial* (kin to *colleague*) is often used in reference to professional or academic relationships, and *friendly* has no such connotation. If the difference between two words is too great, then they should not be called synonyms. *Hot* and *warm* are not synonyms because their meanings are too distinct. A good way to determine whether two words are synonyms is to substitute one word for the other word and verify that the meaning of the sentence has not changed. Substituting *warm* for *hot* in a sentence would convey a different meaning. Although warm and hot may seem close in meaning, warm generally means that the temperature is moderate, and hot generally means that the temperature is excessively high.

Antonyms are words with opposite meanings. *Light* and *dark*, *up* and *down*, *right* and *left*, *good* and *bad*: these are all sets of antonyms. Be careful to distinguish between antonyms and pairs of words that are simply different. *Black* and *gray*, for instance, are not antonyms because gray is not the opposite of black. *Black* and *white*, on the other hand, are antonyms. Not every word has an antonym. For instance, many nouns do not:

What would be the antonym of chair? During your exam, the questions related to antonyms are more likely to concern adjectives. You will recall that adjectives are words that describe a noun. Some common adjectives include *purple*, *fast*, *skinny*, and *sweet*. From those four adjectives, *purple* is the item that lacks a group of obvious antonyms.

> **Review Video: Synonyms and Antonyms**
> Visit mometrix.com/academy and enter code: 105612

Synonym and Antonym Examples

For this section, you will have one word and four choices for a synonym or antonym of that word. Before you look at the choices, try to think of a few words that could be a synonym or antonym for your question. Then, check the choices for a synonym or antonym of the question. Some words may seem close to the question, but you are looking for the best choice. So, don't let your first reaction be your final decision.

Example 1
Insatiable most nearly means:
- A. Compensated
- B. Content
- C. Fulfilled
- D. Unsatisfied

Example 2
Adherent means the opposite of:
- A. Antagonist
- B. Disciple
- C. Piquant
- D. Submissive

Example 3
Protrude most nearly means:
- A. Contract
- B. Evocative
- C. Secede
- D. Swell

Example 4
Unkempt means the opposite of:
- A. Disorder
- B. Flaunt
- C. Unblemished
- D. Volatile

Answers

Example 1: D, Unsatisfied (Synonym)

Example 2: A, Antagonist (Antonym)

Example 3: D, Swell (Synonym)

Example 4: C, Unblemished (Antonym)

Quantitative Skills

Sequences

A **sequence** is an ordered set of numbers that continues in a defined pattern. The function that defines a sequence has a domain composed of the set of positive integers. Each member of the sequence is an element, or individual term. Each element is identified by the notation a_n, where a is the term of the sequence, and n is the integer identifying which term in the sequence a is.

There are two different ways to represent a sequence that contains the element a_n. The first is the simple notation $\{a_n\}$. The second is the expanded notation of a sequence: $a_1, a_2, a_3, \ldots a_n, \ldots$. Notice that the expanded form does not end with the nth term. There is no indication that the nth term is the last term in the sequence, only that the nth term is an element of the sequence.

ARITHMETIC SEQUENCES

An **arithmetic sequence**, or arithmetic progression, is a special kind of sequence in which a specific quantity, called the common difference, is added to each term to make the next term. The common difference may be positive or negative. The general form of an arithmetic sequence containing n terms is $a_1, a_1 + d, a_1 + 2d, \ldots, a_1 + (n-1)d$, where d is the common difference. The general formula for any term of an arithmetic sequence is $a_n = a_1 + (n-1)d$, where a_n is the term you are looking for and d is the common difference. To find the sum of the first n terms of an arithmetic sequence, use the formula $s_n = \frac{n}{2}(a_1 + a_n)$.

> **Review Video: Arithmetic Sequence**
> Visit mometrix.com/academy and enter code: 676885

MONOTONIC SEQUENCES

A **monotonic sequence** is a sequence that is either nonincreasing or nondecreasing. A **nonincreasing** sequence is one whose terms either get progressively smaller in value or remain the same. Such a sequence is always bounded above, that is, all elements of the sequence must be less than some real number. A **nondecreasing** sequence is one whose terms either get progressively larger in value or remain the same. Such a sequence is always bounded below, that is, all elements of the sequence must be greater than some real number.

RECURSIVE SEQUENCES

When one element of a sequence is defined in terms of a previous element or elements of the sequence, the sequence is a **recursive sequence**. For example, given the recursive definition $a_1 = 1$; $a_2 = 1$; $a_n = a_{n-1} + a_{n-2}$ for all $n > 2$, you get the sequence $1,1,2,3,5,8,\ldots$. This is known as the Fibonacci sequence: a continuing sequence of numbers in which each number (after a_2) is the sum of the two previous numbers. The Fibonacci sequence can be defined as starting with either 1,1 or 0,1. Both definitions are considered correct in mathematics. Make sure you know which definition you are working with when dealing with Fibonacci numbers.

Sometimes in a recursive sequence, the terms can be found using a general formula that does not involve the previous terms of the sequence. Such a formula is called a **closed-form** expression for a recursive definition—an alternate formula that will generate the same sequence of numbers. However, not all sequences based on recursive definitions will have a closed-form expression. Some sequences will require the use of the recursive definition.

THE GOLDEN RATIO AND THE FIBONACCI SEQUENCE

The golden ratio is approximately 1.6180339887 and is often represented by the Greek letter phi, Φ. The exact value of Φ is $\frac{(1+\sqrt{5})}{2}$ and it is one of the solutions to $x - \frac{1}{x} = 1$. The golden ratio can be found using the Fibonacci sequence, since the ratio of a term to the previous term approaches Φ as the sequence approaches infinity:

n	a_n	a_{n-1}	$\frac{a_n}{a_{n-1}}$
3	2	1	2
4	3	2	1.5
5	5	3	$1.\overline{6}$
6	8	5	1.6
7	13	8	1.625
8	21	13	$1.\overline{615384}$
9	34	21	$1.\overline{619047}$
⋮	⋮	⋮	⋮
20	6,765	4,181	1.618033963 …

GEOMETRIC SEQUENCES

A geometric sequence is a sequence in which each term is multiplied by a constant number (called the common ratio) to get the next term. Essentially, it's the same concept as an arithmetic sequence, but with multiplication instead of addition.

Consider the following example of a geometric sequence: Andy opens a savings account with $10. During each subsequent week, he plans to double the amount from the previous week.

Sequence: 10, 20, 40, 80, 160, …

Function: $a_n = 10 \times 2^{n-1}$

This is a geometric sequence with a common ratio of 2. All geometric sequences represent exponential functions. The nth term in any geometric sequence is $a_n = a_1 \times r^{n-1}$, where a_n represents the value of the nth term, a_1 is the initial term, r is the common ratio, and n is the number of terms. Thus, substituting the initial value of 10 and common ratio of 2 gives the function $a_n = 10 \times 2^{n-1}$.

> **Review Video: Geometric Sequences**
> Visit mometrix.com/academy and enter code: 140779

Types of Reasoning

INDUCTIVE REASONING

Inductive reasoning is a method used to make a conjecture, based on patterns and observations. The conclusion of an inductive argument may be true or false.

Mathematical Example:

A cube has 6 faces, 8 vertices, and 12 edges. A square pyramid has 5 faces, 5 vertices, and 8 edges. A triangular prism has 5 faces, 6 vertices, and 9 edges. Thus, the sum of the numbers of faces and vertices, minus the number of edges, will always equal 2, for any solid.

Non-Mathematical Example:

Almost all summer days in Tucson are hot. It is a summer day in Tucson. Therefore, it will probably be hot.

DEDUCTIVE REASONING

Deductive reasoning is a method that proves a hypothesis or set of premises. The conclusion of a valid deductive argument will be true, given that the premises are true. Deductive reasoning utilizes logic to determine a conclusion. For instance, consider the following application of the chain rule:

If a ding is a dong, then a ping is a pong.	$p \to q$
If a ping is a pong, then a ring is a ting.	$q \to r$
A ding is a dong.	p
Therefore, a ring is a ting.	$\therefore r$

FORMAL REASONING

Formal reasoning, in mathematics, involves justification using formal steps and processes to arrive at a conclusion. Formal reasoning is utilized when writing proofs and using logic. For example, when applying logic, validity of a conclusion is determined by truth tables. A set of premises will yield a given conclusion. This type of thinking is formal reasoning. Writing a geometric proof also employs formal reasoning. Example:

If a quadrilateral has four congruent sides, it is a rhombus.
If a shape is a rhombus, then the diagonals are perpendicular.
A quadrilateral has four congruent sides.
Therefore, the diagonals are perpendicular.

INFORMAL REASONING

Informal reasoning, in mathematics, uses patterns and observations to make conjectures. The conjecture may be true or false. Several, or even many, examples may show a certain pattern, shedding light on a possible conclusion. However, informal reasoning does not provide a justifiable conclusion. A conjecture may certainly be deemed as likely or probable. However, informal reasoning will not reveal a certain conclusion. Consider the following example:

Mathematical Idea – Given a sequence that starts with 1 and each term decreases by a factor of $\frac{1}{2}$, the limit of the sum of the sequence will be 2.

Informal Reasoning – The sum of 1 and $\frac{1}{2}$ is $1\frac{1}{2}$. The sum of 1, $\frac{1}{2}$, and $\frac{1}{4}$ is $1\frac{3}{4}$. The sum of 1, $\frac{1}{2}$, $\frac{1}{4}$, and $\frac{1}{8}$ is $1\frac{7}{8}$. Thus, it appears that as the sequence approaches infinity, the sum of the sequence approaches 2.

The questions on this section of the test are largely applied math—that is, they require you to use concepts and principles of arithmetic, algebra, and geometry you already know in order to solve new types of problems. In light of this, there is no additional instructional content for this section, but practice problems are provided to help you become familiar with the types of questions you are likely to see on the test.

Practice

NUMBER SERIES

P1. Find the next number in the series: 64, 57, 60, 53, 56, ___

P2. What is the missing number in the sequence: 11, 22, 33, ___, 55, 66

P3. Find the next number in the series: 1, 4, 9, 16, ___

QUANTITATIVE REASONING

P1. What is the sum of 13^2 and 9^2?

P2. What is the product of $\frac{4}{5}$ and the average of 10 and 20?

GEOMETRIC COMPARISON

P1. Which of the following values are equivalent?

1. The diameter of a circle with circumference 12π
2. The area of a rectangle with a length of 3 and a width of 4
3. The radius of a circle with area 144π

P2. Which of the following values are equivalent?

1. The volume of a cube with side length 3
2. The volume of a sphere with radius 3
3. The area of a circle with radius 6

NON-GEOMETRIC COMPARISON

P1. Which of the following statements are equivalent?

1. $4\sqrt{36} - 7$
2. $2 \cdot 20 - 23$
3. $6^2 - 14$

P2. Which of the following statements are equivalent?

1. $\sqrt{4x^2} + 9x \cdot 0$
2. $2(x^2 + 4) - \sqrt{36x^4}$
3. $6(x + 2) - 2(2x + 6)$

Practice Solutions

NUMBER SERIES

P1. The pattern is: subtract 7 from the previous number and then add 3. 53 + 3 = 56, so the next number is 56 − 7 = 49.

P2. The pattern is adding 11 to the previous number, so the missing number is 44.

P3. The pattern is the list of perfect squares starting with 1. $4^2 = 16$, so the next number must be $5^2 = 25$.

QUANTITATIVE REASONING

P1. This is the same as $13^2 + 9^2$. $13^2 = 169$ and $9^2 = 81$ so $169 + 81 = 250$.

P2. First find the average of 10 and 20; $\frac{10+20}{2} = \frac{30}{2} = 15$. The word 'product' indicates multiplication, so $\frac{4}{5} \times 15 = 12$.

GEOMETRIC COMPARISON

P1. To solve this problem, first calculate the value of each statement, then compare them to one another:

1. The formula for circumference is $C = \pi d$. With a circumference of 12π, the diameter (d) is equal to 12.
2. The area of a rectangle is found by multiplying its length by its width, $3 \times 4 = 12$.
3. The area of a circle is found using the formula $A = \pi r^2$. With an area of 144π, the radius (r) is $\sqrt{144} = 12$.

The value of each statement is 12, so they are all equivalent.

P2. To solve this problem, first calculate the value of each statement, then compare them to one another:

1. The volume of a cube with side length 3 is found by cubing 3, $3^3 = 27$.
2. The volume of a sphere is found using the formula $V = \frac{4}{3}\pi r^3$. Plugging in 3 for the radius results in $V = \frac{4}{3}\pi(3)^3 = \frac{4}{3}\pi(27) = 36\pi$.
3. The area of a circle is found using the formula $A = \pi r^2$. Plugging in a radius of 6 results in: $A = \pi(6)^2 = 36\pi$.

Therefore, the values of statements II and III are equivalent.

Non-Geometric Comparison

P1.

$$4\sqrt{36} - 7 = 4 \cdot 6 - 7 = 24 - 7 = 17$$

$$2 \cdot 20 - 23 = 40 - 23 = 17$$

$$6^2 - 14 = 36 - 14 = 22$$

Therefore, statements I and II are equivalent.

P2.

$$\sqrt{4x^2} + 9x \cdot 0 = 2x + 9x \cdot 0 = 2x + 0 = 2x$$

$$2(x^2 + 4) - \sqrt{36x^4} = 2x^2 + 8 - \sqrt{36x^4} = 2x^2 + 8 - 6x^2 = 8 - 4x^2$$

$$6(x - 2) - 2(2x + 6) = 6x + 12 - 4x - 12 = 2x$$

Therefore, statements I and III are equivalent.

Mathematics

Transform passive reading into active learning! After immersing yourself in this chapter, put your comprehension to the test by taking a quiz. The insights you gained will stay with you longer this way. Scan the QR code to go directly to the chapter quiz interface for this study guide. If you're using a computer, simply visit the online resources page at **mometrix.com/resources719/hspt-28350** and click the Chapter Quizzes link.

Numbers and Numeration

NUMBER BASICS
CLASSIFICATIONS OF NUMBERS

Numbers are the basic building blocks of mathematics. Specific features of numbers are identified by the following terms:

Integer – any positive or negative whole number, including zero. Integers do not include fractions $\left(\frac{1}{3}\right)$, decimals (0.56), or mixed numbers $\left(7\frac{3}{4}\right)$.

Prime number – any whole number greater than 1 that has only two factors, itself and 1; that is, a number that can be divided evenly only by 1 and itself.

Composite number – any whole number greater than 1 that has more than two different factors; in other words, any whole number that is not a prime number. For example: The composite number 8 has the factors of 1, 2, 4, and 8.

Even number – any integer that can be divided by 2 without leaving a remainder. For example: 2, 4, 6, 8, and so on.

Odd number – any integer that cannot be divided evenly by 2. For example: 3, 5, 7, 9, and so on.

Decimal number – any number that uses a decimal point to show the part of the number that is less than one. Example: 1.234.

Decimal point – a symbol used to separate the ones place from the tenths place in decimals or dollars from cents in currency.

Decimal place – the position of a number to the right of the decimal point. In the decimal 0.123, the 1 is in the first place to the right of the decimal point, indicating tenths; the 2 is in the second place, indicating hundredths; and the 3 is in the third place, indicating thousandths.

The **decimal**, or base 10, system is a number system that uses ten different digits (0, 1, 2, 3, 4, 5, 6, 7, 8, 9). An example of a number system that uses something other than ten digits is the **binary**, or base 2, number system, used by computers, which uses only the numbers 0 and 1. It is thought that the decimal system originated because people had only their 10 fingers for counting.

Rational numbers include all integers, decimals, and fractions. Any terminating or repeating decimal number is a rational number.

Irrational numbers cannot be written as fractions or decimals because the number of decimal places is infinite and there is no recurring pattern of digits within the number. For example, pi (π) begins with 3.141592 and continues without terminating or repeating, so pi is an irrational number.

Real numbers are the set of all rational and irrational numbers.

> **Review Video: Classification of Numbers**
> Visit mometrix.com/academy and enter code: 461071
>
> **Review Video: Prime and Composite Numbers**
> Visit mometrix.com/academy and enter code: 565581

NUMBERS IN WORD FORM AND PLACE VALUE

When writing numbers out in word form or translating word form to numbers, it is essential to understand how a place value system works. In the decimal or base-10 system, each digit of a number represents how many of the corresponding place value—a specific factor of 10—are contained in the number being represented. To make reading numbers easier, every three digits to the left of the decimal place is preceded by a comma. The following table demonstrates some of the place values:

Power of 10	10^3	10^2	10^1	10^0	10^{-1}	10^{-2}	10^{-3}
Value	1,000	100	10	1	0.1	0.01	0.001
Place	thousands	hundreds	tens	ones	tenths	hundredths	thousandths

For example, consider the number 4,546.09, which can be separated into each place value like this:

4: thousands
5: hundreds
4: tens
6: ones
0: tenths
9: hundredths

This number in word form would be *four thousand five hundred forty-six and nine hundredths*.

> **Review Video: Place Value**
> Visit mometrix.com/academy and enter code: 205433

NUMBER LINES

A number line is a graph to see the distance between numbers. Basically, this graph shows the relationship between numbers. So a number line may have a point for zero and may show negative numbers on the left side of the line. Any positive numbers are placed on the right side of the line. For example, consider the points labeled on the following number line:

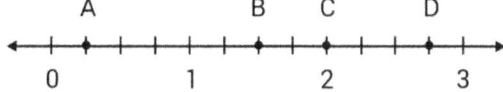

We can use the dashed lines on the number line to identify each point. Each dashed line between two whole numbers is $\frac{1}{4}$. The line halfway between two numbers is $\frac{1}{2}$.

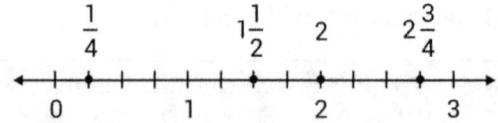

> **Review Video: The Number Line**
> Visit mometrix.com/academy and enter code: 816439

COMPARING NUMBERS
INEQUALITY NOTATION
The symbols < and > mean "is less than" and "is greater than," respectively. For instance, $3 < 5$ means "3 is less than 5," and $7 > 4$ means "7 is greater than 4." Statements like $3 < 5$ and $7 > 4$ are **inequalities**, and the symbols < and > are **inequality symbols**.

WHOLE NUMBERS AND DECIMAL NUMBERS
To compare whole or decimal numbers, we look at the most significant place (the leftmost digit) at which they differ. The number with the larger digit in that place is larger. For instance, 0.3<u>8</u>74 and 0.3<u>9</u> differ in the hundredths place (underlined). Since 8 is smaller than 9, we see $0.3874 < 0.39$. This is clearer if we make the decimals equal in length by writing extra zeroes: $0.3874 < 0.3900$. Similarly, 2<u>3</u>.984 < 2<u>5</u>.112 because 3 is smaller than 5, or 23 is smaller than 25.

FRACTIONS
If fractions have the same denominator, the fraction with the larger numerator is larger. For instance, $\frac{2}{7} < \frac{5}{7}$ since $2 < 5$. We compare fractions with different denominators by finding a common denominator. When comparing the fractions with a common denominator we only compare the numerator, so as a shortcut, we can multiply each numerator by the denominator of the other fraction. The numerator that produces the larger product belongs to the larger fraction. For example, to compare $\frac{7}{8}$ and $\frac{5}{6}$, we note that $7 \cdot 6 = 42$ is larger than $5 \cdot 8 = 40$. Since the numerator 7 produces the larger product, we see $\frac{7}{8} > \frac{5}{6}$. We can also compare fractions by converting them to decimals. For instance, since $\frac{3}{4} = 0.75$ and $\frac{4}{5} = 0.8$ and $0.75 < 0.8$, we conclude $\frac{3}{4} < \frac{4}{5}$.

MIXED NUMBERS
To compare mixed numbers we compare their whole number parts. If those are equal, then we compare their fractional parts. For instance, $5\frac{3}{8} > 4\frac{7}{8}$ because $5 > 4$, but $3\frac{5}{9} < 3\frac{8}{9}$ because $\frac{5}{9} < \frac{8}{9}$.

SQUARE ROOTS
To compare square roots, we convert it to a decimal, usually with a calculator. To compare two square roots, we compare their radicands. For instance, $\sqrt{11} < \sqrt{14}$ because $11 < 14$.

NEGATIVE NUMBERS
A negative number is always less than a positive number. Two negative numbers compare in the reverse order of their opposites. For instance, $-6 < -2$ (that is, -6 is smaller, more negative, than -2) because $6 > 2$.

ROUNDING AND ESTIMATION

Rounding is reducing the digits in a number while still trying to keep the value similar. The result will be less accurate but in a simpler form and easier to use. Whole numbers can be rounded to the nearest ten, hundred, or thousand, for instance.

To round a number, we make it a little smaller (rounding down) or a little larger (rounding up) to get a number that ends in zeros. We specify the number of zeros by naming the last place that we will not "zero out." For example, to round 8,327 to the nearest hundred, we round down to 8,300, zeroing out every digit to the right of the hundreds place. To round 4,728 to the nearest thousand, we round up to 5,000, increasing the thousands digit by one (to make the number larger) and zeroing out every digit to the right of the thousands place.

We decide whether to round down or up by looking at the first digit we are going to zero out. If it is less than 5 (namely, 0, 1, 2, 3, or 4) we round down. If it is greater than or equal to 5 (namely, 5, 6, 7, 8, or 9) we round up by adding 1 to the place we are rounding to. So, rounding 8,327 to the nearest hundred, we round down to 8,300 because the tens digit, 2, is less than 5. And rounding 4,728 to the nearest thousand, we round up to 5,000, increasing the thousands digit by 1, because the hundreds digit, 7, is greater than or equal to 5.

This even works with decimals. For example, rounding 39.7426 to the nearest tenth, we round down to 39.7000 (or simply 39.7) because the hundredths digit, 4, is less than 5. And rounding 0.019823 to the nearest thousandth, we round up to 0.020000 (or simply 0.02) by increasing the thousandths digit by 1, because the ten-thousandths digit, 8, is greater than or equal to 5.

When you are asked to estimate the solution to a problem, you will need to provide only an approximate figure or **estimation** for your answer. In this situation, you will need to round each number in the calculation to the level indicated (nearest hundred, nearest thousand, etc.) or to a level that makes sense for the numbers involved. When estimating a sum **all numbers must be rounded to the same level**. You cannot round one number to the nearest thousand while rounding another to the nearest hundred.

For instance, suppose you are considering buying four pieces of equipment for your home office. Their prices are $485, $1,217, $750, and $643. To estimate their total cost, you might round each price to the nearest hundred and add the rounded figures, getting an estimate of $500 + $1,200 + $800 + $600 = $3,100. By estimating instead of making an exact calculation, you give up a little accuracy to get a simpler calculation.

> **Review Video: Rounding and Estimation**
> Visit mometrix.com/academy and enter code: 126243

ABSOLUTE VALUE

A precursor to working with negative numbers is understanding what **absolute values** are. A number's absolute value is simply the distance away from zero a number is on the number line. The absolute value of a number is always positive and is written $|x|$. For example, the absolute value of 3, written as $|3|$, is 3 because the distance between 0 and 3 on a number line is three units. Likewise, the absolute value of −3, written as $|-3|$, is 3 because the distance between 0 and −3 on a number line is three units. So $|3| = |-3|$.

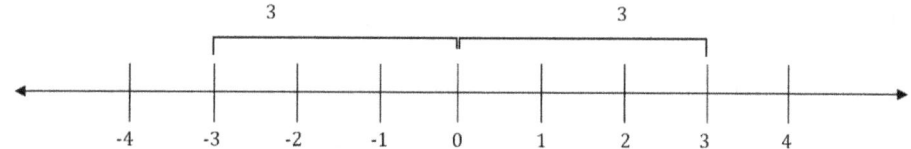

> **Review Video: Absolute Value**
> Visit mometrix.com/academy and enter code: 314669

OPERATIONS

An **operation** is simply a mathematical process that takes some value(s) as input(s) and produces an output. Elementary operations are often written in the following form: *value operation value*. For instance, in the expression $1 + 2$ the values are 1 and 2 and the operation is addition. Performing the operation gives the output of 3. In this way we can say that $1 + 2$ and 3 are equal, or $1 + 2 = 3$.

ADDITION

Addition increases the value of one quantity by the value of another quantity (both called **addends**). Example: $2 + 4 = 6$ or $8 + 9 = 17$. The result is called the **sum**. With addition, the order does not matter, $4 + 2 = 2 + 4$.

When adding signed numbers, if the signs are the same simply add the absolute values of the addends and apply the original sign to the sum. For example, $(+4) + (+8) = +12$ and $(-4) + (-8) = -12$. When the original signs are different, take the absolute values of the addends and subtract the smaller value from the larger value, then apply the original sign of the larger value to the difference. Example: $(+4) + (-8) = -4$ and $(-4) + (+8) = +4$.

SUBTRACTION

Subtraction is the opposite operation to addition; it decreases the value of one quantity (the **minuend**) by the value of another quantity (the **subtrahend**). For example, $6 - 4 = 2$ or $17 - 8 = 9$. The result is called the **difference**. Note that with subtraction, the order does matter, $6 - 4 \neq 4 - 6$.

For subtracting signed numbers, change the sign of the subtrahend and then follow the same rules used for addition. Example: $(+4) - (+8) = (+4) + (-8) = -4$

MULTIPLICATION

Multiplication can be thought of as repeated addition. One number (the **multiplier**) indicates how many times to add the other number (the **multiplicand**) to itself. Example: $3 \times 2 = 2 + 2 + 2 = 6$. With multiplication, the order does not matter, $2 \times 3 = 3 \times 2$ or $3 + 3 = 2 + 2 + 2$, either way the result (the **product**) is the same.

If the signs are the same, the product is positive when multiplying signed numbers. Example: $(+4) \times (+8) = +32$ and $(-4) \times (-8) = +32$. If the signs are opposite, the product is negative. Example: $(+4) \times (-8) = -32$ and $(-4) \times (+8) = -32$. When more than two factors are multiplied together, the sign of the product is determined by how many negative factors are present. If there are an odd number of negative factors then the product is negative, whereas an even number of negative factors indicates a positive product. Example: $(+4) \times (-8) \times (-2) = +64$ and $(-4) \times (-8) \times (-2) = -64$.

DIVISION

Division is the opposite operation to multiplication; one number (the **divisor**) tells us how many parts to divide the other number (the **dividend**) into. The result of division is called the **quotient**. Example: $20 \div 4 = 5$. If 20 is split into 4 equal parts, each part is 5. With division, the order of the numbers does matter, $20 \div 4 \neq 4 \div 20$.

The rules for dividing signed numbers are similar to multiplying signed numbers. If the dividend and divisor have the same sign, the quotient is positive. If the dividend and divisor have opposite signs, the quotient is negative. Example: $(-4) \div (+8) = -0.5$.

> **Review Video: Mathematical Operations**
> Visit mometrix.com/academy and enter code: 208095

PARENTHESES

Parentheses are used to designate which operations should be done first when there are multiple operations. Example: $4 - (2 + 1) = 1$; the parentheses tell us that we must add 2 and 1, and then subtract the sum from 4, rather than subtracting 2 from 4 and then adding 1 (this would give us an answer of 3).

> **Review Video: Mathematical Parentheses**
> Visit mometrix.com/academy and enter code: 978600

EXPONENTS

An **exponent** is a superscript number placed next to another number at the top right. It indicates how many times the base number is to be multiplied by itself. Exponents provide a shorthand way to write what would be a longer mathematical expression, Example: $2^4 = 2 \times 2 \times 2 \times 2$. A number with an exponent of 2 is said to be "squared," while a number with an exponent of 3 is said to be "cubed." The value of a number raised to an exponent is called its power. So 8^4 is read as "8 to the 4th power," or "8 raised to the power of 4."

> **Review Video: Exponents**
> Visit mometrix.com/academy and enter code: 600998

ROOTS

A **root**, such as a square root, is another way of writing a fractional exponent. Instead of using a superscript, roots use the radical symbol ($\sqrt{}$) to indicate the operation. A radical will have a number underneath the bar, and may sometimes have a number in the upper left: $\sqrt[n]{a}$, read as "the nth root of a." The relationship between radical notation and exponent notation can be described by this equation:

$$\sqrt[n]{a} = a^{\frac{1}{n}}$$

The two special cases of $n = 2$ and $n = 3$ are called square roots and cube roots. If there is no number to the upper left, the radical is understood to be a square root ($n = 2$). Nearly all of the roots you encounter will be square roots. A square root is the same as a number raised to the one-half power. When we say that a is the square root of b ($a = \sqrt{b}$), we mean that a multiplied by itself equals b: ($a \times a = b$).

A **perfect square** is a number that has an integer for its square root. There are 10 perfect squares from 1 to 100: 1, 4, 9, 16, 25, 36, 49, 64, 81, 100 (the squares of integers 1 through 10).

> **Review Video: Roots**
> Visit mometrix.com/academy and enter code: 795655
>
> **Review Video: Perfect Squares and Square Roots**
> Visit mometrix.com/academy and enter code: 648063

WORD PROBLEMS AND MATHEMATICAL SYMBOLS

When working on word problems, you must be able to translate verbal expressions or "math words" into math symbols. This chart contains several "math words" and their appropriate symbols:

Phrase	Symbol
equal, is, was, will be, has, costs, gets to, is the same as, becomes	=
times, of, multiplied by, product of, twice, doubles, halves, triples	×
divided by, per, ratio of/to, out of	÷
plus, added to, sum, combined, and, more than, totals of	+
subtracted from, less than, decreased by, minus, difference between	−
what, how much, original value, how many, a number, a variable	x, n, etc.

Review Video: Understanding Word Problems
Visit mometrix.com/academy and enter code: 499199

EXAMPLES OF TRANSLATED MATHEMATICAL PHRASES

- The phrase four more than twice a number can be written algebraically as $2x + 4$.
- The phrase half a number decreased by six can be written algebraically as $\frac{1}{2}x - 6$.
- The phrase the sum of a number and the product of five and that number can be written algebraically as $x + 5x$.
- You may see a test question that says, "Olivia is constructing a bookcase from seven boards. Two of them are for vertical supports and five are for shelves. The height of the bookcase is twice the width of the bookcase. If the seven boards total 36 feet in length, what will be the height of Olivia's bookcase?" You would need to make a sketch and then create the equation to determine the width of the shelves. The height can be represented as double the width. (If x represents the width of the shelves in feet, then the height of the bookcase is $2x$. Since the seven boards total 36 feet, $2x + 2x + x + x + x + x + x = 36$ or $9x = 36$; $x = 4$. The height is twice the width, or 8 feet.)

SUBTRACTION WITH REGROUPING

A great way to make use of some of the features built into the decimal system would be regrouping when attempting longform subtraction operations. When subtracting within a place value, sometimes the minuend is smaller than the subtrahend, **regrouping** enables you to 'borrow' a unit from a place value to the left in order to get a positive difference. For example, consider subtracting 189 from 525 with regrouping.

First, set up the subtraction problem in vertical form:

```
   525
-  189
```

Notice that the numbers in the ones and tens columns of 525 are smaller than the numbers in the ones and tens columns of 189. This means you will need to use regrouping to perform subtraction:

```
   5  2  5
-  1  8  9
```

To subtract 9 from 5 in the ones column you will need to borrow from the 2 in the tens columns:

```
   5  1  15
-  1  8   9
           6
```

Next, to subtract 8 from 1 in the tens column you will need to borrow from the 5 in the hundreds column:

```
  4  11  15
-  1   8   9
          3   6
```

Last, subtract the 1 from the 4 in the hundreds column:

```
  4  11  15
-  1   8   9
  3   3   6
```

> **Review Video: Subtracting Large Numbers**
> Visit mometrix.com/academy and enter code: 603350

ORDER OF OPERATIONS

The **order of operations** is a set of rules that dictates the order in which we must perform each operation in an expression so that we will evaluate it accurately. If we have an expression that includes multiple different operations, the order of operations tells us which operations to do first. The most common mnemonic for the order of operations is **PEMDAS**, or "Please Excuse My Dear Aunt Sally." PEMDAS stands for parentheses, exponents, multiplication, division, addition, and subtraction. It is important to understand that multiplication and division have equal precedence, as do addition and subtraction, so those pairs of operations are simply worked from left to right in order.

For example, evaluating the expression $5 + 20 \div 4 \times (2 + 3)^2 - 6$ using the correct order of operations would be done like this:

- **P:** Perform the operations inside the parentheses: $(2 + 3) = 5$
- **E:** Simplify the exponents: $(5)^2 = 5 \times 5 = 25$
  - The expression now looks like this: $5 + 20 \div 4 \times 25 - 6$
- **MD:** Perform multiplication and division from left to right: $20 \div 4 = 5$; then $5 \times 25 = 125$
  - The expression now looks like this: $5 + 125 - 6$
- **AS:** Perform addition and subtraction from left to right: $5 + 125 = 130$; then $130 - 6 = 124$

> **Review Video: Order of Operations**
> Visit mometrix.com/academy and enter code: 259675

PROPERTIES OF OPERATIONS
THE COMMUTATIVE PROPERTY

The commutative property applies to addition and multiplication and states that these operations can be completed in any order. The **commutative property of addition** states that numbers and terms can be added together in any order to still get the same value. For example, $3 + 4 = 7$ and $4 + 3 = 7$. Also, we can use the commutative property of addition to show that $3x + 4 + 2^2$ is equivalent to $4 + 3x + 2^2$ and $2^2 + 4 + 3x$. When adding terms, you can add in any order and get the same value.

The **commutative property of multiplication** states that numbers and terms can be multiplied in any order to get the same value. For example, 12×3 is equivalent to 3×12. Additionally, we can use the commutative property of multiplication to assume that $(5 + 3) \times (36 - 6)$ is equivalent to $(36 - 6) \times (5 + 3)$. You can multiply terms in any order and still get the same value.

The Associative Property

The **associative property of addition** states that if three or more terms are being added together, the value is the same regardless of the groupings.

For example, given the expression $3 + 4 + 6$, these terms can be grouped and added in any form. $3 + 4 + 6$ is equivalent to $(3 + 4) + 6$ and is also equivalent to $3 + (4 + 6)$. This can be applied to write equivalent expressions in a variety of ways.

For example, suppose we are given the expression $5 + (y + 2) + 4$. We can generate equivalent expressions knowing the associative property. Knowing that when three or more terms are added, the grouping is irrelevant, we can say that this expression is equivalent to $5 + y + (2 + 4)$, and it is equivalent to $(5 + y) + (2 + 4)$. It is even equivalent to $5 + y + 2 + 4$.

The **associative property of multiplication** states that if three or more terms are being multiplied together, the value is the same regardless of the grouping. We can use this property to identify and generate equivalent expressions.

For example, given the expression $2 \times 7 \times 3$, these terms can be grouped in any way and still get the same value. $2 \times 7 \times 3$ is equivalent to $(2 \times 7) \times 3$ or $2 \times (7 \times 3)$.

The Identity Property

The **identity property of multiplication** states that when a number is multiplied by 1, you get the same number. That is, anything multiplied by 1 is itself. For example, $2 \times 1 = 2$, or $1 \times -36 = -36$. Using the identity property of multiplication, we can identify and generate equivalent expressions. Let's say that we are given the expression $15 - (3 \times 4)$. We can generate equivalent expressions using the identity property. One equivalent expression example would be $(15 \times 1) - (3 \times 4)$. Another example would be $15 - (1 \times 3 \times 4)$. We can say these expressions are equivalent because the identity property of multiplication states that we can multiply any portion of an expression by 1 to get the same value.

The **identity property of addition** states that when 0 is added to a number, you get the same number. For example, $2 + 0 = 2$, or $0 + -3 = -3$. We can also use this property to identify and generate equivalent expressions. For example, if we are given the expression $2 \times (1 + 2)$, we could write the equivalent expressions $2 \times (0 + 1 + 2)$ or $(2 + 0) \times (1 + 2)$.

The Inverse Property

The **inverse property of addition** states that the sum of a number and its opposite is always equal to 0. Remember, the opposite of a number is a number that is opposite on the number line from zero, or the same number with the opposite sign. For example, -4 is opposite to 4, and $1{,}726.9$ is opposite to $-1{,}726.9$. So, the inverse property of addition states that if you add opposite numbers, their sum is zero. For example, $5 + (-5) = 0$ and $-5 + 5 = 0$.

The **inverse property of multiplication** states that a number multiplied by its reciprocal is always equal to 1. The **reciprocal** of a number is its "flipped" fraction. For example, the reciprocal of 5 is $\frac{1}{5}$, or the reciprocal of $\frac{2}{3}$ is $\frac{3}{2}$. The inverse property of multiplication can be applied for these values, $5 \times \frac{1}{5} = 1$ and $\frac{2}{3} \times \frac{3}{2} = 1$. This is because when you multiply across, you get a fraction that is equal to 1.

$$\frac{2}{3} \times \frac{3}{2} = \frac{6}{6} = 1$$

The Distributive Property

The **distributive property** explains how multiplication and addition interact. It says that when multiplying one number by the sum of two other numbers, the same result can also be obtained by multiplying the one number by each of the numbers individually and then adding the products. For example, to multiply 2 by the sum of 7 and 3, the direct approach says, "the sum of 7 and 3 is 10, and 2 times 10 is 20." This would be expressed as $2 \times (7 + 3) = 2 \times 10 = 20$. On the other hand, the distributive property states that the same answer can be achieved by multiplying each number inside the parentheses and adding the products. That is, "the product of 2 and 7 is 14, the product of 2 and 3 is 6, and the sum of 14 and 6 is 20." This would be expressed as $2 \times (7 + 3) = 2 \times 7 + 2 \times 3 = 14 + 6 = 20$, and it is demonstrated below.

$$2 \times (7 + 3) = 2 \times 7 + 2 \times 3$$

This same concept can be used when multiplying a number by the difference of two numbers. For example, $5 \times (10 - 4) = 5 \times 10 - 5 \times 4$. Since $5 \times 10 = 50$ and $5 \times 4 = 20$, the result is $50 - 20 = 30$. This answer can be checked by subtracting inside the parentheses first and then multiplying: $5 \times (10 - 4) = 5 \times 6 = 30$.

> **Review Video: Commutative, Associative, and Distributive Properties**
> Visit mometrix.com/academy and enter code: 483176

PROPERTIES OF EXPONENTS

The properties of exponents are as follows:

Property	Description
$a^1 = a$	Any number to the power of 1 is equal to itself
$1^n = 1$	The number 1 raised to any power is equal to 1
$a^0 = 1$	Any number raised to the power of 0 is equal to 1
$a^n \times a^m = a^{n+m}$	Add exponents to multiply powers of the same base number
$a^n \div a^m = a^{n-m}$	Subtract exponents to divide powers of the same base number
$(a^n)^m = a^{n \times m}$	When a power is raised to a power, the exponents are multiplied
$(a \times b)^n = a^n \times b^n$	Multiplication and division operations inside parentheses can be raised to a power. This is the same as each term being raised to that power.
$(a \div b)^n = a^n \div b^n$	
$a^{-n} = \dfrac{1}{a^n}$	A negative exponent is the same as the reciprocal of a positive exponent

Note that exponents do not have to be integers. Fractional or decimal exponents follow all the rules above as well. Example: $5^{\frac{1}{4}} \times 5^{\frac{3}{4}} = 5^{\frac{1}{4}+\frac{3}{4}} = 5^1 = 5$.

> **Review Video: Properties of Exponents**
> Visit mometrix.com/academy and enter code: 532558

SCIENTIFIC NOTATION

Scientific notation is a way of writing large numbers in a shorter form. The form $a \times 10^n$ is used in scientific notation, where a is greater than or equal to 1 but less than 10, and n is the number of places the decimal must move to get from the original number to a. Example: The number 230,400,000 is cumbersome to write. To write the value in scientific notation, place a decimal point between the first and second numbers, and include all digits through the last non-zero digit ($a = 2.304$). To find the appropriate power of 10, count the number of places the decimal point had to move ($n = 8$). The number is positive if the decimal moved to the left, and negative if it moved to the right. We can then write 230,400,000 as 2.304×10^8. If we look instead at the number 0.00002304, we have the same value for a, but this time the decimal moved 5 places to the right ($n =$

−5). Thus, 0.00002304 can be written as 2.304×10^{-5}. Using this notation makes it simple to compare very large or very small numbers. By comparing exponents, it is easy to see that 3.28×10^4 is smaller than 1.51×10^5, because 4 is less than 5.

> **Review Video: Scientific Notation**
> Visit mometrix.com/academy and enter code: 976454

FACTORS AND MULTIPLES

FACTORS AND GREATEST COMMON FACTOR

A whole number a is a **factor** (or **divisor**) of a whole number b if a divides b evenly. In other words, a is a factor of b if the quotient $b \div a$ is a whole number with a remainder of 0. For instance, 3 is a factor of 12 because $12 \div 3 = 4$ with no remainder. Another way to say this is that a is a factor of b if we can multiply a by another whole number to get b. So, we can also show that 3 is a factor of 12 by noting that $3 \times 4 = 12$.

Every positive whole number has 1 and itself as factors. If a whole number greater than one has *only* 1 and itself as factors, we call it a **prime number**. For instance, 5 is a prime number because its only factors are 1 and 5. The first several prime numbers are 2, 3, 5, 7, 11, and 13.

If a whole number greater than 1 is not prime—that is, if it has factors besides 1 and itself—then it is a **composite number.** For instance, 10 is a composite number because it has factors 2 and 5 in addition to 1 and 10. The first several composite numbers are 4, 6, 8, 9, 10, 12, 14, and 15.

A **prime factor** of a whole number is a factor that is also a prime number. For example, the prime factors of 12 are 2 and 3. The prime factors of 15 are 3 and 5.

A **common factor** of two (or more) whole numbers is a number that is a factor of both (or all) of them. For example, the factors of 12 are 1, 2, 3, 4, 6, and 12, while the factors of 15 are 1, 3, 5, and 15. The common factors (underlined) of 12 and 15 are 1 and 3.

The **greatest common factor** (GCF) of two (or more) whole numbers is the largest number that is a factor of both (or all) of them. For example, the factors of 15 are 1, 3, 5, and 15; the factors of 35 are 1, 5, 7, and 35. Therefore, the greatest common factor of 15 and 35 is 5.

> **Review Video: Factors**
> Visit mometrix.com/academy and enter code: 920086
>
> **Review Video: Prime Numbers and Factorization**
> Visit mometrix.com/academy and enter code: 760669

MULTIPLES AND LEAST COMMON MULTIPLE

A whole number b is a **multiple** of a whole number a when a is a factor of b. This means that b is the product of a and another whole number. For example, the multiples of 7 are $0 \times 7 = 0$, $1 \times 7 = 7$, $2 \times 7 = 14$, $3 \times 7 = 21$, $4 \times 7 = 28$, $5 \times 7 = 35$, ... Dividing 0, 7, 14, 21, 28, and 35 by 7 results in the whole numbers 0, 1, 2, 3, 4, and 5, respectively, showing that 7 is a factor of these numbers.

The least common multiple (**LCM**) of two (or more) whole numbers is the smallest number that is a multiple of both (or all) of them. For example, the multiples of 3 are 3, 6, 9, 12, 15, ...; the multiples of 5 are 5, 10, 15, 20, ... The smallest number that appears in both lists is 15, so the least common multiple of 3 and 5 is 15.

> **Review Video: Multiples**
> Visit mometrix.com/academy and enter code: 626738
>
> **Review Video: Greatest Common Factor and Least Common Multiple**
> Visit mometrix.com/academy and enter code: 838699

FRACTIONS

A **fraction** is a number that is expressed as one integer written above another integer, with a dividing line between them $\left(\frac{x}{y}\right)$. It represents the **quotient** of the two numbers "x divided by y." It can also be thought of as x out of y equal parts.

The top number of a fraction is called the **numerator**, and it represents the number of parts under consideration. The 1 in $\frac{1}{4}$ means that 1 part out of the whole is being considered in the calculation. The bottom number of a fraction is called the **denominator**, and it represents the total number of equal parts. The 4 in $\frac{1}{4}$ means that the whole consists of 4 equal parts. A fraction cannot have a denominator of zero; this is referred to as "*undefined.*"

Fractions can be manipulated, without changing the value of the fraction, by multiplying or dividing (but not adding or subtracting) both the numerator and denominator by the same number. If you divide both numbers by a common factor, you are **reducing** or simplifying the fraction. Two fractions that have the same value but are expressed differently are known as **equivalent fractions**. For example, $\frac{2}{10}, \frac{3}{15}, \frac{4}{20}$, and $\frac{5}{25}$ are all equivalent fractions. They can also all be reduced or simplified to $\frac{1}{5}$.

When two fractions are manipulated so that they have the same denominator, this is known as finding a **common denominator**. The number chosen to be that common denominator should be the least common multiple of the two original denominators. Example: $\frac{3}{4}$ and $\frac{5}{6}$; the least common multiple of 4 and 6 is 12. Manipulating to achieve the common denominator: $\frac{3}{4} = \frac{9}{12}$; $\frac{5}{6} = \frac{10}{12}$.

> **Review Video: Overview of Fractions**
> Visit mometrix.com/academy and enter code: 262335

PROPER FRACTIONS AND MIXED NUMBERS

A fraction whose denominator is greater than its numerator is known as a **proper fraction**, while a fraction whose numerator is greater than its denominator is known as an **improper fraction**. Proper fractions have values *less than one* and improper fractions have values *greater than one*.

A **mixed number** is a number that contains both an integer and a fraction. Any improper fraction can be rewritten as a mixed number. Example: $\frac{8}{3} = \frac{6}{3} + \frac{2}{3} = 2 + \frac{2}{3} = 2\frac{2}{3}$. Similarly, any mixed number can be rewritten as an improper fraction. Example: $1\frac{3}{5} = 1 + \frac{3}{5} = \frac{5}{5} + \frac{3}{5} = \frac{8}{5}$.

> **Review Video: Proper and Improper Fractions and Mixed Numbers**
> Visit mometrix.com/academy and enter code: 211077

ADDING AND SUBTRACTING FRACTIONS

If two fractions have a common denominator, they can be added or subtracted simply by adding or subtracting the two numerators and retaining the same denominator. If the two fractions do not already have the same denominator, one or both of them must be manipulated to achieve a common denominator before they can be added or subtracted. Example: $\frac{1}{2} + \frac{1}{4} = \frac{2}{4} + \frac{1}{4} = \frac{3}{4}$.

> **Review Video: Adding and Subtracting Fractions**
> Visit mometrix.com/academy and enter code: 378080

MULTIPLYING FRACTIONS

Two fractions can be multiplied by multiplying the two numerators to find the new numerator and the two denominators to find the new denominator. Example: $\frac{1}{3} \times \frac{2}{3} = \frac{1 \times 2}{3 \times 3} = \frac{2}{9}$.

DIVIDING FRACTIONS

Two fractions can be divided by flipping the numerator and denominator of the second fraction and then proceeding as though it were a multiplication problem. Example: $\frac{2}{3} \div \frac{3}{4} = \frac{2}{3} \times \frac{4}{3} = \frac{8}{9}$.

> **Review Video: Multiplying and Dividing Fractions**
> Visit mometrix.com/academy and enter code: 473632

MULTIPLYING A MIXED NUMBER BY A WHOLE NUMBER OR A DECIMAL

When multiplying a mixed number by something, it is usually best to convert it to an improper fraction first. Additionally, if the multiplicand is a decimal, it is most often simplest to convert it to a fraction. For instance, to multiply $4\frac{3}{8}$ by 3.5, begin by rewriting each quantity as a whole number plus a proper fraction. Remember, a mixed number is a fraction added to a whole number and a decimal is a representation of the sum of fractions, specifically tenths, hundredths, thousandths, and so on:

$$4\frac{3}{8} \times 3.5 = \left(4 + \frac{3}{8}\right) \times \left(3 + \frac{1}{2}\right)$$

Next, the quantities being added need to be expressed with the same denominator. This is achieved by multiplying and dividing the whole number by the denominator of the fraction. Recall that a whole number is equivalent to that number divided by 1:

$$= \left(\frac{4}{1} \times \frac{8}{8} + \frac{3}{8}\right) \times \left(\frac{3}{1} \times \frac{2}{2} + \frac{1}{2}\right)$$

When multiplying fractions, remember to multiply the numerators and denominators separately:

$$= \left(\frac{4 \times 8}{1 \times 8} + \frac{3}{8}\right) \times \left(\frac{3 \times 2}{1 \times 2} + \frac{1}{2}\right)$$

$$= \left(\frac{32}{8} + \frac{3}{8}\right) \times \left(\frac{6}{2} + \frac{1}{2}\right)$$

Now that the fractions have the same denominators, they can be added:

$$= \frac{35}{8} \times \frac{7}{2}$$

Finally, perform the last multiplication and then simplify:

$$= \frac{35 \times 7}{8 \times 2} = \frac{245}{16} = \frac{240}{16} + \frac{5}{16} = 15\frac{5}{16}$$

COMPARING FRACTIONS

It is important to master the ability to compare and order fractions. This skill is relevant to many real-world scenarios. For example, carpenters often compare fractional construction nail lengths when preparing for a project, and bakers often compare fractional measurements to have the correct ratio of ingredients. There are three commonly used strategies when comparing fractions. These strategies are referred to as the common denominator approach, the decimal approach, and the cross-multiplication approach.

USING A COMMON DENOMINATOR TO COMPARE FRACTIONS

The fractions $\frac{2}{3}$ and $\frac{4}{7}$ have different denominators. $\frac{2}{3}$ has a denominator of 3, and $\frac{4}{7}$ has a denominator of 7. In order to precisely compare these two fractions, it is necessary to use a common denominator. A common denominator is a common multiple that is shared by both denominators. In this case, the denominators 3 and 7 share a multiple of 21. In general, it is most efficient to select the least common multiple for the two denominators.

Rewrite each fraction with the common denominator of 21. Then, calculate the new numerators as illustrated below.

$$\frac{2}{3} \overset{\times 7}{\underset{\times 7}{=}} \frac{14}{21} \qquad \frac{4}{7} \overset{\times 3}{\underset{\times 3}{=}} \frac{12}{21}$$

For $\frac{2}{3}$, multiply the numerator and denominator by 7. The result is $\frac{14}{21}$.

For $\frac{4}{7}$, multiply the numerator and denominator by 3. The result is $\frac{12}{21}$.

Now that both fractions have a denominator of 21, the fractions can accurately be compared by comparing the numerators. Since 14 is greater than 12, the fraction $\frac{14}{21}$ is greater than $\frac{12}{21}$. This means that $\frac{2}{3}$ is greater than $\frac{4}{7}$.

Using Decimals to Compare Fractions

Sometimes decimal values are easier to compare than fraction values. For example, $\frac{5}{8}$ is equivalent to 0.625 and $\frac{3}{5}$ is equivalent to 0.6. This means that the comparison of $\frac{5}{8}$ and $\frac{3}{5}$ can be determined by comparing the decimals 0.625 and 0.6. When both decimal values are extended to the thousandths place, they become 0.625 and 0.600, respectively. It becomes clear that 0.625 is greater than 0.600 because 625 thousandths is greater than 600 thousandths. In other words, $\frac{5}{8}$ is greater than $\frac{3}{5}$ because 0.625 is greater than 0.6.

Using Cross-Multiplication to Compare Fractions

Cross-multiplication is an efficient strategy for comparing fractions. This is a shortcut for the common denominator strategy. Start by writing each fraction next to one another. Multiply the numerator of the fraction on the left by the denominator of the fraction on the right. Write down the result next to the fraction on the left. Now multiply the numerator of the fraction on the right by the denominator of the fraction on the left. Write down the result next to the fraction on the right. Compare both products. The fraction with the larger result is the larger fraction.

Consider the fractions $\frac{4}{7}$ and $\frac{5}{9}$.

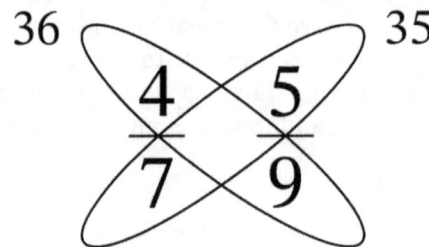

36 is greater than 35. Therefore, $\frac{4}{7}$ is greater than $\frac{5}{9}$.

Decimals

Decimals are one way to represent parts of a whole. Using the place value system, each digit to the right of a decimal point denotes the number of units of a corresponding *negative* power of ten. For example, consider the decimal 0.24. We can use a model to represent the decimal. Since a dime is worth one-tenth of a dollar and a penny is worth one-hundredth of a dollar, one possible model to represent this fraction is to have 2 dimes representing the 2 in the tenths place and 4 pennies representing the 4 in the hundredths place:

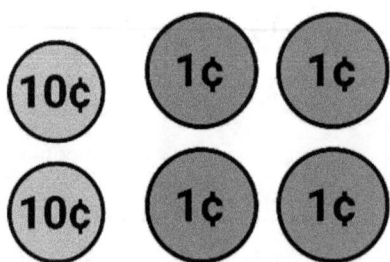

To write the decimal as a fraction, put the decimal in the numerator with 1 in the denominator. Multiply the numerator and denominator by tens until there are no more decimal places. Then simplify the fraction to lowest terms. For example, converting 0.24 to a fraction:

$$0.24 = \frac{0.24}{1} = \frac{0.24 \times 100}{1 \times 100} = \frac{24}{100} = \frac{6}{25}$$

Review Video: Decimals
Visit mometrix.com/academy and enter code: 837268

OPERATIONS WITH DECIMALS
ADDING AND SUBTRACTING DECIMALS

When adding and subtracting decimals, the decimal points must always be aligned. Adding decimals is just like adding regular whole numbers. Example: $4.5 + 2.0 = 6.5$.

If the problem-solver does not properly align the decimal points, an incorrect answer of 4.7 may result. An easy way to add decimals is to align all of the decimal points in a vertical column visually. This will allow you to see exactly where the decimal should be placed in the final answer. Begin adding from right to left. Add each column in turn, making sure to carry the number to the left if a column adds up to more than 9. The same rules apply to the subtraction of decimals.

Review Video: Adding and Subtracting Decimals
Visit mometrix.com/academy and enter code: 381101

MULTIPLYING DECIMALS

A simple multiplication problem has two components: a **multiplicand** and a **multiplier**. When multiplying decimals, work as though the numbers were whole rather than decimals. Once the final product is calculated, count the number of places to the right of the decimal in both the multiplicand and the multiplier. Then, count that number of places from the right of the product and place the decimal in that position.

For example, 12.3×2.56 has a total of three places to the right of the respective decimals. Multiply 123×256 to get 31,488. Now, beginning on the right, count three places to the left and insert the decimal. The final product will be 31.488.

Review Video: How to Multiply Decimals
Visit mometrix.com/academy and enter code: 731574

DIVIDING DECIMALS

Every division problem has a **divisor** and a **dividend**. The dividend is the number that is being divided. In the problem $14 \div 7$, 14 is the dividend and 7 is the divisor. In a division problem with decimals, the divisor must be converted into a whole number. Begin by moving the decimal in the divisor to the right until a whole number is created. Next, move the decimal in the dividend the same number of spaces to the right. For example, 4.9 into 24.5 would become 49 into 245. The decimal was moved one space to the right to create a whole number in the divisor, and then the same was done for the dividend. Once the whole numbers are created, the problem is carried out normally: $245 \div 49 = 5$.

Review Video: Dividing Decimals
Visit mometrix.com/academy and enter code: 560690

Review Video: Dividing Decimals by Whole Numbers
Visit mometrix.com/academy and enter code: 535669

PERCENTAGES

Percentages can be thought of as fractions that are based on a whole of 100; that is, one whole is equal to 100%. The word **percent** means "per hundred." Percentage problems are often presented in three main ways:

- Find what percentage of some number another number is.
  - Example: What percentage of 40 is 8?
- Find what number is some percentage of a given number.
  - Example: What number is 20% of 40?
- Find what number another number is a given percentage of.
  - Example: What number is 8 20% of?

There are three components in each of these cases: a **whole** (W), a **part** (P), and a **percentage** (%). These are related by the equation: $P = W \times \%$. This can easily be rearranged into other forms that may suit different questions better: $\% = \frac{P}{W}$ and $W = \frac{P}{\%}$. Percentage problems are often also word problems. As such, a large part of solving them is figuring out which quantities are what. For example, consider the following word problem:

In a school cafeteria, 7 students choose pizza, 9 choose hamburgers, and 4 choose tacos. What percentage of student choose tacos?

To find the whole, you must first add all of the parts: $7 + 9 + 4 = 20$. The percentage can then be found by dividing the part by the whole $\left(\% = \frac{P}{W}\right): \frac{4}{20} = \frac{20}{100} = 20\%$.

> **Review Video: Computation with Percentages**
> Visit mometrix.com/academy and enter code: 693099

CALCULATING PERCENT CHANGE

Suppose a quantity has a particular value (the *old value*) and then we add something (the *change*) to it to get another value (the *new value*). We can describe this process by the simple equation (old value) + change = (new value). If we know the old and new values, we can rearrange this equation to find the change, getting change = (new value) − (old value). For instance, if a store's price for a box of computer paper goes from $20 last week to $25 this week, this is a change of (new value) − (old value) = $25 − $20 = $5. Or, if the size of the freshman class at a college goes from 500 students one year to 440 students the next year, this is a change of (new value) − (old value) = 440 − 500 = −60 students. So, we see that change can be positive or negative.

Instead of the word *change*, we sometimes use the words *increase* or *decrease* to specify whether the value goes up or down, respectively. In the examples above, the price of computer paper increases by $5 and the freshman class decreases by 60 students. Note that the decrease is 60 students and not −60 because the word *decrease* already means that the value goes down. So, *increase* is the same as positive change and *decrease* is the opposite or negative change.

If the changing quantity represents an amount (how much of something there is), we can also calculate the **percent change**. This is the change expressed as a percentage of the old amount. To calculate this, we divide the change by the old amount and express the quotient as a percent. That is, we use the formula percent change = $\frac{\text{change}}{\text{old value}}$, converting the resulting decimal answer to a percent. In the examples above, the price of a box of computer paper has a percent change of $\frac{\text{change in price}}{\text{old price}} = \frac{\$5}{\$20} = 0.25 = 25\%$, and the size of the freshman class at the college has a percent change of $\frac{\text{change in enrollment}}{\text{old enrollment}} = \frac{-60}{500} = -0.12 = -12\%$. We can also use the terms *percent increase* and *percent decrease*, saying that the price of computer paper increases by 25%

and the size of the freshman class decreases by 12%. Note that the denominator is always the old amount, never the new amount.

Example: Your landlord raises your rent from $1,500 to $1,700 per month. To find the percent change in your rent (rounded to the nearest tenth of a percent), you calculate as follows.

$$\text{percent change in rent} = \frac{\text{change in rent}}{\text{old rent}} = \frac{(\text{new rent}) - (\text{old rent})}{\text{old rent}}$$
$$= \frac{\$1,700 - \$1,500}{\$1,500} = \frac{\$200}{\$1,500} = 0.1333\ldots \approx 13.3\%$$

Therefore, the percent change in your rent is approximately 13.3%.

> **Review Video: Percent Change**
> Visit mometrix.com/academy and enter code: 907890

CONVERTING BETWEEN PERCENTAGES, FRACTIONS, AND DECIMALS

Converting decimals to percentages and percentages to decimals is as simple as moving the decimal point. To *convert from a decimal to a percentage*, move the decimal point **two places to the right**. To *convert from a percentage to a decimal*, move it **two places to the left**. It may be helpful to remember that the percentage number will always be larger than the equivalent decimal number. Example:

$$0.23 = 23\% \quad 5.34 = 534\% \quad 0.007 = 0.7\%$$
$$700\% = 7.00 \quad 86\% = 0.86 \quad 0.15\% = 0.0015$$

To convert a fraction to a decimal, simply divide the numerator by the denominator in the fraction. To convert a decimal to a fraction, put the decimal in the numerator with 1 in the denominator. Multiply the numerator and denominator by tens until there are no more decimal places. Then simplify the fraction to lowest terms. For example, converting 0.24 to a fraction:

$$0.24 = \frac{0.24}{1} = \frac{0.24 \times 100}{1 \times 100} = \frac{24}{100} = \frac{6}{25}$$

Fractions can be converted to a percentage by finding equivalent fractions with a denominator of 100. Example:

$$\frac{7}{10} = \frac{70}{100} = 70\% \quad \frac{1}{4} = \frac{25}{100} = 25\%$$

To convert a percentage to a fraction, divide the percentage number by 100 and reduce the fraction to its simplest possible terms. Example:

$$60\% = \frac{60}{100} = \frac{3}{5} \quad 96\% = \frac{96}{100} = \frac{24}{25}$$

> **Review Video: Converting Fractions to Percentages and Decimals**
> Visit mometrix.com/academy and enter code: 306233
>
> **Review Video: Converting Percentages to Decimals and Fractions**
> Visit mometrix.com/academy and enter code: 287297
>
> **Review Video: Converting Decimals to Fractions and Percentages**
> Visit mometrix.com/academy and enter code: 986765
>
> **Review Video: Converting Decimals, Improper Fractions, and Mixed Numbers**
> Visit mometrix.com/academy and enter code: 696924

RATIONAL AND IRRATIONAL NUMBERS

The term **rational** means that the number can be expressed as a ratio or fraction. That is, a number, r, is rational if and only if it can be represented by a fraction $\frac{a}{b}$ where a and b are integers and b does not equal 0. The set of rational numbers includes integers and decimals. If there is no finite way to represent a value with a fraction of integers, then the number is **irrational**. Common irrational numbers are π and the square roots of whole numbers that are not perfect squares (e.g., $\sqrt{5}$ or $\sqrt{21}$). The sum or product of an integer and an irrational number is always irrational (e.g., 3π or $7 + \sqrt{6}$).

> **Review Video: Rational and Irrational Numbers**
> Visit mometrix.com/academy and enter code: 280645
>
> **Review Video: Ordering Rational Numbers**
> Visit mometrix.com/academy and enter code: 419578
>
> **Review Video: Irrational Numbers on a Number Line**
> Visit mometrix.com/academy and enter code: 433866

Measurements

METRIC AND CUSTOMARY MEASUREMENTS
METRIC MEASUREMENT PREFIXES

Giga-	One billion	1 *giga*watt is one billion watts
Mega-	One million	1 *mega*hertz is one million hertz
Kilo-	One thousand	1 *kilo*gram is one thousand grams
Deci-	One-tenth	1 *deci*meter is one-tenth of a meter
Centi-	One-hundredth	1 *centi*meter is one-hundredth of a meter
Milli-	One-thousandth	1 *milli*liter is one-thousandth of a liter
Micro-	One-millionth	1 *micro*gram is one-millionth of a gram

Review Video: How the Metric System Works
Visit mometrix.com/academy and enter code: 163709

MEASUREMENT CONVERSION

When converting between units, the goal is to maintain the same meaning but change the way it is displayed. In order to go from a larger unit to a smaller unit, multiply the number of the known amount by the equivalent amount. When going from a smaller unit to a larger unit, divide the number of the known amount by the equivalent amount.

For complicated conversions, it may be helpful to set up conversion fractions. In these fractions, one fraction is the **conversion factor**. The other fraction has the unknown amount in the numerator. So, the known value is placed in the denominator. Sometimes, the second fraction has the known value from the problem in the numerator and the unknown in the denominator. Multiply the two fractions to get the converted measurement. Note that since the numerator and the denominator of the factor are equivalent, the value of the fraction is 1. That is why we can say that the result in the new units is equal to the result in the old units even though they have different numbers.

It can often be necessary to chain known conversion factors together. As an example, consider converting 512 square inches to square meters. We know that there are 2.54 centimeters in an inch and 100 centimeters in a meter, and we know we will need to square each of these factors to achieve the conversion we are looking for.

$$\frac{512 \text{ in}^2}{1} \times \left(\frac{2.54 \text{ cm}}{1 \text{ in}}\right)^2 \times \left(\frac{1 \text{ m}}{100 \text{ cm}}\right)^2 = \frac{512 \text{ in}^2}{1} \times \left(\frac{6.4516 \text{ cm}^2}{1 \text{ in}^2}\right) \times \left(\frac{1 \text{ m}^2}{10{,}000 \text{ cm}^2}\right) = 0.330 \text{ m}^2$$

Review Video: Measurement Conversions
Visit mometrix.com/academy and enter code: 316703

Review Video: Converting Kilograms to Pounds
Visit mometrix.com/academy and enter code: 241463

COMMON UNITS AND EQUIVALENTS
METRIC EQUIVALENTS

1000 µg (microgram)	1 mg
1000 mg (milligram)	1 g
1000 g (gram)	1 kg
1000 kg (kilogram)	1 metric ton
1000 mL (milliliter)	1 L
1000 µm (micrometer)	1 mm
1000 mm (millimeter)	1 m
100 cm (centimeter)	1 m
1000 m (meter)	1 km

DISTANCE AND AREA MEASUREMENT

Unit	Abbreviation	US equivalent	Metric equivalent
Inch	in	1 inch	2.54 centimeters
Foot	ft	12 inches	0.305 meters
Yard	yd	3 feet	0.914 meters
Mile	mi	5280 feet	1.609 kilometers
Acre	ac	4840 square yards	0.405 hectares
Square Mile	sq. mi. or mi.^{2}	640 acres	2.590 square kilometers

CAPACITY MEASUREMENTS

Unit	Abbreviation	US equivalent	Metric equivalent
Fluid Ounce	fl oz	8 fluid drams	29.573 milliliters
Cup	c	8 fluid ounces	0.237 liter
Pint	pt.	16 fluid ounces	0.473 liter
Quart	qt.	2 pints	0.946 liter
Gallon	gal.	4 quarts	3.785 liters
Teaspoon	t or tsp.	1 fluid dram	5 milliliters
Tablespoon	T or tbsp.	4 fluid drams	15 or 16 milliliters
Cubic Centimeter	cc or cm^3	0.271 drams	1 milliliter

WEIGHT MEASUREMENTS

Unit	Abbreviation	US equivalent	Metric equivalent
Ounce	oz	16 drams	28.35 grams
Pound	lb	16 ounces	453.6 grams
Ton	tn.	2,000 pounds	907.2 kilograms

VOLUME AND WEIGHT MEASUREMENT CLARIFICATIONS

Always be careful when using ounces and fluid ounces. They are not equivalent.

1 pint = 16 fluid ounces	1 fluid ounce ≠ 1 ounce
1 pound = 16 ounces	1 pint ≠ 1 pound

Having one pint of something does not mean you have one pound of it. In the same way, just because something weighs one pound does not mean that its volume is one pint.

In the United States, the word "ton" by itself refers to a short ton or a net ton. Do not confuse this with a long ton (also called a gross ton) or a metric ton (also spelled *tonne*), which have different measurement equivalents.

$$1 \text{ US ton} = 2000 \text{ pounds} \quad \neq \quad 1 \text{ metric ton} = 1000 \text{ kilograms}$$

TEMPERATURE CONVERSIONS

TEMPERATURE CONVERSION

Converting between Fahrenheit (°F) and Celsius (°C) is slightly more involved than a direct proportion. From the following equations, we can see that a change of one degree Celsius is greater than a change of one degree Fahrenheit.

Conversion	Equation	Example
°F → °C	$°C = \frac{5}{9}(°F - 32)$	Convert 200 °F to °C. $\frac{5}{9}(200 - 32) = \frac{5}{9}(168)$ $\approx 93.33 \, °C$
°C → °F	$°F = \frac{9}{5}(°C) + 32$	Convert 24 °C to °F. $\frac{9}{5}(24) + 32 = 43.2 + 32$ $= 75.2 \, °F$

Geometry

POINTS, LINES, AND PLANES

POINTS AND LINES

A **point** is a fixed location in space, has no size or dimensions, and is commonly represented by a dot. A **line** is a set of points that extends infinitely in two opposite directions. It has length, but no width or depth. A line can be defined by any two distinct points that it contains. A **line segment** is a portion of a line that has definite endpoints. A **ray** is a portion of a line that extends from a single point on that line in one direction along the line. It has a definite beginning, but no ending.

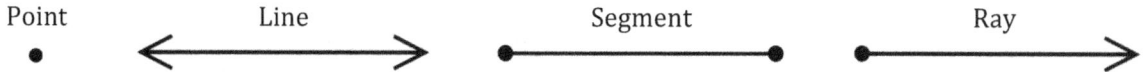

Points are **collinear** if there is a single line that passes through all of them. Otherwise, they are noncollinear. Two points are always collinear since two points define a line. Three points may be noncollinear. For example, the three vertices of a triangle are noncollinear since there is no line that goes through all three of them.

INTERACTIONS BETWEEN LINES

Intersecting lines are lines that have exactly one point in common. **Concurrent lines** are multiple lines that intersect at a single point. **Perpendicular lines** are lines that intersect at right angles. They are represented by the symbol ⊥. The shortest distance from a line to a point not on the line is a perpendicular segment from the point to the line. **Parallel lines** are lines in the same plane that have no points in common and never meet. Two distinct lines in a given plane are always either intersecting or parallel. **Skew lines** are two distinct lines in a three dimensional space that do not intersect and may also not be parallel because there is no single plane that contains them both.

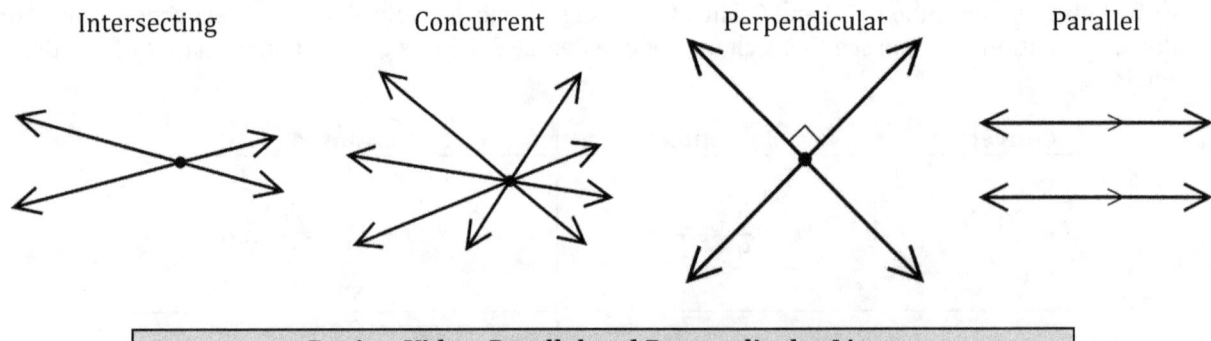

Review Video: Parallel and Perpendicular Lines
Visit mometrix.com/academy and enter code: 815923

A **transversal** is a line that intersects at least two other lines, which may or may not be parallel to one another. A transversal that intersects parallel lines is a common occurrence in geometry. A **bisector** is a line or line segment that divides another line segment into two equal lengths. A **perpendicular bisector** of a line segment is composed of points that are equidistant from the endpoints of the segment it is dividing.

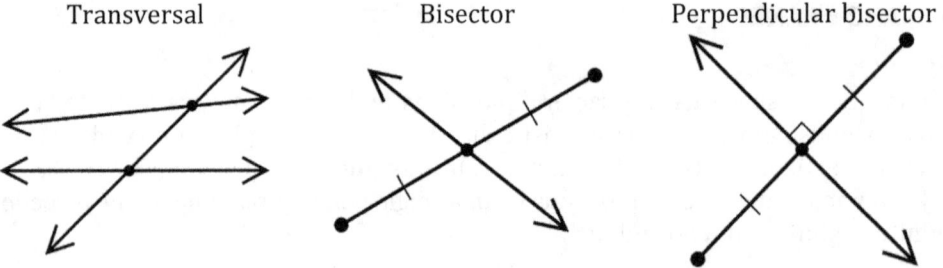

The **projection of a point on a line** is the point at which a perpendicular line drawn from the given point to the given line intersects the line. This is also the shortest distance from the given point to the line. The **projection of a segment on a line** is a segment whose endpoints are the points formed when perpendicular lines are drawn from the endpoints of the given segment to the given line. This is similar to the length a diagonal line appears to be when viewed from above.

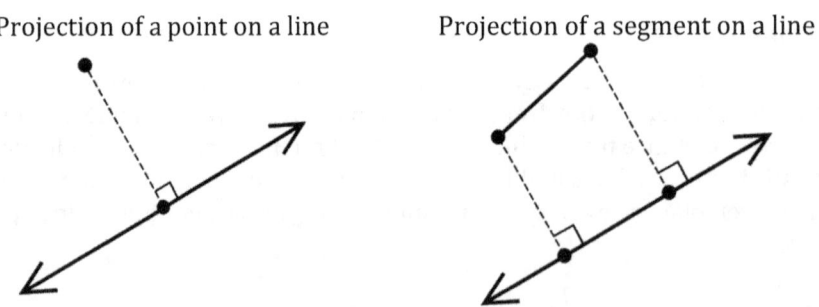

PLANES

A **plane** is a two-dimensional flat surface defined by three non-collinear points. A plane extends an infinite distance in all directions in those two dimensions. It contains an infinite number of points, parallel lines and segments, intersecting lines and segments, as well as parallel or intersecting rays. A plane will never contain a three-dimensional figure or skew lines. Two given planes are either parallel or they intersect at a line. A plane may intersect a circular conic surface to form **conic sections**, such as a parabola, hyperbola, circle or ellipse.

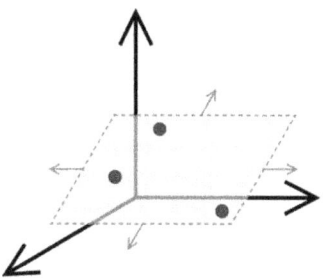

> **Review Video: Lines and Planes**
> Visit mometrix.com/academy and enter code: 554267

ANGLES
ANGLES AND VERTICES

An **angle** is formed when two lines or line segments meet at a common point. It may be a common starting point for a pair of segments or rays, or it may be the intersection of lines. Angles are represented by the symbol ∠.

The **vertex** is the point at which two segments or rays meet to form an angle. If the angle is formed by intersecting rays, lines, and/or line segments, the vertex is the point at which four angles are formed. The pairs of angles opposite one another are called vertical angles, and their measures are equal.

- An **acute** angle is an angle with a degree measure less than 90°.
- A **right** angle is an angle with a degree measure of exactly 90°.
- An **obtuse** angle is an angle with a degree measure greater than 90° but less than 180°.
- A **straight angle** is an angle with a degree measure of exactly 180°.
- A **reflex angle** is an angle with a degree measure greater than 180° but less than 360°.
- A **full angle** is an angle with a degree measure of exactly 360°.

> **Review Video: Angles**
> Visit mometrix.com/academy and enter code: 264624

RELATIONSHIPS BETWEEN ANGLES

Two angles whose sum is exactly 90° are said to be **complementary**. The two angles may or may not be adjacent. In a right triangle, the two acute angles are complementary.

Two angles whose sum is exactly 180° are said to be **supplementary**. The two angles may or may not be adjacent. Two intersecting lines always form two pairs of supplementary angles. Adjacent supplementary angles will always form a straight line.

Two angles that have the same vertex and share a side are said to be **adjacent**. Vertical angles are not adjacent because they share a vertex but no common side.

> **Review Video: Adjacent Angles**
> Visit mometrix.com/academy and enter code: 100375

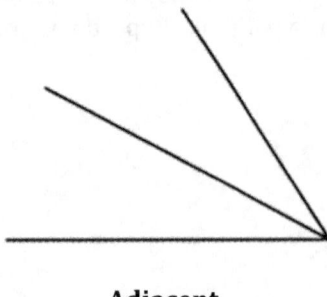
Adjacent
Share vertex and side

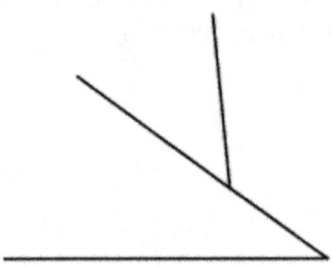
Not adjacent
Share part of a side, but not vertex

When two lines are cut by a transversal, the angles that are between the two lines are **interior angles**. In the diagram below, angles 3, 4, 5, and 6 are interior angles.

When two lines are cut by a transversal, the angles that are outside the lines are **exterior angles**. In the diagram below, angles 1, 2, 7, and 8 are exterior angles.

When two lines are cut by a transversal, the angles that are in the same position relative to the transversal and the cut lines are **corresponding angles**. The diagram below has four pairs of corresponding angles: angles 1 and 5, angles 2 and 6, angles 3 and 7, and angles 4 and 8. Corresponding angles formed by parallel lines are congruent.

When two lines are cut by a transversal, the two interior angles that are on opposite sides of the transversal are called **alternate interior angles**. In the diagram below, there are two pairs of alternate interior angles: angles 3 and 6, and angles 4 and 5. Alternate interior angles formed by parallel lines are congruent. Similarly, the two interior angles on the same side of the transversal (angles 3 and 5, and angles 4 and 6) are supplementary when the transversed lines are parallel. Some books call these angles **same side interior angles**.

When two lines are cut by a transversal, the two exterior angles that are on opposite sides of the transversal are called **alternate exterior angles**. In the diagram below, there are two pairs of alternate exterior angles: angles 1 and 8, and angles 2 and 7. Alternate exterior angles formed by parallel lines are congruent. Similarly, the two exterior angles on the same side of the transversal (angles 1 and 7, and angles 2 and 8) are supplementary when the transversed lines are parallel. Some books call these angles **same side exterior angles**.

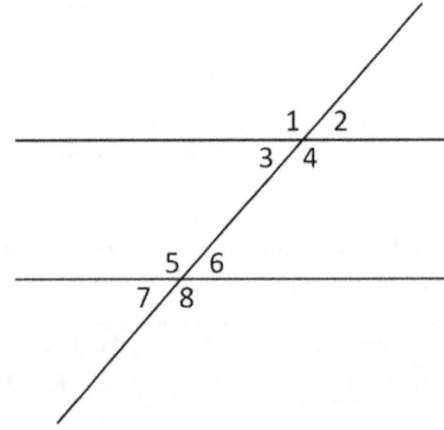

When two lines intersect, four angles are formed. The non-adjacent angles at this vertex are called vertical angles. Vertical angles are congruent. In the diagram, $\angle ABD \cong \angle CBE$ and $\angle ABC \cong \angle DBE$. The other pairs of angles, ($\angle ABC, \angle CBE$) and ($\angle ABD, \angle DBE$), are supplementary, meaning the pairs sum to 180°.

Review Video: **Congruent Angles**
Visit mometrix.com/academy and enter code: 642874

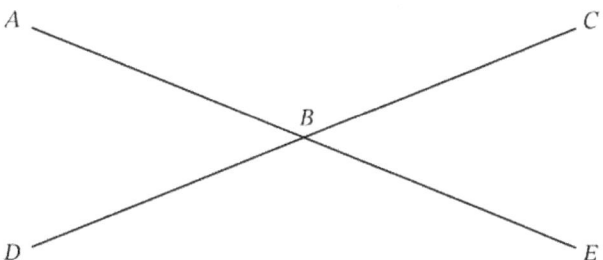

POLYGONS

A **polygon** is a closed, two-dimensional figure with three or more straight line segments called **sides**. The point at which two sides of a polygon intersect is called the **vertex**. In a polygon, the number of sides is always equal to the number of vertices. A polygon with all sides congruent and all angles equal is called a **regular polygon**. Common polygons are:

$$\begin{aligned}
\text{Triangle} &= 3 \text{ sides} \\
\text{Quadrilateral} &= 4 \text{ sides} \\
\text{Pentagon} &= 5 \text{ sides} \\
\text{Hexagon} &= 6 \text{ sides} \\
\text{Heptagon} &= 7 \text{ sides} \\
\text{Octagon} &= 8 \text{ sides} \\
\text{Nonagon} &= 9 \text{ sides} \\
\text{Decagon} &= 10 \text{ sides} \\
\text{Dodecagon} &= 12 \text{ sides}
\end{aligned}$$

More generally, an n-gon is a polygon that has n angles and n sides.

Review Video: **Intro to Polygons**
Visit mometrix.com/academy and enter code: 271869

The sum of the interior angles of an n-sided polygon is $(n - 2) \times 180°$. For example, in a triangle $n = 3$. So the sum of the interior angles is $(3 - 2) \times 180° = 180°$. In a quadrilateral, $n = 4$, and the sum of the angles is $(4 - 2) \times 180° = 360°$.

Review Video: **Sum of Interior Angles**
Visit mometrix.com/academy and enter code: 984991

CONVEX AND CONCAVE POLYGONS

A **convex polygon** is a polygon whose diagonals all lie within the interior of the polygon. A **concave polygon** is a polygon with at least one diagonal that is outside the polygon. In the diagram below, quadrilateral $ABCD$ is concave because diagonal $\overline{AC}$ lies outside the polygon and quadrilateral $EFGH$ is convex because both diagonals lie inside the polygon.

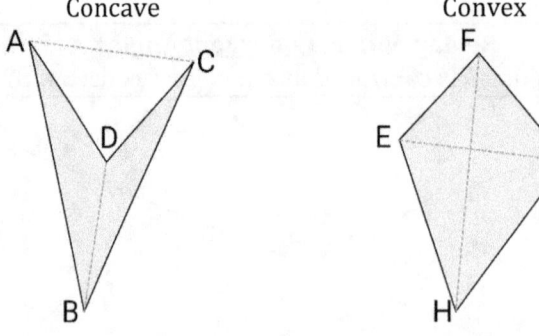

APOTHEM AND RADIUS

A line segment from the center of a regular polygon that is perpendicular to a side of the polygon is called the **apothem**. A line segment from the center of a regular polygon to a vertex of the polygon is called a **radius**. In a regular polygon, the apothem can be used to find the area of the polygon using the formula $A = \frac{1}{2}ap$, where a is the apothem, and p is the perimeter.

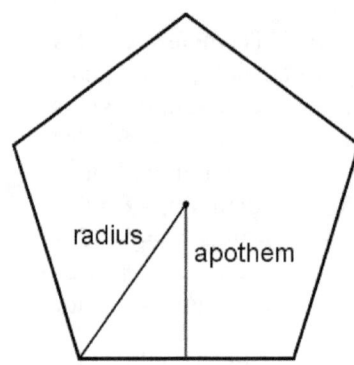

A **diagonal** is a line segment that joins two non-adjacent vertices of a polygon. The number of diagonals a polygon has can be found by using the formula:

$$\text{number of diagonals} = \frac{n(n-3)}{2}$$

Note that n is the number of sides in the polygon. This formula works for all polygons, not just regular polygons.

CONGRUENCE AND SIMILARITY

Congruent figures are geometric figures that have the same size and shape. For congruent polygons all corresponding angle measures are equal, and all corresponding side lengths are equal. Congruence is indicated by the symbol $\cong$. For instance, the expression $ABC \cong DEF$ indicates that the triangles below are congruent.

The order of the letters is important, indicating which parts of the polygons correspond to each other. For example, since the letters A and D both come first, ∠A and ∠D have the same measure.

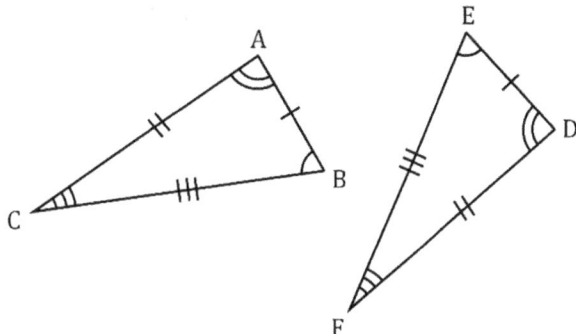

Similar figures are geometric figures that have the same shape, but do not necessarily have the same size. For similar polygons all corresponding angle measures are equal, and all corresponding side lengths are proportional, but they do not have to be equal. It is indicated by the symbol ~. For instance, the expression $ABC \sim DEF$ indicates that the triangles below are similar. Again, the order of the letters indicates which parts of the polygons correspond to each other.

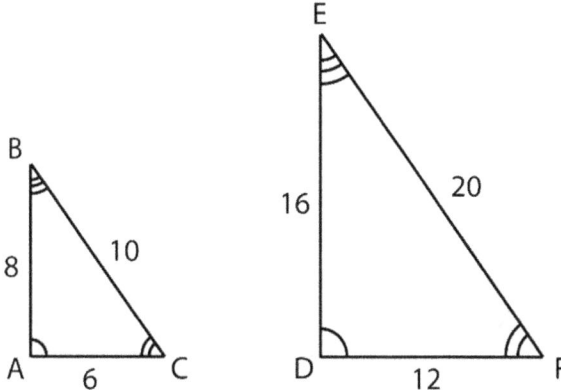

Note that all congruent figures are also similar, but not all similar figures are congruent.

> **Review Video: Congruent Shapes**
> Visit mometrix.com/academy and enter code: 492281

LINE OF SYMMETRY

A line that divides a figure or object into congruent parts that are mirror images of each other across the line is called a **line of symmetry**. An object may have no lines of symmetry, one line of symmetry, or multiple (i.e., more than one) lines of symmetry.

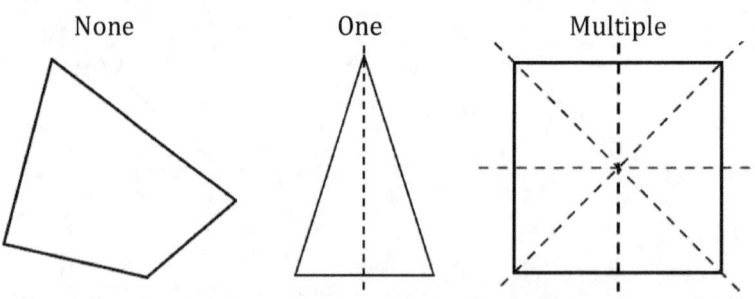

> **Review Video: Symmetry**
> Visit mometrix.com/academy and enter code: 528106

TRIANGLES

A triangle is a three-sided figure with the sum of its interior angles being 180°. The **perimeter of any triangle** is found by summing the three side lengths; $P = a + b + c$. For an equilateral triangle, this is the same as $P = 3a$, where a is any side length, since all three sides are the same length.

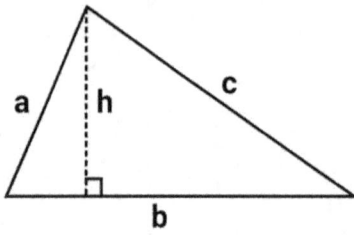

> **Review Video: Proof that a Triangle is 180 Degrees**
> Visit mometrix.com/academy and enter code: 687591
>
> **Review Video: Area and Perimeter of a Triangle**
> Visit mometrix.com/academy and enter code: 853779

The **area of any triangle** can be found by taking half the product of one side length referred to as the base, often given the variable b and the perpendicular distance from that side to the opposite vertex called the altitude or height and given the variable h. In equation form that is $A = \frac{1}{2}bh$. Another formula that works for any triangle is $A = \sqrt{s(s-a)(s-b)(s-c)}$, where s is the semiperimeter: $\frac{a+b+c}{2}$, and a, b, and c are the lengths of the three sides. Special cases include isosceles triangles, $A = \frac{1}{2}b\sqrt{a^2 - \frac{b^2}{4}}$, where b is the unique side and a is the length of one of the two congruent sides, and equilateral triangles, $A = \frac{\sqrt{3}}{4}a^2$, where a is the length of a side.

> **Review Video: Area of Any Triangle**
> Visit mometrix.com/academy and enter code: 138510

PARTS OF A TRIANGLE

An **altitude** of a triangle is a line segment drawn from one vertex perpendicular to the opposite side. In the diagram that follows, $\overline{BE}$, $\overline{AD}$, and $\overline{CF}$ are altitudes. The length of an altitude is also called the height of the triangle. The three altitudes in a triangle are always concurrent. The point of concurrency of the altitudes of a triangle, O, is called the **orthocenter**. Note that in an obtuse triangle, the orthocenter will be outside the triangle, and in a right triangle, the orthocenter is the vertex of the right angle.

A **median** of a triangle is a line segment drawn from one vertex to the midpoint of the opposite side. In the diagram that follows, $\overline{BH}$, $\overline{AG}$, and $\overline{CI}$ are medians. This is not the same as the altitude, except the altitude to the base of an isosceles triangle and all three altitudes of an equilateral triangle. The point of concurrency of the medians of a triangle, T, is called the **centroid**. This is the same point as the orthocenter only in an equilateral triangle. Unlike the orthocenter, the centroid is always inside the triangle. The centroid can also be considered the exact center of the triangle. Any shape triangle can be perfectly balanced on a tip placed at the centroid. The centroid is also the point that is two-thirds the distance from the vertex to the opposite side.

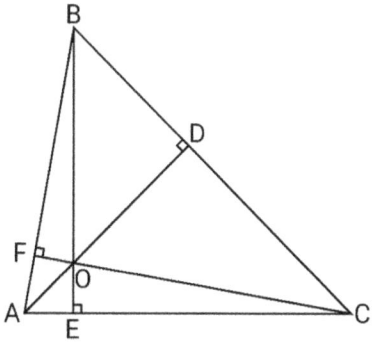 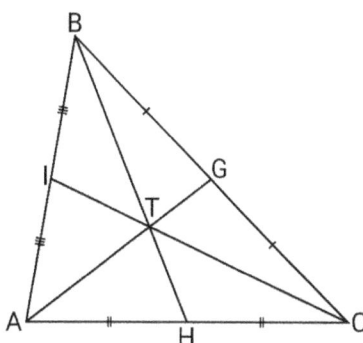

Review Video: Centroid, Incenter, Circumcenter, and Orthocenter
Visit mometrix.com/academy and enter code: 598260

TRIANGLE PROPERTIES

CLASSIFICATIONS OF TRIANGLES

A **scalene triangle** is a triangle with no congruent sides. A scalene triangle will also have three angles of different measures. The angle with the largest measure is opposite the longest side, and the angle with the smallest measure is opposite the shortest side. An **acute triangle** is a triangle whose three angles are all less than 90°. If two of the angles are equal, the acute triangle is also an **isosceles triangle**. An isosceles triangle will also have two congruent angles opposite the two congruent sides. If the three angles are all equal, the acute triangle is also an **equilateral triangle**. An equilateral triangle will also have three congruent angles, each 60°. All equilateral triangles are also acute triangles. An **obtuse triangle** is a triangle with exactly one angle greater than 90°. The other two angles may or may not be equal. If the two remaining angles are equal, the obtuse triangle is also an isosceles triangle. A **right triangle** is a triangle with exactly one angle equal to 90°. All right triangles follow the Pythagorean theorem. A right triangle can never be acute or obtuse.

The table below illustrates how each descriptor places a different restriction on the triangle:

Sides \ Angles	Acute: All angles < 90°	Obtuse: One angle > 90°	Right: One angle = 90°
Scalene: No equal side lengths	$90° > \angle a > \angle b > \angle c$ $x > y > z$	$\angle a > 90° > \angle b > \angle c$ $x > y > z$	$90° = \angle a > \angle b > \angle c$ $x > y > z$
Isosceles: Two equal side lengths	$90° > \angle a, \angle b, \text{ or } \angle c$ $\angle b = \angle c, \quad y = z$	$\angle a > 90° > \angle b = \angle c$ $x > y = z$	$\angle a = 90°$ $\angle b = \angle c = 45°$ $x > y = z$
Equilateral: Three equal side lengths	$60° = \angle a = \angle b = \angle c$ $x = y = z$		

Review Video: Introduction to Types of Triangles
Visit mometrix.com/academy and enter code: 511711

GENERAL RULES FOR TRIANGLES

The **triangle inequality theorem** states that the sum of the measures of any two sides of a triangle is always greater than the measure of the third side. If the sum of the measures of two sides were equal to the third side, a triangle would be impossible because the two sides would lie flat across the third side and there would be no vertex. If the sum of the measures of two of the sides was less than the third side, a closed figure would be impossible because the two shortest sides would never meet. In other words, for a triangle with sides lengths $A, B,$ and C: $A + B > C$, $B + C > A$, and $A + C > B$.

The sum of the measures of the interior angles of a triangle is always 180°. Therefore, a triangle can never have more than one angle greater than or equal to 90°.

In any triangle, the angles opposite congruent sides are congruent, and the sides opposite congruent angles are congruent. The largest angle is always opposite the longest side, and the smallest angle is always opposite the shortest side.

The line segment that joins the midpoints of any two sides of a triangle is always parallel to the third side and exactly half the length of the third side.

> **Review Video: General Rules (Triangle Inequality Theorem)**
> Visit mometrix.com/academy and enter code: 166488

SIMILARITY AND CONGRUENCE RULES

Similar triangles are triangles whose corresponding angles are equal and whose corresponding sides are proportional. Represented by AAA. Similar triangles whose corresponding sides are congruent are also congruent triangles.

Triangles can be shown to be **congruent** in 5 ways:

- **SSS**: Three sides of one triangle are congruent to the three corresponding sides of the second triangle.
- **SAS**: Two sides and the included angle (the angle formed by those two sides) of one triangle are congruent to the corresponding two sides and included angle of the second triangle.
- **ASA**: Two angles and the included side (the side that joins the two angles) of one triangle are congruent to the corresponding two angles and included side of the second triangle.
- **AAS**: Two angles and a non-included side of one triangle are congruent to the corresponding two angles and non-included side of the second triangle.
- **HL**: The hypotenuse and leg of one right triangle are congruent to the corresponding hypotenuse and leg of the second right triangle.

> **Review Video: Similar Triangles**
> Visit mometrix.com/academy and enter code: 398538

QUADRILATERALS

A **quadrilateral** is a closed two-dimensional geometric figure that has four straight sides. The sum of the interior angles of any quadrilateral is 360°.

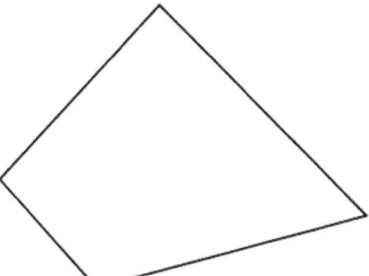

> **Review Video: Diagonals of Parallelograms, Rectangles, and Rhombi**
> Visit mometrix.com/academy and enter code: 320040

KITE

A **kite** is a quadrilateral with two pairs of adjacent sides that are congruent. A result of this is perpendicular diagonals. A kite can be concave or convex and has one line of symmetry.

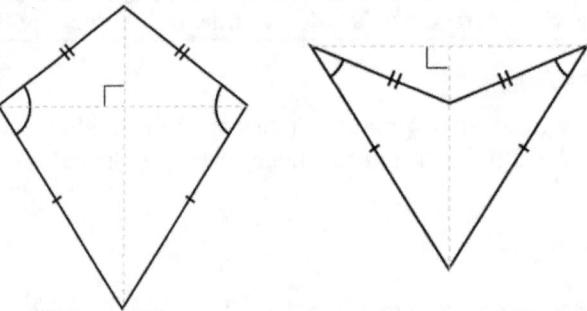

TRAPEZOID

Trapezoid: A trapezoid is defined as a quadrilateral that has at least one pair of parallel sides. There are no rules for the second pair of sides. So, there are no rules for the diagonals and no lines of symmetry for a trapezoid.

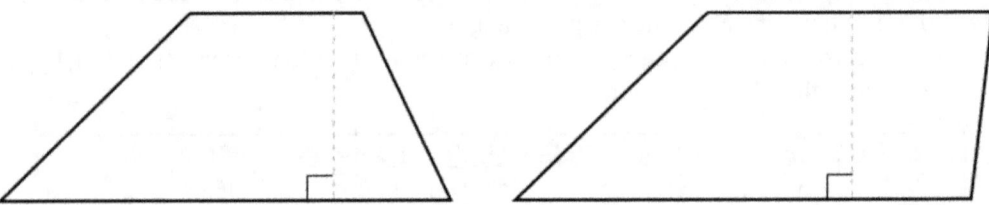

The **area of a trapezoid** is found by the formula $A = \frac{1}{2}h(b_1 + b_2)$, where h is the height (segment joining and perpendicular to the parallel bases), and b_1 and b_2 are the two parallel sides (bases). Do not use one of the other two sides as the height unless that side is also perpendicular to the parallel bases.

The **perimeter of a trapezoid** is found by the formula $P = a + b_1 + c + b_2$, where a, b_1, c, and b_2 are the four sides of the trapezoid.

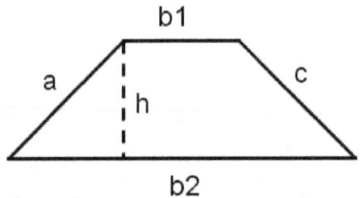

Review Video: Area and Perimeter of a Trapezoid
Visit mometrix.com/academy and enter code: 587523

Isosceles trapezoid: A trapezoid with equal base angles. This gives rise to other properties including: the two nonparallel sides have the same length, the two non-base angles are also equal, and there is one line of symmetry through the midpoints of the parallel sides.

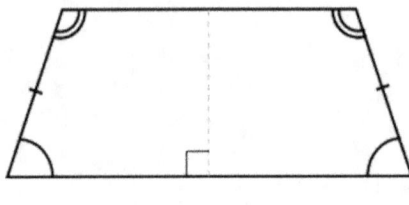

PARALLELOGRAM

A **parallelogram** is a quadrilateral that has two pairs of opposite parallel sides. As such it is a special type of trapezoid. The sides that are parallel are also congruent. The opposite interior angles are always congruent, and the consecutive interior angles are supplementary. The diagonals of a parallelogram divide each other. Each diagonal divides the parallelogram into two congruent triangles. A parallelogram has no line of symmetry, but does have 180-degree rotational symmetry about the midpoint.

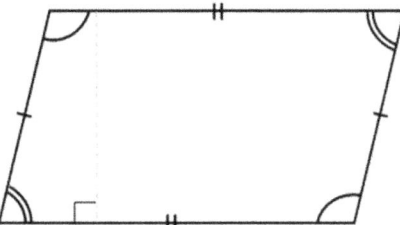

The **area of a parallelogram** is found by the formula $A = bh$, where b is the length of the base, and h is the height. Note that the base and height correspond to the length and width in a rectangle, so this formula would apply to rectangles as well. Do not confuse the height of a parallelogram with the length of the second side. The two are only the same measure in the case of a rectangle.

The **perimeter of a parallelogram** is found by the formula $P = 2a + 2b$ or $P = 2(a + b)$, where a and b are the lengths of the two sides.

> **Review Video: Area and Perimeter of a Parallelogram**
> Visit mometrix.com/academy and enter code: 718313

RECTANGLE

A **rectangle** is a quadrilateral with four right angles. All rectangles are parallelograms and trapezoids, but not all parallelograms or trapezoids are rectangles. The diagonals of a rectangle are congruent. Rectangles have two lines of symmetry (through each pair of opposing midpoints) and 180-degree rotational symmetry about the midpoint.

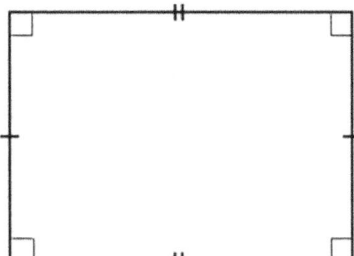

The **area of a rectangle** is found by the formula $A = lw$, where A is the area of the rectangle, l is the length (usually considered to be the longer side) and w is the width (usually considered to be the shorter side). The numbers for l and w are interchangeable.

The **perimeter of a rectangle** is found by the formula $P = 2l + 2w$ or $P = 2(l + w)$, where l is the length, and w is the width. It may be easier to add the length and width first and then double the result, as in the second formula.

RHOMBUS

A **rhombus** is a quadrilateral with four congruent sides. All rhombuses are parallelograms and kites; thus, they inherit all the properties of both types of quadrilaterals. The diagonals of a rhombus are perpendicular to each other. Rhombi have two lines of symmetry (along each of the diagonals) and 180° rotational symmetry. The

area of a rhombus is half the product of the diagonals: $A = \frac{d_1 d_2}{2}$ and the perimeter of a rhombus is: $P = 2\sqrt{(d_1)^2 + (d_2)^2}$.

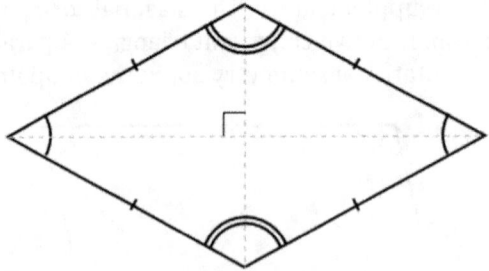

SQUARE

A **square** is a quadrilateral with four right angles and four congruent sides. Squares satisfy the criteria of all other types of quadrilaterals. The diagonals of a square are congruent and perpendicular to each other. Squares have four lines of symmetry (through each pair of opposing midpoints and along each of the diagonals) as well as 90° rotational symmetry about the midpoint.

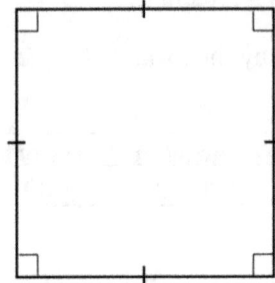

The **area of a square** is found by using the formula $A = s^2$, where s is the length of one side. The **perimeter of a square** is found by using the formula $P = 4s$, where s is the length of one side. Because all four sides are equal in a square, it is faster to multiply the length of one side by 4 than to add the same number four times. You could use the formulas for rectangles and get the same answer.

> **Review Video: Area and Perimeter of Rectangles and Squares**
> Visit mometrix.com/academy and enter code: 428109

HIERARCHY OF QUADRILATERALS

The hierarchy of quadrilaterals is as follows:

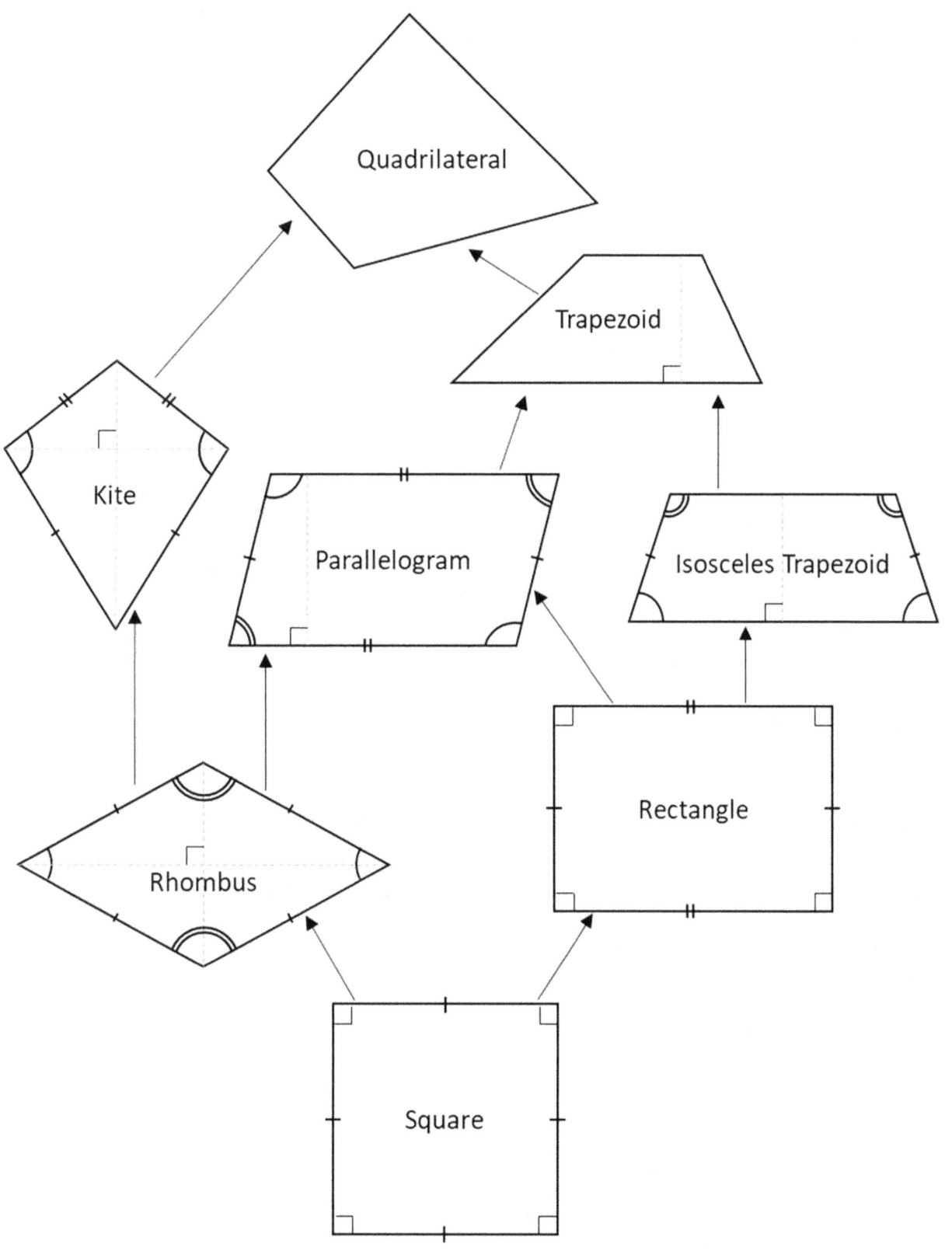

CIRCLES

The **center** of a circle is the single point from which every point on the circle is **equidistant**. The **radius** is a line segment that joins the center of the circle and any one point on the circle. All radii of a circle are equal. Circles that have the same center but not the same length of radii are **concentric**. The **diameter** is a line segment that passes through the center of the circle and has both endpoints on the circle. The length of the diameter is exactly twice the length of the radius. Point O in the diagram below is the center of the circle, segments $\overline{OX}$, $\overline{OY}$, and $\overline{OZ}$ are radii; and segment $\overline{XZ}$ is a diameter.

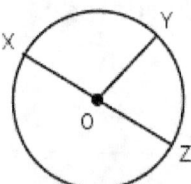

> **Review Video: Points of a Circle**
> Visit mometrix.com/academy and enter code: 420746
>
> **Review Video: Diameter, Radius, and Circumference**
> Visit mometrix.com/academy and enter code: 448988

The **area of a circle** is found by the formula $A = \pi r^2$, where r is the length of the radius. If the diameter of the circle is given, remember to divide it in half to get the length of the radius before proceeding.

The **circumference** of a circle is found by the formula $C = 2\pi r$, where r is the radius. Again, remember to convert the diameter if you are given that measure rather than the radius.

> **Review Video: Area and Circumference of a Circle**
> Visit mometrix.com/academy and enter code: 243015

INSCRIBED AND CIRCUMSCRIBED FIGURES

These terms can both be used to describe a given arrangement of figures, depending on perspective. If each of the vertices of figure A lie on figure B, then it can be said that figure A is **inscribed** in figure B, but it can also be said that figure B is **circumscribed** about figure A. The following table and examples help to illustrate the concept. Note that the figures cannot both be circles, as they would be completely overlapping and neither would be inscribed or circumscribed.

Given	Description	Equivalent Description	Figures
Each of the sides of a pentagon is tangent to a circle	The circle is inscribed in the pentagon	The pentagon is circumscribed about the circle	
Each of the vertices of a pentagon lie on a circle	The pentagon is inscribed in the circle	The circle is circumscribed about the pentagon	

3D SHAPES

SOLIDS

The **surface area of a solid object** is the area of all sides or exterior surfaces. For objects such as prisms and pyramids, a further distinction is made between base surface area (B) and lateral surface area (LA). For a prism, the total surface area (SA) is $SA = LA + 2B$. For a pyramid or cone, the total surface area is $SA = LA + B$.

The **surface area of a sphere** can be found by the formula $A = 4\pi r^2$, where r is the radius. The volume is given by the formula $V = \frac{4}{3}\pi r^3$, where r is the radius. Both quantities are generally given in terms of π.

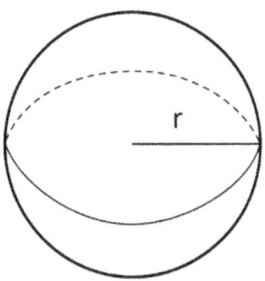

Review Video: Volume and Surface Area of a Sphere
Visit mometrix.com/academy and enter code: 786928

Review Video: How to Calculate the Volume of 3D Objects
Visit mometrix.com/academy and enter code: 163343

The **volume of any prism** is found by the formula $V = Bh$, where B is the area of the base, and h is the height (perpendicular distance between the bases). The surface area of any prism is the sum of the areas of both bases and all sides. It can be calculated as $SA = 2B + Ph$, where P is the perimeter of the base.

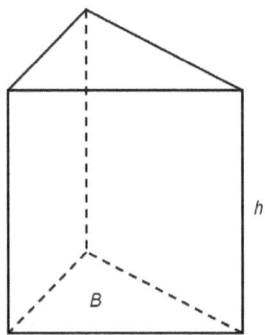

Review Video: Volume and Surface Area of a Prism
Visit mometrix.com/academy and enter code: 420158

For a **rectangular prism**, the volume can be found by the formula $V = lwh$, where V is the volume, l is the length, w is the width, and h is the height. The surface area can be calculated as $SA = 2lw + 2hl + 2wh$ or $SA = 2(lw + hl + wh)$.

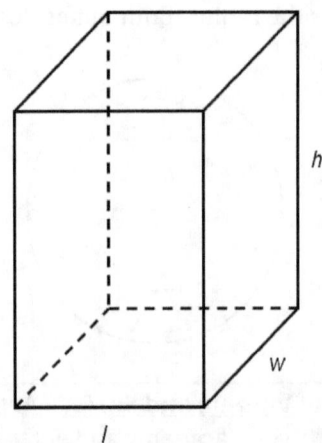

> **Review Video: Volume and Surface Area of a Rectangular Prism**
> Visit mometrix.com/academy and enter code: 282814

The **volume of a cube** can be found by the formula $V = s^3$, where s is the length of a side. The surface area of a cube is calculated as $SA = 6s^2$, where SA is the total surface area and s is the length of a side. These formulas are the same as the ones used for the volume and surface area of a rectangular prism, but simplified since all three quantities (length, width, and height) are the same.

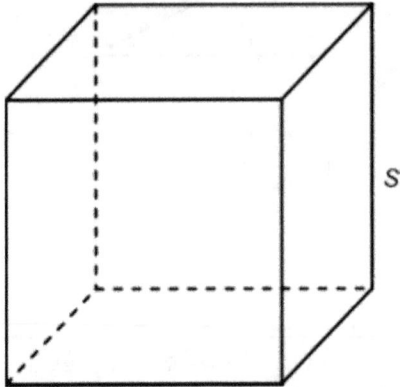

> **Review Video: Volume and Surface Area of a Cube**
> Visit mometrix.com/academy and enter code: 664455

The **volume of a cylinder** can be calculated by the formula $V = \pi r^2 h$, where r is the radius, and h is the height. The surface area of a cylinder can be found by the formula $SA = 2\pi r^2 + 2\pi rh$. The first term is the base area multiplied by two, and the second term is the perimeter of the base multiplied by the height.

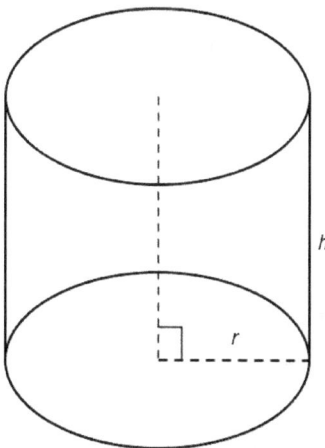

Review Video: Volume and Surface Area of a Right Circular Cylinder
Visit mometrix.com/academy and enter code: 226463

The **volume of a pyramid** is found by the formula $V = \frac{1}{3}Bh$, where B is the area of the base, and h is the height (perpendicular distance from the vertex to the base). Notice this formula is the same as $\frac{1}{3}$ times the volume of a prism. Like a prism, the base of a pyramid can be any shape.

Finding the **surface area of a pyramid** is not as simple as the other shapes we've looked at thus far. If the pyramid is a right pyramid, meaning the base is a regular polygon and the vertex is directly over the center of that polygon, the surface area can be calculated as $SA = B + \frac{1}{2}Ph_s$, where P is the perimeter of the base, and h_s is the slant height (distance from the vertex to the midpoint of one side of the base). If the pyramid is irregular, the area of each triangle side must be calculated individually and then summed, along with the base.

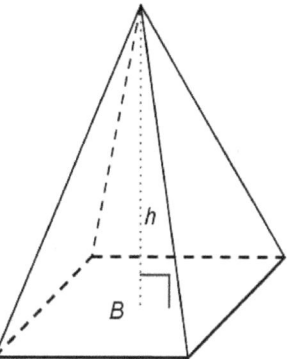

Review Video: Volume and Surface Area of a Pyramid
Visit mometrix.com/academy and enter code: 621932

The **volume of a cone** is found by the formula $V = \frac{1}{3}\pi r^2 h$, where r is the radius, and h is the height. Notice this is the same as $\frac{1}{3}$ times the volume of a cylinder. The surface area can be calculated as $SA = \pi r^2 + \pi rs$, where s

is the slant height. The slant height can be calculated using the Pythagorean theorem to be $\sqrt{r^2 + h^2}$, so the surface area formula can also be written as $SA = \pi r^2 + \pi r\sqrt{r^2 + h^2}$.

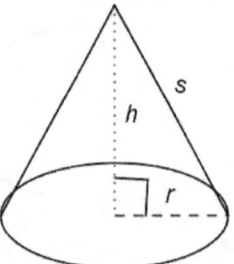

Review Video: **Volume and Surface Area of a Right Circular Cone**
Visit mometrix.com/academy and enter code: 573574

PYTHAGOREAN THEOREM

The side of a triangle opposite the right angle is called the **hypotenuse**. The other two sides are called the legs. The Pythagorean theorem states a relationship among the legs and hypotenuse of a right triangle: $(a^2 + b^2 = c^2)$, where a and b are the lengths of the legs of a right triangle, and c is the length of the hypotenuse. Note that this formula will only work with right triangles.

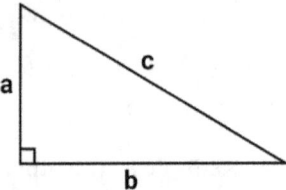

Review Video: **Pythagorean Theorem**
Visit mometrix.com/academy and enter code: 906576

Algebra

PROPORTIONS AND RATIOS

PROPORTIONS

There is a **proportion** between two variable quantities if there is a constant relationship between their products or quotients, a relationship that does not change as the quantities themselves change.

Given variable quantities x and y, we say that they are **directly proportional** (or that y **varies directly with** x) if their quotient or *ratio* is constant—that is, if there is a constant k such that $\frac{y}{x} = k$ is always true. Another way of saying this is that y is a constant multiple of x, so that $y = kx$ is always true. We call the number k the **constant of proportionality**. For example, if you drive at a constant 50 miles per hour, then the distance, y, that you travel in miles is 50 times the number of hours, x, that you drive. In symbols, $y = 50x$ miles (or $\frac{y}{x} = 50$ mph). So, the distance you travel, y, is directly proportional to (or varies directly with) the time you travel, x, with constant of proportionality $k = 50$ mph.

The quantities x and y are **inversely proportional** (or y varies inversely with x) if their product is constant—that is, if there is a constant k such that $xy = k$ is always true. Another way of saying this is to say that y is a constant multiple of the reciprocal of x so that $y = \frac{k}{x}$ is always true. For instance, suppose you drive at speed (rate) y mph for x hours, going a total of 120 miles. Since rate × time = distance, we get $xy = 120$ miles (or

$y = \frac{120}{x}$ miles per hour). Thus, your driving speed, y, is inversely proportional to (or varies inversely with) your drive time, x, with constant of proportionality $k = 120$ miles.

> **Review Video: Proportions**
> Visit mometrix.com/academy and enter code: 505355

RATIOS

A **ratio** expresses the sizes of two quantities relative to each other. For instance, suppose we have 3 copies of sheet music to share among 6 singers. We can divide the singers into groups of 2 and give each group 1 copy of the music. Thus, there is 1 copy of the music for every 2 singers, and we say that the **ratio** of sheet music to singers is 1 to 2, which we write either as a fraction $\frac{1}{2}$ or using a colon 1 : 2. Of course, it is also true there are 3 copies for every 6 singers so that the ratio of sheet music to singers is also 3 to 6, which we write as $\frac{3}{6}$ or 3 : 6. So, the ratios $\frac{1}{2}$ and $\frac{3}{6}$ express the same relative quantities of music and singers. We say that these ratios are equal or **equivalent**, and we note that ratios are equal precisely when their fractions are equal (so, in this case, $\frac{1}{2} = \frac{3}{6}$ as fractions). We can also express the quantities in the other order and say that the ratio of singers to music is $\frac{2}{1}$ or 2 : 1 (or $\frac{6}{3}$ or 6 : 3).

> **Review Video: Ratios**
> Visit mometrix.com/academy and enter code: 996914

CONSTANT OF PROPORTIONALITY

If variable quantities x and y are proportional and we know a pair of corresponding values for them, then we can find their constant of proportionality. If they are directly proportional, we use the formula $\frac{y}{x} = k$. If they are inversely proportional, we use the formula $xy = k$

Example: The cost in dollars, y, of buying fence posts is directly proportional to the number, x, that you buy. If it costs $51 to buy 17 fence posts, what is the constant of proportionality? Because of direct proportionality, we know that $\frac{y}{x} = k$. Since this works for every pair of corresponding x- and y-values, it also works for $x = 17$ and $y = 51$. This gives us $\frac{51}{17} = k$, which simplifies to $k = 3$. Note also that this is the unit price, namely $3 per fence post.

WORK/UNIT RATE

Unit rate expresses a quantity of one thing in terms of one unit of another. For example, if you travel 30 miles every two hours, a unit rate expresses this comparison in terms of one hour: in one hour you travel 15 miles, so your unit rate is 15 miles per hour. Other examples are how much one ounce of food costs (price per ounce) or figuring out how much one egg costs out of the dozen (price per 1 egg, instead of price per 12 eggs). The denominator of a unit rate is always 1. Unit rates are used to compare different situations to solve problems. For example, to make sure you get the best deal when deciding which kind of soda to buy, you can find the unit rate of each. If soda #1 costs $1.50 for a 1-liter bottle, and soda #2 costs $2.75 for a 2-liter bottle, it would be a better deal to buy soda #2, because its unit rate is only $1.375 per 1-liter, which is cheaper than soda #1. Unit rates can also help determine the length of time a given event will take. For example, if you can paint 2 rooms in 4.5 hours, you can determine how long it will take you to paint 5 rooms by solving for the unit rate per room and then multiplying that by 5.

> **Review Video: Rates and Unit Rates**
> Visit mometrix.com/academy and enter code: 185363

CROSS MULTIPLICATION
FINDING AN UNKNOWN IN EQUIVALENT EXPRESSIONS

It is often necessary to apply information given about a rate or proportion to a new scenario. For example, if you know that Jedha can run a marathon (26.2 miles) in 3 hours, how long would it take her to run 10 miles at the same pace? Start by setting up equivalent expressions:

$$\frac{26.2 \text{ mi}}{3 \text{ hr}} = \frac{10 \text{ mi}}{x \text{ hr}}$$

Now, cross multiply and solve for x:

$$26.2x = 30$$
$$x = \frac{30}{26.2} = \frac{15}{13.1}$$
$$x \approx 1.15 \text{ hrs } or \text{ } 1 \text{ hr } 9 \text{ min}$$

So, at this pace, Jedha could run 10 miles in about 1.15 hours or about 1 hour and 9 minutes.

> **Review Video: Cross Multiplying Fractions**
> Visit mometrix.com/academy and enter code: 893904

LINEAR EXPRESSIONS
TERMS AND COEFFICIENTS

Mathematical expressions consist of a combination of one or more values arranged in terms that are added together. As such, an expression could be just a single number, including zero. A **variable term** is the product of a real number, also called a **coefficient**, and one or more variables, each of which may be raised to an exponent. Expressions may also include numbers without a variable, called **constants** or **constant terms**. The expression $6s^2$, for example, is a single term where the coefficient is the real number 6 and the variable term is s^2. Note that if a term is written as simply a variable to some exponent, like t^2, then the coefficient is 1, because $t^2 = 1t^2$.

LINEAR EXPRESSIONS

A **single variable linear expression** is the sum of a single variable term, where the variable has no exponent, and a constant, which may be zero. For instance, the expression $2w + 7$ has $2w$ as the variable term and 7 as the constant term. It is important to realize that terms are separated by addition or subtraction. Since an expression is a sum of terms, expressions such as $5x - 3$ can be written as $5x + (-3)$ to emphasize that the constant term is negative. A real-world example of a single variable linear expression is the perimeter of a square, four times the side length, often expressed: $4s$.

In general, a **linear expression** is the sum of any number of variable terms so long as none of the variables have an exponent and none of the terms have two variables multiplied together. For example, $3m + 8n - \frac{1}{4}p + 5.5q - 1$ is a linear expression, but $3y^3$ and $5xy$ are not. In the same way, the expression for the perimeter of a general triangle $(a + b + c)$ is linear, but the expression for the area of a square (s^2) is not.

SLOPE
FINDING SLOPE GIVEN GRAPH OR TABLE

On a graph with two points, (x_1, y_1) and (x_2, y_2), the **slope** is found with the formula $m = \frac{y_2 - y_1}{x_2 - x_1}$; where $x_1 \neq x_2$ and m stands for slope. If the value of the slope is **positive**, the line has an *upward direction* from left to right. If the value of the slope is **negative**, the line has a *downward direction* from left to right. Consider the following example:

A new book goes on sale in bookstores and online stores. In the first month, 5,000 copies of the book are sold. Over time, the book continues to grow in popularity. The data for the number of copies sold is in the table below.

# of Months on Sale	1	2	3	4	5
# of Copies Sold (In Thousands)	5	10	15	20	25

So, the number of copies that are sold and the time that the book is on sale is a proportional relationship. In this example, an equation can be used to show the data: $y = 5x$, where x is the number of months that the book is on sale. Also, y is the number of copies sold. So, the slope of the corresponding line is $\frac{\text{rise}}{\text{run}} = \frac{5}{1} = 5$.

FINDING SLOPE GIVEN AN EQUATION

When given an equation of a line, it is necessary to solve for y to determine the slope of the line. Given the equation $6x + 2y = 8$, find the slope. First, subtract $6x$ from both sides of the equation, resulting in $2y = -6x + 8$. Then divide both sides of the equation by 2, resulting in $y = -3x + 4$. This then allows us to conclude that the slope of the line is $m = -3$, the coefficient of x. Once an equation is in the form $y = mx + b$, the slope and y-intercept can easily be determined. For this reason, we refer to the equation $y = mx + b$ as "slope-intercept form" of the equation of a line.

> **Review Video: Finding the Slope of a Line**
> Visit mometrix.com/academy and enter code: 766664

LINEAR EQUATIONS

Equations like $5x = 100$ and $8x - 120 = 200$ and $6x + 4y = 240$ are **linear equations**. Linear equations are named based off the number of distinct variables they include. For example, the equation $3x + 30 = 8x$ is a **one-variable linear equation** because it involves only the single variable x. It does not matter that x appears more than once. Any equations that can be written as $ax + b = 0$, where $a \neq 0$, falls into this category. Furthermore, the equation $3x - 5y = 14 + 9y$ is a **two-variable linear equation** because it involves the two variables x and y. The equation $7x + 8y - 12z + 14w = 56$ is a linear equation in four variables.

SATISFYING THE EQUATION

When given a one-variable linear equation, the goal is typically to solve it. This means that we want to find the number that makes the equation true if we substitute it for the variable. That number is the **solution,** or root, of the equation. For instance, the equation $5x = 10$ has the solution $x = 2$. This is true because when 2 is substituted for x, the result is $5 \cdot 2 = 10$, which is true. On the other hand, $x = 6$ can not be a solution because $5 \cdot 6 \neq 10$, so it is false. Two equations with the same solution are **equivalent equations**. For example, the equations $5x = 10$ and $5x + 3 = 13$ are equivalent because both have the same solution of $x = 2$.

DETERMINING A SOLUTION SET

The **solution set** is the set of all solutions of an equation. In the previous example, the solution set would be 2. Solutions to a linear equation in two variables consist of pairs of numbers. For instance, the equation $6x + 4y = 240$ has the solution $x = 20$ and $y = 30$ since $6 \cdot 20 + 4 \cdot 30 = 240$ is true. We can write this solution as the ordered pair (20,30) and plot it as a point on the coordinate plane. Such equations usually have infinitely many solutions; and if we plot the points for all these solutions we get a line, which is a picture of all the solutions. We call this **graphing the equation**. When an equation has no true solutions, it is referred to as an **empty set**.

LINEAR EQUATION FORMS

Linear equations can be written many ways. Below is a list of some forms linear equations can take:

- **Standard Form**: $Ax + By = C$; the slope is $\frac{-A}{B}$ and the y-intercept is $\frac{C}{B}$

- **Slope Intercept Form**: $y = mx + b$, where m is the slope and b is the y-intercept
- **Point-Slope Form**: $y - y_1 = m(x - x_1)$, where m is the slope and (x_1, y_1) is a point on the line
- **Two-Point Form**: $\frac{y - y_1}{x - x_1} = \frac{y_2 - y_1}{x_2 - x_1}$, where (x_1, y_1) and (x_2, y_2) are two points on the given line
- **Intercept Form**: $\frac{x}{x_1} + \frac{y}{y_1} = 1$, where $(x_1, 0)$ is the point at which a line intersects the x-axis, and $(0, y_1)$ is the point at which the same line intersects the y-axis

> **Review Video: Slope-Intercept and Point-Slope Forms**
> Visit mometrix.com/academy and enter code: 113216
>
> **Review Video: Converting Between Standard and Slope-Intercept Forms**
> Visit mometrix.com/academy and enter code: 982828
>
> **Review Video: Linear Equations Basics**
> Visit mometrix.com/academy and enter code: 793005

SOLVING EQUATIONS
MANIPULATING EQUATIONS
LIKE TERMS

Like terms are terms in an equation that have the same variable, regardless of whether they also have the same coefficient. This includes terms that *lack* a variable; all constants (i.e., numbers without variables) are considered like terms. If the equation involves terms with a variable raised to different powers, the like terms are those that have the variable raised to the same power.

For example, consider the equation $x^2 + 3x + 2 = 2x^2 + x - 7 + 2x$. In this equation, 2 and –7 are like terms; they are both constants. The terms $3x$, x, and $2x$ are like terms, they all include the variable x raised to the first power. The terms x^2 and $2x^2$ are like terms, they both include the variable x, raised to the second power. The terms $2x$ and $2x^2$ are not like terms; although they both involve the variable x, the variable is not raised to the same power in both terms. The fact that they have the same coefficient, 2, is not relevant.

> **Review Video: Rules for Manipulating Equations**
> Visit mometrix.com/academy and enter code: 838871

CARRYING OUT THE SAME OPERATION ON BOTH SIDES OF AN EQUATION

When solving an equation, the general procedure is to carry out a series of operations on both sides of an equation, choosing operations that simplify the equation when doing so. The reason why the same operation must be carried out on both sides of the equation is because that leaves the meaning of the equation unchanged, and yields a result that is equivalent to the original equation. This would not be the case if we carried out an operation on one side of an equation and not the other. Consider what an equation means: it is a statement that two values or expressions are equal. If we carry out the same operation on both sides of the equation—add 3 to both sides, for example—then the two sides of the equation are changed in the same way, and so remain equal. If we do that to only one side of the equation—add 3 to one side but not the other—then that wouldn't be true; if we change one side of the equation but not the other then the two sides are no longer equal.

COMBINING LIKE TERMS

Combining like terms refers to adding or subtracting like terms—terms with the same variable—and therefore reducing sets of like terms to a single term. The main advantage of doing this is that it simplifies the equation. Often, combining like terms can be done as the first step in solving an equation, though it can also be done later, such as after distributing terms in a product.

For example, consider the equation $2(x + 3) + 3(2 + x + 3) = -4$. The 2 and the 3 in the second set of parentheses are like terms, and we can combine them, yielding $2(x + 3) + 3(x + 5) = -4$. Now we can carry out the multiplications implied by the parentheses, distributing the outer 2 and 3 accordingly: $2x + 6 + 3x + 15 = -4$. The $2x$ and the $3x$ are like terms, and we can add them together: $5x + 6 + 15 = -4$. Now, the constants 6, 15, and –4 are also like terms, and we can combine them as well: subtracting 6 and 15 from both sides of the equation, we get $5x = -4 - 6 - 15$, or $5x = -25$, which simplifies further to $x = -5$.

> **Review Video: Solving Equations by Combining Like Terms**
> Visit mometrix.com/academy and enter code: 668506

CANCELING TERMS ON OPPOSITE SIDES OF AN EQUATION

Two terms on opposite sides of an equation can be canceled if and only if they *exactly* match each other. They must have the same variable raised to the same power and the same coefficient. For example, in the equation $3x + 2x^2 + 6 = 2x^2 - 6$, $2x^2$ appears on both sides of the equation and can be canceled, leaving $3x + 6 = -6$. The 6 on each side of the equation *cannot* be canceled, because it is added on one side of the equation and subtracted on the other. While they cannot be canceled, however, the 6 and -6 are like terms and can be combined, yielding $3x = -12$, which simplifies further to $x = -4$.

It's also important to note that the terms to be canceled must be independent terms and cannot be part of a larger term. For example, consider the equation $2(x + 6) = 3(x + 4) + 1$. We cannot cancel the x's, because even though they match each other they are part of the larger terms $2(x + 6)$ and $3(x + 4)$. We must first distribute the 2 and 3, yielding $2x + 12 = 3x + 12 + 1$. Now we see that the terms with the x's do not match, but the 12s do, and can be canceled, leaving $2x = 3x + 1$, which simplifies to $x = -1$.

ISOLATING VARIABLES

To isolate a variable means to manipulate the equation so that the variable appears by itself on one side of the equation, and does not appear at all on the other side. Generally, an equation or inequality is considered to be solved once the variable is isolated and the other side of the equation or inequality is simplified as much as possible. In the case of a two-variable equation or inequality, only one variable needs to be isolated; it will not usually be possible to simultaneously isolate both variables.

For a linear equation—an equation in which the variable only appears raised to the first power—isolating a variable can be done by first moving all the terms with the variable to one side of the equation and all other terms to the other side. (*Moving* a term really means adding the inverse of the term to both sides; when a term is *moved* to the other side of the equation its sign is flipped.) Then combine like terms on each side. Finally, divide both sides by the coefficient of the variable, if applicable. The steps need not necessarily be done in this order, but this order will always work.

> **Review Video: Solving Equations for Specific Variables**
> Visit mometrix.com/academy and enter code: 130695
>
> **Review Video: Solving Equations Involving Algebraic Fractions**
> Visit mometrix.com/academy and enter code: 237770
>
> **Review Video: Solving One-Step Equations**
> Visit mometrix.com/academy and enter code: 777004

SOLVING ONE-VARIABLE LINEAR EQUATIONS
EQUATIONS WITH ONE SOLUTION (THE USUAL CASE)

To solve a one-variable linear equation, we use the techniques above to isolate the variable.

1. If any coefficients or constants are fractions, it is often helpful first to multiply both sides of the equation by the least common denominator (of all fractions) to clear the fractions.

2. Simplify both sides of the equation by combining any like terms.
3. Put all terms with the variable on one side of the equation and all constant terms on the other side, by adding or subtracting the same terms on both sides of the equation.
4. Divide both sides by the coefficient of the variable (or multiply both sides by its reciprocal).
5. When we have a value for the variable, we can check it by substituting the value into the original equation to make sure it produces a true result.

Consider the following example for solving the equation $\frac{2}{3}x + 8 = 14$:

$3 \cdot \left(\frac{2}{3}x + 8\right) = 3 \cdot 14$ Clear fractions by multiplying both sides by 3.

$2x + 24 = 42$ Simplify, remembering to apply the distributive property.

$2x + 24 - 24 = 42 - 24$ Subtract 24 from both sides to isolate $2x$.

$2x = 18$ Simplify by combining like terms.

$\frac{2x}{2} = \frac{18}{2}$ Divide both sides by 2 to isolate x.

$x = 9$ Simplify

Finally, we check this answer by substituting $x = 9$ into the original equation to make sure we get a true result.

$$\frac{2}{3}x + 8 = \frac{2}{3}(9) + 8 = 6 + 8 = 14$$

This is correct, so the value of x is 9.

> **Review Video: Solving Equations Using the Distributive Property**
> Visit mometrix.com/academy and enter code: 765499

EQUATIONS WITH MORE THAN ONE SOLUTION

Some types of non-linear equations, such as equations involving squares of variables, may have more than one solution. For example, the equation $x^2 = 4$ has two solutions: 2 and –2. Equations with absolute values can also have multiple solutions: $|x| = 1$ has the solutions $x = 1$ and $x = -1$.

It is possible for a linear equation to have more than one solution but only if the equation is true regardless of the value of the variable. We call such an equation an **identity**. In this case, the equation has infinitely many solutions, because every possible value of the variable is a solution. We discover that a linear equation is an identity when our attempts to isolate the variable cause the variable to disappear, leaving a *true* equation involving only constants. For example, consider the equation $2(3x + 5) = x + 5(x + 2)$. Distributing, we get $6x + 10 = x + 5x + 10$; combining like terms gives $6x + 10 = 6x + 10$, and the $6x$-terms cancel to leave $10 = 10$. This is clearly true, so the original equation is an identity. We could also cancel the 10's leaving $0 = 0$, which is also is clearly true—in general if both sides of the equation can be reduced to match one another exactly, the original equation is an identity.

EQUATIONS WITH NO SOLUTION

Some types of non-linear equations, such as equations involving squares of variables, may have no solution. For example, the equation $x^2 = -2$ has no solutions in the real numbers because the square of a real number must be positive. Similarly, $|x| = -1$ has no solution because the absolute value of a number is always positive.

It is also possible for a linear equation to have no solution. We call such an equation a **contradiction**. We discover that a linear equation is a contradiction when our attempts to isolate the variable cause the variable to disappear, leaving a *false* equation involving only constants. For example, the equation $2(x + 3) + x = 3x$

has no solution. We can see this by trying to solve it: first we distribute, leaving $2x + 6 + x = 3x$. Combining like terms gives us $3x + 6 = 3x$, and cancelling the term $3x$ on both sides leaves us with $6 = 0$. This is clearly false, so the original equation is a contradiction, having no solutions.

FEATURES OF EQUATIONS THAT REQUIRE SPECIAL TREATMENT

A linear equation is an equation in which variables only appear by themselves: not multiplied together, not with exponents other than one, and not inside absolute value signs or any other functions. For example, the equation $x + 1 - 3x = 5 - x$ is a linear equation; while x appears multiple times, it never appears with an exponent other than one, or inside any function. The two-variable equation $2x - 3y = 5 + 2x$ is also a linear equation. In contrast, the equation $x^2 - 5 = 3x$ is *not* a linear equation, because it involves the term x^2. The equation $\sqrt{x} = 5$ is not linear, because it involves a square root. The equation $(x - 1)^2 = 4$ is not linear because even though there's no exponent on the x directly, it appears as part of an expression that is squared. The two-variable equation $x + xy - y = 5$ is not linear because it includes the term xy, where two variables are multiplied together.

As we see above, linear equations can always be solved (or shown to have no solution) by combining like terms and performing simple operations on both sides of the equation. Some non-linear equations can be solved by similar methods, but others may require more advanced methods of solution, if they can be solved analytically at all.

SOLVING EQUATIONS INVOLVING ROOTS

In an equation involving roots, the first step is to isolate the term with the root, if possible, and then raise both sides of the equation to the appropriate power to eliminate it. Consider an example equation, $2\sqrt{x + 1} - 1 = 3$. In this case, begin by adding 1 to both sides, yielding $2\sqrt{x + 1} = 4$, and then dividing both sides by 2, yielding $\sqrt{x + 1} = 2$. Now square both sides, yielding $x + 1 = 4$. Finally, subtracting 1 from both sides yields $x = 3$.

Squaring both sides of an equation (or raising both sides to any *even* power) may, however, yield a spurious solution—a solution to the squared equation that is *not* a solution of the original equation. It's therefore necessary to plug the solution back into the original equation to make sure it works. In this case, it does: $2\sqrt{3 + 1} - 1 = 2\sqrt{4} - 1 = 2(2) - 1 = 4 - 1 = 3$.

The same procedure applies for other roots as well. For example, given the equation $3 + \sqrt[3]{2x} = 5$, we can first subtract 3 from both sides, yielding $\sqrt[3]{2x} = 2$ and isolating the root. Raising both sides to the third power yields $2x = 2^3$; i.e., $2x = 8$. We can now divide both sides by 2 to get $x = 4$.

> **Review Video: Solving Equations Involving Roots**
> Visit mometrix.com/academy and enter code: 297670

SOLVING EQUATIONS WITH EXPONENTS

In solving an equation with powers of a variable, sometimes it is possible to eliminate all but one term involving the variable. In that case, we can isolate the power of the variable and then take the appropriate root of both sides to eliminate the exponent. For instance, for the equation $2x^3 + 17 = 5x^3 - 7$, we can subtract $5x^3$ from both sides to get $-3x^3 + 17 = -7$, and then subtract 17 from both sides to get $-3x^3 = -24$. Finally, we can divide both sides by -3 to get $x^3 = 8$. Since this isolates the cube of the variable, we can take the cube root of both sides to get $x = \sqrt[3]{8} = 2$.

One important but often overlooked point is that equations with an exponent greater than 1 may have more than one answer. The solution to $x^2 = 9$ isn't simply $x = 3$; it's $x = \pm 3$ (that is, $x = 3$ or $x = -3$). For a slightly more complicated example, consider the equation $(x - 1)^2 - 1 = 3$. Adding 1 to both sides yields $(x - 1)^2 = 4$; taking the square root of both sides yields $x - 1 = 2$. We can then add 1 to both sides to get $x = 3$. However, there's a second solution. We also have the possibility that $x - 1 = -2$, in which case $x = -1$. Both $x = 3$ and $x = -1$ are valid solutions, as can be verified by substituting them both into the original equation.

> **Review Video: Solving Equations with Exponents**
> Visit mometrix.com/academy and enter code: 514557
>
> **Review Video: Adding and Subtracting with Exponents**
> Visit mometrix.com/academy and enter code: 875756

SOLVING EQUATIONS WITH ABSOLUTE VALUES

When solving an equation with an absolute value, the first step is to isolate the absolute value term. We then consider two possibilities: when the expression inside the absolute value is positive or when it is negative. In the former case, the expression in the absolute value equals the expression on the other side of the equation; in the latter, it equals the additive inverse of that expression—the expression times negative one. We consider each case separately and finally check for spurious solutions.

For instance, consider solving $|2x - 1| + x = 5$ for x. We can first isolate the absolute value by moving the x to the other side: $|2x - 1| = -x + 5$. Now, we have two possibilities. First, that $2x - 1$ is positive, and hence $2x - 1 = -x + 5$. Rearranging and combining like terms yields $3x = 6$, and hence $x = 2$. The other possibility is that $2x - 1$ is negative, and hence $2x - 1 = -(-x + 5) = x - 5$. In this case, rearranging and combining like terms yields $x = -4$. Substituting $x = 2$ and $x = -4$ back into the original equation, we see that they are both valid solutions.

Note that the absolute value of a sum or difference applies to the sum or difference as a whole, not to the individual terms; in general, $|2x - 1|$ is not equal to $|2x + 1|$ or to $|2x| - 1$.

> **Review Video: Solving Absolute Value Equations**
> Visit mometrix.com/academy and enter code: 501208

EXTRANEOUS SOLUTIONS

An **extraneous solution** may arise when we square both sides of an equation (or raise both sides to an even power) as a step in solving it or under certain other operations on the equation. It is a solution to the squared or otherwise modified equation that is *not* a solution of the original equation. To identify an extraneous solution, it's useful when you solve an equation involving roots or absolute values to plug the solution back into the original equation to make sure it's valid.

TWO-VARIABLE EQUATIONS

Similar to methods for a one-variable equation, solving a two-variable equation involves isolating a variable: manipulating the equation so that a variable appears by itself on one side of the equation, and not at all on the other side. However, in a two-variable equation, you will usually only be able to isolate one of the variables; the other variable may appear on the other side along with constant terms, or with exponents or other functions. If an equation has multiple variables, the problem should tell you which variable to isolate.

> **Review Video: Solving Equations with Variables on Both Sides**
> Visit mometrix.com/academy and enter code: 402497

GRAPHING EQUATIONS
GRAPHICAL SOLUTIONS TO EQUATIONS

When equations are shown graphically, they are usually shown on a **Cartesian coordinate plane**. The Cartesian coordinate plane consists of two number lines placed perpendicular to each other and intersecting at the zero point, also known as the origin. The horizontal number line is known as the x-axis, with positive values to the right of the origin, and negative values to the left of the origin. The vertical number line is known as the y-axis, with positive values above the origin, and negative values below the origin. Any point on the plane can be identified by an ordered pair in the form (x, y), called coordinates. The x-value of the coordinate is called the abscissa, and the y-value of the coordinate is called the ordinate. The two number lines divide the plane into **four quadrants**: I, II, III, and IV.

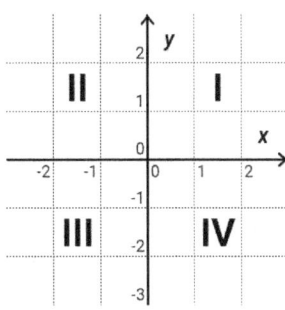

Note that in quadrant I $x > 0$ and $y > 0$, in quadrant II $x < 0$ and $y > 0$, in quadrant III $x < 0$ and $y < 0$, and in quadrant IV $x > 0$ and $y < 0$.

Recall that if the value of the slope of a line is positive, the line slopes upward from left to right. If the value of the slope is negative, the line slopes downward from left to right. If the y-coordinates are the same for two points on a line, the slope is 0 and the line is a **horizontal line**. If the x-coordinates are the same for two points on a line, there is no slope and the line is a **vertical line**. Two or more lines that have equivalent slopes are **parallel lines**. **Perpendicular lines** have slopes that are negative reciprocals of each other, such as $\frac{a}{b}$ and $\frac{-b}{a}$.

> **Review Video: Cartesian Coordinate Plane and Graphing**
> Visit mometrix.com/academy and enter code: 115173

GRAPHING EQUATIONS IN TWO VARIABLES

One way of graphing an equation in two variables is to plot enough points to get an idea for its shape and then draw the appropriate curve through those points. A point can be plotted by substituting in a value for one variable and solving for the other. If the equation is linear, we only need two points and can then draw a straight line between them.

For example, consider the equation $y = 2x - 1$. This is a linear equation—both variables only appear raised to the first power—so we only need two points. When $x = 0$, $y = 2(0) - 1 = -1$. When $x = 2$, $y = 2(2) - 1 = 3$. We can therefore choose the points $(0, -1)$ and $(2, 3)$, and draw a line between them:

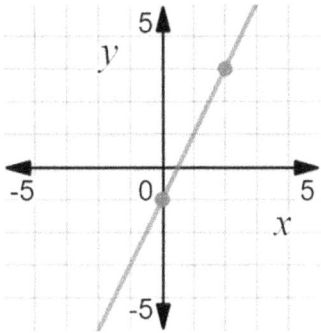

INEQUALITIES

Commonly in algebra and other upper-level fields of math you find yourself working with mathematical expressions that do not equal each other. The statement comparing such expressions with symbols such as < (less than) or > (greater than) is called an *inequality*. An example of an inequality is $7x > 5$. To solve for x, simply divide both sides by 7 and the solution is shown to be $x > \frac{5}{7}$. Graphs of the solution set of inequalities are represented on a number line. Open circles are used to show that an expression approaches a number but is never quite equal to that number.

> **Review Video: Solving One-Step Inequalities**
> Visit mometrix.com/academy and enter code: 229684
>
> **Review Video: Solving Multi-Step Inequalities**
> Visit mometrix.com/academy and enter code: 347842
>
> **Review Video: Solving Inequalities Using All 4 Basic Operations**
> Visit mometrix.com/academy and enter code: 401111

TYPES OF INEQUALITIES

Conditional inequalities are those with certain values for the variable that will make the condition true and other values for the variable where the condition will be false. **Absolute inequalities** can have any real number as the value for the variable to make the condition true, while there is no real number value for the variable that will make the condition false. Solving inequalities is done by following the same rules for solving equations with the exception that when multiplying or dividing by a negative number the direction of the inequality sign must be flipped or reversed. **Double inequalities** are situations where two inequality statements apply to the same variable expression. Example: $-c < ax + b < c$.

> **Review Video: Conditional and Absolute Inequalities**
> Visit mometrix.com/academy and enter code: 980164

SOLVING INEQUALITIES

DETERMINING SOLUTIONS TO INEQUALITIES

To determine whether a coordinate is a solution of an inequality, you can substitute the values of the coordinate into the inequality, simplify, and check whether the resulting statement holds true. For instance, to determine whether $(-2,4)$ is a solution of the inequality $y \geq -2x + 3$, substitute the values into the inequality, $4 \geq -2(-2) + 3$. Simplify the right side of the inequality and the result is $4 \geq 7$, which is a false statement. Therefore, the coordinate is not a solution of the inequality. You can also use this method to determine which part of the graph of an inequality is shaded. The graph of $y \geq -2x + 3$ includes the solid line $y = -2x + 3$ and, since it excludes the point $(-2,4)$ to the left of the line, it is shaded to the right of the line.

> **Review Video: Graphing Linear Inequalities**
> Visit mometrix.com/academy and enter code: 439421
>
> **Review Video: Graphing Solutions to Inequalities**
> Visit mometrix.com/academy and enter code: 391281

FLIPPING INEQUALITY SIGNS

When given an inequality, we can always turn the entire inequality around, swapping the two sides of the inequality and changing the inequality sign. For instance, $x + 2 > 2x - 3$ is equivalent to $2x - 3 < x + 2$. Aside from that, normally the inequality does not change if we carry out the same operation on both sides of the inequality. There is, however, one principal exception: if we *multiply* or *divide* both sides of the inequality by a *negative number*, the inequality is flipped. For example, if we take the inequality $-2x < 6$ and divide both sides by -2, the inequality flips and we are left with $x > -3$. This *only* applies to multiplication and division, and only with negative numbers. Multiplying or dividing both sides by a positive number, or adding or subtracting any number regardless of sign, does not flip the inequality. Another special case that flips the inequality sign is when reciprocals are used. For instance, $3 > 2$ but the relation of the reciprocals is $\frac{1}{3} < \frac{1}{2}$.

COMPOUND INEQUALITIES

A **compound inequality** is an equality that consists of two inequalities combined with *and* or *or*. The two components of a proper compound inequality must be of opposite type: that is, one must be greater than (or greater than or equal to), the other less than (or less than or equal to). For instance, "$x + 1 < 2$ or $x + 1 > 3$" is a compound inequality, as is "$2x \geq 4$ and $2x \leq 6$." An *and* inequality can be written more compactly by having one inequality on each side of the common part: "$2x \geq 1$ and $2x \leq 6$," can also be written as $1 \leq 2x \leq 6$.

In order for the compound inequality to be meaningful, the two parts of an *and* inequality must overlap; otherwise, no numbers satisfy the inequality. On the other hand, if the two parts of an *or* inequality overlap, then *all* numbers satisfy the inequality and as such the inequality is usually not meaningful.

Solving a compound inequality requires solving each part separately. For example, given the compound inequality "$x + 1 < 2$ or $x + 1 > 3$," the first inequality, $x + 1 < 2$, reduces to $x < 1$, and the second part, $x + 1 > 3$, reduces to $x > 2$, so the whole compound inequality can be written as "$x < 1$ or $x > 2$." Similarly, $1 \leq 2x \leq 6$ can be solved by dividing each term by 2, yielding $\frac{1}{2} \leq x \leq 3$.

> **Review Video: Compound Inequalities**
> Visit mometrix.com/academy and enter code: 786318

SOLVING INEQUALITIES INVOLVING ABSOLUTE VALUES

To solve an inequality involving an absolute value, first isolate the term with the absolute value. Then proceed to treat the two cases separately as with an absolute value equation, but flipping the inequality in the case where the expression in the absolute value is negative (since that essentially involves multiplying both sides by -1.) The two cases are then combined into a compound inequality; if the absolute value is on the greater side of the inequality, then it is an *or* compound inequality, if on the lesser side, then it's an *and*.

Consider the inequality $2 + |x - 1| \geq 3$. We can isolate the absolute value term by subtracting 2 from both sides: $|x - 1| \geq 1$. Now, we're left with the two cases $x - 1 \geq 1$ or $x - 1 \leq -1$: note that in the latter, negative case, the inequality is flipped. $x - 1 \geq 1$ reduces to $x \geq 2$, and $x - 1 \leq -1$ reduces to $x \leq 0$. Since in the inequality $|x - 1| \geq 1$ the absolute value is on the greater side, the two cases combine into an *or* compound inequality, so the final, solved inequality is "$x \leq 0$ or $x \geq 2$."

> **Review Video: Solving Absolute Value Inequalities**
> Visit mometrix.com/academy and enter code: 997008

SOLVING INEQUALITIES INVOLVING SQUARE ROOTS

Solving an inequality with a square root involves two parts. First, we solve the inequality as if it were an equation, isolating the square root and then squaring both sides of the equation. Second, we restrict the solution to the set of values of x for which the value inside the square root sign is non-negative.

For example, in the inequality, $\sqrt{x - 2} + 1 < 5$, we can isolate the square root by subtracting 1 from both sides, yielding $\sqrt{x - 2} < 4$. Squaring both sides of the inequality yields $x - 2 < 16$, so $x < 18$. Since we can't take the square root of a negative number, we also require the part inside the square root to be non-negative. In this case, that means $x - 2 \geq 0$. Adding 2 to both sides of the inequality yields $x \geq 2$. Our final answer is a compound inequality combining the two simple inequalities: $x \geq 2$ and $x < 18$, or $2 \leq x < 18$.

Note that we only get a compound inequality if the two simple inequalities are in opposite directions; otherwise, we take the one that is more restrictive.

The same technique can be used for other even roots, such as fourth roots. It is *not*, however, used for cube roots or other odd roots—negative numbers *do* have cube roots, so the condition that the quantity inside the root sign cannot be negative does not apply.

> **Review Video: Solving Inequalities Involving Square Roots**
> Visit mometrix.com/academy and enter code: 800288

SPECIAL CIRCUMSTANCES

Sometimes an inequality involving an absolute value or an even exponent is true for all values of x, and we don't need to do any further work to solve it. This is true if the inequality, once the absolute value or exponent term is isolated, says that term is greater than a negative number (or greater than or equal to zero). Since an absolute value or a number raised to an even exponent is *always* non-negative, this inequality is always true.

GRAPHING INEQUALITIES
GRAPHING SIMPLE INEQUALITIES

To graph a simple inequality, we first mark on the number line the value that signifies the end point of the inequality. If the inequality is strict (involves a less than or greater than), we use a hollow circle; if it is not strict (less than or equal to or greater than or equal to), we use a solid circle. We then fill in the part of the number line that satisfies the inequality: to the left of the marked point for less than (or less than or equal to), to the right for greater than (or greater than or equal to).

For example, we would graph the inequality $x < 5$ by putting a hollow circle at 5 and filling in the part of the line to the left:

GRAPHING COMPOUND INEQUALITIES

To graph a compound inequality, we fill in both parts of the inequality for an *or* inequality, or the overlap between them for an *and* inequality. More specifically, we start by plotting the endpoints of each inequality on the number line. For an *or* inequality, we then fill in the appropriate side of the line for each inequality. Typically, the two component inequalities do not overlap, which means the shaded part is *outside* the two points. For an *and* inequality, we instead fill in the part of the line that meets both inequalities.

For the inequality "$x \leq -3$ or $x > 4$," we first put a solid circle at –3 and a hollow circle at 4. We then fill the parts of the line *outside* these circles:

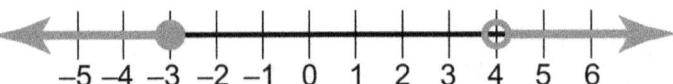

GRAPHING INEQUALITIES INCLUDING ABSOLUTE VALUES

An inequality with an absolute value can be converted to a compound inequality. To graph the inequality, first convert it to a compound inequality, and then graph that normally. If the absolute value is on the greater side of the inequality, we end up with an *or* inequality; we plot the endpoints of the inequality on the number line and fill in the part of the line *outside* those points. If the absolute value is on the smaller side of the inequality, we end up with an *and* inequality; we plot the endpoints of the inequality on the number line and fill in the part of the line *between* those points.

For example, the inequality $|x + 1| \geq 4$ can be rewritten as $x \geq 3$ or $x \leq -5$. We place solid circles at the points 3 and −5 and fill in the part of the line *outside* them:

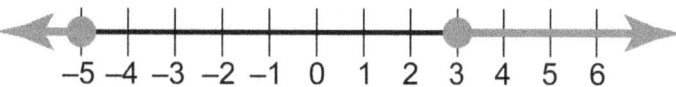

GRAPHING INEQUALITIES IN TWO VARIABLES

To graph an inequality in two variables, we first graph the border of the inequality. This means graphing the equation that we get if we replace the inequality sign with an equals sign. If the inequality is strict ($>$ or $<$), we graph the border with a dashed or dotted line; if it is not strict ($\geq$ or $\leq$), we use a solid line. We can then test any point not on the border to see if it satisfies the inequality. If it does, we shade in that side of the border; if not, we shade in the other side. As an example, consider $y > 2x + 2$. To graph this inequality, we first graph the border, $y = 2x + 2$. Since it is a strict inequality, we use a dashed line. Then, we choose a test point. This can be any point not on the border; in this case, we will choose the origin, (0,0). (This makes the calculation easy and is generally a good choice unless the border passes through the origin.) Putting this into the original inequality, we get $0 > 2(0) + 2$, i.e., $0 > 2$. This is *not* true, so we shade in the side of the border that does *not* include the point (0,0):

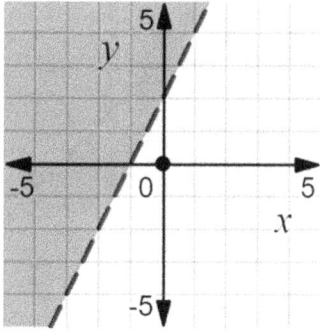

GRAPHING COMPOUND INEQUALITIES IN TWO VARIABLES

One way to graph a compound inequality in two variables is to first graph each of the component inequalities. For an *and* inequality, we then shade in only the parts where the two graphs overlap; for an *or* inequality, we shade in any region that pertains to either of the individual inequalities.

Consider the graph of "$y \geq x - 1$ and $y \leq -x$":

We first shade in the individual inequalities:

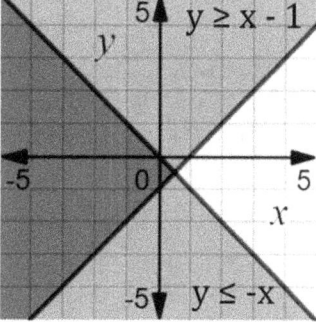

Now, since the compound inequality has an *and*, we only leave shaded the overlap—the part that pertains to *both* inequalities:

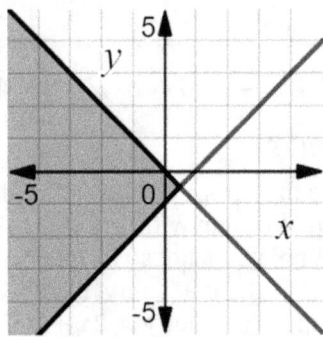

If instead the inequality had been "$y \geq x - 1$ or $y \leq -x$," our final graph would involve the *total* shaded area:

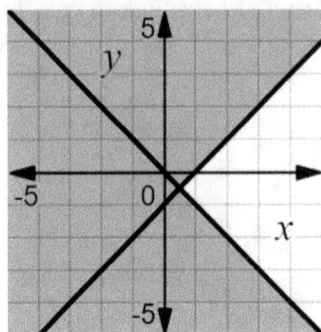

> **Review Video: Graphing Solutions to Inequalities**
> Visit mometrix.com/academy and enter code: 391281

Systems of Equations
Solving Systems of Equations

A **system of equations** is a set of simultaneous equations that all use the same variables. A solution to a system of equations must be true for each equation in the system. **Consistent systems** are those with at least one solution. **Inconsistent systems** are systems of equations that have no solution.

> **Review Video: Solving Systems of Linear Equations**
> Visit mometrix.com/academy and enter code: 746745

Substitution

To solve a system of linear equations by **substitution**, start with the easier equation and solve for one of the variables. Express this variable in terms of the other variable. Substitute this expression in the other equation and solve for the other variable. The solution should be expressed in the form (x, y). Substitute the values into both of the original equations to check your answer. Consider the following system of equations:

$$x + 6y = 15$$
$$3x - 12y = 18$$

Solving the first equation for x: $x = 15 - 6y$

Substitute this value in place of x in the second equation, and solve for y:

$$3(15 - 6y) - 12y = 18$$
$$45 - 18y - 12y = 18$$
$$30y = 27$$
$$y = \frac{27}{30} = \frac{9}{10} = 0.9$$

Plug this value for y back into the first equation to solve for x:

$$x = 15 - 6(0.9) = 15 - 5.4 = 9.6$$

Check both equations if you have time:

$$\begin{array}{ll} 9.6 + 6(0.9) = 15 & 3(9.6) - 12(0.9) = 18 \\ 9.6 + 5.4 = 15 & 28.8 - 10.8 = 18 \\ 15 = 15 & 18 = 18 \end{array}$$

Therefore, the solution is (9.6, 0.9).

> **Review Video: The Substitution Method**
> Visit mometrix.com/academy and enter code: 565151
>
> **Review Video: Substitution and Elimination**
> Visit mometrix.com/academy and enter code: 958611

ELIMINATION

To solve a system of equations using **elimination**, begin by rewriting both equations in standard form $Ax + By = C$. Check to see if the coefficients of one pair of like variables add to zero. If not, multiply one or both of the equations by a non-zero number to make one set of like variables add to zero. Add the two equations to solve for one of the variables. Substitute this value into one of the original equations to solve for the other variable. Check your work by substituting into the other equation. Now, let's look at solving the following system using the elimination method:

$$5x + 6y = 4$$
$$x + 2y = 4$$

If we multiply the second equation by -3, we can eliminate the y-terms:

$$5x + 6y = 4$$
$$-3x - 6y = -12$$

Add the equations together and solve for x:

$$2x = -8$$
$$x = \frac{-8}{2} = -4$$

Plug the value for x back in to either of the original equations and solve for y:

$$-4 + 2y = 4$$
$$y = \frac{4+4}{2} = 4$$

Check both equations if you have time:

$$5(-4) + 6(4) = 4 \qquad\qquad -4 + 2(4) = 4$$
$$-20 + 24 = 4 \qquad\qquad -4 + 8 = 4$$
$$4 = 4 \qquad\qquad 4 = 4$$

Therefore, the solution is $(-4, 4)$.

> **Review Video: The Elimination Method**
> Visit mometrix.com/academy and enter code: 449121

GRAPHICALLY

To solve a system of linear equations **graphically**, plot both equations on the same graph. The solution of the equations is the point where both lines cross. If the lines do not cross (are parallel), then there is **no solution**.

For example, consider the following system of equations:

$$y = 2x + 7$$
$$y = -x + 1$$

Since these equations are given in slope-intercept form, they are easy to graph; the y-intercepts of the lines are $(0,7)$ and $(0,1)$. The respective slopes are 2 and -1, thus the graphs look like this:

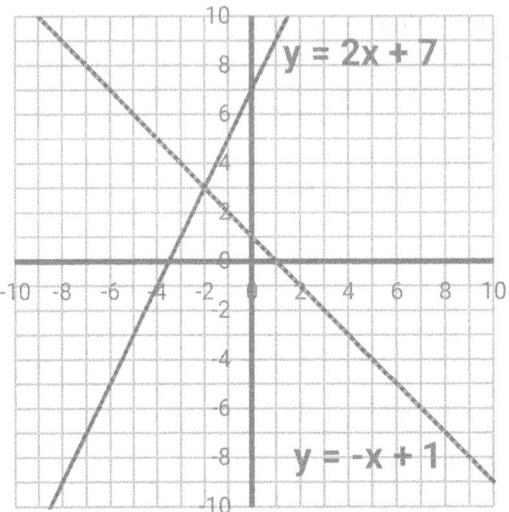

The two lines intersect at the point $(-2, 3)$, thus this is the solution to the system of equations.

Solving a system graphically is generally only practical if both coordinates of the solution are integers; otherwise the intersection will lie between gridlines on the graph and the coordinates will be difficult or impossible to determine exactly. It also helps if, as in this example, the equations are in slope-intercept form or some other form that makes them easy to graph. Otherwise, another method of solution (by substitution or elimination) is likely to be more useful.

Review Video: Solving Systems by Graphing
Visit mometrix.com/academy and enter code: 634812

SOLVING SYSTEMS OF EQUATIONS USING THE TRACE FEATURE

Using the trace feature on a calculator requires that you rewrite each equation, isolating the y-variable on one side of the equal sign. Enter both equations in the graphing calculator and plot the graphs simultaneously. Use the trace cursor to find where the two lines cross. Use the zoom feature if necessary to obtain more accurate results. Always check your answer by substituting into the original equations. The trace method is likely to be less accurate than other methods due to the resolution of graphing calculators but is a useful tool to provide an approximate answer.

MIDPOINT AND DISTANCE FORMULAS

If you know the coordinates of the endpoints of a line segment, you can calculate the midpoint and length of the line segment. Conveniently, the length of the line segment is also the distance between the two endpoints.

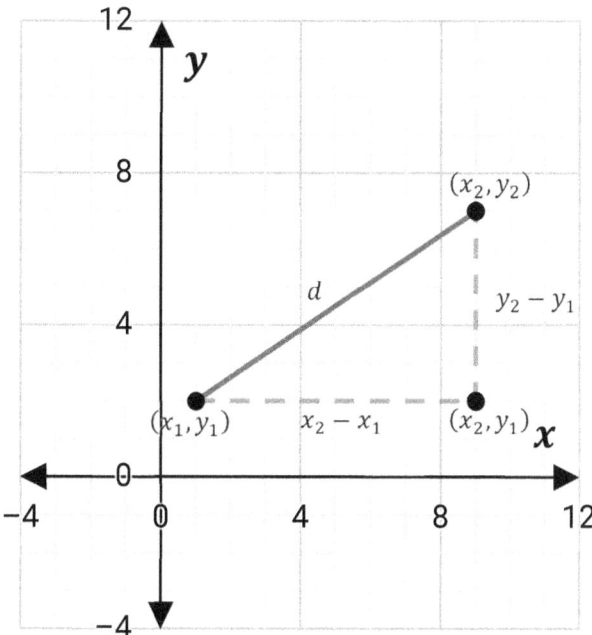

To find the **midpoint** of the line segment with endpoints (x_1, y_1) and (x_2, y_2), average the x-coordinates to get the x-coordinate of the midpoint, and average the y-coordinates to get the y-coordinate of the midpoint. Thus, the **midpoint formula** is:

$$\left(\frac{x_1 + x_2}{2}, \frac{y_1 + y_2}{2}\right)$$

The **distance** between points (x_1, y_1) and (x_2, y_2) is the same as the length of the hypotenuse of a right triangle with the two given points as endpoints, and the two sides of the right triangle parallel to the x-axis and y-axis, respectively. The length of the segment parallel to the x-axis is the difference between the x-coordinates of the two points. The length of the segment parallel to the y-axis is the difference between the y-coordinates of the two points. Use the Pythagorean theorem $a^2 + b^2 = c^2$ or $c = \sqrt{a^2 + b^2}$ to find the distance. Thus, the **distance formula** is:

$$d = \sqrt{(x_2 - x_1)^2 + (y_2 - y_1)^2}$$

> **Review Video: Calculations Using Points on a Graph**
> Visit mometrix.com/academy and enter code: 883228

BASICS OF FUNCTIONS
DEFINITION OF A FUNCTION

A function is a rule that assigns to every number in a given set (called the **domain**) exactly one corresponding value. For example, if our domain is the set $\{-2,1,2,3\}$, we can define a function by assigning to each number its square. This function assigns to -2 the value 4, to 1 the value 1, to 2 the value 4, and to 3 the value 9 (since $(-2)^2 = 4$, $1^2 = 1$, $2^2 = 4$, and $3^2 = 9$). The set of all the values assigned by a function is the **range** of the function. The range of the function in our example is the set $\{1, 4, 9\}$. We may think of a function as a kind of machine: we give it a number as an input, and it uses its rule to produce a number as an output. In the squaring function above, the input 3 produces the output 9.

> **Review Video: What is a Function?**
> Visit mometrix.com/academy and enter code: 784611

FUNCTION NOTATION

We usually name a function by a letter, often the letter f (for *function*—if we need to talk about more than one function, we name the second one g, the third one h, etc.). To specify the value (the output) corresponding to a particular number in the domain (the input), we write the function letter followed by the input number in parentheses. For instance, in the example above the notation $f(3)$ means the value that the function assigns to the number 3, namely 9—that is, $f(3) = 9$. We read the symbols $f(3)$ as, "f of 3," and we call 3 the **argument** of the function and 9 the **value** of the function (so *argument* means *input* and *value* means *output*).

Using function notation we can define the squaring function above by listing the values the function assigns to each argument in the domain: $f(-2) = 4$. $f(1) = 1$, $f(2) = 4$, and $f(3) = 9$. More efficiently, we can define the function by the single equation $f(x) = x^2$, which says that if x is a number from the domain, then we calculate the value assigned to it by substituting the number x in the formula x^2. For instance, we calculate $f(5) = 5^2 = 25$. Similarly, if we define a function g by the equation $g(x) = x^2 - 4x + 7$, then we calculate the value $g(3)$ by substituting 3 for each x in the formula: $g(3) = 3^2 - 4 \cdot 3 + 7 = 9 - 12 + 7 = 4$.

OTHER WAYS TO DEFINE FUNCTIONS

Instead of denoting the value of the function by $f(x)$, sometimes we simply use another letter, usually y. For instance, instead of defining the squaring function by the equation $f(x) = x^2$, we might use the equation $y = x^2$. In this case, we refer to x (the input) as the **independent variable** and y (the output) as the **dependent variable** because the value, y, depends on the number we choose for x.

A formula (with y or $f(x)$) is the most common way to define a function; but sometimes, if the domain is small enough, we prefer to list explicitly the possible inputs and their corresponding outputs. Some ways of doing this appear above, but a more common approach is to put the input-output pairs in a table. For instance, we can define the squaring function above by the table

x	-2	1	2	3
y	4	1	4	9

We see that the domain of this function is the set of all numbers in the x-row and the range is the set of all numbers in the y-row. We note that numbers cannot repeat in the x-row (because a function assigns exactly one value to each argument in the domain) but they can repeat in the y-row (because the function can assign the same value to multiple arguments—for instance, the number 4 appears twice in the y-row).

We can also define a function by writing the inputs and corresponding outputs as ordered pairs of x- and y-values. For instance, we can write the squaring function above as the set of ordered pairs $\{(-2,4),(1,1),(2,4),(3,9)\}$. Further, by treating these ordered pairs as coordinates and plotting the corresponding points on the coordinate plane, we get the **graph** of the function:

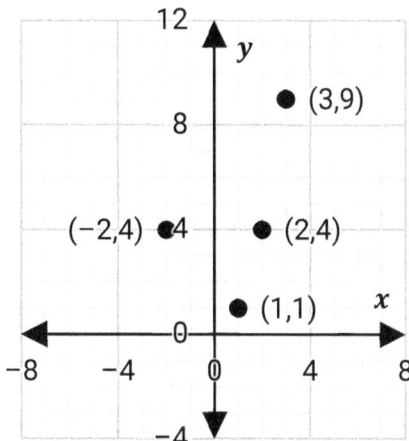

Turning this around, we can potentially use a graph to define a function, namely the function consisting of the coordinate pairs of all the points in the graph. This always works unless the graph has two points with the same x-coordinate (because then the function would assign two different y-values to the same x). It is easy to detect such points: because they have the same x-coordinate, a vertical line passes through both of them. Thus, a graph always defines a function unless it is possible to draw a vertical line that intersects the graph in two or more points. We call this condition the **vertical line test**. For example, if our graph is a circle, then by the Vertical Line Test the graph does not define a function because there are vertical lines that will intersect the circle in two different points.

MORE ON DOMAINS AND RANGES

When we define a function by a formula and do not specify the domain, then by default the domain consists of all real numbers for which the formula produces an answer. For instance, suppose we define a function f by the formula $f(x) = 1/x$. If $x = 0$, then $1/x = 1/0$, which is undefined. But if x is any other real number, then we can calculate the value of $1/x$. So, the default domain of this function is all real numbers except zero. Because of this domain convention, the graph of a function defined by a formula usually consists of infinitely many points that "connect to" each other in a way that produces a line or curve (see examples below) rather than the isolated points we see in the squaring function above.

If we have the graph of a function, its domain consists of all numbers on the x-axis with corresponding points on the graph and its range consists of all numbers on the y-axis with corresponding points on the graph. For example, consider the function $f(x) = x^2 + 3$:

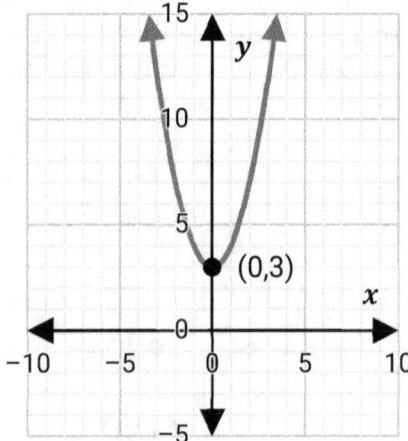

Since the graph continues infinitely to the left and right beyond what we can see, every point on the x-axis has a corresponding point on the graph; so, the domain of this function is all real numbers. On the other hand, the lowest point on this graph has a y-value of 3, and the graph passes through all higher y-values. So, the range of this function is all real numbers greater than or equal to 3, which we can denote algebraically by $y \geq 3$ or, using interval notation, by $[3, \infty)$.

> **Review Video: How to Find Domain and Range**
> Visit mometrix.com/academy and enter code: 778133
>
> **Review Video: Domain and Range of Quadratic Functions**
> Visit mometrix.com/academy and enter code: 331768

MONOTONIC AND EVEN/ODD FUNCTIONS

A function, f, is **increasing** if it always assigns larger values to larger arguments. It is **decreasing** if it always assigns smaller values to larger arguments. That is, f is increasing if $a < b$ always guarantees $f(a) < f(b)$, and it is decreasing if $a < b$ always guarantees $f(a) > f(b)$. The graph of an increasing function consistently rises from left to right, and the graph of a decreasing function consistently falls from left to right. For example, the function $f(x) = 2x$ is an increasing function because doubling a larger number always gives us a larger result than doubling a smaller number. The graph of $f(x) = 2x$ is a line with slope $m = 2$, which, as we expect, rises from left to right. We call a function **monotonic** if it is either increasing or decreasing.

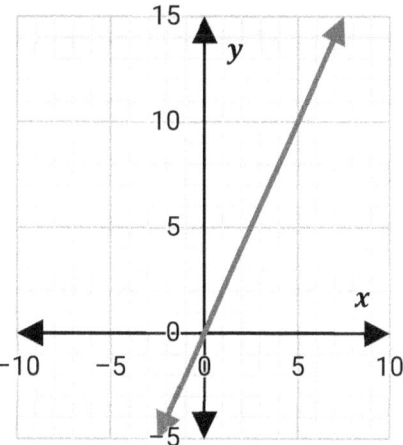

A function, f, is **even** if changing the sign of its argument produces the same value. It is **odd** if changing the sign of its argument produces the same value except with the opposite sign. That is, f is even if $f(-x) = f(x)$ and odd if $f(-x) = -f(x)$ for every argument x. The function $f(x) = x^2 + 3$ is even because substituting opposite arguments always produces the same value. For instance, $f(5) = 28$ and $f(-5) = 28$ because $5^2 + 3 = 25 + 3 = 28$ and $(-5)^2 + 3 = 25 + 3 = 28$. The function $f(x) = 2x$ is odd because substituting opposite arguments always produces opposite values. For instance, $f(10) = 20$ and $f(-10) = -20$ because $2(10) = 20$ and $2(-10) = -20$. The graph of an even function is always symmetric with respect to the y-axis, making the left and right halves of the graph mirror images of each other, as in the graph of the even function $f(x) = x^2 + 3$ above. The graph of an odd function is always symmetric with respect to the origin. This means that if we rotate the graph 180° around the origin (think of sticking a pin through the origin on a sheet of graph paper and rotating the paper halfway around) the graph looks the same, as in the graph of the odd function $f(x) = 2x$ above.

It is worth noting that most functions are neither increasing nor decreasing (that is, they are not monotonic) and most functions are neither even nor odd. For example, the function $f(x) = x^2 - x$ is neither increasing nor decreasing and neither even nor odd: its graph neither rises nor falls consistently, and it is symmetric with respect to neither the y-axis nor the origin.

> **Review Video: Even and Odd Functions**
> Visit mometrix.com/academy and enter code: 278985

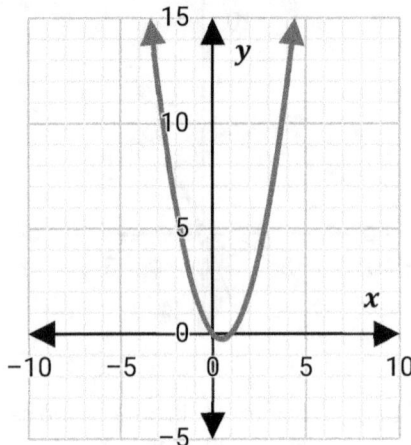

INVERTIBLE (ONE-TO-ONE) FUNCTIONS

A function, f, is one-to-one if it never assigns the same value to different arguments—that is, if $f(a)$ and $f(b)$ are different whenever a and b are different. The graph of a one-to-one function never has two points that lie on the same horizontal line because such points would have different x-values but the same y-value. Thus, a function is one-to-one if it is impossible to draw a horizontal line that intersects its graph in more than one point. We call this condition the **horizonal line test**. For example, the graph of the function $f(x) = 2x$ above is a line that rises from left to right. Every horizontal line intersects this line in exactly one point, so the function $f(x) = 2x$ is one-to-one. This is also clear without the graph because it is impossible to double two different numbers and get the same answer.

When a function, f, is one-to-one, it is possible to define its inverse function, f^{-1}, that "undoes" what f does, assigning to each output from f the input that produced it. That is, for each x in the domain of f, if $y = f(x)$, then $f^{-1}(y) = x$. For example, the inverse of the function $f(x) = 2x$ above is $f^{-1}(y) = y/2$. So, for instance, $f(5) = 2 \cdot 5 = 10$, and $f^{-1}(10) = 10/2 = 5$ (and similarly for every other value of x). Thus, the domain of f^{-1} is the range of f and vice versa. If a function, f, has an inverse, we say that f is **invertible**. Since a function has an inverse precisely when it is one-to-one, the terms *invertible* and *one-to-one* are synonyms.

If f is an invertible function defined by a formula, then to find its inverse we simply write the equation $y = f(x)$ and solve it for x (that is, we isolate the x). The result will be the equation $f^{-1}(y) = x$. For instance, starting with the function $f(x) = 2x$, we write $y = 2x$ and isolate the x by dividing both sides of the equation by 2. This gives us $y/2 = x$, so we know that $f^{-1}(y) = y/2$. Although this procedure is theoretically simple, in practice the algebra can be difficult.

COMMON FUNCTIONS

Certain functions and certain kinds of functions are particularly useful, coming up frequently in mathematics and its applications. Once we know some basic function terminology and concepts, it is useful to begin developing a mental library of the most common and useful functions.

> **Review Video: Common Functions**
> Visit mometrix.com/academy and enter code: 629798

CONSTANT FUNCTIONS

A function of the form $f(x) = a$, where a is a real number, is a **constant function**. This function assigns the same value, a, to every real argument x. For instance, given the constant function $f(x) = 5$, we have $f(2) = 5$, $f(100) = 5$, and $f(-7.1) = 5$.

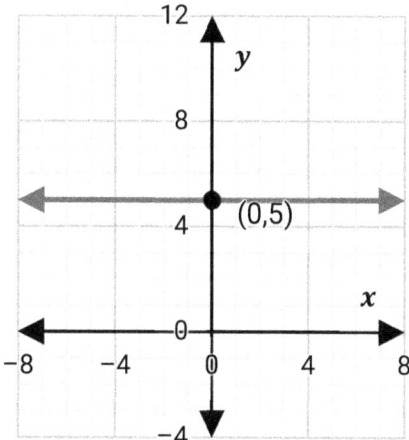

The domain of a constant function is the set of all real numbers, and the range is the set containing the single number a. Its graph is a horizontal line passing through the number $y = a$ on the y-axis (we call the number at which a function's graph intersects the y-axis the **y-intercept** of the function).

THE IDENTITY FUNCTION

The function $f(x) = x$ is the **identity function**. Its value always equals its argument. Thus, for instance, $f(2) = 2$, $f(100) = 100$, and $f(-7.1) = -7.1$.

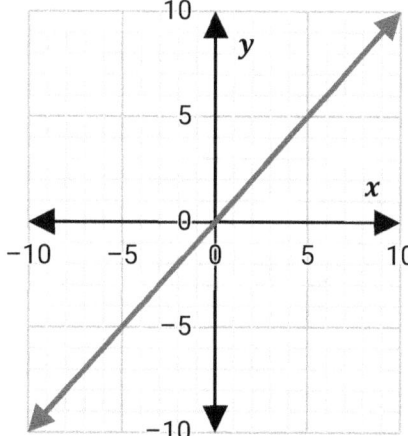

Its domain and range are the set of all real numbers. It is both an increasing function and an odd function. Its graph is a line that passes through the origin and rises from left to right at a 45° angle to the horizontal. Since it passes through the origin, its y intercept is $y = 0$ and it also has an **x-intercept** (a number at which the function's graph intersects the x-axis) of $x = 0$.

LINEAR FUNCTIONS

A function of the form $f(x) = ax + b$, where a and b are real numbers (with $a \neq 0$), is a **linear function** (the identity function is a linear function with $a = 1$ and $b = 0$). Its domain and range are the set of all real numbers. Its graph is a line (the word *linear* contains the root word *line*) with one x-intercept (at $x = -b/a$), with a y-intercept at $y = b$, and with a direction and steepness that depend on the coefficient a, which we call the **slope**. Specifically, the slope a is the amount the y-value increases for each increase of 1 in the x-value. Thus, for $a > 0$, the line rises from left to right (making f an increasing function), and larger values of a produce steeper ascents. Similarly, for $a < 0$, the line falls from left to right (making f a decreasing function), and smaller (more negative) values of a produce steeper descents. For instance, the graph of the linear function $f(x) = (1/2)x + 3$ is a line that passes through the point $y = 3$ on the y-axis and that rises by $1/2$ unit for every unit that x increases.

> **Review Video: Linear Functions**
> Visit mometrix.com/academy and enter code: 200735
>
> **Review Video: Graphing Linear Functions**
> Visit mometrix.com/academy and enter code: 699478

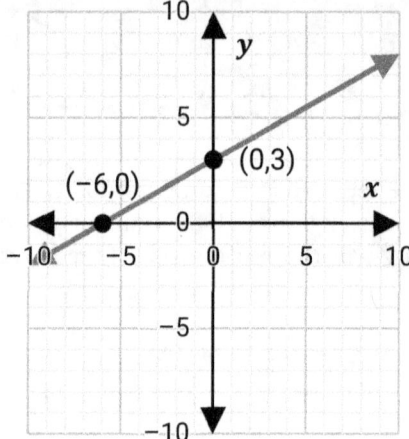

In many contexts it is standard to use the letter m for slope and thus to write the general form of a linear function as $f(x) = mx + b$, known as **slope-intercept form**.

THE SQUARING FUNCTION

The function $f(x) = x^2$ is the **squaring function**.

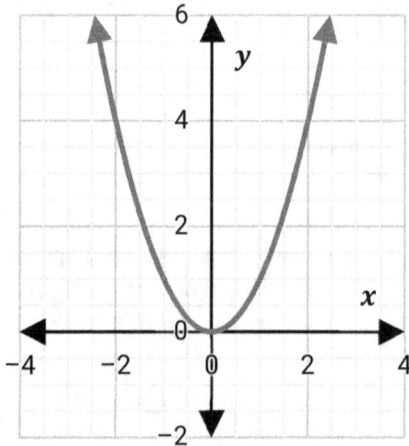

Its graph is U-shaped, opening upward as shown, a shape known as a **parabola**. It has a lowest point, its **vertex**, at the origin, which is also the location of its single x-intercept and single y-intercept. Thus, its **minimum** is $y = 0$, its domain is the set of all real numbers, and its range is the set of nonnegative real numbers (that is, $y \geq 0$). It is an even function and thus symmetric with respect to the y-axis (which we call the **axis of symmetry**), meaning that the left half of the graph is the mirror image of the right half, with the mirror standing on the y-axis.

QUADRATIC FUNCTIONS

A function of the form $f(x) = ax^2 + bx + c$, where a, b, and c are real numbers (with $a \neq 0$), is a **quadratic function** (the squaring function is a quadratic function with $a = 1$, $b = 0$, and $c = 0$). Its domain is the set of all real numbers, and its graph is a parabola. It is symmetric with respect to its axis of symmetry, the vertical line $x = -b/(2a)$. If $a > 0$, the parabola opens upward, so that its vertex is at its lowest point (its minimum) and its range consists of all real numbers greater than or equal to this minimum y-value. If $a < 0$, the parabola opens downward, so that its vertex is at its highest point (its maximum) and its range consists of all real numbers less than or equal to this maximum y-value. Its y-intercept is $y = c$ since $f(0) = c$, and it may have zero, one, or two x-intercepts. For example, the function $f(x) = x^2 - 6x + 5$ has $a = 1$, $b = -6$, and $c = 5$.

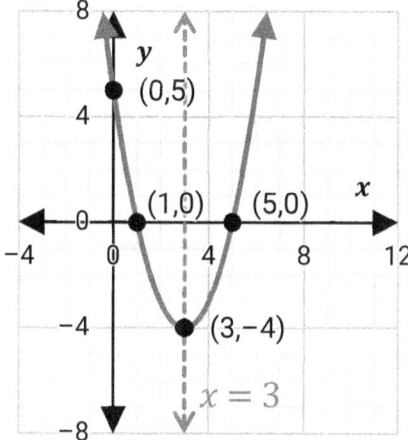

Its graph opens upward (because $a > 0$) and its axis of symmetry is the vertical line $x = 3$ (since $-b/(2a) = -(-6)/(2 \cdot 1) = 3$). Its y-intercept is at $y = 5$. It turns out to have its vertex at the point $(3, -4)$, making its minimum value $y = -4$. So, its domain is the set of all real numbers, and its range is $y \geq -4$. It also turns out to have two x-intercepts, at $x = 1$ and at $x = 5$ (since $f(1) = 0$ and $f(5) = 0$).

POLYNOMIAL FUNCTIONS

A function of the form $f(x) = a_n x^n + a_{n-1} x^{n-1} + \cdots + a_2 x^2 + a_1 x + a_0$, where n is a whole number and $a_0, a_1, a_2, \ldots a_{n-1}, a_n$ are real numbers, is a **polynomial function of degree n**. Its domain is the set of all real numbers (it is complicated to describe its range in general), and its y-intercept is $y = a_0$ (since $f(0) = a_0$). Constant functions, linear functions, and quadratic functions are polynomial functions of degrees 0, 1, and 2, respectively. In general, a polynomial function of degree n has up to n zeros (x-intercepts) and up to $n - 1$ "bends." For example, the fourth degree polynomial function $f(x) = x^4 - 11x^3 + 41x^2 - 61x + 30$, whose graph appears here, has four x-intercepts (at $x = 1$, $x = 2$, $x = 3$, and $x = 5$) and three "bends," and its y-intercept (not visible on the graph) is at $y = 30$.

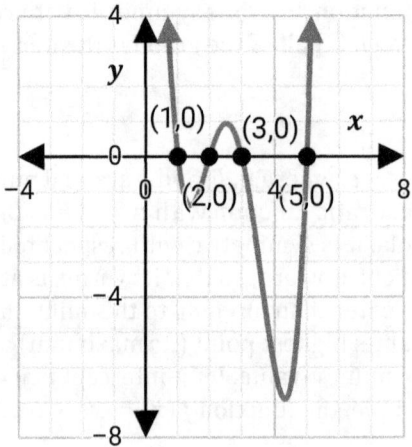

RATIONAL FUNCTIONS

A function of the form $f(x) = P(x)/Q(x)$, where P and Q are polynomials, is a rational function (we note that the word <u>rational</u> includes the root word <u>ratio</u>, indicating that a rational function is a ratio of polynomial functions). The domain of a rational function is all real numbers except the zeros of $Q(x)$ since division by zero is undefined (the range can be difficult to describe in general). Its y-intercept is $f(0)$, if this is defined; and its x-intercepts are the zeros of $P(x)$ that are in the domain of f, if there are any. A rational function may also have vertical asymptotes (vertical lines that the graph approaches without crossing) and a horizontal asymptote (a horizontal line that the curve approaches as x becomes very small or very large (toward the left and right edges of the graph). For example, the rational function $f(x) = (2x^2 + x - 1)/(x^2 + x - 2)$ has as its domain the set of all real numbers except $x = -2$ and $x = 1$ (since those numbers make the denominator zero).

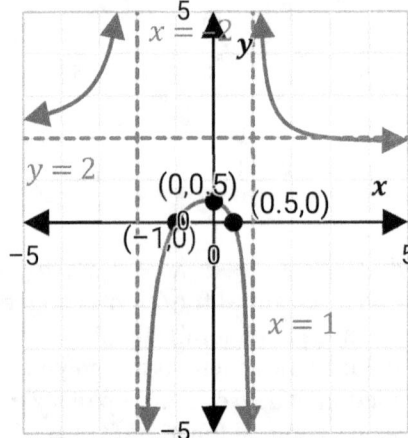

It has a y-intercept of $y = 1/2$ since $f(0) = (-1)/(-2) = 1/2$, and it has x-intercepts at $x = -1$ and at $x = 1/2$ since those numbers make the numerator zero. It has vertical asymptotes at $x = -2$ and $x = 1$ (not coincidentally, these are the numbers omitted from the domain) and a horizontal asymptote at $y = 2$. It is important to note that vertical asymptotes cannot be crossed in rational functions, but horizontal asymptotes can be crossed if the function tends near the asymptote at infinity and does not go past all possible turning points.

> **Review Video: Simplifying Rational Polynomial Functions**
> Visit mometrix.com/academy and enter code: 351038
>
> **Review Video: Horizontal Asymptotes**
> Visit mometrix.com/academy and enter code: 747796

THE SQUARE ROOT FUNCTION

The function $f(x) = \sqrt{x}$ is the square root function.

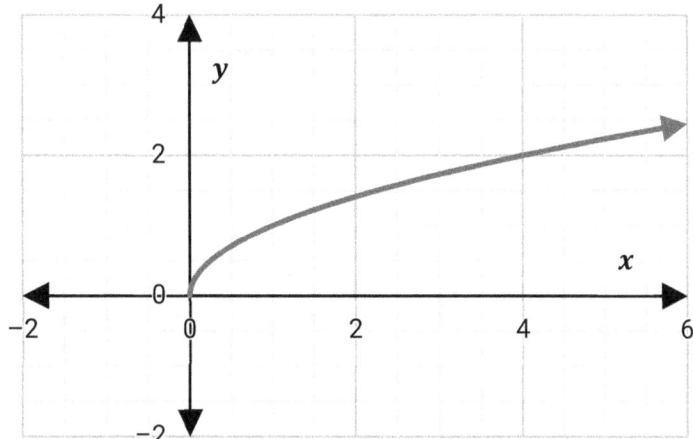

It is an increasing function, and its domain and range are both the set of all nonnegative real numbers. It has one x-intercept and one y-intercept, both appearing at the origin. Its graph is the upper half of a parabola opening to the right. The square root function is the inverse of the squaring function with domain restricted to the nonnegative real numbers (that is, $f(x) = x^2$ for $x \geq 0$).

PIECEWISE-DEFINED FUNCTIONS

As the name suggests, a **piecewise-defined function** (or, simply, a **piecewise function**) is a function defined by different rules on different pieces of the domain. We define such a function using the following form:

Function Name	Rule to Apply	Piece of the Domain on Which the Rule Applies
$f(x) =$	$\begin{cases} \text{Rule 1,} \\ \text{Rule 2,} \\ \text{Rule 3,} \\ \text{etc.,} \end{cases}$	First Piece of the Domain Second Piece of the Domain Third Piece of the Domain etc.

The pieces of the domain should not overlap, and together they should cover the whole domain. For example, we might craft a piecewise-defined function by

$$f(x) = \begin{cases} x^2, & \text{if } x < 2 \\ 3x - 5, & \text{if } x \geq 2 \end{cases}$$

The two pieces of the domain—namely, $x < 2$ and $x \geq 2$—do not overlap, and together they include all real numbers. To evaluate the function for a particular argument x, we determine which piece of the domain includes x and then apply the corresponding rule. For instance, to find $f(4)$, we note that $4 \geq 2$; so, we apply the rule $3x - 5$ to get the value $f(4) = 3 \cdot 4 - 5 = 7$. Similarly, to find $f(-6)$, we note that $-6 < 2$; so, we apply the rule x^2 to get the value $f(-6) = (-6)^2 = 36$.

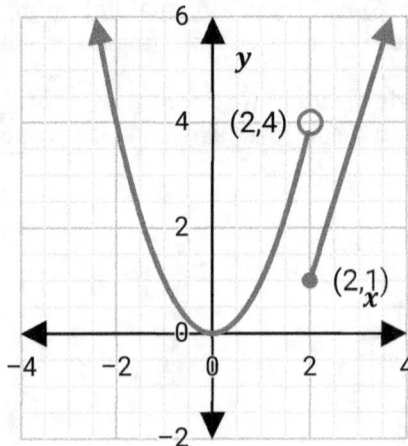

To graph this function, we sketch the graph of the parabola $y = x^2$ on the part of the plane where $x < 2$ and we sketch the line $y = 3x - 5$ on the part of the plane where $x \geq 2$. This produces a graph with a jump at $x = 2$ (a discontinuity—piecewise-defined functions are useful for producing graphs with discontinuities). We plot an open circle at the point $(2,4)$, the end of the left part of the graph, to show that this point is not part of the graph. And we plot a solid dot at the point $(2,1)$, the start of the right part of the graph, to show that this point *is* part of the graph.

Review Video: Piecewise Functions
Visit mometrix.com/academy and enter code: 707921

THE ABSOLUTE VALUE FUNCTION

A particularly useful piecewise-defined function is the absolute value function. It is so important that instead of naming it $f(x)$ or $g(x)$, we denote it using the special notation $|x|$. Its definition is

$$|x| = \begin{cases} -x, & \text{if } x < 0 \\ x, & \text{if } x \geq 0 \end{cases}$$

For instance, $|8| = 8$ (since $8 \geq 0$) and $|-5| = -(-5) = 5$, since $-5 < 0$. So, the absolute value function acts like the identity function for nonnegative numbers (it leaves them unchanged), and it gives the opposite of negative numbers (it effectively strips off the minus sign). Thus, we can think of the absolute value of a real number as its distance from zero on the number line, without taking into consideration whether the number is larger than or smaller than zero. For instance, $|-3| = 3$ and $|3| = 3$, showing that both -3 and 3 are three units away from zero. The absolute value function is an even function with a V-shaped graph that looks like the line $y = x$ (the identity function) on the right "half" of the plane (for $x \geq 0$) and the line $y = -x$ on the left "half" of the plane (for $x < 0$).

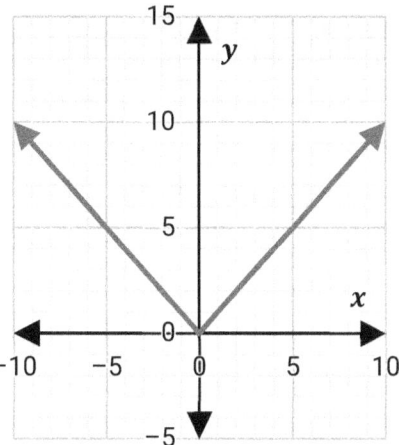

WORKING WITH FUNCTIONS
MANIPULATION OF FUNCTIONS

Translation occurs when values are added to or subtracted from the x- or y-values. If a constant is added to the y-portion of each point, the graph shifts up. If a constant is subtracted from the y-portion of each point, the graph shifts down. This is represented by the expression $f(x) \pm k$, where k is a constant. If a constant is added to the x-portion of each point, the graph shifts left. If a constant is subtracted from the x-portion of each point, the graph shifts right. This is represented by the expression $f(x \pm k)$, where k is a constant.

Stretching, compression, and reflection occur when different parts of a function are multiplied by different groups of constants. If the function as a whole is multiplied by a real number constant greater than 1, $(k \times f(x))$, the graph is stretched vertically. If k in the previous equation is greater than zero but less than 1, the graph is compressed vertically. If k is less than zero, the graph is reflected about the x-axis, in addition to being either stretched or compressed vertically if k is less than or greater than -1, respectively. If instead, just the x-term is multiplied by a constant greater than 1 $(f(k \times x))$, the graph is compressed horizontally. If k in the previous equation is greater than zero but less than 1, the graph is stretched horizontally. If k is less than zero, the graph is reflected about the y-axis, in addition to being either stretched or compressed horizontally if k is greater than or less than -1, respectively.

> **Review Video: Manipulation of Functions**
> Visit mometrix.com/academy and enter code: 669117

APPLYING THE BASIC OPERATIONS TO FUNCTIONS

For each of the basic operations, we will use these functions as examples: $f(x) = x^2$ and $g(x) = x$.

To find the sum of two functions f and g, assuming the domains are compatible, simply add the two functions together: $(f + g)(x) = f(x) + g(x) = x^2 + x$.

To find the difference of two functions f and g, assuming the domains are compatible, simply subtract the second function from the first: $(f - g)(x) = f(x) - g(x) = x^2 - x$.

To find the product of two functions f and g, assuming the domains are compatible, multiply the two functions together: $(f \times g)(x) = f(x) \times g(x) = x^2 \times x = x^3$.

To find the quotient of two functions f and g, assuming the domains are compatible, divide the first function by the second: $\left(\frac{f}{g}\right)(x) = \frac{f(x)}{g(x)} = \frac{x^2}{x} = x \,;\, x \neq 0$.

The example given in each case is fairly simple, but on a given problem, if you are looking only for the value of the sum, difference, product, or quotient of two functions at a particular x-value, it may be simpler to solve the functions individually and then perform the given operation using those values.

The composite of two functions f and g, written as $(f \circ g)(x)$ simply means that the output of the second function is used as the input of the first. This can also be written as $f(g(x))$. In general, this can be solved by substituting $g(x)$ for all instances of x in $f(x)$ and simplifying. Using the example functions $f(x) = x^2 - x + 2$ and $g(x) = x + 1$, we can find that $(f \circ g)(x)$ or $f(g(x))$ is equal to $f(x + 1) = (x + 1)^2 - (x + 1) + 2$, which simplifies to $x^2 + x + 2$.

It is important to note that $(f \circ g)(x)$ is not necessarily the same as $(g \circ f)(x)$. The process is not always commutative like addition or multiplication expressions. It *can* be commutative, but most often this is not the case.

EVALUATING LINEAR FUNCTIONS

A **function** can be expressed as an equation that relates an input to an output where each input corresponds to exactly one output. The input of a function is defined by the x-variable, and the output is defined by the y-variable. For example, consider the function $y = 2x + 6$. The value of y, the output, is determined by the value of the x, the input. If the value of x is 3, the value of y is $y = 2(3) + 6 = 6 + 6 = 12$. This means that when $x = 3$, $y = 12$. This can be expressed as the ordered pair (3,12).

It is common for function equations to use the form $f(x) =$ instead of $y =$. However, $f(x)$ and y represent the same thing. We read $f(x)$ as "f of x." The expression "f of x" implies that the value of f depends on the value of x. The function used in the example above could be expressed as $y = 2x + 6$ or $f(x) = 2x + 6$. Both functions represent the same line when graphed.

Functions that are expressed in the form $f(x) =$ are evaluated in the same way the equations are evaluated in the form $y =$. For example, when evaluating the function $f(x) = 3x - 2$ for $f(6)$, substitute 6 in for x, and simplify. In this case, $f(x) = 3x - 2$ becomes $f(6) = 3(6) - 2 = 18 - 2 = 16$. When x is 6, $f(x)$ is 16.

Example: To find the value of $f(8)$, calculate as follows:

$$f(x) = 3x - 2$$
$$f(8) = 3(8) - 2$$
$$f(8) = 22$$

> **Review Video: Evaluating Functions**
> Visit mometrix.com/academy and enter code: 588515

Statistics and Probability

PROBABILITY

Probability is the likelihood of a certain outcome occurring for a given event. An **event** is any situation that produces a result. It could be something as simple as flipping a coin or as complex as launching a rocket. Determining the probability of an outcome for an event can be equally simple or complex. As such, there are specific terms used in the study of probability that need to be understood:

- **Compound event**—an event that involves two or more independent events (rolling a pair of dice and taking the sum)
- **Desired outcome** (or success)—an outcome that meets a particular set of criteria (a roll of 1 or 2 if we are looking for numbers less than 3)
- **Independent events**—two or more events whose outcomes do not affect one another (two coins tossed at the same time)
- **Dependent events**—two or more events whose outcomes affect one another (two cards drawn consecutively from the same deck)
- **Certain outcome**—probability of outcome is 100% or 1
- **Impossible outcome**—probability of outcome is 0% or 0
- **Mutually exclusive outcomes**—two or more outcomes whose criteria cannot all be satisfied in a single event (a coin coming up heads and tails on the same toss)
- **Random variable**—refers to all possible outcomes of a single event which may be discrete or continuous.

> **Review Video: Intro to Probability**
> Visit mometrix.com/academy and enter code: 212374

SAMPLE SPACE

The total set of all possible results of a test or experiment is called a **sample space**, or sometimes a universal sample space. The sample space, represented by one of the variables S, Ω, or U (for universal sample space) has individual elements called outcomes. Other terms for outcome that may be used interchangeably include elementary outcome, simple event, or sample point. The number of outcomes in a given sample space could be infinite or finite, and some tests may yield multiple unique sample sets. For example, tests conducted by drawing playing cards from a standard deck would have one sample space of the card values, another sample space of the card suits, and a third sample space of suit-denomination combinations. For most tests, the sample spaces considered will be finite.

An **event**, represented by the variable E, is a portion of a sample space. It may be one outcome or a group of outcomes from the same sample space. If an event occurs, then the test or experiment will generate an outcome that satisfies the requirement of that event. For example, given a standard deck of 52 playing cards as the sample space, and defining the event as the collection of face cards, then the event will occur if the card drawn is a J, Q, or K. If any other card is drawn, the event is said to have not occurred.

For every sample space, each possible outcome has a specific likelihood, or probability, that it will occur. The probability measure, also called the **distribution**, is a function that assigns a real number probability, from zero to one, to each outcome. For a probability measure to be accurate, every outcome must have a real number probability measure that is greater than or equal to zero and less than or equal to one. Also, the probability measure of the sample space must equal one, and the probability measure of the union of multiple outcomes must equal the sum of the individual probability measures.

Probabilities of events are expressed as real numbers from zero to one. They give a numerical value to the chance that a particular event will occur. The probability of an event occurring is the sum of the probabilities of the individual elements of that event. For example, in a standard deck of 52 playing cards as the sample space and the collection of face cards as the event, the probability of drawing a specific face card is $\frac{1}{52} = 0.019$, but the probability of drawing any one of the twelve face cards is $12(0.019) = 0.228$. Note that rounding of numbers can generate different results. If you multiplied 12 by the fraction $\frac{1}{52}$ before converting to a decimal, you would get the answer $\frac{12}{52} = 0.231$.

THEORETICAL AND EXPERIMENTAL PROBABILITY

Theoretical probability can usually be determined without actually performing the event. The likelihood of an outcome occurring, or the probability of an outcome occurring, is given by the formula:

$$P(A) = \frac{\text{Number of acceptable outcomes}}{\text{Number of possible outcomes}}$$

Note that $P(A)$ is the probability of an outcome A occurring, and each outcome is just as likely to occur as any other outcome. If each outcome has the same probability of occurring as every other possible outcome, the outcomes are said to be equally likely to occur. The total number of acceptable outcomes must be less than or equal to the total number of possible outcomes. If the two are equal, then the outcome is certain to occur and the probability is 1. If the number of acceptable outcomes is zero, then the outcome is impossible and the probability is 0. For example, if there are 20 marbles in a bag and 5 are red, then the theoretical probability of randomly selecting a red marble is 5 out of 20, $\left(\frac{5}{20} = \frac{1}{4}, 0.25, \text{ or } 25\%\right)$.

If the theoretical probability is unknown or too complicated to calculate, it can be estimated by an experimental probability. **Experimental probability**, also called empirical probability, is an estimate of the likelihood of a certain outcome based on repeated experiments or collected data. In other words, while theoretical probability is based on what *should* happen, experimental probability is based on what *has* happened. Experimental probability is calculated in the same way as theoretical probability, except that actual outcomes are used instead of possible outcomes. The more experiments performed or datapoints gathered, the better the estimate should be.

Theoretical and experimental probability do not always line up with one another. Theoretical probability says that out of 20 coin-tosses, 10 should be heads. However, if we were actually to toss 20 coins, we might record just 5 heads. This doesn't mean that our theoretical probability is incorrect; it just means that this particular experiment had results that were different from what was predicted. A practical application of empirical probability is the insurance industry. There are no set functions that define lifespan, health, or safety. Insurance companies look at factors from hundreds of thousands of individuals to find patterns that they then use to set the formulas for insurance premiums.

> **Review Video: Empirical Probability**
> Visit mometrix.com/academy and enter code: 513468

OBJECTIVE AND SUBJECTIVE PROBABILITY

Objective probability is based on mathematical formulas and documented evidence. Examples of objective probability include raffles or lottery drawings where there is a pre-determined number of possible outcomes and a predetermined number of outcomes that correspond to an event. Other cases of objective probability include probabilities of rolling dice, flipping coins, or drawing cards. Most gambling games are based on objective probability.

In contrast, **subjective probability** is based on personal or professional feelings and judgments. Often, there is a lot of guesswork following extensive research. Areas where subjective probability is applicable include sales trends and business expenses. Attractions set admission prices based on subjective probabilities of attendance based on varying admission rates in an effort to maximize their profit.

COMPLEMENT OF AN EVENT

Sometimes it may be easier to calculate the possibility of something not happening, or the **complement of an event**. Represented by the symbol $\bar{A}$, the complement of A is the probability that event A does not happen. When you know the probability of event A occurring, you can use the formula $P(\bar{A}) = 1 - P(A)$, where $P(\bar{A})$ is the probability of event A not occurring, and $P(A)$ is the probability of event A occurring.

ADDITION RULE

The **addition rule** for probability is used for finding the probability of a compound event. Use the formula $P(A \cup B) = P(A) + P(B) - P(A \cap B)$, where $P(A \cap B)$ is the probability of both events occurring to find the probability of a compound event. The probability of both events occurring at the same time must be subtracted to eliminate any overlap in the first two probabilities.

CONDITIONAL PROBABILITY

Given two events A and B, the **conditional probability** $P(A|B)$ is the probability that event A will occur, given that event B has occurred. The conditional probability cannot be calculated simply from $P(A)$ and $P(B)$; these probabilities alone do not give sufficient information to determine the conditional probability. It can, however, be determined if you are also given the probability of the intersection of events A and B, $P(A \cap B)$, the probability that events A and B both occur. Specifically, $P(A|B) = \frac{P(A \cap B)}{P(B)}$. For instance, suppose you have a jar containing two red marbles and two blue marbles, and you draw two marbles at random. Consider event A being the event that the first marble drawn is red, and event B being the event that the second marble drawn is blue. If we want to find the probability that B occurs given that A occurred, $P(B|A)$, then we can compute it using the fact that $P(A)$ is $\frac{1}{2}$, and $P(A \cap B)$ is $\frac{1}{3}$. (The latter may not be obvious, but may be determined by finding the product of $\frac{1}{2}$ and $\frac{2}{3}$). Therefore $P(B|A) = \frac{P(A \cap B)}{P(A)} = \frac{1/3}{1/2} = \frac{2}{3}$.

CONDITIONAL PROBABILITY IN EVERYDAY SITUATIONS

Conditional probability often arises in everyday situations in, for example, estimating the risk or benefit of certain activities. The conditional probability of having a heart attack given that you exercise daily may be smaller than the overall probability of having a heart attack. The conditional probability of having lung cancer given that you are a smoker is larger than the overall probability of having lung cancer. Note that changing the order of the conditional probability changes the meaning: the conditional probability of having lung cancer given that you are a smoker is a very different thing from the probability of being a smoker given that you have lung cancer. In an extreme case, suppose that a certain rare disease is caused only by eating a certain food, but even then, it is unlikely. Then the conditional probability of having that disease given that you eat the dangerous food is nonzero but low, but the conditional probability of having eaten that food given that you have the disease is 100%!

> **Review Video: Conditional Probability**
> Visit mometrix.com/academy and enter code: 397924

INDEPENDENCE

The conditional probability $P(A|B)$ is the probability that event A will occur given that event B occurs. If the two events are independent, we do not expect that whether or not event B occurs should have any effect on whether or not event A occurs. In other words, we expect $P(A|B) = P(A)$.

This can be proven using the usual equations for conditional probability and the joint probability of independent events. The conditional probability $P(A|B) = \frac{P(A \cap B)}{P(B)}$. If A and B are independent, then $P(A \cap B) = P(A)P(B)$. So $P(A|B) = \frac{P(A)P(B)}{P(B)} = P(A)$. By similar reasoning, if A and B are independent then $P(B|A) = P(B)$.

MULTIPLICATION RULE

The **multiplication rule** can be used to find the probability of two independent events occurring using the formula $P(A \cap B) = P(A) \times P(B)$, where $P(A \cap B)$ is the probability of two independent events occurring, $P(A)$ is the probability of the first event occurring, and $P(B)$ is the probability of the second event occurring.

The multiplication rule can also be used to find the probability of two dependent events occurring using the formula $P(A \cap B) = P(A) \times P(B|A)$, where $P(A \cap B)$ is the probability of two dependent events occurring and $P(B|A)$ is the probability of the second event occurring after the first event has already occurred.

Use a **combination of the multiplication** rule and the rule of complements to find the probability that at least one outcome of the element will occur. This is given by the general formula P(at least one event occurring) $= 1 - P$(no outcomes occurring). For example, to find the probability that at least one even number will show when a pair of dice is rolled, find the probability that two odd numbers will be rolled (no even numbers) and subtract from one. You can always use a tree diagram or make a chart to list the possible outcomes when the sample space is small, such as in the dice-rolling example, but in most cases it will be much faster to use the multiplication and complement formulas.

> **Review Video: Multiplication Rule**
> Visit mometrix.com/academy and enter code: 782598

UNION AND INTERSECTION OF TWO SETS OF OUTCOMES

If A and B are each a set of elements or outcomes from an experiment, then the **union** (symbol ∪) of the two sets is the set of elements found in set A or set B. For example, if $A = \{2, 3, 4\}$ and $B = \{3, 4, 5\}$, $A \cup B = \{2, 3, 4, 5\}$. Note that the outcomes 3 and 4 appear only once in the union. For statistical events, the union is equivalent to "or"; $P(A \cup B)$ is the same thing as $P(A \text{ or } B)$. The **intersection** (symbol ∩) of two sets is the set of outcomes common to both sets. For the above sets A and B, $A \cap B = \{3, 4\}$. For statistical events, the intersection is equivalent to "and"; $P(A \cap B)$ is the same thing as $P(A \text{ and } B)$. It is important to note that union and intersection operations commute. That is:

$$A \cup B = B \cup A \text{ and } A \cap B = B \cap A$$

MEASURES OF CENTRAL TENDENCY

A **measure of central tendency** is a statistical value that gives a reasonable estimate for the center of a group of data. There are several different ways of describing the measure of central tendency. Each one has a unique way it is calculated, and each one gives a slightly different perspective on the data set. Whenever you give a measure of central tendency, always make sure the units are the same. If the data has different units, such as hours, minutes, and seconds, convert all the data to the same unit, and use the same unit in the measure of central tendency. If no units are given in the data, do not give units for the measure of central tendency.

MEAN

The **statistical mean** of a group of data is the same as the arithmetic average of that group. To find the mean of a set of data, first convert each value to the same units, if necessary. Then find the sum of all the values, and count the total number of data values, making sure you take into consideration each individual value. If a value appears more than once, count it more than once. Divide the sum of the values by the total number of values and apply the units, if any. Note that the mean does not have to be one of the data values in the set, and may not divide evenly.

$$\text{mean} = \frac{\text{sum of the data values}}{\text{quantity of data values}}$$

For instance, the mean of the data set {88, 72, 61, 90, 97, 68, 88, 79, 86, 93, 97, 71, 80, 84, 89} would be the sum of the fifteen numbers divided by 15:

$$\frac{88 + 72 + 61 + 90 + 97 + 68 + 88 + 79 + 86 + 93 + 97 + 71 + 80 + 84 + 89}{15} = \frac{1242}{15} = 82.8$$

While the mean is relatively easy to calculate and averages are understood by most people, the mean can be very misleading if it is used as the sole measure of central tendency. If the data set has outliers (data values that are unusually high or unusually low compared to the rest of the data values), the mean can be very distorted, especially if the data set has a small number of values. If unusually high values are countered with unusually low values, the mean is not affected as much. For example, if five of twenty students in a class get a 100 on a test, but the other 15 students have an average of 60 on the same test, the class average would appear as 70. Whenever the mean is skewed by outliers, it is always a good idea to include the median as an alternate measure of central tendency.

A **weighted mean**, or weighted average, is a mean that uses "weighted" values. The formula is weighted mean $= \frac{w_1 x_1 + w_2 x_2 + w_3 x_3 \ldots + w_n x_n}{w_1 + w_2 + w_3 + \cdots + w_n}$. Weighted values, such as $w_1, w_2, w_3, \ldots w_n$ are assigned to each member of the set $x_1, x_2, x_3, \ldots x_n$. When calculating the weighted mean, make sure a weight value for each member of the set is used.

> **Review Video: All About Averages**
> Visit mometrix.com/academy and enter code: 176521

MEDIAN

The **statistical median** is the value in the middle of the set of data. To find the median, list all data values in order from smallest to largest or from largest to smallest. Any value that is repeated in the set must be listed the number of times it appears. If there are an odd number of data values, the median is the value in the middle of the list. If there is an even number of data values, the median is the arithmetic mean of the two middle values.

For example, the median of the data set {88, 72, 61, 90, 97, 68, 88, 79, 86, 93, 97, 71, 80, 84, 88} is 86 since the ordered set is {61, 68, 71, 72, 79, 80, 84, **86**, 88, 88, 88, 90, 93, 97, 97}.

The big disadvantage of using the median as a measure of central tendency is that is relies solely on a value's relative size as compared to the other values in the set. When the individual values in a set of data are evenly dispersed, the median can be an accurate tool. However, if there is a group of rather large values or a group of rather small values that are not offset by a different group of values, the information that can be inferred from the median may not be accurate because the distribution of values is skewed.

MODE

The **statistical mode** is the data value that occurs the greatest number of times in the data set. It is possible to have exactly one mode, more than one mode, or no mode. To find the mode of a set of data, arrange the data like you do to find the median (all values in order, listing all multiples of data values). Count the number of times each value appears in the data set. If all values appear an equal number of times, there is no mode. If one value appears more than any other value, that value is the mode. If two or more values appear the same number of times, but there are other values that appear fewer times and no values that appear more times, all of those values are the modes.

For example, the mode of the data set {**88**, 72, 61, 90, 97, 68, **88**, 79, 86, 93, 97, 71, 80, 84, **88**} is 88.

The main disadvantage of the mode is that the values of the other data in the set have no bearing on the mode. The mode may be the largest value, the smallest value, or a value anywhere in between in the set. The mode only tells which value or values, if any, occurred the greatest number of times. It does not give any suggestions about the remaining values in the set.

Review Video: Mean, Median, and Mode
Visit mometrix.com/academy and enter code: 286207

DISPLAYING INFORMATION
FREQUENCY TABLES

Frequency tables show how frequently each unique value appears in a set. A **relative frequency table** is one that shows the proportions of each unique value compared to the entire set. Relative frequencies are given as percentages; however, the total percent for a relative frequency table will not necessarily equal 100 percent due to rounding. An example of a frequency table with relative frequencies is below.

Favorite Color	Frequency	Relative Frequency
Blue	4	13%
Red	7	22%
Green	3	9%
Purple	6	19%
Cyan	12	38%

Review Video: Data Interpretation of Graphs
Visit mometrix.com/academy and enter code: 200439

CIRCLE GRAPHS

Circle graphs, also known as *pie charts*, provide a visual depiction of the relationship of each type of data compared to the whole set of data. The circle graph is divided into sections by drawing radii to create central angles whose percentage of the circle is equal to the individual data's percentage of the whole set. Each 1% of data is equal to 3.6° in the circle graph. Therefore, data represented by a 90° section of the circle graph makes up 25% of the whole. When complete, a circle graph often looks like a pie cut into uneven wedges. The pie chart below shows the data from the frequency table referenced earlier where people were asked their favorite color.

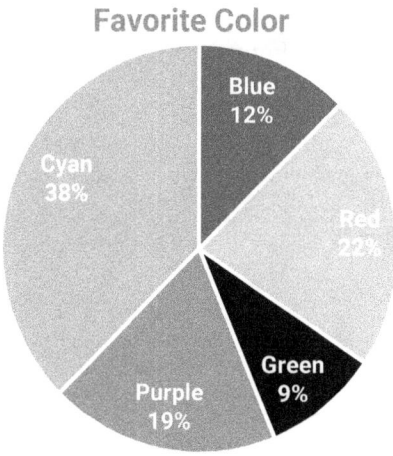

PICTOGRAPHS

A **pictograph** is a graph, generally in the horizontal orientation, that uses pictures or symbols to represent the data. Each pictograph must have a key that defines the picture or symbol and gives the quantity each picture or symbol represents. Pictures or symbols on a pictograph are not always shown as whole elements. In this case, the fraction of the picture or symbol shown represents the same fraction of the quantity a whole picture or symbol stands for. For example, a row with $3\frac{1}{2}$ ears of corn, where each ear of corn represents 100 stalks of corn in a field, would equal $3\frac{1}{2} \times 100 = 350$ stalks of corn in the field.

Name	Number of ears of corn eaten	Field	Number of stalks of corn
Michael	🌽🌽🌽🌽🌽	Field 1	🌽🌽🌽🌽🌽
Tara	🌽🌽	Field 2	🌽🌽🌽 (partial)
John	🌽🌽🌽🌽	Field 3	🌽🌽🌽🌽
Sara	🌽	Field 4	🌽
Jacob	🌽🌽🌽	Field 5	🌽🌽🌽🌽 (partial)

Each 🌽 represents 1 ear of corn eaten.   Each 🌽 represents 100 stalks of corn.

> **Review Video: Pictographs**
> Visit mometrix.com/academy and enter code: 147860

LINE GRAPHS

Line graphs have one or more lines of varying styles (solid or broken) to show the different values for a set of data. The individual data are represented as ordered pairs, much like on a Cartesian plane. In this case, the x- and y-axes are defined in terms of their units, such as dollars or time. The individual plotted points are joined by line segments to show whether the value of the data is increasing (line sloping upward), decreasing (line sloping downward), or staying the same (horizontal line). Multiple sets of data can be graphed on the same line graph to give an easy visual comparison. An example of this would be graphing achievement test scores for different groups of students over the same time period to see which group had the greatest increase or decrease in performance from year to year (as shown below).

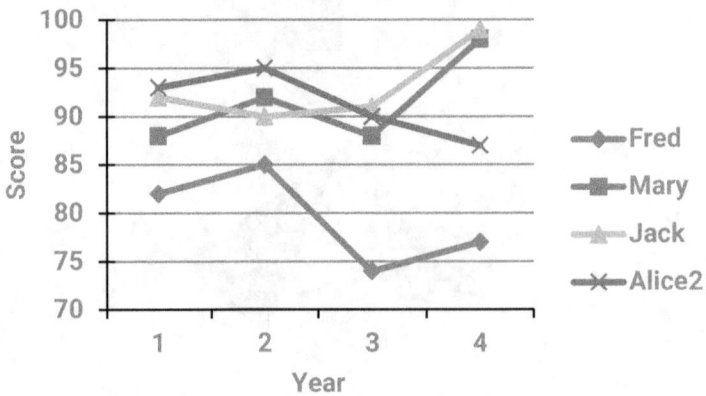

Review Video: How to Create a Line Graph
Visit mometrix.com/academy and enter code: 480147

LINE PLOTS

A **line plot**, also known as a *dot plot*, has plotted points that are not connected by line segments. In this graph, the horizontal axis lists the different possible values for the data, and the vertical axis lists the number of times the individual value occurs. A single dot is graphed for each value to show the number of times it occurs. This graph is more closely related to a bar graph than a line graph. Do not connect the dots in a line plot or it will misrepresent the data.

Review Video: Line Plot
Visit mometrix.com/academy and enter code: 754610

STEM AND LEAF PLOTS

A **stem and leaf plot** is useful for depicting groups of data that fall into a range of values. Each piece of data is separated into two parts: the first, or left, part is called the stem; the second, or right, part is called the leaf. Each stem is listed in a column from smallest to largest. Each leaf that has the common stem is listed in that stem's row from smallest to largest. For example, in a set of two-digit numbers, the digit in the tens place is the stem, and the digit in the ones place is the leaf. With a stem and leaf plot, you can easily see which subset of numbers (10s, 20s, 30s, etc.) is the largest. This information is also readily available by looking at a histogram, but a stem and leaf plot also allows you to look closer and see exactly which values fall in that range. Using a sample set of test scores (82, 88, 92, 93, 85, 90, 92, 95, 74, 88, 90, 91, 78, 87, 98, 99), we can assemble a stem and leaf plot like the one below.

Test Scores

7	4	8					
8	2	5	7	8	8		
9	0	0	1	2	2	3	5	8	9

Review Video: Stem and Leaf Plots
Visit mometrix.com/academy and enter code: 302339

BAR GRAPHS

A **bar graph** is one of the few graphs that can be drawn correctly in two different configurations – both horizontally and vertically. A bar graph is similar to a line plot in the way the data is organized on the graph. Both axes must have their categories defined for the graph to be useful. Rather than placing a single dot to mark the point of the data's value, a bar, or thick line, is drawn from zero to the exact value of the data, whether it is a number, percentage, or other numerical value. Longer bar lengths correspond to greater data values. To read a bar graph, read the labels for the axes to find the units being reported. Then, look where the bars end in relation to the scale given on the corresponding axis and determine the associated value.

The bar chart below represents the responses from our favorite-color survey.

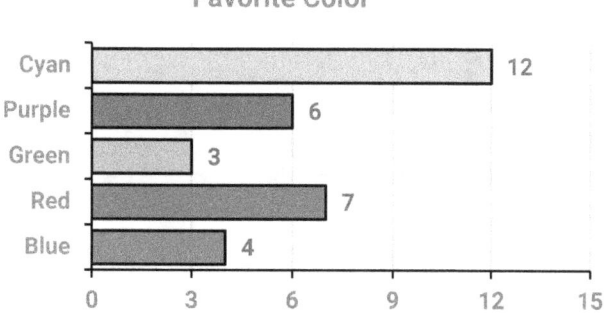

HISTOGRAMS

At first glance, a **histogram** looks like a vertical bar graph. The difference is that a bar graph has a separate bar for each piece of data and a histogram has one continuous bar for each *range* of data. For example, a histogram may have one bar for the range 0–9, one bar for 10–19, etc. While a bar graph has numerical values on one axis, a histogram has numerical values on both axes. Each range is of equal size, and they are ordered left to right from lowest to highest. The height of each column on a histogram represents the number of data values within that range. Like a stem and leaf plot, a histogram makes it easy to glance at the graph and quickly determine which range has the greatest quantity of values. A simple example of a histogram is below.

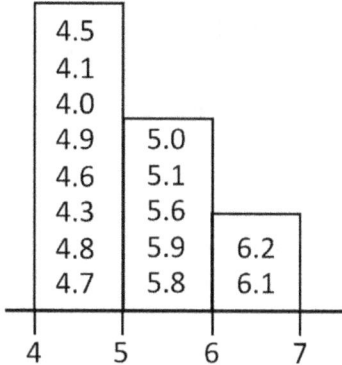

5-NUMBER SUMMARY

The **5-number summary** of a set of data gives a very informative picture of the set. The five numbers in the summary include the minimum value, maximum value, and the three quartiles. This information gives the reader the range and median of the set, as well as an indication of how the data is spread about the median.

BOX AND WHISKER PLOTS

A **box-and-whiskers plot** is a graphical representation of the 5-number summary. To draw a box-and-whiskers plot, plot the points of the 5-number summary on a number line. Draw a box whose ends are through the points for the first and third quartiles. Draw a vertical line in the box through the median to divide the box in half. Draw a line segment from the first quartile point to the minimum value, and from the third quartile point to the maximum value.

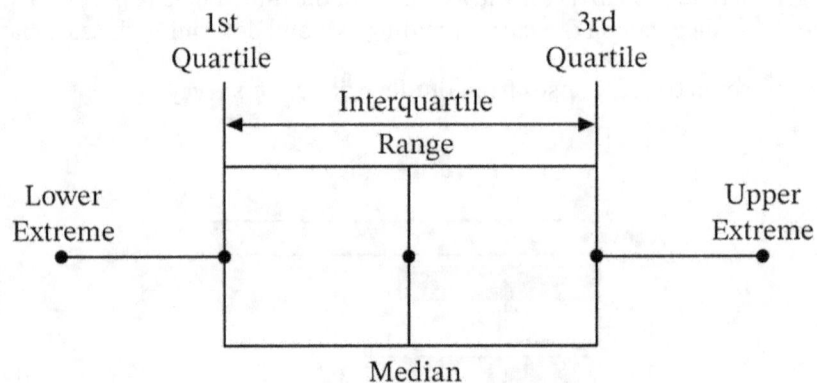

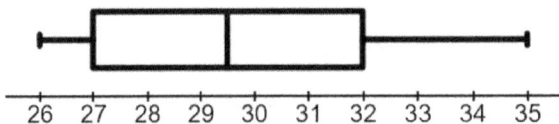

Review Video: Box and Whisker Plots
Visit mometrix.com/academy and enter code: 810817

EXAMPLE

Given the following data (32, 28, 29, 26, 35, 27, 30, 31, 27, 32), we first sort it into numerical order: 26, 27, 27, 28, 29, 30, 31, 32, 32, 35. We can then find the median. Since there are ten values, we take the average of the 5th and 6th values to get 29.5. We find the lower quartile by taking the median of the data smaller than the median. Since there are five values, we take the 3rd value, which is 27. We find the upper quartile by taking the median of the data larger than the overall median, which is 32. Finally, we note our minimum and maximum, which are simply the smallest and largest values in the set: 26 and 35, respectively. Now we can create our box plot:

This plot is fairly "long" on the right whisker, showing one or more unusually high values (but not quite outliers). The other quartiles are similar in length, showing a fairly even distribution of data.

INTERQUARTILE RANGE

The **interquartile range, or IQR**, is the difference between the upper and lower quartiles. It measures how the data is dispersed: a high IQR means that the data is more spread out, while a low IQR means that the data is clustered more tightly around the median. To find the IQR, subtract the lower quartile value (Q_1) from the upper quartile value (Q_3).

EXAMPLE

To find the upper and lower quartiles, we first find the median and then take the median of all values above it and all values below it. In the following data set (16, 18, 13, 24, 16, 51, 32, 21, 27, 39), we first rearrange the values in numerical order: 13, 16, 16, 18, 21, 24, 27, 32, 39, 51. There are 10 values, so the median is the average of the 5th and 6th: $\frac{21+24}{2} = \frac{45}{2} = 22.5$. We do not actually need this value to find the upper and lower quartiles. We look at the set of numbers below the median: 13, 16, 16, 18, 21. There are five values, so the 3rd is the median (16), or the value of the lower quartile (Q_1). Then we look at the numbers above the median: 24, 27, 32, 39, 51. Again there are five values, so the 3rd is the median (32), or the value of the upper quartile (Q_3). We find the IQR by subtracting Q_1 from Q_3: $32 - 16 = 16$.

68-95-99.7 Rule

The **68–95–99.7 rule** describes how a normal distribution of data should appear when compared to the mean. This is also a description of a normal bell curve. According to this rule, 68 percent of the data values in a normally distributed set should fall within one standard deviation of the mean (34 percent above and 34 percent below the mean), 95 percent of the data values should fall within two standard deviations of the mean (47.5 percent above and 47.5 percent below the mean), and 99.7 percent of the data values should fall within three standard deviations of the mean, again, equally distributed on either side of the mean. This means that only 0.3 percent of all data values should fall more than three standard deviations from the mean. On the graph below, the normal curve is centered on the y-axis. The x-axis labels are how many standard deviations away from the center you are. Therefore, it is easy to see how the 68-95-99.7 rule can apply.

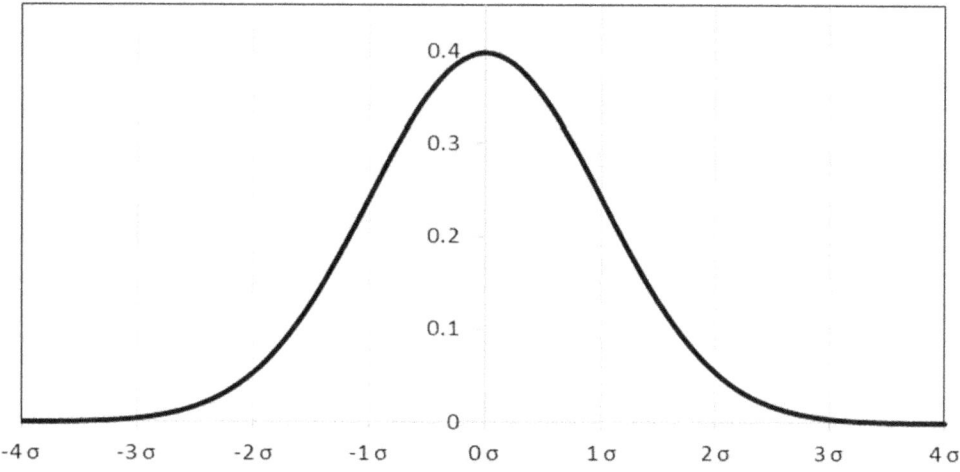

Chapter Quiz

Ready to see how well you retained what you just read? Scan the QR code to go directly to the chapter quiz interface for this study guide. If you're using a computer, simply visit the online resources page at **mometrix.com/resources719/hspt-28350** and click the Chapter Quizzes link.

Optional HSPT Assessments

The HSPT also offers three optional assessments, one or more of which may be part of your exam. Be sure to check with your school about which, if any, of the optional assessments they expect you to take:

1. Science
2. Catholic Religion
3. Mechanical Aptitude

Note that while these optional assessments will not be part of your composite score, your school may still use the results for placement decisions.

HSPT Practice Test #1

Want to take this practice test in an online interactive format?
Check out the online resources page, which includes interactive practice questions and much more: **mometrix.com/resources719/hspt-28350**

Reading—Comprehension

Refer to the following for questions 1–6:

It is a truth universally acknowledged, that a single man in possession of a good fortune, must be in want of a wife.

However little known the feelings or views of such a man may be on his first entering a neighbourhood, this truth is so well fixed in the minds of the surrounding families, that he is considered the rightful property of some one or other of their daughters.

"My dear Mr. Bennet," said his lady to him one day, "have you heard that Netherfield Park is let at last?"

Mr. Bennet replied that he had not.

"But it is," returned she; "for Mrs. Long has just been here, and she told me all about it."

Mr. Bennet made no answer.

"Do you not want to know who has taken it?" cried his wife impatiently.

"You want to tell me, and I have no objection to hearing it."

This was invitation enough.

"Why, my dear, you must know, Mrs. Long says that Netherfield is taken by a young man of large fortune from the north of England; that he came down on Monday in a chaise and four to see the place, and was so much delighted with it, that he agreed with Mr. Morris immediately; that he is to take possession before Michaelmas, and some of his servants are to be in the house by the end of next week."

"What is his name?"

"Bingley."

"Is he married or single?"

"Oh! Single, my dear, to be sure! A single man of large fortune; four or five thousand a year. What a fine thing for our girls!"

"How so? How can it affect them?"

"My dear Mr. Bennet," replied his wife, "how can you be so tiresome! You must know that I am thinking of his marrying one of them."

"Is that his design in settling here?"

"Design! Nonsense, how can you talk so! But it is very likely that he may fall in love with one of them, and therefore you must visit him as soon as he comes."

"I see no occasion for that. You and the girls may go, or you may send them by themselves, which perhaps will be still better, for as you are as handsome as any of them, Mr. Bingley may like you the best of the party."

[Adapted from Jane Austen, *Pride and Prejudice* (1813)]

1. What is the central idea of this selection?
    a. A new neighbor is due to arrive who may become good friends with Mr. and Mrs. Bennet.
    b. A new neighbor is due to arrive who may be a prospective husband for one of the Bennet daughters.
    c. A new neighbor is due to arrive who may be a good business connection for Mr. Bennet.
    d. A new neighbor is due to arrive who has already expressed an interest in marrying one of the Bennet daughters.

2. Which of the following statements best describes Mrs. Bennet's feelings about her husband as indicated by this selection?
    a. Mrs. Bennet is tired of her husband.
    b. Mrs. Bennet is exasperated by her husband.
    c. Mrs. Bennet is afraid of her husband.
    d. Mrs. Bennet is indifferent toward her husband.

3. This selection is set in England at the beginning of the 19th century. Drawing on information from this selection, what could you conclude was a primary goal for young women in England during this time period?
    a. To marry a man who wants a wife
    b. To marry a man with money
    c. To entertain the neighbors
    d. To find and attract wealthy neighbors to move nearby

4. "Is that his design in settling here?"

What does the word design mean in the context of this selection?
    a. Intention
    b. Drawing
    c. Creation
    d. Improvisation

5. "It is a truth universally acknowledged, that a single man in possession of a good fortune, must be in want of a wife."

Which of the following most nearly matches the meaning of the underlined phrase?
    a. Everyone knows
    b. The universe has decided
    c. It is a documented fact
    d. It is best to tell the truth

6. How does Mrs. Bennet feel about the arrival of Mr. Bingley?
   a. Mrs. Bennet is excited about the arrival of Mr. Bingley.
   b. Mrs. Bennet is nervous about the arrival of Mr. Bingley.
   c. Mrs. Bennet is afraid the arrival of Mr. Bingley will upset Mr. Bennet.
   d. Mrs. Bennet is indifferent to the arrival of Mr. Bingley.

Refer to the following for questions 7–10:

> Margaritte stood nervously in the wings of the stage, waiting for her cue. The music from the orchestra swelled around her. She could almost see the colors and shapes it made in the air. With one foot, Margaritte kept time with the beat. Any minute now, it would be her turn. The note sounded, and Margaritte flew from the wings.

7. Which of the following would be the best introductory sentence for this paragraph?
   a. Margaritte wore her favorite pink tutu.
   b. Margaritte looked at the other dancers waiting with her backstage.
   c. Margaritte had been taking dance lessons since she was nine years old.
   d. Margaritte was about to begin the most important performance of her dancing career.

8. Which of the following would be the best sentence to add sensory detail to this paragraph?
   a. The people in the audience looked like a garden in their colorful attire.
   b. The stage was draped in black so that the dancers' costumes stood out.
   c. The sound of the music reverberated in Margaritte's chest, becoming a part of her.
   d. Margaritte's tights felt itchy against her legs.

9. Which of the following would be the best sentence to add descriptive detail to this paragraph?
   a. The music formed the shapes of birds that soared above the stage and disappeared over the audience.
   b. This was Margaritte's favorite music to dance to.
   c. Tapping her toe to the beat of the music, Margaritte found herself growing increasingly nervous.
   d. Margaritte felt the audience would see her nervousness as soon as she stepped onto the stage.

10. Which of the following would be the best concluding sentence for this paragraph?
    a. Margaritte danced onto the stage as the music swirled around her.
    b. Margaritte danced onto the stage; her moment had finally come.
    c. When the dance recital was over, Margaritte was tired.
    d. The other dancers moved onto the stage with Margaritte.

Refer to the following for questions 11–13:

> Many fears about snakes arise from misconceptions. People are often afraid that all snakes are venomous creatures looking for people to bite. However, of the approximately 2400 species of snakes, only 270 are venomous. Venomous snakes have fangs, hollow teeth with tiny holes at the bottom through which venom is released. Although venomous snakes should be treated carefully, there is no need to fear that a snake will bite you without provocation. Like many other animals, snakes will only attack when they feel threatened.

11. Which of the following would be the best introductory sentence for this paragraph?
    a. Many people think snakes have slimy skin, but they do not.
    b. Gaining knowledge about snakes is the best way to learn to live harmoniously with these misunderstood reptiles.
    c. A rattlesnake will sound its rattle to warn people not to come near.
    d. Snakes shed their skin when it gets too small.

12. **Which of the following sentences is not essential to explain the primary premise of the paragraph?**
    a. People are often afraid that all snakes are venomous creatures looking for people to bite.
    b. However, of the approximately 2400 species of snakes, only 270 are venomous.
    c. Venomous snakes have fangs, hollow teeth with tiny holes at the bottom through which venom is released.
    d. Although venomous snakes should be treated carefully, there is no need to fear that a snake will bite you without provocation.

13. **Which of the following would be the best concluding sentence for this paragraph?**
    a. There is no need to be fearful of snakes as long as you are careful.
    b. People in the desert are the only ones who should be afraid of snakes.
    c. You should learn the names of each species of snake.
    d. Snakes are more afraid of people than people are of them.

Refer to the following for questions 14–18:

Puck

(1) It was the second week of an unseasonably cool July. The sun had finally made a rare weekend appearance, and the suburban neighborhood sizzled with possibility. As the day slipped lazily into evening, sun-baked residents trickled back to their homes from the lakeshore and the park and the community pool. The air smelled of sunscreen, charcoal smoke, sweat, overcooked meat.

(2) Will Jensen tossed a football across the yard to his best friend, Troy Coons. Dusk was settling around them, but the thought of retreating to the confines of the house seemed sacrilegious.

(3) "Can you believe we're going to college in a few weeks?" Troy asked, lobbing the ball back to Will.

(4) "What I can't believe is that you and I will be six hundred miles apart," Will said, catching the ball easily. "I don't think we've gone more than three days without seeing each other since kindergarten."

(5) "Except for when you had chicken pox," Troy said. "And the time I went to Hawaii with my grandparents. Remember how we begged them to let you come in my luggage?"

(6) Will laughed and tossed the ball back. "Those things don't count," he argued.

(7) The ball went sideways and Troy lunged for it, tripping over a ragged little terrier lounging lazily on the lawn. Troy collapsed in a tangled heap and the ball bounced down, just beyond his outstretched hand.

(8) "Puck!" Troy groaned. "No dogs on the field!"

(9) Will sauntered over and scooped up the little dog. He plopped down onto the crisp brown grass and laughed at Troy. Will reached over and rolled the ball toward Troy.

(10) "Don't blame Puck for your clumsiness," Will said, idly scratching the dog's fuzzy scalp. "How was he supposed to know you'd come stumbling through his daydreams?"

(11) Troy chuckled. Then they sat in silence as darkness swirled around them. Light glowed from windows thrown hopefully open to the faint breeze. Above them, the stars

winked on in the charcoal sky. In the distance, leftover fireworks crackled and fizzed. The night was ripe with memories to be made.

(12) "Are you taking Puck with you?" Troy finally asked, breaking the silence.

(13) "Nah. No dogs in the dorm. Besides, Puck would hate being locked up in a room. He's spent the last sixteen years being king of the castle. He'll be happier here. That way he can greet me whenever I make it back home."

(14) Will lifted Puck and held him in mid-air. Puck wriggled playfully and licked Will's nose with his doughy pink tongue. Will laughed and set him down.

(15) "I sure will miss him, though," Will said, wiping Puck's saliva from his nose. "Puck's been a part of every memory I've had since I was really little."

(16) Troy faked a sniffle. "Stop, man. Just stop. I'm tearing up over here."

(17) Will punched Troy's arm good-naturedly. "Shut up!"

(18) A low, loud car careened around the corner, shattering the stupor of the summer night. Puck ran barking toward the car as it wove across the street like a wayward pinball.

(19) Seized with sudden panic, Will scrambled to his feet. "Puck, no! Come back!"

(20) As Will reached the sidewalk, Puck darted into the street. In a terrible, slow-motion montage, Will heard the tires squeal and Puck's bark turn to a startled yelp. Then the car sped away, and silence smothered the chaos.

(21) Will ran into the street. People peeked from doorways and windows, searching for the source of the commotion. Will fell beside Puck's limp body. Puck whimpered quietly and struggled to lick Will's hand. Then he was still.

(22) "No, Puck! No!" Will screamed. Shock rang in his ears and he was dizzy with emotion. Troy put a hand on Will's shoulder, but Will shook it off. He didn't want to be comforted. He wanted to wallow and writhe in the pool of pain that was slowly spreading through his soul.

(23) Every memory he had with Puck flooded his mind. This was not how it was supposed to be. Puck was supposed to be waiting for him when he came home from college. He was supposed to watch at the window as Will drove away and be there wagging with excitement whenever Will came home. He was supposed to be the constant in Will's changing life. This was not part of the plan.

(24) Will stayed in the road for a long time, crouched over Puck's familiar, lifeless body. He felt numb, empty, and emotionless. Finally, Will's mother led him gently from the street. Troy and Will's father gathered Puck's body carefully into a sheet. Neighbors watched in sympathy as the sorrowful party crossed the lawn.

(25) They walked in silence as darkness swirled around them. Lights still glowed from windows thrown hopefully open to the faint breeze. Above them, stars still winked on in the charcoal sky. In the distance, leftover fireworks still crackled and fizzed. Everything was the same, and nothing was the same. Puck was gone. And Will knew things would never really be the same again.

14. In paragraph 2, what does "sacrilegious" mean?
    a. Absurdly inappropriate
    b. Nasty and evil
    c. A waste of time
    d. Holy and good

15. Which of the following best describes Will's attitude in paragraph 15?
    a. Angry
    b. Cheerful
    c. Sentimental
    d. Annoyed

16. What type of figurative language is used to describe the stars in paragraph 11?
    a. Simile
    b. Personification
    c. Metaphor
    d. Paradox

17. How is Puck's death an example of irony?
    a. Will was worried about missing Puck while Will was away at college, and now he will miss him forever
    b. Will wanted Puck to die so Will didn't have to think about him while he was away at college
    c. Puck was always quiet and docile, but he was strangely driven to run after that one car
    d. Troy hated Puck, and he wanted Puck to be hit by the passing car

18. Which of the following is a main idea in this story?
    a. The passing car is playing loud music
    b. Troy misses the ball when he trips over Puck
    c. Will and Troy like to play football
    d. Will has had Puck for a very long time

Refer to the following for questions 19–23:

Comets

Comets are bodies that orbit the sun. They are distinguishable from asteroids by the presence of comas or tails. In the outer solar system, comets remain frozen and are so small that they are difficult to detect from Earth. As a comet approaches the inner solar system, solar radiation causes the materials within the comet to vaporize and trail off the nuclei. The released dust and gas forms a fuzzy atmosphere called the coma, and the force exerted on the coma causes a tail to form, pointing away from the sun.

Comet nuclei are made of ice, dust, rock and frozen gases and vary widely in size: from 100 meters or so to tens of kilometers across. The comas may be even larger than the Sun. Because of their low mass, they do not become spherical and have irregular shapes.

There are over 3,500 known comets, and the number is steadily increasing. This represents only a small portion of the total comets existing, however. Most comets are too faint to be visible without the aid of a telescope; the number of comets visible to the naked eye is around one a year.

Comets leave a trail of solid debris behind them. If a comet's path crosses the Earth's path, there will likely be meteor showers as Earth passes through the trail of debris.

Many comets and asteroids have collided into Earth. Some scientists believe that comets hitting Earth about 4 billion years ago brought a significant proportion of the water in Earth's oceans. There are still many near-Earth comets.

Most comets have oval shaped orbits that take them close to the Sun for part of their orbit and then out further into the Solar System for the remainder of the orbit. Comets are often classified according to the length of their orbital period: short period comets have orbital periods of less than 200 years, long period comets have orbital periods of more than 200 years, single apparition comets have trajectories which cause them to permanently leave the solar system after passing the Sun once.

19. What does the passage claim distinguishes comets from asteroids?
   a. The make-up of their nuclei
   b. The presence of comas or tails
   c. Their orbital periods
   d. Their irregular shapes

20. According to the passage, which of the following is true?
   a. There are 350 known comets, and the number is steadily increasing.
   b. There are 3,500 known comets, and the number is staying the same.
   c. There are 3,500 known comets, and many more comets that aren't known.
   d. Most comets are visible to the naked eye.

21. According to the passage, why do comets have irregular shapes?
   a. Because they are not spherical
   b. Because they have orbital periods
   c. Because of their low mass
   d. Because of their tails

22. What does the passage claim about the size of comets?
   a. Some are tens of kilometers across and can be seen without the use of a telescope
   b. Some are tens of kilometers across, and the coma is never larger than the Sun.
   c. Some are 100 meters across, and the coma is never larger than the Sun.
   d. The smallest comet is at least a kilometer, and the coma can be larger than the Sun.

23. According to the last paragraph, what does the name "single apparition comets" mean?
   a. They only appear during the part of their orbit that is nearer to the Sun.
   b. They stay in the solar system even though they are only apparent once.
   c. Their orbital periods are so long they only appear once across millennia.
   d. They only remain in the solar system long enough to pass the Sun once.

Refer to the following for questions 24–29:

Selection of "The Gettysburg Address" by Abraham Lincoln

Four score and seven years ago our fathers brought forth, upon this continent, a new nation, conceived in Liberty, and dedicated to the proposition that all men are created equal.

Now we are engaged in a great civil war, testing whether that nation, or any nation so conceived, and so dedicated, can long endure. We are met here on a great battlefield of that war. We have come to dedicate a portion of it as a final resting place for those who here gave their lives that that nation might live. It is altogether fitting and proper that we should do this.

But in a larger sense we cannot dedicate—we cannot consecrate—we cannot hallow this ground. The brave men, living and dead, who struggled here, have consecrated it far above our poor power to add or detract. The world will little note, nor long remember, what we say here, but can never forget what they did here.

It is for us, the living, rather to be dedicated here to the unfinished work which they have, thus far, so nobly carried on. It is rather for us to be here dedicated to the great task remaining before us—that from these honored dead we take increased devotion to that cause for which they here gave the last full measure of devotion—that we here highly resolve that these dead shall not have died in vain; that this nation shall have a new birth of freedom; and that this government of the people, by the people, for the people, shall not perish from the earth.

24. What is the main message of this speech?
   a. Those who died in this battle honor this land we are dedicating today better than anyone else.
   b. As we honor those who died in this battle, we should move forward with renewed dedication to ensuring the nation our founding fathers created continues to function the way they intended.
   c. We need to put the regrets of the past aside, without remembering the sacrifices of those who gave their lives for our country.
   d. The war we are fighting is far from over, as evidenced by the number of lives lost in this battle.

25. The phrase "the world will little note" means what?
   a. The world will not soon forget.
   b. The world will record what we say here.
   c. The world will not pay much attention.
   d. The world will recall what we do with perfect accuracy.

26. There were nearly 100 years between the American Revolution and the Civil War. The speech connects ideas about these two conflicts by saying that the ideas of the Civil War:
   a. Threaten those of the Revolution.
   b. Are similar to those of the Revolution.
   c. Are newer than those of the Revolution.
   d. Are better than those of the Revolution.

27. Why does Lincoln most likely talk about the past before he talks about the present?
   a. To incite listeners of his message to protest
   b. To remember what has been lost in the past
   c. To establish context for his main message
   d. To try to get listeners to side with his position

28. What is the following sentence addressing?
Now we are engaged in a great civil war, testing whether that nation, or any nation so conceived, and so dedicated, can long endure.
   a. Whether or not a nation based on ideas of freedom and equality can survive for any significant length of time
   b. Whether or not the Union will be able to preserve the existing structure of the United States by preventing the Confederacy from seceding
   c. Whether or not the Confederacy will be successful in seceding from the United States and surviving on its own
   d. Whether or not Lincoln should continue dedicating troops to the war

29. In paragraph 4, the word *vain* most nearly means:
a. Decisive
b. Frivolous
c. Momentous
d. Practical

Refer to the following for questions 30–34:

Black History Month

Black History Month is still a meaningful observance. Despite the election of our first African American president being a huge achievement, education about African American history is still unmet to a substantial degree. Black History Month is a powerful tool in working towards meeting that need. There is no reason to give up that tool now, and it can easily coexist with an effort to develop a more comprehensive and inclusive yearly curriculum.

Having a month set aside for the study of African American history doesn't limit its study and celebration to that month; it merely focuses complete attention on it for that month. There is absolutely no contradiction between having a set-aside month and having it be present in the curriculum the rest of the year.

Equally important is that the debate itself about the usefulness of Black History Month can, and should, remind parents that they can't necessarily count on schools to teach African American history as thoroughly as many parents would want.

Although Black History Month has, to an extent, become a shallow ritual, it doesn't have to be. Good teachers and good materials could make the February curriculum deeply informative, thought-provoking, and inspiring. The range of material that can be covered is rich, varied, and full of limitless possibilities.

Finally, it is worthwhile to remind ourselves and our children of the key events that happened during the month of February. In 1926, Woodson organized the first Black History Week to honor the birthdays of essential civil rights activists Abraham Lincoln and Frederick Douglass. W. E. B. DuBois was born on February 23, 1868. The 15th Amendment, which granted African Americans the right to vote, was passed on February 3, 1870. The first black U.S. senator, Hiram R. Revels, took his oath of office on February 25, 1870. The National Association for the Advancement of Colored People (NAACP) was founded on February 12, 1909. Malcolm X was shot on February 21, 1965.

30. Based on this passage, what would be the author's argument against the study and celebration of Black History Month being limited to one month of the year?
a. Black History Month is still a meaningful observance.
b. Black History Month is a powerful tool in meeting the need for education about African American history.
c. Having a month set aside for the study of African American history does not limit its study and celebration to that month.
d. Black History Month does not have to be a shallow ritual.

31. **Why does the author believe that the debate itself about Black History Month can be useful?**
    a. The people on opposing sides can come to an intelligent resolution about whether to keep it.
    b. African American history is discussed in the media when the debate is ongoing.
    c. The debate is a reminder to parents that they can't count on schools to teach their children about African American history.
    d. Black History Month doesn't have to be a shallow ritual.

32. **What does the author say about the range of material that can be taught during Black History Month?**
    a. It is rich and varied.
    b. It is important.
    c. It is an unmet need.
    d. It is comprehensive.

33. **The author's tone in this passage can be described as:**
    a. Doubtful
    b. Emboldening
    c. Jovial
    d. Menacing

34. **Which of the following can be inferred from the last paragraph?**
    a. The most important events in black history happened in the 19th century.
    b. Black history has been influenced by more men than women.
    c. There are several avenues from which to draw on larger lessons of black history.
    d. The most influential black figures served in politics.

Refer to the following for questions 35–40:

Plastics

Plastics have long been considered one of the great conveniences of the modern era, but evidence is mounting to indicate that these conveniences have come at an incredible cost. The chief benefit of plastics is their durability, but this benefit turns out to be the same reason plastic has become a significant problem: It takes between two and four hundred years to decompose. All of this plastic has accumulated into a catastrophic mess and has also caused disease in humans.

Between Hawaii and Japan, a giant mass of plastic twice the size of Texas slowly swirls with the currents of the Pacific Ocean. This area has come to be known as the Great Pacific Garbage Patch, and its effects on the ecology of the ocean are unimaginable. According to United Nations researchers, a hundred thousand sea mammals and a million seabirds die each year. They are found with cigarette lighters, syringes, and other plastics that they mistake for food in their stomachs.

Evidence also indicates that the plastic we store our food in poses health risks. For instance, phthalates (pronounced "THEY-lates") have been shown to have detrimental effects on the reproductive system, yet they are found in many plastic products—including baby bottles and water bottles. They have also been linked to various forms of cancer. Additionally, a chemical called bisphenol A that is found in many plastics can mimic the effects of the hormone estrogen, which can also affect the reproductive system.

In short, plastics may turn out to be a lot less convenient than they seem!

35. Which of the following best describes the author's purpose in writing this passage?
    a. To persuade readers to accept the author's point of view.
    b. To explain the benefits of plastic.
    c. To explain the risks of plastic bottles.
    d. To inform the reader of the effects of phthalates in plastics.

36. In the first paragraph, the word "chief" most nearly means:
    a. Main
    b. Least likely
    c. Benefit
    d. Leader of a Native American tribe

37. Which of the following statements can be inferred from paragraph two?
    a. The Great Pacific Garbage Patch is not a significant threat to humans.
    b. No one has determined why sea mammals and seabirds are dying at an alarming rate.
    c. The Great Pacific Garbage Patch is too large to be cleaned up by one country.
    d. Ocean currents carry the plastic to the middle of the ocean.

38. As used in this passage, the word "mimic" most nearly means:
    a. Reduce
    b. Cancerous
    c. Intensify
    d. Resemble

39. Why does this passage not discuss more of plastics' benefits?
    a. Plastics have no benefits.
    b. The passage emphasizes the dangers over the benefits in order to prove that plastics are harmful.
    c. The passage devotes a significant amount of attention to the benefits of plastics.
    d. Discussing the benefits would contradict the author's point that plastics are a necessary evil.

40. According to the passage, the word "durability" most nearly means:
    a. Decomposition
    b. Permanence
    c. Coloration
    d. Poisonous

Reading—Vocabulary

Refer to the following for questions 1–22:

Select the answer that is closest in meaning to the underlined portion.

1. <u>Selecting</u> the best person for the job was difficult.
    a. Locating
    b. Contacting
    c. Choosing
    d. Informing

2. The **smoldering** warehouse
    a. Reeking
    b. Smoking
    c. Empty
    d. Enormous

3. The new car was very **costly**.
    a. expensive
    b. cheap
    c. attractive
    d. rare

4. A **severe** storm
    a. Relentless
    b. Slight
    c. Cold
    d. Immediate

5. Stanley was so **besotted** with his prom date that he spent most of the dance gazing at her adoringly.
    a. infatuated
    b. infuriated
    c. perplexed
    d. engrossed

6. The **stellar** student
    a. Predictable
    b. Unimpressed
    c. Outstanding
    d. Indifferent

7. The woman's **response** to the question was correct.
    a. hesitation
    b. answer
    c. decision
    d. concern

8. The **unanimous** decision
    a. Difficult
    b. Undisputed
    c. Praised
    d. Predictable

9. The unpopular **tariff**
    a. Official
    b. Vote
    c. Law
    d. Tax

10. Chemotherapy is designed to <u>suppress</u> the growth of cancerous cells.
    a. encourage
    b. promote
    c. repress
    d. reveal

11. <u>Ruddy</u> cheeks
    a. Red
    b. Weary
    c. Swollen
    d. Watery

12. His <u>keen</u> remorse
    a. Relative
    b. Sharp
    c. Long
    d. Large

13. He made an <u>oath</u> to his king.
    a. delivery
    b. promise
    c. statement
    d. criticism

14. After a work emergency, the company promised to <u>compensate</u> the employees for working above and beyond their normal required hours.
    a. allocate
    b. contribute
    c. penalize
    d. reimburse

15. They enjoyed the <u>silence</u> of the night.
    a. darkness
    b. excitement
    c. quiet
    d. mood

16. After her traumatic experience, the troubling dream began to <u>recur</u> nearly every night.
    a. concur
    b. disappear
    c. incur
    d. reappear

17. The <u>secluded</u> village
    a. Loud
    b. Remote
    c. Populous
    d. Religious

18. He **modified** his schedule so he could attend the staff lunch.
    a. checked
    b. shortened
    c. considered
    d. changed

19. To **skulk** quietly
    a. Sniff
    b. Plan
    c. Sneak
    d. Talk

20. The child **trembled** with fear.
    a. spoke
    b. shook
    c. wept
    d. ducked

21. The **belated** gift
    a. Beautiful
    b. Overdue
    c. Inexpensive
    d. Sincere

22. She **cleansed** her face in the morning.
    a. examined
    b. washed
    c. touched
    d. dried

Language

1. Identify the sentence that contains an error in usage, punctuation, or grammar. If there are no errors, choose the last option.
   a. Fear of the number thirteen is called "triskaidekaphobia."
   b. The earwig's name originates in the myth that the insect burrows into the human ear to lay its eggs.
   c. The longest word recorded in an English dictionary are "Pneumonoultramicroscopicsilicovolcanokoniosis."
   d. No mistake.

2. Identify the sentence that contains an error in usage, punctuation, or grammar. If no errors are found, choose the last option.
   a. "Stewardesses," "desegregated," and "reverberated" are the longest words a person can type using only his or her left hand.
   b. The largest catfish ever catch is 646 pounds, the size of an adult brown bear.
   c. A flyswatter has holes in it to reduce air resistance.
   d. No mistake.

3. Identify the sentence that contains an error in usage, punctuation, or grammar. If no errors are found, choose the last option.
   a. The canoe cut a clear swath through the algae.
   b. Though widely ridiculed when first proposed, Alfred Wegener's theory of plate tectonics is now an accepted explanation of how continents are formed.
   c. Though a highly influentially anthropologist, Claude Levi-Strauss often took criticism for spending little time in the field studying real cultures.
   d. No mistake.

4. Identify the sentence that contains an error in usage, punctuation, or grammar. If no errors are found, choose the last option.
   a. Fiction writer David Foster Wallace, author of the influential novel *Infinite Jest*, also authored a book surveying all of the significant theories of infinity in the history of mathematics.
   b. The photograph made the Eiffel Tower look like it was balanced on Oswald's palm.
   c. It is easy to get confused when calculating time differences between time zones a useful way to remember them is that the Atlantic Ocean starts with A, as in A.M., and the Pacific Ocean starts with P, as in P.M.
   d. No mistake.

5. Identify the sentence that contains an error in usage, punctuation, or grammar. If no errors are found, choose the last option.
   a. Arnold was disappointed to discover the model airplane he purchased online was half the size he expected.
   b. Computer storage has come a long way since the days of punched paper tape.
   c. The surrealists were a group of artists who believed that art should reflect the subconscious mind, their images are often very dreamlike, showing businessmen falling like rain over a city and melting clocks.
   d. No mistake.

6. Identify the sentence that contains an error in usage, punctuation, or grammar. If no errors are found, choose the last option.
   a. A "moor" is a plot of uncultivated land, similar to prairies in the U.S.
   b. "Orange is my favorite color, but not my favorite fruit." said Lisa.
   c. Some historians believe that the United States would have been too large for one government to control if the telegraph had not been invented in 1837.
   d. No mistake.

7. Identify the sentence that contains an error in usage, punctuation, or grammar. If no errors are found, choose the last option.
   a. The largest volcano in our solar system is found on Mars.
   b. The deepest canyon, too.
   c. The volcano, called the Olympus Mons, is 342 miles in width and 17 miles tall; the canyon, called the Valles Marinaris, is 2,500 miles long.
   d. No mistake.

8. Identify the sentence that contains an error in usage, punctuation, or grammar. If no errors are found, choose the last option.
   a. Pocahontas spent the last year's of her young life in England under the name Rebecca.
   b. Dorine beat me in tennis for three straight matches.
   c. Much of the light given off by stars is blocked by cosmic dust before it reaches the Earth's atmosphere.
   d. No mistake.

9. Identify the sentence that contains an error in usage, punctuation, or grammar. If no errors are found, choose the last option.
   a. The Pima Indians of Arizona have remarkably high rates of diabetes and obesity some scientists believe the gene that causes this present-day health crisis was actually of great value to the Pima's ancestors who had to be able to retain glucose during periods of famine.
   b. Recent research has discovered that some types of incense can create effects in the human brain similar to antidepressants.
   c. Though debate on the topic has been ongoing, some believe that many amphibian species may be on the brink of extinction.
   d. No mistake.

10. Identify the sentence that contains an error in usage, punctuation, or grammar. If no errors are found, choose the last option.
   a. The driver's side fender of my car is caved in because the high-speed winds pulled the door open too quickly.
   b. While there is some truth to the belief that Inuits have many words for snow, it is often overlooked that there are quite a few words for snow in English too: snow, slush, flurry, snowflake, and even more if you count the slang of snowboarders.
   c. Director Alfred Hitchcock make over 60 films in his career.
   d. No mistake.

11. Identify the sentence that contains an error in usage, punctuation, or grammar. If no errors are found, choose the last option.
   a. A good pediatrician should try not to laugh at the fears of new parents.
   b. Some of the most difficult words to spell include "bureaucracy," "sacrilegious," and "millennium."
   c. Sales of digitally downloaded albums have risen from 5.5 million in 2004 to 65.8 million in 2008.
   d. No mistake.

12. Identify the sentence that contains an error in usage, punctuation, or grammar. If no errors are found, choose the last option.
   a. The earliest recording of a human voice was made by Thomas Edison in 1877, when they recorded himself reciting "Mary Had a Little Lamb."
   b. In 2009, *The Simpsons* became the longest running series in television history.
   c. Many say that Reunion Tower in downtown Dallas, Texas, resembles a microphone or a golf ball on a tee.
   d. No mistake.

13. Identify the sentence that contains an error in usage, punctuation, or grammar. If no errors are found, choose the last option.
   a. The *trireme* was a Greek battleship that got its name from the three banks of oars that helped propel the ship into battle.
   b. Our basement floods once a yearly.
   c. The *novitiate* is the period of time before a monk or priest takes his vows to make sure he is suited for the religious life.
   d. No mistake.

14. Identify the sentence that contains an error in usage, punctuation, or grammar. If no errors are found, choose the last option.
   a. The trumpet player said, "I played the song right, just not the notes."
   b. Woody Allen said, "I don't want to achieve immortality through my work. I want to achieve it through not dying."
   c. Samuel Goldwyn is said to have replied to a secretary who asked whether she should destroy files over ten years old, "Yes, but keep copies."
   d. No mistake.

15. Identify the sentence that contains an error in usage, punctuation, or grammar. If no errors are found, choose the last option.
   a. When asked to take a reduction in pay from $20,000 to $7,500 a year, baseball legend Vernon Gomez replied, "You keep the salary and pay me the cut."
   b. The spread of Islam began around 600 A.D. and reached from the Middle East to North Africa, Spain, Central Asia, and India?
   c. Hadrian, Emperor of Rome, is credited with halting the expansion of the Roman Empire to concentrate instead on defending its boundaries.
   d. No mistake.

16. Identify the sentence that contains an error in usage, punctuation, or grammar. If no errors are found, choose the last option.
   a. The Sahara Desert was rarely crossed until the introduction of the camel in 100 A.D.
   b. International time standards were not put in place until 1883.
   c. The names of the days of the week originate in either Latin or Saxon names for deities, Sunday, for instance, is Saxon for "Sun's Day," while Thursday derives from "Thor's Day."
   d. No mistake.

17. Identify the sentence that contains an error in usage, punctuation, or grammar. If no errors are found, choose the last option.
   a. The origin of the clock is usually traced back to Galileo, who in 1583 reportedly watched a chandelier swinging during a church service and imagined a way to use a pendulum as a time-keeping device.
   b. Irvin Hertzel ran a statistical analysis of Monopoly squares and found that players land on some spots more often than others, specifically Illinois Ave., Go, B & O Railroad, and Free Parking.
   c. Held in Georgia, the Masters is an annual golf tournament that professional golfers consider the most valuable title in golf.
   d. No mistake.

18. Identify the sentence that contains an error in usage, punctuation, or grammar. If no errors are found, choose the last option.
   a. Ironically, the namesake of the Nobel Peace Prize, Alfred Nobel, are most noted for his invention of dynamite in the 1860s.
   b. The terms of our lease agreement were long and hard to understand.
   c. Many terms in our legal system are Latin in origin, such as "nolo contendere" (no contest) and "actus rea" (a wrongful act).
   d. No mistake.

19. **Identify the sentence that contains an error in usage, punctuation, or grammar. If no errors are found, choose the last option.**
    a. Loud sounds can causing damage to the hair cells that turn sound waves into electrical signals that the brain perceives as sound.
    b. Debate has raged for over 200 years about whether the U.S. should adopt the metric system.
    c. The metric system recognizes only seven base units of measurement, including the meter for length, the kilogram for mass, and lesser known units used by specialists like the mole for substance and the candela for light intensity.
    d. No mistake.

20. **Identify the sentence that contains an error in usage, punctuation, or grammar. If no errors are found, choose the last option.**
    a. The metric system uses a "base-ten" system of measurement, which means its prefixes indicate multiples of ten.
    b. If you ever need to measure something but do not have access to a ruler, these facts can help: The average credit card is $3\frac{3}{8}$ inches by $2\frac{1}{8}$ inches, the diameter of a quarter is around one inch, and the diameter of a penny is about $\frac{3}{4}$ inch.
    c. Carbon monoxide Poisoning can cause disorientation and delirium, and it can induce a coma.
    d. No mistake.

21. **Identify the sentence that contains an error in usage, punctuation, or grammar. If no errors are found, choose the last option.**
    a. Capgras Syndrome causes the strange delusion that people such as family members and friends are not who they appear to be but are instead imposters.
    b. Yvette belonged to three organizations whose schedules constantly conflicted.
    c. Owen's shirt was stained pink from his popsicle, purple from jelly, and blue from Kool-Aid.
    d. No mistake.

22. **Identify the sentence that contains an error in usage, punctuation, or grammar. If no errors are found, choose the last option.**
    a. They closed the parking deck at midnight, so we could not get no cars out until morning.
    b. "Associationism" is the name given to the theory that memories are linked together so that when one is triggered, associated memories are activated as well.
    c. Some psychologists believe that many emotional disorders, including depression and anxiety, can be traced back to unrealistic expectations and assumptions.
    d. No mistake.

23. **Identify the sentence that contains an error in usage, punctuation, or grammar. If no errors are found, choose the last option.**
    a. Joni designed the grocery stores sign, but Evan painted it.
    b. The "figure-ground phenomenon" is a term used to describe the way we perceive some objects to be in the foreground and others to be in the background.
    c. The Latin professor called his students "quidnuncs" when they asked too many questions about the course; the term is Latin for "what now?"
    d. No mistake.

24. Identify the sentence that contains an error in usage, punctuation, or grammar. If no errors are found, choose the last option.
   a. Outside the apartment, the bus stop is a source of constant noise.
   b. Few people remembered Sydney's birthday except Jon, whose birthday was the same day.
   c. Erin brought cookies and juice on the last day of class.
   d. No mistake.

25. Identify the sentence that contains an error in usage, punctuation, or grammar. If no errors are found, choose the last option.
   a. In math, the "Goldbach conjecture" states that every even number greater than two is the sum of two primes.
   b. Enjil was a complex Sumerian sky god who was at times characterized as wrathful and at others as kind and generous.
   c. Twenty-four leaders of the Nazi party was brought to trial at the end of World War II in what became known as the Nuremberg Trials.
   d. No mistake.

26. Identify the sentence that contains an error in usage, punctuation, or grammar. If no errors are found, choose the last option.
   a. In radio broadcasting, a short jingle called a "bumper" announces the name of the station after commercials.
   b. "There weren't any jobs listed in the newspaper this morning," Ed told his father.
   c. Water is called "hard water" if it do not quickly create lather upon contact with soap because of mineral compounds dissolved in the water.
   d. No mistake.

27. Identify the sentence that contains an error in usage, punctuation, or grammar. If no errors are found, choose the last option.
   a. Halley's Comet, which completes its orbit around the sun once every 76 years, was last seen in 1986 and will not be visible again until 2062.
   b. Ice crystals in the atmosphere, which can create a halo around the sun or moon.
   c. "Abiogenesis" is a term that refers to the discredited belief that living things can be created from nonliving things.
   d. No mistake.

28. Identify the sentence that contains an error in usage, punctuation, or grammar. If no errors are found, choose the last option.
   a. The term "Algebra" comes from the title of a book written in the ninth century that explains how to balance equations.
   b. Atomic clocks keep time by measuring the vibrations of Atoms and molecules.
   c. The chemical formula for the caffeine molecule contains calcium, hydrogen, oxygen, and nitrogen.
   d. No mistake.

29. Identify the sentence that contains an error in usage, punctuation, or grammar. If no errors are found, choose the last option.
   a. Heat was once believes to be a type of fluid called "caloric," which flowed into objects and raised their temperature.
   b. Streams of protons and neutrons that escape the sun during solar flares are called "solar wind."
   c. The "heat death of the universe" is a theory that predicts the universe will eventually run out of usable energy.
   d. No mistake.

30. Identify the sentence that contains an error in usage, punctuation, or grammar. If no errors are found, choose the last option.
   a. The epicenter of an earthquake is the point on the Earth's surface that is above the hypocenter, or the point inside the Earth where the earthquake occurs.
   b. Apart from a sine wave created by an electronic device, most sounds are not "pure" because they contain many different vibrations at different frequencies pure tones vibrate at only one frequency.
   c. Though Chicago is known as the "Windy City" with winds that average 10.4 miles per hour, its winds are far slower than those of Mt. Washington, New Hampshire, where winds average 35.3 miles per hour.
   d. No mistake.

31. Identify the sentence that contains an error in usage, punctuation, or grammar. If no errors are found, choose the last option.
   a. Arthur, realizing that bugs were turning the roots of his zucchini plants to mush.
   b. The Earth moves at different speeds depending on where one stands in relation to the poles; the North Pole spins at about zero miles per hour, while the equator spins at over 1,000 miles per hour.
   c. Because maps must distort the size of certain continents to represent a sphere stretched over a two-dimensional plane, Greenland is often depicted as similar in size to South America, even though it is about eight times smaller.
   d. No mistake.

32. Identify the sentence that contains an error in usage, punctuation, or grammar. If no errors are found, choose the last option.
   a. The Earth is believed to be about 4.6 billion years old.
   b. Sequoyah, who created a written script for the Cherokee language, compared the task to "catching a wild animal and taming it."
   c. The discovery of gold on Cherokee land in 1828 is considered a significant motivation for the passage of the Indian Removal Act of 1830, which forced Native Americans from their homes.
   d. No mistake.

33. Identify the sentence that contains an error in usage, punctuation, or grammar. If no errors are found, choose the last option.
   a. In 1803, Robert Livingston and James Monroe, two of Thomas Jefferson's aides, purchased all of the French territories in America.
   b. They paid the remarkably low price of $15 million to Napoleon, who wanted to sell the land to finance his military campaigns.
   c. This figure amounts to about four cents per acre, or eight dollars per square mile.
   d. No mistake.

34. Identify the sentence that contains an error in usage, punctuation, or grammar. If no errors are found, choose the last option.
   a. The narwhal is a member of the dolphin family, easily recognized by its long, spiraling tusk, it is often compared to the mythical unicorn.
   b. The ocean is saltier in regions where the temperature is higher due to a higher rate of evaporation.
   c. The garter snake is often called a "gardener snake" or a "guarder snake" because of the similar sounds of the words.
   d. No mistake.

35. Identify the sentence that contains an error in usage, punctuation, or grammar. If no errors are found, choose the last option.
   a. Long distance calls were placed by an operator until 1951.
   b. The first drive-in movie theater opened in 1933.
   c. The first Ferris' Wheel was built in Chicago, Illinois.
   d. No mistake.

36. Identify the sentence that contains an error in usage, punctuation, or grammar. If no errors are found, choose the last option.
   a. Trees in the Olympic rain forest in northwest Washington State is covered with a thick green moss that is nourished by the 150 annual inches of rainfall.
   b. The sand dunes were prettiest at sunset, when the shadows ran across the landscape like dark ribbons.
   c. Some of the students were sleeping during reading time.
   d. No mistake.

37. Identify the sentence that contains an error in usage, punctuation, or grammar. If no errors are found, choose the last option.
   a. Most published writing goes through many drafts and many readers before it is printed.
   b. Blogs, however, are rarely edited as carefully.
   c. As a result, readers have different expectations of online publications.
   d. No mistake.

38. Identify the sentence that contains an error in usage, punctuation, or grammar. If no errors are found, choose the last option.
   a. When asked what his songs were about, Bob Dylan replied, "Well, some of them are about five minutes, and some of them are about eleven minutes."
   b. I found several fossils of large trilobites on a field trip with my geology class.
   c. I was, hoping to avoid the customs official who was yelling at all of the other travelers.
   d. No mistake.

39. Identify the sentence that contains an error in usage, punctuation, or grammar. If no errors are found, choose the last option.
   a. Reykjavik is the Capitol of Iceland.
   b. It is pronounced "Rake-ya-veek."
   c. The letter "j" is pronounced like a "y" in English.
   d. No mistake.

40. Identify the sentence that contains an error in usage, punctuation, or grammar. If no errors are found, choose the last option.
   a. Jen asked the professor for an extension on her first essay.
   b. She was asking for more time.
   c. The professor added three pages to the required length.
   d. No mistake.

41. Select the sentence with an error in spelling. If no errors are found, choose the last option.
   a. My favorite Beatles' record is <u>Revolver</u>.
   b. My favorite Beatles' song is "Strawberry Fields."
   c. My favorite Beatle is John Lennon.
   d. No mistake.

42. Select the sentence with an error in spelling. If no errors are found, choose the last option.
    a. I had to have a tooth pulled after a bike accident.
    b. When I received the dentist's bill, I was disgruntled.
    c. I was graitful that I couldn't feel a thing.
    d. No mistake.

43. Select the sentence with an error in spelling. If no errors are found, choose the last option.
    a. Mrs. Albom, the music teacher, financed her summer vacation by bagging groceries at Wal-Mart after school.
    b. We put down a tarp and shook the branches to get the mulberries.
    c. The citric acid used in Vitamin C tablets makes them taste sower.
    d. No mistake.

44. Choose the sentence that contains a spelling error. If there are no errors, choose the last option.
    a. Despite being born a slave, Benjamin Banneker went on to play a pivotal role in the planning of Washington D.C.
    b. Andrew Johnson is the only president to serve as a sinator after his time as president, which is ironic because the senate had attempted to impeach him when he was president.
    c. The St. Burchardi Church in Halberstadt, Germany, is currently performing a composition by John Cage entitled "As Slow as Possible," a piece that takes 639 years to complete.
    d. No mistake.

45. Select the sentence with an error in spelling. If no errors are found, choose the last option.
    a. Jan tried to remember her groshery list by turning it into a song that went, "carrots and cashews and rolled toilet tissues."
    b. I thought for sure I had killed the basil plant, but it revived with a little water.
    c. The washing machine died with a load of wet clothes in it.
    d. No mistake.

46. Select the sentence with an error in spelling. If no errors are found, choose the last option.
    a. The rock polisher ran all nite and day for months.
    b. When the bouquet of flowers started to die, it left a little mound of yellow dust under each flower.
    c. Nora wants to become a veterinarian when she grows up.
    d. No mistake.

47. Select the sentence with an error in spelling. If no errors are found, choose the last option.
    a. Eleanor wove baskets from reeds that she pulled from the bank of the nearby lake.
    b. The dog howled whenever the ambulances passed.
    c. Gas station coffee alway tastes watered down to me.
    d. No mistake.

48. Select the sentence with an error in spelling. If no errors are found, choose the last option.
    a. Peter Elbow is famous for his book titled *Writing without Teachers*, in which he promotes "freewriting," or writing for short periods of time without any concern for spelling, grammar, or logic.
    b. John Wilkes Booth's intention in assassinating President Lincoln was to avenge the Confederacy, but in effect, his actions hurt the South because Lincoln did not live to oversee his plan for reconstruction.
    c. Perspective painting uses techniques to give the two-dimentional surface of a painting the appearance of three-dimentional spays.
    d. No mistake.

49. **Select the sentence with an error in spelling. If no errors are found, choose the last option.**
    a. We entered the church from the south, but the family we were supposed to meet was waiting on the north side of the building.
    b. The stained glass cast colorful shadows across the carpet.
    c. I filled out the tax forms incorrectly, and that mistake cost me a quadruple-digit figure.
    d. No mistake.

50. **Select the sentence with an error in spelling. If no errors are found, choose the last option.**
    a. Enrique loved to sketch copies of the images he found in *National Geographic*.
    b. Over 60% of the Netherlands lies below sea level.
    c. Jon submitted three poems to the contest and won one thousand dollars.
    d. No mistake.

51. **Where should the following sentence be placed in the paragraph below?**

    Many people have proposed explanations for this drop.

    (1) Surveys of criminal activity in the United States have shown that the 1990s marked a significant drop in crimes such as vehicle theft, rape, and murder. (2) Economist Rick Nevin argues that one contributing factor is the ban on lead gasoline in the 70s because lead poisoning in children has been linked with criminal behavior later in life. (3) Other theories include the controversial claim that legalizing abortion has led to fewer unwanted children and, as a result, fewer potential criminals. (4) Some politicians, including Rudy Giuliani, even take personal responsibility, identifying their policies as effective deterrents to crime.

    a. After sentence 1
    b. After sentence 2
    c. After sentence 3
    d. After sentence 4

52. **Where should the following sentence be placed in the paragraph below?**

    Insects that carry the disease can develop resistance to the chemicals, or insecticides, that are used to kill the mosquitoes.

    (1) Malaria, a disease spread by insects and parasites, has long proven to be difficult to treat. (2) Part of the explanation has to do with adaptation, or the ability of one generation to pass its strengths on to another. (3) Some insects are simply not affected by these insecticides. (4) Unfortunately, these are the insects that survive and go on to reproduce, creating another generation of insects that are immune to the current insecticides. (5) Many researchers have abandoned hope for insecticides as a cure for malaria, turning their attention instead to other forms of defense, such as protein-blockers that protect humans from the effects of the disease instead of from the carriers.

    a. After sentence 1
    b. After sentence 2
    c. After sentence 3
    d. After sentence 4

53. Choose the word or words that best fill the blank.

    Disney films often use the same voice actors; _____, Sterling Holloway was the voice for Winnie the Pooh, the stork in *Dumbo*, the snake Kaa in *Jungle Book*, and the Cheshire Cat in *Alice in Wonderland*.

    a. but
    b. for instance
    c. thus
    d. so

54. Choose the word or words that best fill the blank.

    Many similarities exist between the film *Star Wars IV: A New Hope* and a Japanese film called *The Hidden Fortress*; _____ , *Star Wars* director George Lucas openly acknowledges the film as a significant influence.

    a. however
    b. or
    c. in fact
    d. yet

55. Choose the word or words that best fill the blank.

    Marty did not realize until he arrived to perform in Philadelphia that he had left his guitar in Pittsburgh; _____, he was fortunate to find a music store that agreed to rent him one for the evening.

    a. however
    b. because
    c. after
    d. while

56. Choose the sentence that is correct and most clearly written.

    a. The novelist David Markson is known for his experimental works, such as "This Is Not a Novel."
    b. Experimental works such as "This Is Not a Novel" have been wrote by David Markson.
    c. Novelist David Markson is knew for his experimental works, such as "This Is Not a Novel."
    d. David Markson is a novelist who is known for experimentation his works include "This Is Not a Novel."

57. Choose the sentence that is correct and most clearly written.

    a. I intended to mow the yard, but I wanted to wait until evening when it are cooler.
    b. I intended to mow the yard, but I wanted to wait until evening when it would be cooler.
    c. I intended to mow the yard, but not until it getting cooler in the evening.
    d. I intended to mow the yard, but I waits until evening when it was cooler.

58. Choose the sentence that is correct and most clearly written.

    a. We used to dump our lawn clippings, but now we compost them for the garden.
    b. Dumping our lawn clippings used to be something done by us, but now composting is done by us for the garden.
    c. We used to dumps our lawn clippings, but now we composts them for the garden.
    d. We used to dump our lawn clippings, but now I compost them for the garden.

59. Which sentence does NOT belong in the following paragraph?

    (1) Though Thomas Jefferson's taste for expensive home furnishings and wine contributed to the substantial debts he faced toward the end of his life, many other factors also contributed. (2) For instance, when Jefferson's father-in-law died, all of his debts were transferred to Jefferson. (3) Additionally, though his holdings in land and slaves were considerable, they were never especially profitable. (4) Jefferson is

believed to have fathered children with one of his slaves. (5) Finally, less than a decade before his death, Jefferson unwisely agreed to endorse a $20,000 loan for a friend, and when the friend unexpectedly died a year later, Jefferson inherited yet another large debt. (6) Jefferson's personal experience with debt may have been part of his motivation in criticizing policies that would increase the national debt.

a. Sentence 2
b. Sentence 3
c. Sentence 4
d. Sentence 5

60. Which sentence does NOT belong in the following paragraph?

(1) Renowned scientist Richard Feynman once said that the atomic theory is one of the most profound discoveries scientists have made. (2) Feynman was also an accomplished percussionist who could play nine beats with one hand while playing ten with the other! (3) "All things are made of atoms," explained Feynman, "little particles that…move around in perpetual motion, attracting each other when they are a little distance apart, but repelling upon being squeezed into one another." (4) He then made the claim that this idea is one of the most illuminating ideas in the history of science: "In that one sentence, you will see, there is an enormous amount of information about the world, if just a little imagination and thinking are applied."

a. Sentence 1
b. Sentence 2
c. Sentence 3
d. Sentence 4

Verbal Skills

1. **Obligation most nearly means:**
    a. Legal
    b. Commitment
    c. Connective
    d. Decay

2. **Purchased most nearly means:**
    a. Sold
    b. Bargained
    c. Complained
    d. Bought

3. **Lesley was born the year before Steve. Steve and Barb both have birthdays in September. Lesley is older than Barb. If the first two statements are true, then the third is:**
    a. True
    b. False
    c. Unknown

4. **Intricate most nearly means:**
    a. Woven
    b. Complex
    c. Unified
    d. Simple

5. Which word does NOT belong with the others?
    a. Indian
    b. Ocean
    c. Pacific
    d. Atlantic

6. Pool is to water as library is to:
    a. A librarian
    b. A student
    c. Books
    d. Computers

7. Punishment is to reprimand as impetuous is to:
    a. Cautious
    b. Considerate
    c. Hasty
    d. Meticulous

8. Eccentric most nearly means:
    a. Egalitarian
    b. Frivolous
    c. Peculiar
    d. Obsolete

9. Eminent means the *opposite* of:
    a. Disliked
    b. Inevitable
    c. Mental
    d. Interior

10. Which word does NOT belong with the others?
    a. Appliance
    b. Washer
    c. Dryer
    d. Refrigerator

11. Which word does NOT belong with the others?
    a. Tropical
    b. Arid
    c. Climate
    d. Temperate

12. Which word does NOT belong with the others?
    a. Small intestine
    b. Kidney
    c. Liver
    d. Anatomy

13. **Charitable most nearly means:**
    a. Stingy
    b. Generous
    c. Poor
    d. Profitable

14. **Powerful means the *opposite* of:**
    a. Commanding
    b. Insignificant
    c. Dominant
    d. Potent

15. **Elevator is to building as:**
    a. Seat is to theater
    b. Apple is to core
    c. Fence is to fence post
    d. Plumber is to pipes

16. **Dexterity means the *opposite* of:**
    a. Awkwardness
    b. Agility
    c. Skill
    d. Discord

17. **Insufficient means the *opposite* of:**
    a. Deaden
    b. Distract
    c. Suction
    d. Adequate

18. **Alleviate means the *opposite* of:**
    a. Hover
    b. Worsen
    c. Intend
    d. Large

19. **Depart most nearly means:**
    a. Leave
    b. Describe
    c. Arrive
    d. Portion

20. **Mackenzie left the daycare right after Austin. Nora left right before Austin. Mackenzie left before Austin. If the first two statements are true, then the third is:**
    a. True
    b. False
    c. Unknown
    d. An opinion

21. Jovial means the *opposite* of:
   a. Revive
   b. Depressed
   c. Obscure
   d. Pretend

22. Declare means the opposite of:
   a. Pronounce
   b. Affirm
   c. Deny
   d. State

23. Reece weighs more than Scott. Scott is heavier than Della. Reece weighs more than Della. If the first two statements are true, then the third is:
   a. True
   b. False
   c. Unknown

24. Approximate means the *opposite* of:
   a. Inexact
   b. Precise
   c. Attempt
   d. Estimate

25. Which word does NOT belong with the others?
   a. Snail
   b. Turtle
   c. Cheetah
   d. Sloth

26. Which word does NOT belong with the others?
   a. Pickup truck
   b. Tugboat
   c. Railroad car
   d. Eighteen-wheeler

27. Which word does NOT belong with the others?
   a. Brick
   b. Bottleneck
   c. Burden
   d. Benchmark

28. Frequently most nearly means:
   a. Difficulty
   b. Freely
   c. Often
   d. Easy

29. **Ubiquitous is the opposite of:**
    a. Seldom
    b. Divisive
    c. Boisterous
    d. Stubborn

30. **Repulsive most nearly means:**
    a. Attractive
    b. Gravitational
    c. Pulse
    d. Disgusting

31. **Flat means the *opposite* of:**
    a. Smooth
    b. Uneven
    c. Even
    d. Level

32. **Support means the *opposite* of:**
    a. Oppose
    b. Encourage
    c. Back
    d. Aid

33. **Initiate means the *opposite* of:**
    a. Stop
    b. Headlong
    c. Internal
    d. Sequence

34. **Pernicious most nearly means:**
    a. Benign
    b. Cautious
    c. Ridiculous
    d. Detrimental

35. **Gigantic most nearly means:**
    a. Small
    b. Great
    c. Huge
    d. Scary

36. **Remark most nearly means:**
    a. Rebuke
    b. Comment
    c. Lecture
    d. Replace

37. **Opportunity most nearly means.**
    a. Event
    b. Plan
    c. Direction
    d. Chance

38. **Sniper is to aim as tightrope walker is to:**
    a. Circus
    b. Net
    c. Balance
    d. Fear

39. **Which word does NOT belong with the others?**
    a. Independence
    b. Irresponsibility
    c. Duty
    d. Maturity

40. **Accidental means the *opposite* of:**
    a. Artificial
    b. Intentional
    c. Chance
    d. Unanticipated

41. **Achilles ran half as far as the tortoise. The rabbit ran twice as far as Achilles. The tortoise and rabbit ran the same distance. If the first two statements are true, then the third is:**
    a. True
    b. False
    c. Uncertain

42. **Which word does NOT belong with the others?**
    a. Mammal
    b. Bear
    c. Lion
    d. Tiger

43. **Entire most nearly means:**
    a. Whole
    b. Divide
    c. Tired
    d. Basic

44. **Coca Cola is to soft drink as Xerox is to:**
    a. Paper
    b. Office
    c. Writing
    d. Copier

45. Passive means the *opposite* of:
    a. Active
    b. Attend
    c. Lassitude
    d. Forlorn

46. Eileen left for the airport after Sara left. David left before Sara. David left after Eileen. If the first two statements are true, then the third is:
    a. True
    b. False
    c. Uncertain

47. Which word does NOT belong with the others?
    a. Helmet
    b. Shoulder pads
    c. Football
    d. Kneepads

48. Aiden earned the same score on his math test as Jessica. Will earned 10 points higher than Jessica. Aiden earned a higher score than Will. If the first two statements are true, then the third statement is:
    a. True
    b. False
    c. Unknown

49. Which word does NOT belong with the others?
    a. Interstate
    b. Asphalt
    c. Highway
    d. Avenue

50. Amber scored fewer soccer goals than Megan. Alise scored three times the number of soccer goals as Amber. Megan scored more soccer goals than Alise. If the first two statements are true, then the third statement is:
    a. True
    b. False
    c. Unknown

51. Light is to hologram as film is to:
    a. Aesthetic
    b. Panoramic
    c. Photographer
    d. Video camera

52. Which word does NOT belong with the others?
    a. Woman
    b. Man
    c. Girl
    d. Female

53. Joni arrived in the canyon after Cass. Jackson arrived before Joni. Cass arrived before Jackson. If the first two statements are true, then the third is:
    a. True
    b. False
    c. Uncertain

54. Change means the *opposite* of:
    a. Remain
    b. Alter
    c. Amend
    d. Transform

55. Which word does NOT belong with the others?
    a. Epidermis
    b. Ribosomes
    c. Nucleolus
    d. Mitochondria

56. Ineligible means the *opposite* of:
    a. Flexible
    b. Legible
    c. Allowed
    d. Banned

57. Which word does NOT belong with the others?
    a. Barren
    b. Desolate
    c. Abundant
    d. Infertile

58. Which word does NOT belong with the others?
    a. Artificial
    b. Synthetic
    c. Natural
    d. Man-made

59. Hot is to cold as veracity is to:
    a. Dishonesty
    b. Impartiality
    c. Accuracy
    d. Distaste

60. Monday is my longest day at work. Tuesday is shorter than Thursday. Thursday is longer than Monday. If the first two statements are true, then the third is:
    a. True
    b. False
    c. Unknown

Quantitative Skills

1. Examine the isosceles triangle in the figure below and select the best answer choice.

   a. $\angle A \cong \angle B \cong \angle C$
   b. $\angle A \cong \angle B$
   c. $\angle B \cong \angle C$
   d. $\angle A \cong \angle C$

2. Examine (I), (II), and (III), and find the best answer.

   (I) $\frac{1}{3}$ of 24
   (II) $\frac{1}{5}$ of 30
   (III) $\frac{3}{4}$ of 20

   a. (II) < (III)
   b. (I) < (II) < (III)
   c. (I) = (II) and (II) < (III)
   d. (I) = (II) and (II) > (III)

3. What number should come next in the sequence 41, 44, 48, 53, 59, ...?

   a. 64
   b. 65
   c. 66
   d. 67

4. Examine (I), (II), and (III), and find the best answer.

   (I) 0.04
   (II) 4%
   (III) $\frac{2}{50}$

   a. (II) > (III)
   b. (I) = (II) = (III)
   c. (II) = (III)
   d. (II) < (III)

5. Given the sequence represented in the table below, where n represents the position of the term and a_n represents the value of the term, which of the following describes the relationship between the position number and the value of the term?

n	1	2	3	4	5	6
a_n	5	2	−1	−4	−7	−10

   a. Multiply n by 2 and subtract 4
   b. Multiply n by 2 and subtract 3
   c. Multiply n by −3 and add 8
   d. Multiply n by −4 and add 1

6. Which of the following sums is the greatest?
   a. $3 + 4 + 16$
   b. $6 + 4 + 5 + 7$
   c. $4 + 5 + 9$
   d. $10 + 4 + 8$

7. The square root of 6 is between which of the following numbers?
   a. 0 and 1
   b. 1 and 2
   c. 2 and 3
   d. 3 and 4

8. Which of the following numbers lies between $\frac{1}{3}$ and $\frac{2}{3}$?
   a. 0.25
   b. 0.30
   c. 0.45
   d. 0.75

9. Examine (I), (II), and (III), and find the best answer.

   (I) 20% of 80
   (II) 50% of 70
   (III) 40% of 90

   a. (II) > (III)
   b. (II) > (I)
   c. (I) < (II) and (II) = (III)
   d. (I) = (II) = (III)

10. What number subtracted from 45 makes 3 times 9?
    a. 27
    b. 21
    c. 18
    d. 16

11. Which of the following sums is the least?
    a. $4 + 3 + 4 + 5$
    b. $3 + 6 + 8$
    c. $9 + 5 + 3$
    d. $1 + 8 + 7 + 2$

12. Examine (I), (II), and (III) and select the best answer.

    (I) 30% of 90
    (II) 10% of 270
    (III) 60% of 45

    a. (I) < (II) < (III)
    b. (I) < (II) = (III)
    c. (I) = (II) < (III)
    d. (I) = (II) = (III)

13. What number should fill the blank in the sequence 8, 12, 16, __, 24?

    a. 18
    b. 20
    c. 22
    d. 26

14. What number should come next in the sequence: 3, 6, 8, 16, 18, 36, ...?

    a. 38
    b. 44
    c. 57
    d. 72

15. Which number should come next in the sequence: 4, 13, 22, 31, ...?

    a. 34
    b. 39
    c. 40
    d. 42

16. One-third of what number is equal to 2 cubed?

    a. 16
    b. 20
    c. 24
    d. 27

17. In the figure below, $\overline{AB} = \overline{CD}$ and $\overline{AC} = \overline{BD}$. Find the best answer concerning the measures of angles ∠A, ∠B, ∠C, and ∠D.

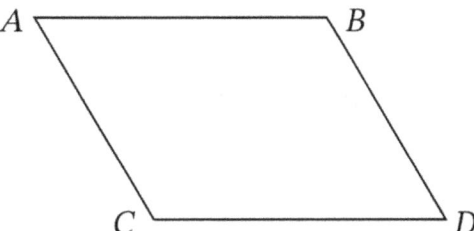

    a. $m\angle A = m\angle B$ and $m\angle C = m\angle D$
    b. $m\angle A = m\angle C$ and $m\angle B = m\angle D$
    c. $m\angle A = m\angle D$ and $m\angle B = m\angle C$
    d. $m\angle A = m\angle B = m\angle C = m\angle D$

18. Examine (I), (II), and (III) and select the best answer.

(I) $\frac{1}{5}$ of 30

(II) $\frac{1}{4}$ of 20

(III) $\frac{1}{3}$ of 15

a. (I) > (II) = (III)
b. (I) = (II) = (III)
c. (I) < (II) = (III)
d. (I) < (II) < (III)

19. Which of the following numbers is greatest?

a. $\frac{1}{3}$
b. 0.25
c. 0.099
d. $\frac{2}{7}$

20. The repeating pattern shown below uses the same four figures repeatedly.

Fig. 1   Fig. 2   Fig. 3   Fig. 4   Fig. 5   Fig. 6 ...

Which of the four figures will the figure in the 31st position look like?

a. Figure 1
b. Figure 2
c. Figure 3
d. Figure 4

21. Which of the following expressions represents "five times a number m squared"?

a. $\frac{5}{m^2}$
b. $5m^2$
c. $(5m)^2$
d. $5 + m^2$

22. If $x = 2y - 3$ and $2x + \frac{1}{2}y = 3$, then what is the value of y?

a. $-\frac{2}{3}$
b. 1
c. 2
d. $\frac{18}{7}$

23. Forty students in a class take a test that is graded on a scale of 1 to 10. The histogram in the figure shows the grade distribution, with the x-axis representing the grades and the y-axis representing the number of students who obtained each grade. If the mean, median, and mode values are represented by n, p, and q, respectively, which of the following is true?

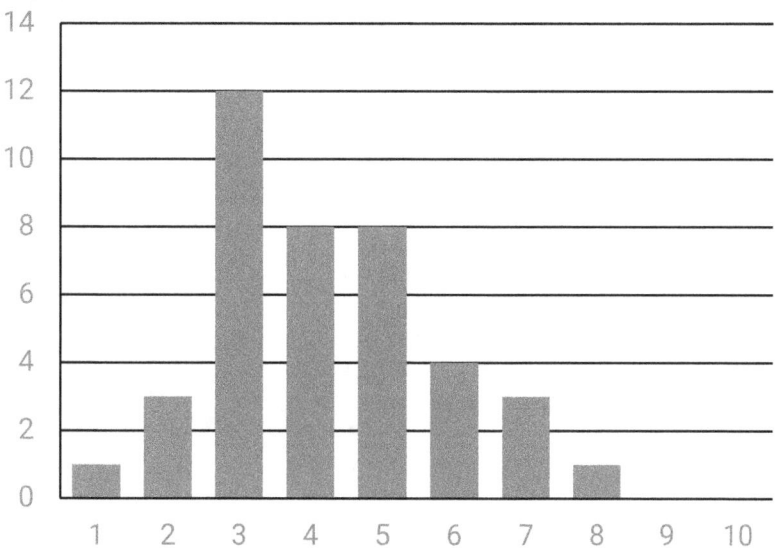

   a. $n > p > q$
   b. $n > q > p$
   c. $q > p > n$
   d. $p > q > n$

24. Which number comes next in the sequence: 1, 4, 9, 16, ...?

   a. 20
   b. 24
   c. 25
   d. 32

25. Rectangle A is 11 feet long and 5 feet wide. Rectangle B is 8 feet long and 7 feet wide. Which statement correctly describes the relative sizes of their perimeters and areas?

   a. Rectangle B has the greater perimeter and the greater area.
   b. Rectangle B has the greater perimeter. Rectangle A has the greater area.
   c. Rectangle A has the greater perimeter. Rectangle B has the greater area.
   d. Rectangle A has the greater perimeter and the greater area.

26. What number should be next in the sequence: 108, 104, 98, 90, 80, ...?

   a. 64
   b. 68
   c. 72
   d. 76

27. Two even integers and one odd integer are multiplied together. Which of the following could be their product?

   a. 3.75
   b. 9
   c. 16.2
   d. 24

28. Examine the figure below, in which $\overline{AB} = \overline{BC}$, and select the best choice.

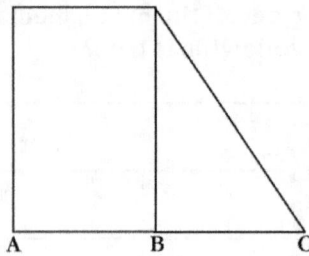

   a. The area of the rectangle equals that of the triangle.
   b. The area of the rectangle is twice that of the triangle.
   c. The area of the rectangle is half that of the triangle.
   d. The area of the rectangle is more than twice that of the triangle.

29. Examine (I), (II), and (III), and find the best answer.
   (I) $\frac{2}{3}$
   (II) $\frac{20}{30}$
   (III) $\frac{30}{45}$

   a. (II) > (III)
   b. (I) = (II) = (III)
   c. (II) = (III)
   d. (II) < (III)

30. The number 5 is multiplied by its reciprocal. What is the result?
   a. 0
   b. $\frac{1}{5}$
   c. 1
   d. 5

31. The point A lies at the intersection of the diagonals of the square in the figure. Examine the regions of the square and find the best answer. Compare the size of the regions (I), (II), and (III).

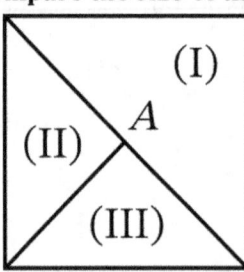

   a. (I) = (II) = (III)
   b. (I) = (II) < (III)
   c. (I) > (II) = (III)
   d. (I) > (II) < (III)

32. How many integers exist between the numbers –4.2 and 6.1?
   a. 2
   b. 6
   c. 10
   d. 11

33. Which numeral comes next in the sequence: 116, 113, 107, 98, ...?
   a. 86
   b. 89
   c. 91
   d. 92

34. Equal numbers of dimes and pennies are placed in a single row on a table. Which of the following must be true?
   a. Every dime will be next to a penny.
   b. If there are two dimes at one end of the row, two pennies must be next to one another.
   c. If there is a dime at one end of the row, there must be a penny at the other end.
   d. If there are two pennies together anywhere in the row, there must be dimes at both ends.

35. Which number comes next in the sequence: 12, 7, 8, 13, 4, 19, 0, ...?
   a. –2
   b. 0
   c. 19
   d. 25

36. If an odd number is added to an even number, then which of the following must be true of the result?
   a. It is odd
   b. It is even
   c. It is positive
   d. It is zero

37. Examine the intersecting line segments in the figure. A, B, C, and D are the measures of the angles. Select the true statement.

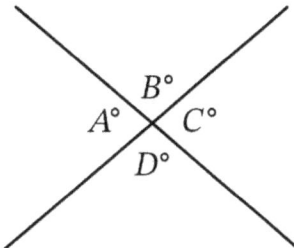

   a. $A = B$ and $C = D$
   b. $A = C$ and $B = C$
   c. $A = C$ and $B = D$
   d. $A = D$ and $B = C$

38. What is the missing number in the sequence: 4, 6, 10, 18, ___, 66?
    a. 22
    b. 34
    c. 45
    d. 54

39. Examine (I), (II), and (III), and find the best answer. Consider only the magnitude of each measurement.
    (I) The perimeter of a rectangle with length of 6 cm and width of 4 cm
    (II) The perimeter of a square with sides 4 cm long
    (III) The area of a square with sides 4 cm long
    a. (II) > (III)
    b. (I) = (II) = (III)
    c. (II) = (III)
    d. (II) < (III)

40. Which numeral comes next in the sequence: 54, 59, 63, 68, 72, ...?
    a. 76
    b. 77
    c. 78
    d. 79

41. Which of the following choices is the missing number from this sequence: 1, 2, 4, ___, 16?
    a. 6
    b. 8
    c. 10
    d. 12

42. Examine the diagram of a circle and find the best answer. The chord shown is a diameter of the circle. The shorter line segment is a radius of the circle. The labels (I), (II), and (III) correspond to segments of the circle.

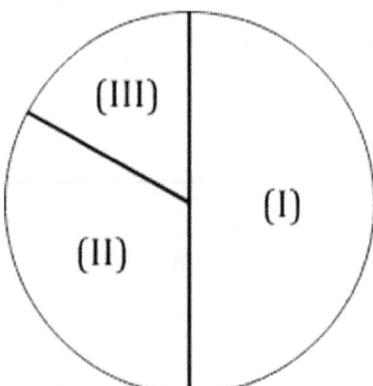

    a. (I) = (II) = (III)
    b. (I) > (II) < (III)
    c. (II) = (I) − (III)
    d. (I) + (III) = (II)

43. What two numbers should come next in the sequence 1, 1, 2, 3, 5, 8, 13, …?
    a. 18, 24
    b. 18, 28
    c. 21, 29
    d. 21, 34

44. In a sequence of prime numbers from least to greatest, which prime number immediately follows 67?
    a. 68
    b. 69
    c. 71
    d. 73

45. Examine the figure below, which shows two lines passing through the center O of a circle, and select the best answer.

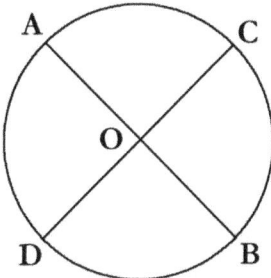

    a. $\overline{AO}$ is greater than $\overline{OC}$ but less than $\overline{CD}$
    b. $\overline{AB}$ is greater than $\overline{CD}$ and greater than $\overline{DO}$
    c. $\overline{AB}$ is greater than $\overline{OC}$ but less than $\overline{CD}$
    d. $\overline{AO}$ is the same length as $\overline{OC}$ but less than $\overline{CD}$

46. Dorothy is half of her sister's age. In 20 years, she will be three-fourths of her sister's age. What is Dorothy's current age?
    a. 10
    b. 15
    c. 20
    d. 25

47. Examine (I), (II), and (III), and find the best answer.
    (I) 5^2
    (II) 2^5
    (III) 25
    a. (III) > (II)
    b. (I) = (II) = (III)
    c. (II) = (III)
    d. (I) = (III) and (III) < (II)

48. Examine (I), (II), and (III), and find the best answer.

(I) A number that is 3 less than 2 times 15
(II) A number that is equal to 3 cubed
(III) A number that is 3 more than 80% of 30

a. (II) > (III)
b. (I) = (II) = (III)
c. (II) < (III)
d. (I) < (II) and (II) > (III)

49. Which of the following statements is true about the sum of two negative numbers?

a. It is always negative.
b. It is always positive.
c. It is sometimes is positive and sometimes is negative.
d. It is always zero.

50. Which number added to itself is $\frac{1}{3}$ of 66?

a. 11
b. 22
c. 33
d. 44

51. Which numeral should fill in the blank in the sequence 2, 4, 8, __, 32, 64?

a. 12
b. 16
c. 20
d. 24

52. Examine the diagram of a square and find the best answer.

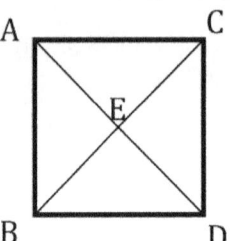

a. $\overline{AD}$ is equal to $\overline{CD}$
b. $\overline{CE}$ is equal to $\overline{AE}$
c. $\overline{BD}$ is equal to $\overline{ED}$
d. $\overline{CB}$ is equal to $\overline{BD}$

Mathematics

1. Hannah draws two supplementary angles. One angle measures 34°. What is the measure of the other angle?

a. 56°
b. 66°
c. 146°
d. 326°

2. A recipe called for 2 ounces of cream. Lindsay didn't have a way to measure ounces, and her measuring cups were in the dishwasher, but she remembered the number of ounces and cups in a pint. The cream carton had a chart showing that a cup contains 16 tablespoons, but all she could find was her teaspoon measuring spoon. She also knew there are 3 teaspoons in a tablespoon. Which of the following shows the calculation for the number of teaspoons of cream Lindsay needs for her recipe?

   a. $2 \times \frac{1}{16} \times 2 \times 16 \times 3$
   b. $2 \times 16 \times \frac{1}{2} \times \frac{1}{16} \times \frac{1}{3}$
   c. $\frac{1}{2} \times 16 \times 2 \times 16 \times \frac{1}{3}$
   d. $\frac{2}{16} \times \frac{1}{2} \times 16 \times \frac{1}{3}$

3. What is the value of $(44 + 3^2) + 2^2$?

   a. 48
   b. 54
   c. 57
   d. 60

4. Which of the following is equal to $4(6 + 1)$?

   a. 14
   b. 25
   c. 28
   d. 50

5. Which of the following statements is true?

   a. Perpendicular lines have opposite slopes.
   b. Perpendicular lines have the same slopes.
   c. Perpendicular lines have reciprocal slopes.
   d. Perpendicular lines have opposite reciprocal slopes.

6. Which of the following are complementary angles?

   a. 71° and 19°
   b. 90° and 90°
   c. 90° and 45°
   d. 15° and 30°

7. Which of the following is equal to $4\sqrt{2^4}$?

   a. 4
   b. 8
   c. 16
   d. 32

8. The cost, in dollars, of shipping x computers to California for sale is $3,000 + 100x$. The amount received when selling these computers is $400x$ dollars. What is the least number of computers that must be shipped and sold so that the amount received is at least equal to the shipping cost?

   a. 10 computers
   b. 15 computers
   c. 20 computers
   d. 25 computers

9. A jar contains pennies and nickels. The ratio of nickels to pennies is 6 : 2. What percentage of the coins are pennies?

   a. 6.7%
   b. 12.5%
   c. 20%
   d. 25%

10. Evaluate $9 + 4(2 + 3)$
    a. 20
    b. 22
    c. 24
    d. 29

11. The average of six numbers is 4. If the average of two of those numbers is 2, what is the average of the other four numbers?

    a. 5
    b. 6
    c. 7
    d. 8

12. What is the area of a square with a perimeter of 16 feet?

    a. 4 ft^2
    b. 16 ft^2
    c. 32 ft^2
    d. 256 ft^2

13. Which of these is NOT a net of a cube?

    a. 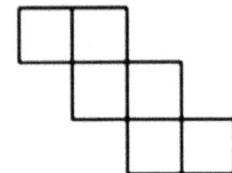   b. 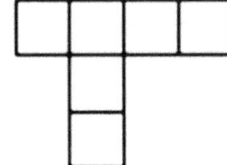   c. 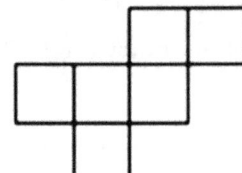   d.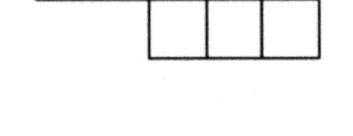

14. Enrique is a full-time employee who earns $12.00 per hour. If he works overtime, he receives time-and-a-half (where each hour worked over 40 hours is compensated at 1.5 times the regular rate). If Enrique works 45 hours, how much money will he earn?

    a. $510
    b. $540
    c. $570
    d. $600

15. Jonas jogs three times faster than he walks. Which graph best represents the situation?

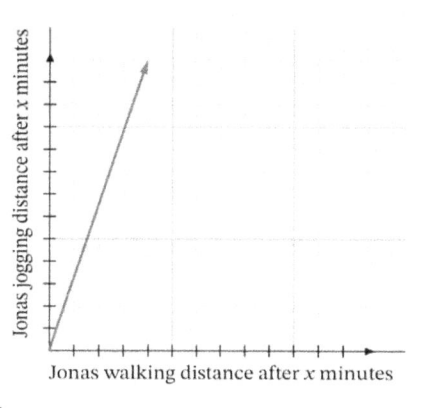
a.

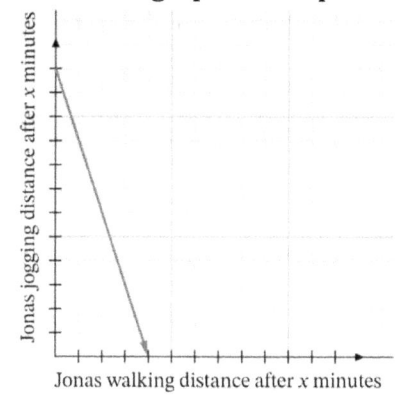
c.

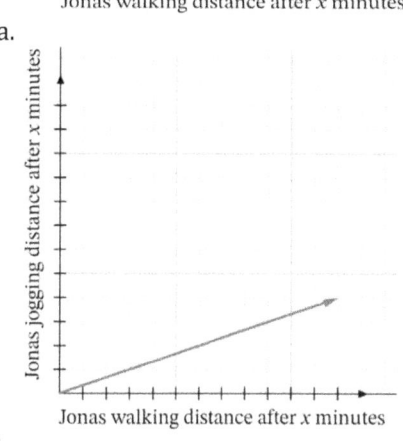
b.

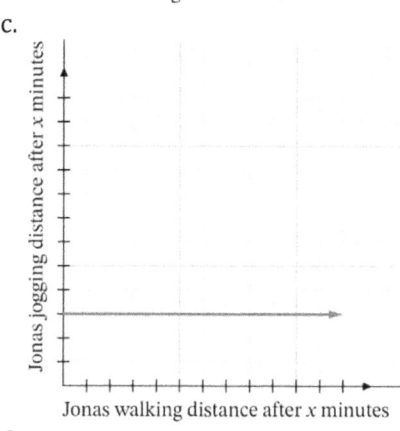
d.

16. In a class of 24 students, 18 students completed their projects on time. What fraction of the students failed to complete their projects on time?

   a. $\frac{1}{4}$
   b. $\frac{2}{3}$
   c. $\frac{3}{4}$
   d. $\frac{5}{8}$

17. Mrs. Patterson's classroom has sixteen empty chairs. All the chairs are occupied when every student is present. If $\frac{2}{5}$ of the students are absent, how many students make up her entire class?

   a. 16 students
   b. 24 students
   c. 32 students
   d. 40 students

18. If 12 inches = 1 foot, and 3 feet = 1 yard, how many inches are there in 2.5 yards?

   a. 86
   b. 90
   c. 94
   d. 96

19. Richard buys two cups of coffee every day except Saturday and Sunday. On Saturday he buys only one cup, and on Sunday he buys none. If a cup of coffee costs $2.25, how much does Richard spend on coffee every week?
   a. $25.00
   b. $23.50
   c. $24.75
   d. $25.25

20. A bullet travels at 5×10^6 feet per hour. If it strikes its target in 2×10^{-4} hours, how far has it traveled?
   a. 50 feet
   b. 100 feet
   c. 200 feet
   d. 1,000 feet

21. An airplane travels at 300 mph relative to the air. It moves against a headwind of 15 mph. What is its speed relative to the ground?
   a. 270 mph
   b. 285 mph
   c. 300 mph
   d. 315 mph

22. Which function represents the graph?

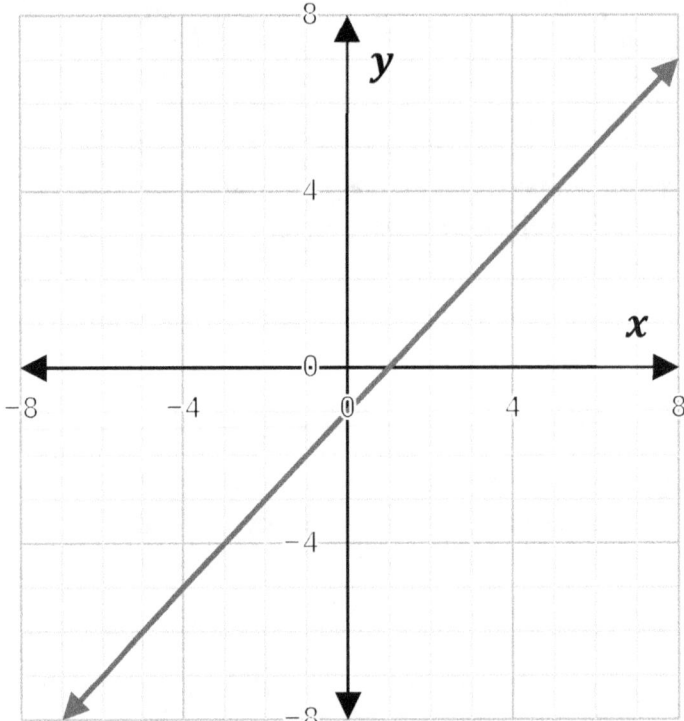

   a. $y = x + 1$
   b. $y = x - 1$
   c. $y = -x + 1$
   d. $y = -x - 1$

23. The sides of a triangle are equal to integer values of units. Two sides are 4 and 6 units long, respectively. What is the minimum value for the triangle's perimeter?
    a. 10 units
    b. 11 units
    c. 12 units
    d. 13 units

24. How many meters are equivalent to 336 millimeters?
    a. 336,000
    b. 33,600
    c. 3.36
    d. 0.336

25. A dartboard is divided into 8 black and 8 white wedge-shaped sectors so that when a dart is thrown it has a 50% chance of landing on white and a 50% chance of landing on black. If a dart is thrown 3 times in a row and lands on black each time, what is the chance that it will land again on black if it is thrown a fourth time?
    a. 12.5%
    b. 25%
    c. 50%
    d. 100%

26. Archie's gas tank is $\frac{1}{3}$ full. If Archie adds 3 gallons of gas to the tank, it will be $\frac{1}{2}$ full. What is the capacity of Archie's tank?
    a. 12 gallons
    b. 18 gallons
    c. 20 gallons
    d. 28 gallons

27. There are 16 ounces in a pound. If one apple weighs 6 ounces, what is the weight of 12 apples?
    a. 12 pounds
    b. 6 pounds 6 ounces
    c. 6 pounds
    d. 4 pounds 8 ounces

28. Given that $3(4x + 3) = 45$, what is the value of x?
    a. 2
    b. 3
    c. 4
    d. 5

29. A dress is marked down by 20% and placed on a clearance rack, under a sign reading "Take an extra 25% off already reduced merchandise." What fraction of the original price is the final sale price of the dress?
    a. $\frac{2}{5}$
    b. $\frac{9}{20}$
    c. $\frac{3}{5}$
    d. $\frac{11}{20}$

30. Four people decide to adopt a dog and take turns caring for it. Person A thinks he can take care of the dog $\frac{1}{4}$ of the time. Person B thinks she can handle $\frac{1}{8}$. Person C thinks he can take care of the dog $\frac{1}{2}$ of the time. What part is left for the fourth person to cover?

    a. $\frac{1}{8}$
    b. $\frac{1}{4}$
    c. $\frac{1}{3}$
    d. $\frac{1}{2}$

31. A skyscraper is 548 meters high. The building's owners decide to increase its height by 3%. How high would the skyscraper be after the increase? Round to the nearest whole number.

    a. 551 meters
    b. 555 meters
    c. 562 meters
    d. 564 meters

32. Which of the following numbers is a multiple of 23?

    a. 39
    b. 48
    c. 92
    d. 101

33. A woman wants to stack two small bookcases beneath a window that is $26\frac{1}{2}$ inches from the floor. The larger bookcase is $14\frac{1}{2}$ inches tall. The other bookcase is $8\frac{3}{4}$ inches tall. How tall will the two bookcases be when they are stacked together?

    a. 12 inches
    b. $23\frac{1}{4}$ inches
    c. $35\frac{1}{4}$ inches
    d. 41 inches

34. Based on the histogram below, how many students scored 75 points or fewer on the math test?

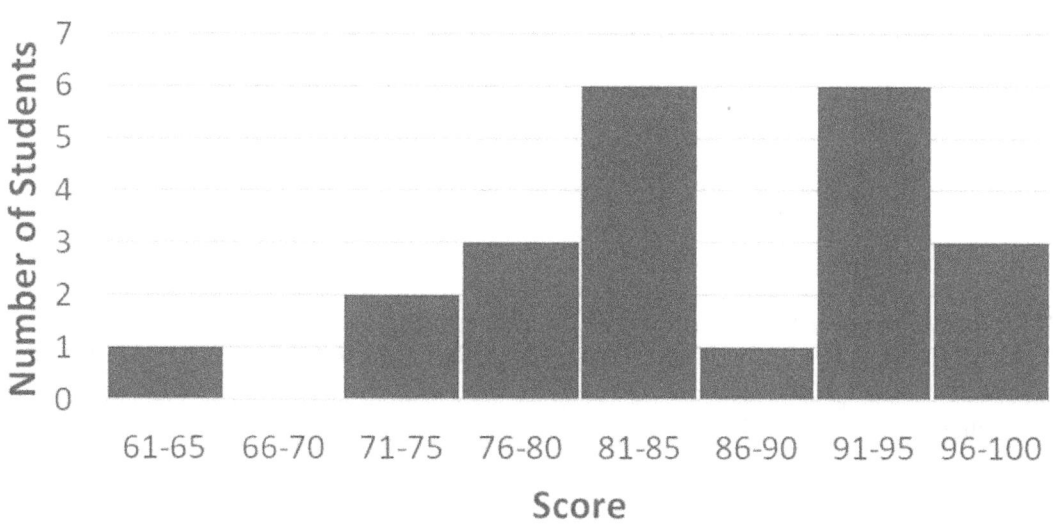

a. 0 students
b. 2 students
c. 3 students
d. 6 students

Refer to the following for question 35:

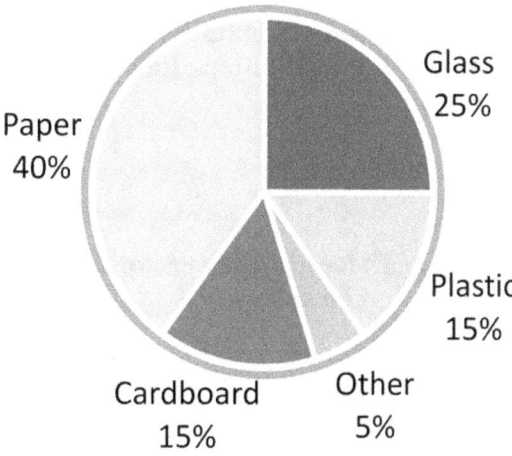

35. The Charleston Recycling Company collects 50,000 tons of recyclable material every month. The chart shows the kinds of materials that are collected by the company's five trucks. What is the second most common material that is recycled?

a. Cardboard
b. Glass
c. Paper
d. Plastic

36. A bag contains six marbles: two green, two blue, and two red. If two marbles are drawn at random, what is the probability that they are of the same color?

   a. 3%
   b. 20%
   c. 25%
   d. 33%

37. A clothing store offers a red tag sale during which items are offered at 5% off the marked price. Margaret selects a dress with a marked price of $120. How much will she have to pay for it?

   a. $115
   b. $114
   c. $110
   d. $96

38. A metal rod used in manufacturing must be as close as possible to 15 inches in length. The tolerance of the length, L, in inches, is specified by the inequality $|L - 15| \leq 0.01$. What is the minimum length permissible for the rod?

   a. 14.9 inches
   b. 14.99 inches
   c. 15.01 inches
   d. 15.1 inches

39. Jerry needs to load 4 pieces of equipment onto a factory elevator that has a weight limit of 800 pounds. Jerry weighs 200 pounds. What would the average weight of each item have to be so that the elevator's weight limit is not exceeded, assuming Jerry accompanies the equipment?

   a. 128 pounds
   b. 150 pounds
   c. 175 pounds
   d. 180 pounds

40. To begin making her soup, Jennifer poured 4 containers of chicken broth and 1 liter of water into the pot. Each container of chicken broth is 410 milliliters. How much liquid is in the pot?

   a. 1.64 liters
   b. 2.64 liters
   c. 5.44 liters
   d. 6.12 liters

41. Bob spends $17.90 on sodas and snacks for his study group. The expenses are to be split evenly between five people. How much is each person's share?

   a. $3.45
   b. $3.58
   c. $3.65
   d. $3.73

Refer to the following for question 42:

An MP3 player is set to play songs at random from the 15 songs it contains in memory. Any song can be played at any time, even if it is repeated. There are 5 songs by Band A, 3 songs by Band B, 2 by Band C, and 5 by Band D.

42. If the player has just played two songs in a row by Band D, what is the probability that the next song will also be by Band D?

   a. $\frac{1}{3}$
   b. $\frac{1}{5}$
   c. $\frac{1}{9}$
   d. $\frac{1}{27}$

43. Which number equals 2^{-3}?

   a. $\frac{1}{2}$
   b. $\frac{1}{4}$
   c. $\frac{1}{8}$
   d. $\frac{1}{16}$

44. Which number is the least common multiple of 2 and 4?

   a. 2
   b. 4
   c. 8
   d. 12

45. The town of Fram will build a water storage tank on a hill overlooking the town. The tank will be a right, circular cylinder of radius r and height h. The plot of ground selected for the installation is large enough to accommodate a circular tank 60 feet in diameter. The planning commission wants the tank to hold 1,000,000 cubic feet of water, and they intend to use the full area available. Which of the following is the minimum acceptable height? Use 3.14 for π.

   a. 654 ft
   b. 455 ft
   c. 354 ft
   d. 255 ft

46. If $10x + 2 = 7$, what is the value of $2x$?

   a. −0.5
   b. 0.5
   c. 1
   d. 5

47. Marc purchased pizza from five different locations (Stores A, B, C, D, and E) to test quality and pricing. If the pizza from Store C cost $2 more than the pizza from store E, and Store B was the least expensive, which of the following graphs could model Marc's pizza purchases? Cost in dollars is represented on the y-axis and location on the x-axis.

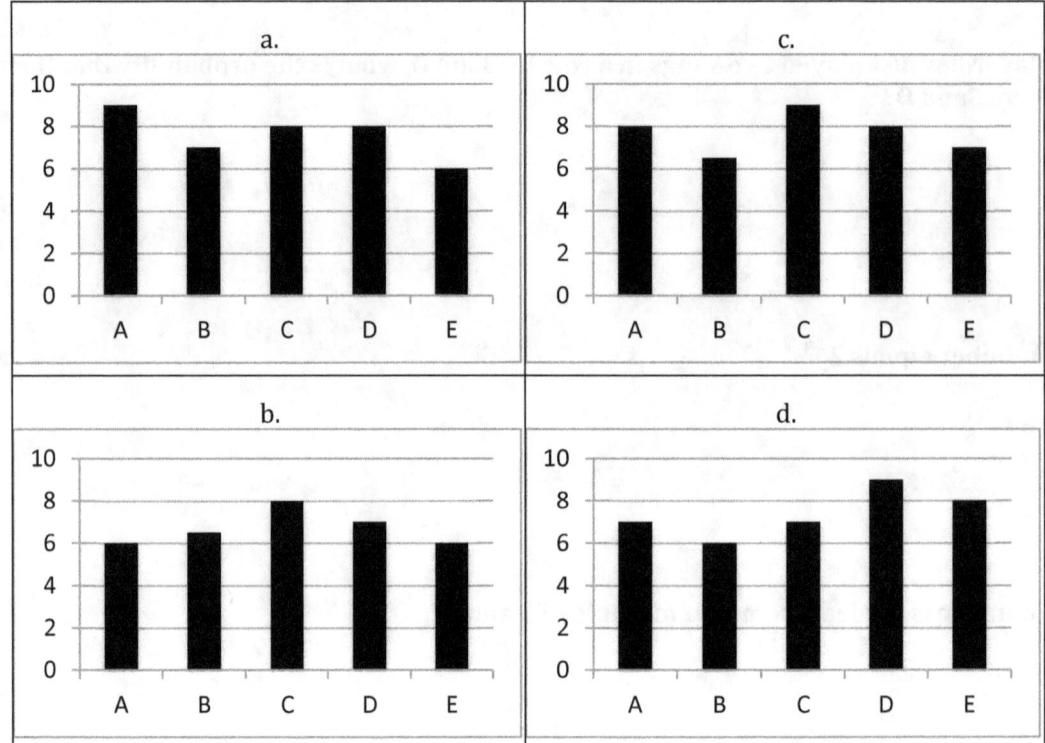

48. Evaluate $3 + [(12 \div 4) \times 6] - 20$.
    a. 0
    b. 1
    c. 6
    d. 8

49. How many centimeters are in 6 meters?
    a. 0.06
    b. 60
    c. 600
    d. 6,000

50. Which of the following represents the value of the "5" in 452?
    a. 5×1
    b. 5×10
    c. 5×100
    d. 5×0.1

51. What is the approximate diameter of a circle with an area of 314 square inches?
    a. 20 inches
    b. 10 inches
    c. 100 inches
    d. 31.4 inches

52. Which of the following letters has a vertical line of symmetry?

a. E

b. V

c. K

d. B

53. What is the area of a square inscribed in a circle of radius r?
   a. $2r^2$
   b. $2r^3$
   c. $2\pi r$
   d. $4r^2$

54. Richard sells cell phones. He is paid a commission of 10% for every phone he sells. The phones cost $140 each. How many phones must Richard sell in order to be paid $840?
   a. 40
   b. 50
   c. 60
   d. 70

55. A commuter survey counts the people riding in cars on a highway in the morning. Each car contains only one man, only one woman, or both one man and one woman. Out of 25 cars, 13 contain a woman and 20 contain a man. How many contain both a man and a woman?
   a. 0
   b. 7
   c. 8
   d. 12

56. A rectangle is twice as long as it is wide. If it were 3 inches shorter and 3 inches wider, it would be a square. What is the width in inches of the rectangle?
   a. 4
   b. 6
   c. 8
   d. 12

57. Haley's violin instructor insists that she practice a minimum of 3.5 hours per week. If she practices 45 minutes on both Sunday and Monday, 25 minutes on both Tuesday and Wednesday, how many minutes does she have left to practice this week?
   a. 70 minutes
   b. 75 minutes
   c. 80 minutes
   d. 85 minutes

58. Nancy had $17.25 from her part-time job. She spent $3.15 on a magazine and $6.75 on snacks and drinks. How much does she have left?
   a. $7.20
   b. $7.35
   c. $7.40
   d. $9.90

59. If 35% of a paycheck was deducted for taxes and 4% for insurance, what is the total percentage taken out of the paycheck?
   a. 20%
   b. 31%
   c. 39%
   d. 42%

60. In the figure below, what are the coordinates of the point A?

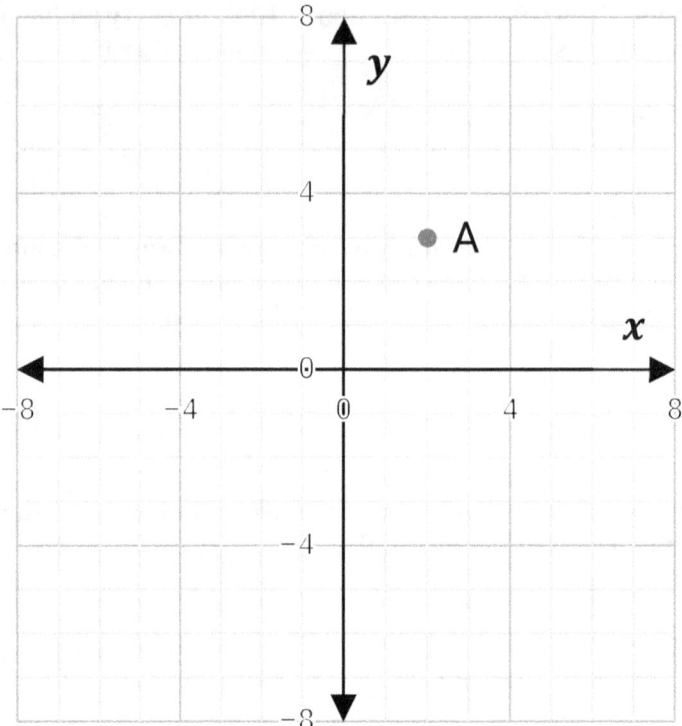

   a. $(-2, -3)$
   b. $(2, 3)$
   c. $(3, 2)$
   d. $(3, 3)$

61. Refer to the following chart. Which month shows the greatest increase in rainfall compared to the preceding month?

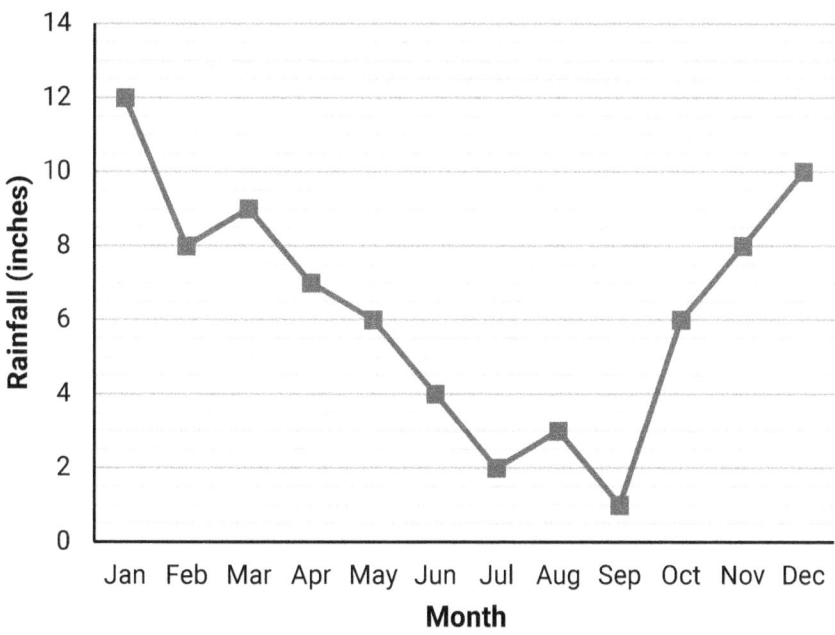

   a. January
   b. March
   c. August
   d. October

62. Chan receives a bonus from his job. He pays 30% in taxes, gives 30% to charity, and uses another 25% to pay off an old debt. He has $600 left. What was the total amount of Chan's bonus?
   a. $4,000
   b. $3,600
   c. $3,200
   d. $3,000

63. If $\frac{4}{x-3} - \frac{2}{x} = 1$, then what is the value of x?
   a. −6
   b. −1
   c. −6 or −1
   d. −1 or 6

64. Which of the following figures has rotational symmetry?

a.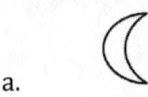

b.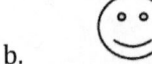

c.

d.

Answer Key and Explanations for Test #1

Reading—Comprehension

1. B: There is no indication in the passage that the Bennets are interested in becoming friends with Mr. Bingley (A), that Mr. Bingley would be a valuable business connection (C), or that Mr. Bingley has any prior knowledge of the Bennet daughters (D). Mrs. Bennet tells her husband that a new neighbor is moving in: "Mrs. Long says that Netherfield is taken by a young man of large fortune." Mrs. Bennet is sure he will make an excellent husband for one of her daughters: "You must know that I am thinking of his marrying one of them."

2. B: Mrs. Bennet is exasperated by her husband, meaning that she is frustrated or annoyed and fed up with her husband's seeming indifference to Mr. Bingley: "'My dear Mr. Bennet,' replied his wife, 'how can you be so tiresome!'" Being annoyed would indicate that she is not indifferent toward him. She also is the person who initiated the dialog and seems to eagerly want to talk to him about her ideas. This would indicate that she is neither tired nor afraid of her husband.

3. B: The evidence in this selection indicates that marrying a man with money was a primary goal for young women. Mrs. Bennet tells Mr. Bennet that Mr. Bingley is "A single man of large fortune; four or five thousand a year." Mrs. Bennet further indicates that she is thrilled with the news because of Mr. Bingley's potential as a husband for one of her daughters: "What a fine thing for our girls... You must know that I am thinking of his marrying one of them."

4. A: Mr. Bennet is facetiously asking if the idea of marriage (particularly to one of his own daughters) was Mr. Bingley's intention when he agreed to rent Netherfield Park.

5. A: "It is a truth universally acknowledged" means that something is understood to be true by the general public.

6. A: Mrs. Bennet feels that Mr. Bingley is likely to marry one of her daughters. She tells her husband that Mr. Bingley is a "single man of large fortune; four or five thousand a year. What a fine thing for our girls!"

7. D: Choices A and C are detail sentences that do not convey the setting or event of the rest of the paragraph. Choice B references other dancers not mentioned anywhere else in the paragraph.

8. C: This is the only choice that expands on Margaritte's feelings about the music and echoes the tension of the event. Choices A and B refer to people (the audience, the other dancers) outside of Margaritte and her experience with the music as she waits for her cue, which is not the point of the passage. Choice D talks about Margaritte's clothing, which is not mentioned anywhere else in the paragraph.

9. A: Choices B, C, and D are details, but do not invoke a particular image.

10. B: This sentence tells what is happening at the moment and reflects on the tension that is apparent throughout the rest of the paragraph. Choice A only tells what is happening at the moment. Choice C refers to a time beyond the time referenced in the paragraph. Choice D introduces other dancers not mentioned previously in the paragraph.

11. B: The other choices are detail sentences and do not express the main idea of the paragraph.

12. C: Of the choices given, this sentence does not add anything to the paragraph's central premise that people should educate themselves about snakes instead of believing that snakes are looking for someone to attack.

13. A: This is the only choice that sums up the tone and purpose of the paragraph.

14. A: Choice A is the best choice because the best definition of "sacrilegious" as it appears in paragraph 2 is "absurdly inappropriate." B, C, and D are not the best choices because they do not express proper definitions of "sacrilegious" as it appears in paragraph 2.

15. C: Choice C is the best choice because Will's attitude in paragraph 15 is best described as sentimental. A, B, and D are not the best choices because Will's attitude in paragraph 15 is not angry, cheerful, or annoyed.

16. B: Choice B is the best choice because personification is used to describe the stars in paragraph 11. A, C, and D are not the best choices because simile, metaphor, and paradox are not used to describe the stars in paragraph 11.

17. A: Choice A is the best choice because it best illustrates how Puck's death is an example of irony. B, C, and D are not the best choices because they do not effectively illustrate how Puck's death is an example of irony.

18. D: Choice D is the best choice because it is the only option that is a main idea in this story. A, B, and C are not the best choices because they are all supporting ideas, not main ideas in the story.

19. B: The second sentence in the passage notes that comets are distinguishable from asteroids by the presence of comas or tails.

20. C: The third paragraph notes that there are over 3,500 known comets. It also notes that this represents only a small portion of those in existence.

21. C: The second paragraph notes that because they have low mass, they don't become spherical and have irregular shapes.

22. D: The second paragraph notes that some comets may be tens of kilometers across. The passage also notes that comas may be larger than the sun.

23. D: The passage defines single apparition comets as those whose trajectories make them pass the Sun once and then exit our solar system permanently. It also describes most comets as having oval orbits wherein they are nearer to the Sun during part of their orbit, and then move farther away from the Sun *within the solar system* for the rest of the orbit; hence (A) is incorrect. While single apparition comets are only apparent once, they are NOT still in the solar system (B). The passage defines short and long orbital periods, but does not include long orbital periods in that definition (C).

24. B: Lincoln begins this speech by discussing the founding of the US and what the original purpose of the US was. Then, he goes on to talk about how the US is currently engaged in a war intended to fracture the nation, and he states that the battle being discussed was one large tragedy that came out of the war. Next, Lincoln says that his speech and even the memorial itself can't truly honor those who died, and that it's up to those who survived to continue the fight to ensure the nation does not break apart. Choice B best communicates this message.

25. C: The sentence in which this phrase is found is: "The world will little note, nor long remember, what we say here, but can never forget what they did here." In this context, the phrase "the world will little note" means that no one outside of those in attendance or possibly those outside the country will pay attention to the speech or the ceremony. This eliminates all of the choices except choice C.

26. A: The ideals of the revolution are addressed in the first paragraph: "Four score and seven years ago our fathers brought forth, upon this continent, a new nation, conceived in Liberty, and dedicated to the proposition that all men are created equal." This introduces the point that Lincoln is trying to make about the battle at hand and the war as a whole: the Civil War is threatening the ideas upon which the nation was created.

27. C: There is a comparison between the ideas of the Revolution and the Civil War in this speech. To facilitate understanding of this comparison, Lincoln has to set the stage by telling his audience about the past event he is referencing. This establishes the context of his message.

28. A: This line directly references the idea in the previous paragraph, which is that the US is a nation that was created to ensure liberty and equality. This sentence talks about how the Civil War is testing whether or not a nation that was created to ensure liberty and equality can really survive.

29. B: When President Lincoln argues that the people who died at Gettysburg did not die in vain, he asserts that their passing was not frivolous or unimportant or meaningless.

30. C: The author points out that just because there is a month focused on African American history, this doesn't mean that African American history must be ignored for the rest of the year.

31. C: The author points out in paragraph 3 that the debate about how to meet the need to teach children about African American history can remind parents that this need is not yet fully met.

32. A: In paragraph 4, the author states that the material available is rich and varied.

33. B: Throughout the passage, the author continues to instill hope and encouragement that Black History Month still has a vital role to play in American culture despite opposing attitudes. Therefore, the best choice is emboldening.

34. C: Choices A and D cannot be correct because the paragraph contains only a handful of moments that are important to black history which are narrowed further by occurring in February. While the final paragraph contains only men, you should not make the conclusion of choice B. Nowhere in the passage does the author make a distinction between male and female influence in black history. Many women have made a remarkable difference in black history. Rosa Parks, Barbara Jordan, Diane Nash, and Septima Poinsette Clark are only a few. The number of men or women to make a significant impact on black history is not the author's point. Instead, you should conclude that regardless of a person's background, ethnicity, or position in society, there are many vital moments and people that connect to black history and those should be known by every individual.

35. A: This passage attempts to persuade readers to accept its point of view. While some of the other choices are true of particular statements found in the passage, only choice A is true of the passage as a whole.

36. A: Choice A is best. The chief benefit, in this context, means the main benefit.

37. D: Only choice D can be correctly inferred from the second paragraph.

38. D: To mimic is to resemble. Choice D is best.

39. B: Choice B best answers the question: the author excludes discussion of plastics' benefits in order to focus on their dangers.

40. B: Durability in this sense means permanence.

Reading—Vocabulary

1. C: When a selection is being made, it involves making a choice between several options. Selecting something is the same as choosing something.

2. B: Smoldering means to burn without flames or smoke heavily.

3. A: Something that is costly is expensive. It costs a lot of money.

4. A: The word with the closest meaning to <u>severe</u> in this context is relentless.

5. A: Besotted means infatuated.

6. C: In this context, <u>stellar</u> means exceptional or outstanding.

7. B: A response is also commonly known as an answer. A response to a question carries the same meaning as an answer to a question.

8. B: Unanimous means undisputed.

9. D: Whereas several of these choices could be associated with <u>tariffs</u> or the people who create them, the closest synonym is <u>tax</u>.

10. C: Suppress most nearly has the same meaning as repress.

11. A: <u>Ruddy</u> means red.

12. B: <u>Keen</u> is another word for sharp.

13. B: An oath is a promise. For example, if you make an oath to keep a secret, you are promising to keep that secret.

14. D: Compensate most nearly has the same meaning as reimburse.

15. C: "Silent" or "silence" indicates quiet and calm. To enjoy the silence of the night is to enjoy the complete quiet of the night.

16. D: Recur most nearly has the same meaning as reappear.

17. B: The word with the nearest meaning to the word <u>secluded</u> is remote.

18. D: Something that has been modified has been changed. Saying you modified your plans means that you changed them.

19. C: <u>Skulk</u> means to move about in a stealthy manner or <u>sneak</u>.

20. B: Tremble is another word for shake. To say somebody or something trembled means that it shook or shuddered.

21. B: <u>Belated</u> means <u>overdue</u> or untimely.

22. B: To cleanse something is to clean or wash it. Saying you cleansed your face or clothes is the same as saying you washed them.

Language

1. C: The longest word recorded in an English dictionary are "Pneumonoultramicroscopicsilicovolcanokoniosis."

Error: Subject-verb disagreement

The subject of this sentence is the singular noun "word," so the plural verb "are" disagrees with the subject. The verb used here should be the singular "is."

2. B: The largest catfish ever catch is 646 pounds, the size of an adult brown bear.

   Error: Incorrect verb tense

   The verb "catch" is not in the appropriate tense. It should be written in the past tense, "caught."

3. C: Though a highly influentially anthropologist, Claude Levi-Strauss often took criticism for spending little time in the field studying real cultures.

   Error: Adverb / adjective error

   The adverb "influentially" is being used to modify the noun "anthropologist." Since adverbs cannot modify nouns, "influentially" should be written in adjective form: "influential."

4. C: It is easy to get confused when calculating time differences between time zones a useful way to remember them is that the Atlantic Ocean starts with A, as in A.M., and the Pacific Ocean starts with P, as in P.M.

   Error: Run-on sentence

   Choice C contains two complete thoughts, each with its own subject and predicate. The second complete thought begins, "a useful way to remember them…." A sentence composed of two complete thoughts joined together without appropriate punctuation is called a "run-on." A period or semicolon should appear between the phrases "time zones" and "a useful way."

5. C: The surrealists were a group of artists who believed that art should reflect the subconscious mind, their images are often very dreamlike, showing businessmen falling like rain over a city and melting clocks.

   Error: Comma splice

   There are two complete sentences here joined by only a comma. A period or semicolon should replace the comma after "mind."

6. B: "Orange is my favorite color, but not my favorite fruit." said Lisa.

   Error: Punctuation

   The period that appears at the end of the quote should be a comma.

7. B: The deepest canyon, too.

   Error: Fragment

   This phrase contains a subject, but it does not contain a predicate, which makes it a sentence fragment.

8. A: Pocahontas spent the last year's of her young life in England under the name Rebecca.

   Error: Apostrophe

   The apostrophe in the word "year's" is unnecessary. The sentence should read, "Pocahontas spent the last years…."

9. A: The Pima Indians of Arizona have remarkably high rates of diabetes and obesity some scientists believe the gene that causes this present-day health crisis was actually of great value to the Pima's ancestors who had to be able to retain glucose during periods of famine.

> Error: Run-on sentence
>
> A sentence composed of two complete thoughts joined together without appropriate punctuation is called a "run-on." A period or semicolon should appear between "obesity" and "some scientists."

10. C: Director Alfred Hitchcock make over 60 films in his career.

> Error: Subject-verb disagreement
>
> The subject "Alfred Hitchcock" is a singular subject, which requires a singular verb. "Make" should be "makes."

11. D: No error.

12. A: The earliest recording of a human voice was made by Thomas Edison in 1877, when they recorded himself reciting "Mary Had a Little Lamb."

> Error: Pronoun-antecedent agreement
>
> Thomas Edison is singular, so the plural pronoun "they" is incorrect. It should read "he."

13. B: Our basement floods once a yearly.

> Error: Adjective/adverb
>
> Here the adverb "yearly" is incorrectly used. It should be replaced with the noun "year."

14. D: No error.

15. B: The spread of Islam began around 600 AD and reached from the Middle East to North Africa, Spain, Central Asia, and India?

> Error: Punctuation
>
> Since this is a declarative sentence and not a question, the question mark should be a period.

16. C: The names of the days of the week originate in either Latin or Saxon names for deities, Sunday, for instance, is Saxon for "Sun's Day," while Thursday derives from "Thor's Day."

> Error: Comma Splice
>
> There are two complete sentences here joined by only a comma. A period or semicolon should replace the comma after "deities."

17. D: No error.

18. A: Ironically, the namesake of the Nobel Peace Prize, Alfred Nobel, are most noted for his invention of dynamite in the 1860s.

Error: Subject-verb disagreement

The subject of this sentence is the singular noun "namesake." The plural verb "are" is incorrect. It should be replaced with the singular verb "is."

19. A: Loud sounds can causing damage to the hair cells that turn sound waves into electrical signals, which the brain perceives as sound.

Error: Verb tense

The verb "causing" is the progressive tense, which is the incorrect tense for this sentence. The sentence should read, "Loud sounds can cause...."

20. C: Carbon monoxide Poisoning can cause disorientation and delirium, and it can induce a coma.

Error: Capitalization

The word "poisoning" does not need to be capitalized because it is not a proper noun.

21. D: No error.

22. A: They closed the parking deck at midnight, so we could not get no cars out until morning.

Error: Double negative

The phrase "could not get no" is an example of a double negative. The phrase should read, "could not get any ...."

23. A: Joni designed the grocery stores sign, but Evan painted it.

Error: *Apostrophe*

Since the sign belongs to the grocery store, an apostrophe should be used to indicate possession. The sentence should read, "...the grocery store's sign...."

24. D: No error.

25. C: Twenty-four leaders of the Nazi party was brought to trial at the end of World War II in what became known as the Nuremberg Trials.

Error: *Subject-verb disagreement*

The subject of this sentence is the plural noun "leaders," which requires a plural verb. "Was" is a singular verb. The sentence should use the plural verb "*were*."

26. C: Water is called "hard water" if it do not quickly create lather upon contact with soap because of mineral compounds dissolved in the water.

Error: *Subject-verb disagreement*

The pronoun "it" is singular, and the verb "do" is plural. The sentence should read, "if it does not quickly create...."

27. B: Ice crystals in the atmosphere, which can create a halo around the sun or moon.

Error: *Sentence fragment*

This sentence contains a subject, but it does not contain a predicate, which makes it a fragment. *Rule of thumb*: Watch out for words such as "which" or "that" in a sentence because the verb that comes afterward *oftentimes does not function* as the main verb of the sentence. One way to correct this sentence would be to delete the comma and the word "which." "Ice crystals in the atmosphere can create a halo around the sun or moon" is a complete thought because it contains a subject, "Ice crystals," and a main verb, "can create."

28. B: Atomic clocks keep time by measuring the vibrations of Atoms and molecules.

Error: *Capitalization*

The word "Atoms" should not be capitalized because it is not a proper noun.

29. A: Heat was once believes to be a type of fluid called "caloric," which flowed into objects and raised their temperature.

Error: *Verb tense*

The verb phrase "was once believes" uses two different tenses: past and present. It should read, "Heat was once *believed*...."

30. B: Apart from a sine wave created by an electronic device, most sounds are not "pure" because they contain many different vibrations at different frequencies pure tones vibrate at only one frequency.

Error: *Run-on sentence*

This sentence contains two complete thoughts without punctuation separating them. The second one begins with the words "pure tones vibrate...." A period or semicolon should be inserted before these words.

31. A: Arthur, realizing that bugs were turning the roots of his zucchini plants to mush.

Error: *Sentence fragment*

These words form an incomplete thought; it does not contain a subject and verb. *Rule of thumb*: Watch out for verbs ending in –ing. These verbs *cannot* be the main verb of a sentence *on their own*. They need another verb (called a "helping verb"), such as "was." The following sentence is a complete thought because the –ing verb is not alone: "Arthur *was realizing* that bugs were turning the roots of his zucchini plants to mush."

32. D: No error.

33. D: No error.

34. A: The narwhal is a member of the dolphin family, easily recognized by its long, spiraling tusk, it is often compared to the mythical unicorn.

Error: *Comma splice*

There are two complete thoughts here, joined together with a comma. The second complete thought begins with the words "it is often...." To correct this sentence, replace the comma after "tusk" with a period or semicolon.

35. C: The first Ferris' Wheel was built in Chicago, Illinois.

> Error: *Apostrophe*
>
> The apostrophe at the end of "Ferris" is incorrect because it is not a possessive noun.

36. A: Trees in the Olympic rain forest in northwest Washington State is covered with a thick green moss that is nourished by the 150 annual inches of rainfall.

> Error: *Subject-verb agreement*
>
> The subject of the sentence is "trees," which is a plural form; the verb "is" does not agree with the subject because it is singular. The main verb in this sentence should be "are." *Rule of thumb:* Watch out for sentences that have a lot of words between the subject and verb. Often, these sentences contain subject-verb verb errors.

37. D: No error.

38. C: I was, hoping to avoid the customs official who was yelling at all of the other travelers.

> Error: *Comma*
>
> The comma between "was" and "hoping" is incorrect. A single comma should not come between a helping verb and an –ing verb.

39. A: Reykjavik is the Capitol of Iceland.

> Error: Capitalization
>
> The word "Capitol" does not need to be capitalized because it is not a proper noun.

40. D: No error.

41. D: No error.

42. C: "Graitful" should be spelled "grateful."

43. C: "Sower" should be spelled "sour."

44. B: "Sinator" should be spelled "senator."

45. A: "Groshery" should be spelled "grocery."

46. A: Though "nite" has become a common informal spelling, the formal spelling of the word is "night."

47. C: "Alway" should be spelled "always."

48. C: "Spays" should be spelled "space."

49. D: No error.

50. D: No error.

51. A: The sentence "Many people have proposed explanations for this drop" provides an introduction to the short explanations that follow. It should come after the first sentence.

52. B: The third sentence of this passage refers to "these insecticides," but there is no earlier reference to any insecticides in the paragraph. The sentence, "Insects that carry the disease can develop resistance to the chemicals, or insecticides, that are used to kill the mosquitoes," needs to be placed after sentence 2 for sentence 3 to make sense.

53. B: Since the second part of this sentence goes on to list examples that help support the point made in the first sentence, "for instance" is the best transitional phrase.

54. C: The second part of the sentence adds additional evidence to prove the claim made in the first part. "In fact" is the best transition to introduce supporting evidence.

55. A: The second part of the sentence contrasts with the first. "However" is the most appropriate transition to use to help create that sense of contrast.

56. A: All of the sentences except sentence A contain errors. Sentences B and C contain verb errors; sentence D is a run-on sentence.

57. B: All of the sentences except sentence B contain verb errors.

58. A: Sentence A contains no errors. Sentence B is less clear than sentence A because it is awkwardly written in the passive voice. Sentence C contains a subject-verb agreement error. Sentence C switches pronouns from "We" to "I" in mid-sentence.

59. C: Sentence 4, regarding Jefferson's affair with one of his slaves, is not directly relevant to the main topic at hand, which is Jefferson's debts.

60. B: Sentence 2, regarding Feynman's musicianship, is of little relevance to the discussion of the atomic theory.

Verbal Skills

1. B: Obligation most nearly means commitment.

2. D: Saying that somebody purchased something and saying they bought something conveys the same meaning.

3. C: Unknown
The first sentence can be diagrammed as follows: Lesley>Steve. But it is unclear from the second sentence whether Steve is older or younger than Barb. Therefore, it is impossible to tell if Lesley is older or younger than Barb.

4. B: Intricate most nearly means complex.

5. B: Ocean is the general category which contains all the other items in the list.

6. C: A pool holds water; a library holds books.

7. C: This analogy focuses on synonyms. *Reprimand* and *punishment* are close synonyms. *Impetuous* is a sudden or impulsive action with little or no thoughtful planning. So, the best choice is *hasty* which means rapid or very quick.

8. C: Eccentric means strange or unconventional, and peculiar means being unusual or out of the ordinary. Therefore, peculiar would be the best choice.

9. A: Eminent means esteemed or distinguished, the opposite of disliked.

10. A: Appliance is the category to which the other answers belong.

11. C: Tropical, arid, and temperate are all different climate types found on Earth. Climate can be understood as the pattern of weather in an area over time and can generally be broken down into 12 different categories, of which tropical, arid, and temperate are examples.

12. D: Small intestine, kidney, and liver are all examples of anatomy.

13. B: Charitable most nearly means generous.

14. B: Powerful means great, which is the opposite of insignificant.

15. A: An elevator is part of a building as a seat is part of a theater. (B) and (C) both contain parts of larger items, but the order is reversed.

16. A: Dexterity means agility, the opposite of awkwardness.

17. D: Insufficient means inadequate, which is the opposite of adequate.

18. B: Alleviate means to ease or lessen, which is the opposite of worsen.

19. A: If somebody or something is departing from somewhere, it means they are leaving. For example, to say the train departed from the station is the same as saying the train left the station.

20. B: We can diagram the first two sentences as follows: Mackenzie > Austin; Nora > Austin. The third sentence, which we could diagram as Mackenzie < Austin, contradicts the first sentence.

21. B: Jovial means happy, which is the opposite of depressed.

22. C: Declare means assert, which is the opposite of deny.

23. A: True

The first two sentences can be diagrammed as follows: Reece>Scott>Della. Sentence three, Reece>Della, is consistent with the first two sentences. It is true.

24. B: Approximate means estimated, the opposite of precise.

25. C: Snail, turtle, and sloth are all animals that can be categorized as slow-moving. Conversely, a cheetah can be categorized as fast-moving.

26. B: Each item except for tugboat runs on land.

27. C: The other words start with the letter "B" and end with the letter "K." So, the correct answer starts with the letter "B," but it ends with the letter "N."

28. C: To say that something is done frequently implies that it is done regularly or often.

29. A: Ubiquitous means frequently present or found everywhere, while seldom means rare or infrequent.

30. D: Repulsive most nearly means disgusting.

31. B: Flat means without any bumps or curves, which is the opposite of uneven.

32. A: Support means help, which is the opposite of oppose.

33. A: Initiate means to start, the opposite of to stop.

34. D: Pernicious means destructive or to have a harmful effect, and detrimental means damaging. Therefore, detrimental is the best choice.

35. C: Something that is described as gigantic is extremely large, or huge, in size.

36. B: A remark is a spoken statement, also commonly known as a comment. To say somebody made a remark conveys the same meaning as saying they made a comment.

37. D: An opportunity is a chance to do something. For example, saying someone was given the *opportunity* to go to school or saying somebody was given the *chance* to go to school conveys the same meaning.

38. C: A sniper must have good aim; a tightrope walker must have good balance.

39. B: Independence, responsibility, and maturity are positive qualities typically associated with adulthood. Irresponsibility is a negative quality that is often associated with youth.

40. B: Accidental means unintentional, the opposite of intentional.

41. A: We can diagram this sequence as follows: A<T, A<R, T=R. If Achilles ran half the distance the tortoise ran, and the rabbit ran twice the distance of Achilles, the tortoise and the rabbit both ran the same distance.

42. A: Lions, tigers, and bears are all different types of animals that can be classified as mammals. Thus, a mammal is the overall category, or classification, that the listed animals belong to.

43. A: Entire is an amount. It usually means the whole amount. For example, if someone says they ate an entire apple, it is the same as saying they ate a whole apple.

44. D: Coca Cola is a brand of soft drink; Xerox is a brand of copier.

45. A: Passive means inactive, or the opposite of active.

46. B: We can diagram this as sequence follows: D>S>E. If it is true that David left for the airport before Sara, then he was the first of the three to leave. The third statement cannot be true.

47. C: Football is the only item in the list that a football player cannot wear.

48. B: We can diagram the first two statements as follows: Aiden=Jessica and Will>Jessica. The third statement says Aiden>Will, which is inconsistent with the first two statements, so it is false.

49. B: Interstate, highway, and avenue are all types of road. Asphalt is used in road construction, but is not a type of road.

50. C: We can diagram the first two statements as follows: Amber<Megan and Alise>Amber. We do not have enough information to determine if Megan scored more goals than Alise.

51. D: A *hologram* is an image that is made up of beams of *light* from a laser. So, we could say that the order of this analogy is a piece of a whole. The start of the next comparison is *film* which would be a piece of a *video camera*.

52. B: Man is the opposite of the other three words, which are all synonyms.

53. C: We can diagram this sequence as follows: Cass<Joni, Jackson<Joni. The relationship between Cass and Jackson is not specified, so the third statement is uncertain.

54. A: Change means modify, which is the opposite of remain.

55. A: Ribosomes, the nucleolus, and mitochondria are all parts of a cell. The epidermis is the outermost layer of skin.

56. C: Ineligible means disqualified, the opposite of allowed.

57. C: Barren, desolate, and infertile all describe conditions in which growth is unsupported or there is emptiness. Conversely, abundant means available in large quantities and represents the opposite of the previous three terms.

58. C: Natural is the opposite of the other words in the series. Artificial, synthetic, and man-made are all words for non-natural processes.

59. A: This analogy focuses on antonyms, or opposites. Hot is the opposite of cold; veracity, or conformity with facts or the truth, is the opposite of dishonesty, or the lack of honesty.

60. B: False

The first two sentences can be diagrammed as follows: Monday>Thursday>Tuesday. Sentence three, Thursday>Monday, is inconsistent with the first two sentences. It is false.

Quantitative Skills

1. C: In an isosceles triangle, two of the sides are congruent, and two of the angles are congruent. In this case, since side $\overline{AB}$ is congruent to side $\overline{AC}$ (and side $\overline{BC}$ is shorter), the angles B and C are congruent and greater than the measure of angle A.

2. A: Find the value of each expression.

$$\frac{1}{3} \times 24 = 8$$
$$\frac{1}{5} \times 30 = 6$$
$$\frac{3}{4} \times 20 = 15$$

$6 < 8 < 15$, so (II) < (I) < (III), which means the statement (II) < (III) is correct.

3. C: In this sequence, the number added to the preceding term goes up by one for each term.

$$41 + 3 = 44$$
$$44 + 4 = 48$$
$$48 + 5 = 53$$
$$53 + 6 = 59$$

Therefore, the next term can be found by adding 7 to 59: $59 + 7 = 66$. Therefore, 66 is the value of the next term.

4. B: A percent is a number divided by 100, so $4\% = \frac{4}{100}$. The decimal 0.04 is also equal to $\frac{4}{100}$. Multiplying both numerator and denominator of $\frac{2}{50}$ by 2 shows that it, too, is equal to $\frac{4}{100}$. Therefore, all three values are equal.

5. C: The equation that represents the relationship between the position number, n, and the value of the term, a_n, is $a_n = -3n + 8$. Notice each n is multiplied by –3, with 8 added to that value. Substituting position number

1 for n gives $a_1 = -3(1) + 8$, which equals 5. Substitution of the remaining position numbers does not provide a counterexample to this procedure.

6. A: Find the sum of each expression.

$$3 + 4 + 16 = 23$$
$$6 + 4 + 5 + 7 = 22$$
$$4 + 5 + 9 = 18$$
$$10 + 4 + 8 = 22$$

Therefore, the greatest sum is $3 + 4 + 16$.

7. C: The square root of a number must lie between the square roots of numbers that are larger and smaller than itself. Since $\sqrt{4} = 2$, and $\sqrt{9} = 3$, and since $4 < 6 < 9$, it follows that $\sqrt{6}$ must lie between 2 and 3.

8. C: Since $\frac{1}{3} \approx 0.33$, and $\frac{2}{3} \approx 0.66$, the correct answer must lie between 0.33 and 0.66. Only choice C satisfies this condition.

9. B: Calculate the value of each expression.

$$20\% \text{ of } 80 = 0.2 \times 80 = 16$$
$$50\% \text{ of } 70 = 0.5 \times 70 = 35$$
$$40\% \text{ of } 90 = 0.4 \times 90 = 36$$

Since $36 > 35 > 16$, the statement (II) > (I) is correct.

10. C: Write an equation to represent the information given.

$$45 - x = 3 \times 9$$

First, simplify the multiplication on the right side.

$$45 - x = 27$$

Then, subtract 45 from both sides.

$$-x = -18$$

Finally, divide both sides by –1.

$$x = 18$$

Therefore, 18 subtracted from 45 makes 3 times 9.

11. A: Find the sum of each expression.

$$4 + 3 + 4 + 5 = 16$$
$$3 + 6 + 8 = 17$$
$$9 + 5 + 3 = 17$$
$$1 + 8 + 7 + 2 = 18$$

Therefore, the expression $4 + 3 + 4 + 5$ has the smallest sum.

12. D: Find the value of each expression.

$$30\% \times 90 = 0.3 \times 90 = 27$$
$$10\% \times 270 = 0.1 \times 270 = 27$$
$$60\% \times 45 = 0.6 \times 45 = 27$$

All three expressions are equal, so the statement (I) = (II) = (III) is true.

13. B: Each term in the sequence is 4 greater than the preceding term. Since $16 + 4 = 20$, 20 is the number that belongs in the blank position.

14. A: In this sequence, each number is either double the preceding number or 2 more than the preceding number, and these procedures alternate. Since $36 = 2 \times 18$, the next element of the sequence will be determined by adding 2. Since $36 + 2 = 38$, the next number in the sequence is 38.

15. C: Each element of the sequence adds 9 to the preceding one. In algebraic terms, $P_n = P_{n-1} + 9$, where P_n is the nth element of the series. Since $31 + 9 = 40$, 40 is the correct answer.

16. C: Set up an equation to represent the given information.

$$\frac{1}{3}x = 2^3$$

First, simplify the cube on the right side.

$$\frac{1}{3}x = 8$$

Then, multiply both sides by 3.

$$x = 24$$

Therefore, one-third of 24 is equal to 2 cubed.

17. C: A quadrilateral with two pairs of equal, opposite sides is called a parallelogram. In all such figures, which include squares and rectangles, the measures of the opposite angles are equal to one another. This means that the statement "$m\angle A = m\angle D$ and $m\angle B = m\angle C$" is correct.

18. A: Find the value of each expression.

$$\frac{1}{5} \times 30 = 6$$
$$\frac{1}{4} \times 20 = 5$$
$$\frac{1}{3} \times 15 = 5$$

Therefore, the statement (I) > (II) = (III) is true.

19. A: Convert all the numbers to fractions and compare. The number 0.099 can be rounded to 0.1. Then, the first 3 choices are $\frac{1}{3}, \frac{1}{4}$, and $\frac{1}{100}$ as fractions. Since the numerators are equal, the number with the smallest denominator is greatest. To compare that with choice D, note that $\frac{1}{3} = \frac{2}{6}$ and $\frac{2}{6} > \frac{2}{7}$.

20. C: Since the pattern repeats the same 4 figures, each multiple of 4 looks like figure 4 (4, 8, 12, ..., 28, 32, ...). The figure in the 31st position is one less than 32, so it should look like the figure left of figure 4, which is figure 3.

21. B: The verbal description "five times a number m squared" means that m must be squared, and the resulting number multiplied by 5. This is represented by the expression $5m^2$. Choice C is incorrect because the value within the parentheses is evaluated first, so that both 5 and m are squared. This results in a value of $25m^2$, which is incorrect.

22. C: The given equations form a system of linear equations. Since the first equation is already given in terms of x, it will be easier to solve it using the substitution method. Start by substituting $2y - 3$ for x in the second equation.

$$2x + \frac{1}{2}y = 3$$
$$2(2y - 3) + \frac{1}{2}y = 3$$

Next, solve the resulting equation for y. Distribute the 2 and then combine like y-terms in the result.

$$4y - 6 + \frac{1}{2}y = 3$$
$$\frac{9}{2}y - 6 = 3$$

Finally, isolate the variable y by adding 6 to both sides and then dividing both sides by the coefficient of y, which is $\frac{9}{2}$.

$$\frac{9}{2}y = 9$$
$$y = 2$$

Therefore, the value of y is 2.

23. A: The mean, or average, of the distribution can be computed by multiplying each grade by the number of students who obtained it, summing all the products, and then dividing by the total number of students. Here, $n = 4.2$. The median is the value where the number of students who received a lower grade is equal to the number of students who received a higher grade. Here, $p = 4$. The mode is the most frequently obtained grade, and here, $q = 3$. Thus, $n > p > q$.

24. C: The sequence consists of the squares of consecutive integers, beginning with 1: $1^2 = 1, 2^2 = 4, 3^2 = 9$, and $4^2 = 16$. In the fifth position, $5^2 = 25$, so 25 is the next number.

25. C: To find the perimeter of rectangle A, we add all its side lengths to get a perimeter of $11 + 5 + 11 + 5 = 32$ feet. Similarly, the perimeter of rectangle B is $8 + 7 + 8 + 7 = 30$ feet. So, rectangle A has the greater perimeter. To find the area of rectangle A, we multiply its length by its width to get an area of $11 \times 5 = 55$ square feet. Similarly, the area of rectangle B is $8 \times 7 = 56$ square feet. Thus, rectangle B has the greater area.

26. B: In this sequence, the number subtracted from the preceding term increases by 2 for each term.

$$108 - 4 = 104$$
$$104 - 6 = 98$$
$$98 - 8 = 90$$
$$90 - 10 = 80$$

For the next term, subtract 12: $80 - 12 = 68$. Therefore, 68 is the next term in the sequence.

27. D: Integers consist of all positive and negative whole numbers and the number zero. The product of three integers must be an integer, so you can eliminate any answer choice that is not an integer. The product of two even integers is even. The product of an even and odd integer is even. The only even choice is 24, and we can see that $2 \times 4 \times 3 = 24$.

28. B: The area of a rectangle is given by $A = \text{length} \times \text{width}$. The area of a triangle is given by $A = \frac{\text{base} \times \text{height}}{2}$. In the figure, the height of the triangle equals the length of the rectangle, and the base of the triangle, $\overline{BC}$, equals the width of the rectangle, $\overline{AB}$. Therefore, the triangle's base × height equals the rectangle's length × width, and since the area of a triangle is half that amount, that area is also half the area of the rectangle.

29. B: Fractions can be simplified by dividing both numerator and denominator by the same number. Divide the numerator and denominator of item (II) by 10, and the result is $\frac{2}{3}$. Divide the numerator and denominator of (III) by 15, the result is $\frac{2}{3}$. Therefore, all three fractions are equal.

30. C: The reciprocal of 5 is $\frac{1}{5}$. When numbers are multiplied by their reciprocals, the result is always 1.

$$5 \times \frac{1}{5} = 1$$

31. C: Since A is at the intersection of the diagonals, the regions (II) and (III) are both quadrants of the square and are equal. Region (I) is one-half of the square and is equal to two quadrants, so it is greater than (II) or (III).

32. D: The integers between –4.2 and 6.1 are –4, –3, –2, –1, 0, 1, 2, 3, 4, 5, and 6. Therefore, there are 11 integers between –4.2 and 6.1.

33. A: Each element of the sequence is a multiple of 3 less than the previous element. Starting with 116, the next element is 1×3 less, or $116 - (1 \times 3) = 113$. The next element is 2×3 less, or $113 - (2 \times 3) = 107$. The next element is 3×3 less, or $107 - (3 \times 3) = 98$. So, the next element will be 4×3 less, or $98 - (4 \times 3) = 86$.

34. B: Since there are equal numbers of each coin in the row, if two of one type are next to each other, two of the other type must also be next to each other someplace within the row or at each end of the row. Since the two dimes take up one end of the row, the two pennies must be together.

35. D: The sequence alternates between subtracting 4 from the number occurring two positions earlier (12, 8, 4, 0) and adding 6 to the number occurring two positions earlier (7, 13, 19). Therefore, the next number should be $19 + 6$, which is 25.

36. A: An odd number can be considered as an even number N plus 1. Two even numbers added together produce an even number, so the result of adding an odd and an even number must be an even number plus 1, which is odd. For example, $4 + 3 = 7$, and 7 is odd.

37. C: When two line segments intersect, vertical angles are congruent and adjacent angles are supplementary. Therefore, the statement "$A = C$ and $B = D$" is the only true statement listed.

38. B: Figure out how much is added from one number to the next.

$$4 + \mathbf{2} = 6$$
$$6 + \mathbf{4} = 10$$
$$10 + \mathbf{8} = 18$$

The pattern is to double the number that is added to the previous number. So, to find the next number in the sequence, add 16 to 18.

$$18 + 16 = 34$$

Therefore, the missing number is 34. We can double check this by adding double of 16, which is 32, to 34 to see if we get 66.

$$34 + 32 = 66$$

39. C: The perimeter of a rectangle of length 6 and width 4 equals $2(6 + 4) = 20$. The perimeter of a square of side length 4 equals $4 + 4 + 4 + 4 = 16$. The area of a square of side length 4 equals $4 \times 4 = 16$. Although the units for the measurement of area differ from those of the perimeters, the magnitude of the measurements for (II) and (III) are the same.

40. B: In this sequence, 5 and 4 are added alternatively to successive numbers to determine the next numeral: $54 + 5 = 59, 59 + 4 = 63$, etc. Since $68 + 4 = 72$, the next element is calculated by adding 5: $72 + 5 = 77$, so 77 is the next term in the sequence.

41. B: The sequence consists of numbers where each number is double the previous number. The number prior to the blank is 4: $2 \times 4 = 8$. The number following the blank is 16: $2 \times 8 = 16$. Since this is true, we know the missing number is 8.

42. C: The straight line separating section (I) from sections (II) and (III) is a diameter. Therefore, section (I) is equal to one half of the circle. Since (II) and (III) together make up the remaining half of the circle, their sum is equal to section (I). Since (II) + (III) = (I), it follows that (II) = (I) − (III).

43. D: In this sequence, each number is the sum of the two preceding numbers. For example, $3 = 1 + 2$, and $5 = 3 + 2$. Therefore, the number following 13 must be $13 + 8 = 21$, and the next number must be $21 + 13 = 34$. This is known as a Fibonacci sequence.

44. C: Prime numbers are those that are only evenly divisible by 1 and themselves. 68 is not a prime number because it is divisible by 1, 2, 4, 17, 34, and 68. 69 is not a prime number because it is divisible by 1, 3, 23, and 69. 70 is not a prime number because it is divisible by 1, 2, 5, 7, 10, 14, 35, and 70. 71 is a prime number because it is only divisible by 1 and itself. Therefore, in a sequence of prime numbers from least to greatest, the number 71 immediately follows 67.

45. D: Since the line segments pass through the center of the circle, both $\overline{AB}$ and $\overline{CD}$ are diameters of equal length, and the four line segments radiating outwards from O are all equal-length radii.

46. A: Let D represent Dorothy's age and S represent her sister's age. Since she is half of her sister's age today, we have $D = \frac{S}{2}$, or $S = 2D$. In twenty years, her age will be $D + 20$, and her sister's age will be $S + 20$. At that time, Dorothy will be $\frac{3}{4}$ of her sister's age. Therefore, $D + 20 = \frac{3}{4}(S + 20)$. Substitute $2D$ for S in this equation.

$$D + 20 = \frac{3}{4}(2D + 20)$$

Use the distributive property and reduce.

$$D + 20 = \frac{3}{2}D + 15$$

From here, solve for D.

$$20 - 15 = \frac{3}{2}D - D$$
$$5 = \frac{1}{2}D$$
$$10 = D$$

Dorothy is 10 years old today, and her sister is 20 years old. In twenty years, Dorothy will be 30 years old, and her sister will be 40 years old.

47. D: $5^2 = 5 \times 5 = 25$, so (I) = (III). However, $2^5 = 2 \times 2 \times 2 \times 2 \times 2 = 32$, which means (II) is greater than (I) or (III). This makes the statement (I) = (III) and (III) < (II) true.

48. B: Find the value of each expression.

$$2 \times 15 - 3 = 30 - 3 = 27$$
$$3^3 = 27$$
$$3 + 80\% \times 30 = 3 + 0.8 \times 30 = 3 + 24 = 27$$

Therefore, all three expressions are equal, and the statement (I) = (II) = (III) is true.

49. A: Negative numbers represent segments extending to the left of zero on the number line. Adding a negative number to another negative number extends the segment even further to the left, or into "negative territory." To add two negative numbers, add the magnitudes and retain the negative sign. Example: $(-3) + (-5) = -8$.

50. A: Start by writing an equation that represents the information.

$$x + x = \frac{1}{3} \times 66$$

Then, simplify both sides of the equation.

$$2x = 22$$

Now, divide both sides of the equation by 2.

$$x = 11$$

Therefore, 11 added to itself is $\frac{1}{3}$ of 66.

51. B: The sequence consists of a series of numbers each of which is double the preceding number. Since $2 \times 8 = 16$, and $2 \times 16 = 32$, the missing term is 16.

52. B: Since $\overline{AB}$, $\overline{BD}$, $\overline{CD}$, and $\overline{AC}$ are sides of the square, they are all equal. They are shorter than the diagonals $\overline{AD}$ and $\overline{CB}$. These diagonals have the same length and bisect one another at the point E, which means that $\overline{AE} = \overline{BE} = \overline{CE} = \overline{DE}$, and are equal to half the length of the full diagonals. Therefore, the statement "$\overline{CE}$ is equal to $\overline{AE}$" is the only true statement listed.

Mathematics

1. C: Supplementary angles add to 180 degrees. Therefore, the other angle is equal to the difference between 180 degrees and 34 degrees: $180° - 34° = 146°$.

2. A: Lindsay used the following calculations to convert 2 ounces to teaspoons:

$$2 \text{ ounces} \times \frac{1 \text{ pint}}{16 \text{ ounces}} \times \frac{2 \text{ cups}}{1 \text{ pint}} \times \frac{16 \text{ tablespoons}}{1 \text{ cup}} \times \frac{3 \text{ teaspoons}}{1 \text{ tablespoon}} = 12 \text{ teaspoons}$$

3. C: Following the order of operations, start by calculating the expression inside the brackets. Calculate the power first: $3^2 = 9$.

$$(44 + 3^2) + 2^2$$
$$(44 + 9) + 2^2$$

Then, fully simplify the bracketed expression.

$$53 + 2^2$$

Next, evaluate 2^2.

$$53 + 4$$

Finally, add the expressions.

$$53 + 4 = 57$$

4. C: The expression within the grouping symbols must be evaluated first: $6 + 1 = 7$. This result is then multiplied by the number outside the grouping symbols: $4 \times 7 = 28$.

5. D: The slopes of perpendicular lines are reciprocals and have the opposite sign. As an example, in the figure below, Line A has a slope of $-\frac{1}{2}$, and Line B has a slope of 2. These lines are perpendicular.

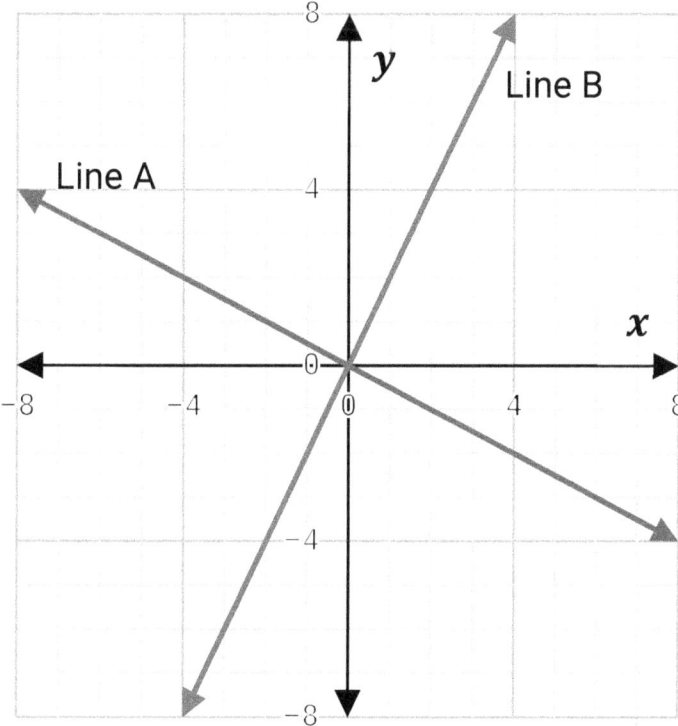

6. A: Complementary angles are two angles that add to 90°. Of the given answer choices, only choice A contains angles that add up to 90° (71° and 19°).

7. C: The square root of a number which is raised to the 4th power is the same number raised to the 2nd power. That is, $\sqrt{2^4} = 2^2 = 4$. Since $4 \times 4 = 16$, choice C is correct.

8. A: Setting the cost of shipping equal to the amount received gives us the equation $3{,}000 + 100x = 400x$. Subtract $100x$ from both sides to get $3{,}000 = 300x$, then divide both sides by 300 to see that $x = 10$. Therefore, the least number of computers that must be shipped and sold is 10.

9. D: If the ratio of nickels to pennies is 6 : 2, then there are 8 total coins because $6 + 2 = 8$. The ratio of pennies to combined coins is 2 : 8. This is $\frac{2}{8}$ as a fraction, which simplifies to $\frac{1}{4}$. This is equivalent to 25%.

10. D: Following the normal order of operations, first calculate the sum in the parentheses: $2 + 3 = 5$. The expression is now equivalent to $9 + 4 \times 5$. Next, perform the multiplication, which makes the expression $9 + 20$. Add the final terms to find that $9 + 20 = 29$.

11. A: A set of six numbers with an average of 4 must have a collective sum of 24 because $6 \times 4 = 24$. The two numbers that average 2 will add up to 4 ($2 \times 2 = 4$), so the remaining numbers must add up to 20 ($24 - 4 = 20$). The average of these four numbers can be calculated by dividing the sum by the amount of numbers: $20 \div 4 = 5$. Therefore, the average of the other four numbers is 5.

12. B: The perimeter of a square is 4 times the length of a side. Therefore, in this case, the side must equal $s = 16 \div 4 = 4$. The area is found by squaring the side length, or $A = s^2 = 4^2 = 16$. Therefore, the area is 16 ft².

13. B: A cube has six square faces. The arrangement of these faces in a two-dimensional figure is a net of a cube if the figure can be folded to form a cube. If choice B is folded, the bottom square in the second column will overlap the fourth square in the top row, so the figure does not represent a net of a cube. The other figures represent three of the eleven possible nets of a cube.

14. C: Enrique gets paid $12/hr for the first 40 hours and $12/hr × 1.5 = $18/hr for every hour of overtime. Since he worked 45 hours, that is 40 hours at the regular rate and 5 hours at the overtime rate.

$$40 \text{ hr} \times (\$12/\text{hr}) + 5 \text{ hr} \times (\$18/\text{hr}) = \$480 + \$90 = \$570$$

Therefore, Enrique will earn $570.

15. A: $(0, 0)$ is a point because if Jonas doesn't walk, then his running speed is also 0. Another point is $(1, 3)$ because if Jonas moves a distance of 1 unit after walking x minutes, then he moves a distance of 3 units after x minutes from jogging. Jonas's jogging distance will always be 3 times his walking distance, as seen in choice A.

16. A: If 18 of 24 students completed their projects on time, then the number of students who failed to complete their projects on time can be found by subtracting 18 from 24.

$$24 - 18 = 6$$

This means that 6 students failed to complete their projects on time. Create a fraction representing how many students failed to complete their projects on time out of the whole class.

$$\frac{6}{24} = \frac{6 \div 6}{24 \div 6} = \frac{1}{4}$$

Therefore, $\frac{1}{4}$ of the students failed to complete their projects on time.

17. D: There are 16 empty chairs. This gives $\frac{2}{5}$ of the total enrollment. So, the full class must be:

$$\text{Class} = \frac{5}{2} \times 16 = 40 \text{ students}$$

Another option is to use proportions.

$$\frac{2}{5} = \frac{16}{x}$$

First, cross multiply to get: $2x = 80$. Then, divide each side by 2 to solve for x. So, $x = 40$, which means there are 40 students in the entire class.

18. B: To make this conversion, set up fractions to convert from one unit to the other.

$$\frac{2.5 \text{ yd}}{1} \times \frac{3 \text{ ft}}{1 \text{ yd}} \times \frac{12 \text{ in}}{1 \text{ ft}} = 90 \text{ in}$$

Therefore, there are 90 inches in 2.5 yards.

19. C: Since he buys two cups per day for five days and one cup on Saturday, the total number of cups that Richard buys each week is 11 cups: $2 \times 5 + 1 = 11$. Since each cup costs $2.25, the amount he spends can be calculated by multiplying 11 by 2.25.

$$11 \times 2.25 = 24.75$$

Richard spends $24.75 on coffee every week.

20. D: Distance is the product of velocity and time.

$$(5 \times 10^6) \times (2 \times 10^{-4}) = (5 \times 2) \times (10^6 \times 10^{-4})$$
$$= 10 \times 10^{6-4}$$
$$= 10 \times 10^2$$
$$= 10^3$$
$$= 1,000$$

Therefore, the bullet traveled 1,000 feet.

21. B: Since the airplane is moving against a headwind, it will be slowed relative to the ground. Therefore, its final speed will be 300 mph − 15 mph = 285 mph.

22. B: The y-intercept of the line is $(0, -1)$. Another point on the line is $(1, 0)$. Slope is the vertical change over horizontal change, which is $m = \frac{0-(-1)}{1-0} = \frac{1}{1} = 1$. Plugging this information into the slope-intercept form $y = mx + b$, the equation is $y = x - 1$.

23. D: The sides of a triangle must all be greater than 0. The sum of the lengths of the two shorter sides must be greater than the length of the third side. Since we are looking for the minimum value of the perimeter, assume the longer of the two given sides, which is 6, is the longest side of the triangle. Then, the third side must be greater than $6 - 4 = 2$. Since we are told the sides are all integers, the last side must be 3 units in length. Thus, the minimum length for the perimeter is $4 + 6 + 3 = 13$ units.

24. D: Since 1 meter equals 1,000 millimeters, the conversion factor is 1,000. Since a millimeter is shorter than a meter, we divide by the conversion factor.

$$336 \text{ mm} \times \frac{1 \text{ m}}{1,000 \text{ mm}} = 0.336 \text{ m}$$

So, 336 millimeters is equal to 0.336 meters.

25. C: Each throw of the dart is an independent event and has no influence on the outcome of any other throw. Every time the dart is thrown, it has a 50% chance of landing on black, irrespective of the results of previous throws.

26. B: This problem can be solved with the following equation, in which x is the total capacity of the tank.

$$\frac{1}{2}x = \frac{1}{3}x + 3$$
$$\left(\frac{1}{2} - \frac{1}{3}\right)x = 3$$
$$\left(\frac{3}{6} - \frac{2}{6}\right)x = 3$$
$$\frac{1}{6}x = 3$$
$$x = 18$$

Therefore, Archie's tank can hold 18 gallons of gas.

27. D: The total weight in ounces is $12 \times 6 = 72$ ounces. Divide 72 by the number of ounces per pound: $72 \div 16 = 4.5$. Since there are 16 ounces in a pound, half a pound is equal to 8 ounces. Therefore, 12 apples weigh 4 pounds 8 ounces.

28. B: Solve this equation by isolating the variable on one side of the equality sign. Start by dividing both sides of the equation by 3.

$$4x + 3 = 15$$

Next, subtract 3 from both sides.

$$4x = 12$$

Finally, divide both sides by 4.

$$x = 3$$

Therefore, the value of x is 3.

29. C: When the dress is marked down by 20%, the cost of the dress is 80% of its original price. Since a percentage can be written as a fraction by placing the percentage over 100, the reduced price of the dress can be written as $\frac{80}{100}x$, or $\frac{4}{5}x$, where x is the original price. When discounted an extra 25%, the dress costs 75% of the reduced price. This results in the expression $\frac{75}{100}\left(\frac{4}{5}x\right)$, which can be simplified to $\frac{3}{4}\left(\frac{4}{5}x\right)$, or $\frac{3}{5}x$. So the final price of the dress is three-fifths of the original price.

30. A: There are three fractions: $\frac{1}{4}, \frac{1}{8}$, and $\frac{1}{2}$. To answer the question, they must be added together. The common denominator is 8, so express each fraction with a denominator of 8 and then add the fractions.

$$\frac{1}{2} + \frac{1}{4} + \frac{1}{8} = \frac{4}{8} + \frac{2}{8} + \frac{1}{8} = \frac{7}{8}$$

Among just the first three people, the dog is being taken care of $\frac{7}{8}$ of the time. Therefore, to calculate the proportion of time the fourth person will have to care for the dog, subtract $\frac{7}{8}$ from 1 whole, or $\frac{8}{8}$.

$$\frac{8}{8} - \frac{7}{8} = \frac{1}{8}$$

Therefore, the fourth person will have to take care of the dog $\frac{1}{8}$ of the time.

31. D: First, calculate 3% of 548 meters.

$$0.03 \times 548 \text{ m} = 16.44 \text{ m}$$

Add this increase to the building's original height.

$$548 \text{ m} + 16.44 \text{ m} = 564.44 \text{ m}$$

Rounding to the nearest whole number, we get 564 meters. Therefore, the new height of the skyscraper will be 564 m.

32. C: Start by listing out the multiples of 23.

$$23 \times 1 = 23$$
$$23 \times 2 = 46$$
$$23 \times 3 = 69$$
$$23 \times 4 = 92$$
$$23 \times 5 = 115$$

The only answer choice that is a part of this list is 92.

33. B: Add the heights of the two bookcases to solve. The height of the window from the floor is not needed for this question. It is extra information. Change the fractions so that they have a common denominator. After you add, simplify the fraction.

$$14\frac{1}{2} + 8\frac{3}{4} = 14\frac{2}{4} + 8\frac{3}{4}$$
$$= 22 + \frac{5}{4}$$
$$= 22 + 1\frac{1}{4}$$
$$= 23\frac{1}{4}$$

Therefore, the bookcases are $23\frac{1}{4}$ inches tall when they are stacked together.

34. C: The question asks us how many students scored "75 points or fewer" on the math test. This means we are looking for all the data contained in the intervals 61–65, 66–70, and 71–75. From the histogram we may not know the exact scores of these students, but we do know that all the scores contained in these intervals must be 75 points or less. Only 1 student scored between 61 and 65 points, 0 students scored between 66 and 70 points, and 2 students scored between 71 and 75 points. Because $1 + 0 + 2 = 3$, we can conclude that 3 students scored 75 points or fewer on the math test.

35. B: This pie chart shows the percentage of the total recyclable material that each material represents. The larger percentages have larger slices of the circle. Also, the percentage for each material is shown next to each slice. In this chart, paper is the most recycled material because it has the largest slice. This is 40% of the total. The next most common is glass at 25% of the total. All of the other materials stand for smaller portions of the total.

36. B: Any color can be drawn the first time, leaving five marbles. At this point, only one of the five is the same color as the one that was drawn the first time. The odds of selecting this marble are one chance in five, or 20%.

37. B: The price is reduced by an amount equal to 5% of the original price.

$$120 \times 0.05 = 6$$

She will save $6. Now, subtract $6 from the original price of $120 to calculate the sale price.

$$120 - 6 = 114$$

Margaret will pay $114 for the dress.

38. B: The inequality specifies that the difference between L and 15 inches must be less or equal to 0.01. Note that $|14.99 - 15| = |-0.01| = 0.01$, which is equal to the specified tolerance and therefore meets the condition.

39. B: To solve, first subtract Jerry's weight from the total permitted weight to find out how much the items can weight together.

$$800 - 200 = 600$$

Since there are 4 pieces of equipment, divide 600 by 4 to find out the average weight of each item.

$$600 \div 4 = 150$$

Each item should weigh about 150 pounds.

40. B: First, determine how many milliliters of chicken broth are in the soup. Since there are 4 containers and 410 milliliters in each container, multiply the values: 410 mL × 4 = 1,640 mL. Then, convert 1,640 mL to liters. There are 1,000 milliliters in 1 liter, so divide 1,640 by 1,000: $\frac{1,640 \text{ mL}}{1,000 \text{ mL/L}} = 1.64$ L. Add the liter of water to find the total amount of liquid in the pot: 1.64 L + 1 L = 2.64 L.

41. B: Since five people are splitting $17.90, each person's share can be calculated by dividing the total price by 5.

$$17.90 \div 5 = 3.58$$

Each person will pay $3.58.

42. A: The probability of playing a song by any band is proportional to the number of songs by that band over the total number of songs, or $\frac{5}{15} = \frac{1}{3}$ for Band D. The probability of playing any particular song is not affected by what has been played previously, so all 15 songs have an equal probability to be played.

43. C: According to the exponent rule $a^{-n} = \frac{1}{a^n}$, the expression 2^{-3} is equivalent to $\frac{1}{2^3}$. Since $2^3 = 2 \times 2 \times 2 = 8$, this expression is equivalent to $\frac{1}{8}$.

44. B: The least common multiple, or LCM, is the smallest number that is a multiple of two numbers. Since $2 \times 2 = 4$, and $1 \times 4 = 4$, 4 is the least common multiple of the two numbers given.

45. C: The volume of a right, circular cylinder is equal to its height multiplied by the area of its base, B.

$$V = Bh$$

The area of the circular base is πr^2, so substitute this value in for B.

$$V = \pi r^2 h$$

Since the diameter is twice the length of the radius, $r = 60$ ft $\div 2 = 30$ ft. From here, substitute the known values for V, π, and r. Then, solve for h.

$$1,000,000 = (3.14)(30)^2 h$$
$$1,000,000 = (3.14)(900)h$$
$$1,000,000 = 2,826h$$
$$353.86 \approx h$$

Since the height of the tank needs to be at least 353.86 ft, the minimum acceptable height is 354 ft.

46. C: To determine this, first solve for x. Start by subtracting 2 from both sides.

$$10x + 2 = 7$$
$$10x = 5$$

Then, divide both sides by 10.

$$x = \frac{5}{10} = \frac{1}{2}$$

Since $x = \frac{1}{2}$, multiply this by 2 to find that $2x = 2\left(\frac{1}{2}\right) = 1$.

47. C: We are looking for a graph with two key pieces of information: a value 2 greater for column C than column E and a value of B that is less than any others. Answer choices A and B show that Store C charges $8 and Store E charges $6, so this fits, but they both show other locations as less expensive than Store B. Answer choice D shows that Store B is the least expensive, but Store C charges less than Store E, not $2 more. Only answer choice C is correct because it shows that Store B charges the least of any store and that store C ($9) is $2 more expensive than Store E ($7).

48. B: First, evaluate the expressions within the grouping symbols, starting from the innermost and working outwards.

$$3 + [(12 \div 4) \times 6] - 20$$
$$3 + [3 \times 6] - 20$$
$$3 + 18 - 20$$

Then, add and subtract in order from left to right.

$$3 + 18 - 20 = 21 - 20 = 1$$

49. C: Since 1 meter equals 100 centimeters, the conversion factor is 100. Since a meter is longer than a centimeter, we multiply by the conversion factor.

$$6 \text{ m} \times \frac{100 \text{ cm}}{1 \text{ m}} = 600 \text{ cm}$$

So, there are 600 centimeters in 6 meters.

50. B: The "5" in 452 occupies the tens place and represents the number of tens in the number, or 5×10.

51. A: The area of a circle is $A = \pi r^2$, where r is the radius. Since π is approximately 3.14, we have $r = \sqrt{\frac{A}{\pi}} \approx \sqrt{\frac{314 \text{ inches}^2}{3.14}} = \sqrt{100 \text{ inches}^2} = 10$ inches. The diameter is twice the radius, or 2×10 inches $= 20$ inches.

52. B: If you draw a vertical line down the center of the letter V, the two sides will be symmetrical. This is not true for the other letters shown.

53. A: The diagonal of the square corresponds to the diameter of the circle. This allows for calculation of the side a by the Pythagorean theorem, where the diameter is $d = 2r$.

$$d^2 = a^2 + a^2$$
$$(2r)^2 = 2a^2$$
$$4r^2 = 2a^2$$
$$2r^2 = a^2$$

Since the area of the square is a^2, we can say the area of a square inscribed within a circle is $2r^2$.

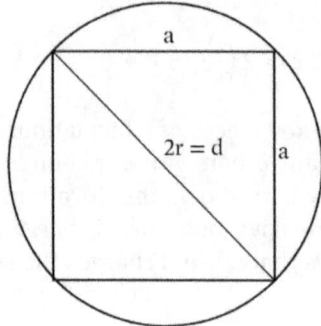

54. C: The amount Richard is paid per phone sale can be calculated by multiplying 140 by 10%.

$$140 \times 10\% = 140 \times 0.1 = 14$$

He makes $14 per phone he sells. To find out how many phones he needs to sell to make $840, divide this number by the amount he makes per phone sale.

$$840 \div 14 = 60$$

Therefore, Richard must sell 60 phones in order to be paid $840.

55. C: The total number of people mentioned is $20 + 13 = 33$, but there are only 25 cars. Therefore, $33 - 25 = 8$ cars must have both a man and a woman inside.

56. B: If x represents the width of the shape, its length is equal to $2x$. Since we are told it would be a square if it were 3 inches shorter and 3 inches wider, and the sides of a square are equal, we can use the following equation to solve for x.

$$2x - 3 = x + 3$$
$$x - 3 = 3$$
$$x = 6$$

So, the shape is 6 inches wide.

57. A: We first convert the number of hours she needs to practice to minutes.

$$3.5 \times 60 = 210$$

Haley needs to practice 210 minutes. The number of minutes Haley has left to practice equal the number required minus the sum of the minutes she's already practiced.

$$210 - (45 + 45 + 25 + 25) = 210 - 140 = 70$$

Haley has 70 minutes left to practice this week.

58. B: Nancy spent a total of $3.15 + $6.75 = $9.90. Subtracting the $9.90 she spent from the $17.25 she started with yields $7.35. Therefore, Nancy has $7.35 left.

59. C: To find the total percentage taken out, add the two percentages.

$$35\% + 4\% = 39\%$$

Therefore, 39% was taken out of the paycheck.

60. B: The coordinates of points in a Cartesian plane are represented in the form (x, y). The point A in the figure is at $x = 2$ and $y = 3$ and is represented as $(2, 3)$.

61. D: Rainfall in October increases to 6 inches, from 1 inch in September. This represents an increase of 5 inches. We don't have information about the month before January, so we cannot know the change in rainfall. The change in amount of rainfall from February to March is 1 inch. The change in amount of rainfall from July to August is also 1 inch. Therefore, the greatest increase happens from September to October.

62. A: Besides the $600 he has remaining, Chan has paid out a total of 85% (30% + 30% + 25%) of his bonus for the expenses described in the question. Therefore, the $600 represents the remaining 15%. Remember that 15% can be written as $\frac{15}{100}$. To determine his total bonus, solve $\frac{15}{100}x = 600$. So, $x = \frac{100}{15} \times 600 = 4{,}000$, and Chan's total bonus is $4,000.

63. D: To solve the equation, first get rid of the denominators by multiplying both sides of the equation by $x(x - 3)$ and simplifying the result.

$$\frac{4}{x-3} - \frac{2}{x} = 1$$
$$x(x-3)\left[\frac{4}{x-3} - \frac{2}{x}\right] = x(x-3) \times 1$$
$$4x - 2(x-3) = x(x-3)$$
$$4x - 2x + 6 = x^2 - 3x$$
$$2x + 6 = x^2 - 3x$$

The result is a quadratic equation. Move everything to one side and then solve for x by factoring the left side and applying the zero-product rule.

$$x^2 - 5x - 6 = 0$$
$$(x+1)(x-6) = 0$$
$$x + 1 = 0 \qquad x - 6 = 0$$
$$x = -1 \qquad x = 6$$

Therefore, the possible solutions are $x = -1$ and $x = 6$. Since neither of these values will cause division by zero when substituted back into the original equation, they are both valid solutions.

64. D: Rotational symmetry is defined as a figure that looks exactly the same after being rotated any amount. The octagon is the only example given that would stay the same if rotated.

HSPT Practice Test #2

To take this additional practice test, visit our online resources page:
mometrix.com/resources719/hspt-28350

How to Overcome Test Anxiety

Just the thought of taking a test is enough to make most people a little nervous. A test is an important event that can have a long-term impact on your future, so it's important to take it seriously and it's natural to feel anxious about performing well. But just because anxiety is normal, that doesn't mean that it's helpful in test taking, or that you should simply accept it as part of your life. Anxiety can have a variety of effects. These effects can be mild, like making you feel slightly nervous, or severe, like blocking your ability to focus or remember even a simple detail.

If you experience test anxiety—whether severe or mild—it's important to know how to beat it. To discover this, first you need to understand what causes test anxiety.

Causes of Test Anxiety

While we often think of anxiety as an uncontrollable emotional state, it can actually be caused by simple, practical things. One of the most common causes of test anxiety is that a person does not feel adequately prepared for their test. This feeling can be the result of many different issues such as poor study habits or lack of organization, but the most common culprit is time management. Starting to study too late, failing to organize your study time to cover all of the material, or being distracted while you study will mean that you're not well prepared for the test. This may lead to cramming the night before, which will cause you to be physically and mentally exhausted for the test. Poor time management also contributes to feelings of stress, fear, and hopelessness as you realize you are not well prepared but don't know what to do about it.

Other times, test anxiety is not related to your preparation for the test but comes from unresolved fear. This may be a past failure on a test, or poor performance on tests in general. It may come from comparing yourself to others who seem to be performing better or from the stress of living up to expectations. Anxiety may be driven by fears of the future—how failure on this test would affect your educational and career goals. These fears are often completely irrational, but they can still negatively impact your test performance.

Elements of Test Anxiety

As mentioned earlier, test anxiety is considered to be an emotional state, but it has physical and mental components as well. Sometimes you may not even realize that you are suffering from test anxiety until you notice the physical symptoms. These can include trembling hands, rapid heartbeat, sweating, nausea, and tense muscles. Extreme anxiety may lead to fainting or vomiting. Obviously, any of these symptoms can have a negative impact on testing. It is important to recognize them as soon as they begin to occur so that you can address the problem before it damages your performance.

The mental components of test anxiety include trouble focusing and inability to remember learned information. During a test, your mind is on high alert, which can help you recall information and stay focused for an extended period of time. However, anxiety interferes with your mind's natural processes, causing you to blank out, even on the questions you know well. The strain of testing during anxiety makes it difficult to stay focused, especially on a test that may take several hours. Extreme anxiety can take a huge mental toll, making it difficult not only to recall test information but even to understand the test questions or pull your thoughts together.

Effects of Test Anxiety

Test anxiety is like a disease—if left untreated, it will get progressively worse. Anxiety leads to poor performance, and this reinforces the feelings of fear and failure, which in turn lead to poor performances on subsequent tests. It can grow from a mild nervousness to a crippling condition. If allowed to progress, test anxiety can have a big impact on your schooling, and consequently on your future.

Test anxiety can spread to other parts of your life. Anxiety on tests can become anxiety in any stressful situation, and blanking on a test can turn into panicking in a job situation. But fortunately, you don't have to let anxiety rule your testing and determine your grades. There are a number of relatively simple steps you can take to move past anxiety and function normally on a test and in the rest of life.

Physical Steps for Beating Test Anxiety

While test anxiety is a serious problem, the good news is that it can be overcome. It doesn't have to control your ability to think and remember information. While it may take time, you can begin taking steps today to beat anxiety.

Just as your first hint that you may be struggling with anxiety comes from the physical symptoms, the first step to treating it is also physical. Rest is crucial for having a clear, strong mind. If you are tired, it is much easier to give in to anxiety. But if you establish good sleep habits, your body and mind will be ready to perform optimally, without the strain of exhaustion. Additionally, sleeping well helps you to retain information better, so you're more likely to recall the answers when you see the test questions.

Getting good sleep means more than going to bed on time. It's important to allow your brain time to relax. Take study breaks from time to time so it doesn't get overworked, and don't study right before bed. Take time to rest your mind before trying to rest your body, or you may find it difficult to fall asleep.

Along with sleep, other aspects of physical health are important in preparing for a test. Good nutrition is vital for good brain function. Sugary foods and drinks may give a burst of energy but this burst is followed by a crash, both physically and emotionally. Instead, fuel your body with protein and vitamin-rich foods.

Also, drink plenty of water. Dehydration can lead to headaches and exhaustion, especially if your brain is already under stress from the rigors of the test. Particularly if your test is a long one, drink water during the breaks. And if possible, take an energy-boosting snack to eat between sections.

Along with sleep and diet, a third important part of physical health is exercise. Maintaining a steady workout schedule is helpful, but even taking 5-minute study breaks to walk can help get your blood pumping faster and clear your head. Exercise also releases endorphins, which contribute to a positive feeling and can help combat test anxiety.

When you nurture your physical health, you are also contributing to your mental health. If your body is healthy, your mind is much more likely to be healthy as well. So take time to rest, nourish your body with healthy food and water, and get moving as much as possible. Taking these physical steps will make you stronger and more able to take the mental steps necessary to overcome test anxiety.

Mental Steps for Beating Test Anxiety

Working on the mental side of test anxiety can be more challenging, but as with the physical side, there are clear steps you can take to overcome it. As mentioned earlier, test anxiety often stems from lack of preparation, so the obvious solution is to prepare for the test. Effective studying may be the most important weapon you have for beating test anxiety, but you can and should employ several other mental tools to combat fear.

First, boost your confidence by reminding yourself of past success—tests or projects that you aced. If you're putting as much effort into preparing for this test as you did for those, there's no reason you should expect to fail here. Work hard to prepare; then trust your preparation.

Second, surround yourself with encouraging people. It can be helpful to find a study group, but be sure that the people you're around will encourage a positive attitude. If you spend time with others who are anxious or cynical, this will only contribute to your own anxiety. Look for others who are motivated to study hard from a desire to succeed, not from a fear of failure.

Third, reward yourself. A test is physically and mentally tiring, even without anxiety, and it can be helpful to have something to look forward to. Plan an activity following the test, regardless of the outcome, such as going to a movie or getting ice cream.

When you are taking the test, if you find yourself beginning to feel anxious, remind yourself that you know the material. Visualize successfully completing the test. Then take a few deep, relaxing breaths and return to it. Work through the questions carefully but with confidence, knowing that you are capable of succeeding.

Developing a healthy mental approach to test taking will also aid in other areas of life. Test anxiety affects more than just the actual test—it can be damaging to your mental health and even contribute to depression. It's important to beat test anxiety before it becomes a problem for more than testing.

Study Strategy

Being prepared for the test is necessary to combat anxiety, but what does being prepared look like? You may study for hours on end and still not feel prepared. What you need is a strategy for test prep. The next few pages outline our recommended steps to help you plan out and conquer the challenge of preparation.

STEP 1: SCOPE OUT THE TEST

Learn everything you can about the format (multiple choice, essay, etc.) and what will be on the test. Gather any study materials, course outlines, or sample exams that may be available. Not only will this help you to prepare, but knowing what to expect can help to alleviate test anxiety.

STEP 2: MAP OUT THE MATERIAL

Look through the textbook or study guide and make note of how many chapters or sections it has. Then divide these over the time you have. For example, if a book has 15 chapters and you have five days to study, you need to cover three chapters each day. Even better, if you have the time, leave an extra day at the end for overall review after you have gone through the material in depth.

If time is limited, you may need to prioritize the material. Look through it and make note of which sections you think you already have a good grasp on, and which need review. While you are studying, skim quickly through the familiar sections and take more time on the challenging parts. Write out your plan so you don't get lost as you go. Having a written plan also helps you feel more in control of the study, so anxiety is less likely to arise from feeling overwhelmed at the amount to cover.

STEP 3: GATHER YOUR TOOLS

Decide what study method works best for you. Do you prefer to highlight in the book as you study and then go back over the highlighted portions? Or do you type out notes of the important information? Or is it helpful to make flashcards that you can carry with you? Assemble the pens, index cards, highlighters, post-it notes, and any other materials you may need so you won't be distracted by getting up to find things while you study.

If you're having a hard time retaining the information or organizing your notes, experiment with different methods. For example, try color-coding by subject with colored pens, highlighters, or post-it notes. If you learn better by hearing, try recording yourself reading your notes so you can listen while in the car, working out, or simply sitting at your desk. Ask a friend to quiz you from your flashcards, or try teaching someone the material to solidify it in your mind.

STEP 4: CREATE YOUR ENVIRONMENT

It's important to avoid distractions while you study. This includes both the obvious distractions like visitors and the subtle distractions like an uncomfortable chair (or a too-comfortable couch that makes you want to fall asleep). Set up the best study environment possible: good lighting and a comfortable work area. If background music helps you focus, you may want to turn it on, but otherwise keep the room quiet. If you are using a computer to take notes, be sure you don't have any other windows open, especially applications like social media, games, or anything else that could distract you. Silence your phone and turn off notifications. Be sure to keep water close by so you stay hydrated while you study (but avoid unhealthy drinks and snacks).

Also, take into account the best time of day to study. Are you freshest first thing in the morning? Try to set aside some time then to work through the material. Is your mind clearer in the afternoon or evening? Schedule your study session then. Another method is to study at the same time of day that you will take the test, so that your brain gets used to working on the material at that time and will be ready to focus at test time.

STEP 5: STUDY!

Once you have done all the study preparation, it's time to settle into the actual studying. Sit down, take a few moments to settle your mind so you can focus, and begin to follow your study plan. Don't give in to distractions or let yourself procrastinate. This is your time to prepare so you'll be ready to fearlessly approach the test. Make the most of the time and stay focused.

Of course, you don't want to burn out. If you study too long you may find that you're not retaining the information very well. Take regular study breaks. For example, taking five minutes out of every hour to walk briskly, breathing deeply and swinging your arms, can help your mind stay fresh.

As you get to the end of each chapter or section, it's a good idea to do a quick review. Remind yourself of what you learned and work on any difficult parts. When you feel that you've mastered the material, move on to the next part. At the end of your study session, briefly skim through your notes again.

But while review is helpful, cramming last minute is NOT. If at all possible, work ahead so that you won't need to fit all your study into the last day. Cramming overloads your brain with more information than it can process and retain, and your tired mind may struggle to recall even previously learned information when it is overwhelmed with last-minute study. Also, the urgent nature of cramming and the stress placed on your brain contribute to anxiety. You'll be more likely to go to the test feeling unprepared and having trouble thinking clearly.

So don't cram, and don't stay up late before the test, even just to review your notes at a leisurely pace. Your brain needs rest more than it needs to go over the information again. In fact, plan to finish your studies by noon or early afternoon the day before the test. Give your brain the rest of the day to relax or focus on other things, and get a good night's sleep. Then you will be fresh for the test and better able to recall what you've studied.

STEP 6: TAKE A PRACTICE TEST

Many courses offer sample tests, either online or in the study materials. This is an excellent resource to check whether you have mastered the material, as well as to prepare for the test format and environment.

Check the test format ahead of time: the number of questions, the type (multiple choice, free response, etc.), and the time limit. Then create a plan for working through them. For example, if you have 30 minutes to take a 60-question test, your limit is 30 seconds per question. Spend less time on the questions you know well so that you can take more time on the difficult ones.

If you have time to take several practice tests, take the first one open book, with no time limit. Work through the questions at your own pace and make sure you fully understand them. Gradually work up to taking a test under test conditions: sit at a desk with all study materials put away and set a timer. Pace yourself to make sure you finish the test with time to spare and go back to check your answers if you have time.

After each test, check your answers. On the questions you missed, be sure you understand why you missed them. Did you misread the question (tests can use tricky wording)? Did you forget the information? Or was it something you hadn't learned? Go back and study any shaky areas that the practice tests reveal.

Taking these tests not only helps with your grade, but also aids in combating test anxiety. If you're already used to the test conditions, you're less likely to worry about it, and working through tests until you're scoring well gives you a confidence boost. Go through the practice tests until you feel comfortable, and then you can go into the test knowing that you're ready for it.

Test Tips

On test day, you should be confident, knowing that you've prepared well and are ready to answer the questions. But aside from preparation, there are several test day strategies you can employ to maximize your performance.

First, as stated before, get a good night's sleep the night before the test (and for several nights before that, if possible). Go into the test with a fresh, alert mind rather than staying up late to study.

Try not to change too much about your normal routine on the day of the test. It's important to eat a nutritious breakfast, but if you normally don't eat breakfast at all, consider eating just a protein bar. If you're a coffee drinker, go ahead and have your normal coffee. Just make sure you time it so that the caffeine doesn't wear off right in the middle of your test. Avoid sugary beverages, and drink enough water to stay hydrated but not so much that you need a restroom break 10 minutes into the test. If your test isn't first thing in the morning, consider going for a walk or doing a light workout before the test to get your blood flowing.

Allow yourself enough time to get ready, and leave for the test with plenty of time to spare so you won't have the anxiety of scrambling to arrive in time. Another reason to be early is to select a good seat. It's helpful to sit away from doors and windows, which can be distracting. Find a good seat, get out your supplies, and settle your mind before the test begins.

When the test begins, start by going over the instructions carefully, even if you already know what to expect. Make sure you avoid any careless mistakes by following the directions.

Then begin working through the questions, pacing yourself as you've practiced. If you're not sure on an answer, don't spend too much time on it, and don't let it shake your confidence. Either skip it and come back later, or eliminate as many wrong answers as possible and guess among the remaining ones. Don't dwell on these questions as you continue—put them out of your mind and focus on what lies ahead.

Be sure to read all of the answer choices, even if you're sure the first one is the right answer. Sometimes you'll find a better one if you keep reading. But don't second-guess yourself if you do immediately know the answer. Your gut instinct is usually right. Don't let test anxiety rob you of the information you know.

If you have time at the end of the test (and if the test format allows), go back and review your answers. Be cautious about changing any, since your first instinct tends to be correct, but make sure you didn't misread any of the questions or accidentally mark the wrong answer choice. Look over any you skipped and make an educated guess.

At the end, leave the test feeling confident. You've done your best, so don't waste time worrying about your performance or wishing you could change anything. Instead, celebrate the successful completion of this test. And finally, use this test to learn how to deal with anxiety even better next time.

Review Video: Test Anxiety
Visit mometrix.com/academy and enter code: 100340

Important Qualification

Not all anxiety is created equal. If your test anxiety is causing major issues in your life beyond the classroom or testing center, or if you are experiencing troubling physical symptoms related to your anxiety, it may be a sign of a serious physiological or psychological condition. If this sounds like your situation, we strongly encourage you to seek professional help.

Online Resources

Due to our efforts to try to keep this book to a manageable length, we've created a link that will give you access to all of your online resources:

mometrix.com/resources719/hspt-28350

www.ingramcontent.com/pod-product-compliance
Lightning Source LLC
Chambersburg PA
CBHW081417230426
43668CB00016B/2260